George Anson, Baron Anson (1697–1762), circumnavigator and First Lord of the Admiralty, entered the Royal Navy in 1712 and progressed rapidly, achieving his first command in 1722. He benefited from the patronage of his uncle Thomas Parker, later the Earl of Macclesfield, who served as Lord Chief Justice and Lord Chancellor until his impeachment for fraud in 1725. Anson first saw action at the Battle of Cape Passaro (1718) under Admiral Sir George Byng but most of his early career was spent as captain of the station ship based at Charleston, South Carolina.

In 1737 he was appointed captain of the 60-gun *Centurion* and sent on patrol to West Africa and the Caribbean. It was in this ship that he circumnavigated the globe (1740-1744) during the war with Spain. Ordered to attack the Pacific coast of Spanish South America, the expedition almost ended in disaster when half of Anson's squadron disappeared as it encountered 'huge deep, hollow seas' during the passage around Cape Horn. Despite further heavy losses, Anson was able to carry out a limited number of raids against coastal targets, but his capture of the Spanish treasure galleon *Nuestra Señora de Covadonga* off the Philippines was a real victory that secured his reputation (and wealth).

On his return Anson, welcomed as a national hero, soon revealed his political ambitions: he joined the opposition Whigs, was elected MP for Hedon and appointed to the Admiralty Board. Although he entered the Board while still a captain, he secured rapid promotion to rear admiral, vice admiral and then admiral of the fleet. Anson returned to sea in command of the Western Squadron in 1746–1747 and his notable victory against the French at the first Battle of Cape Finisterre was a rare example of a British naval success after seven years of war. Anson, who was then raised to the peerage, returned to the Admiralty Board, working with the Duke of Bedford as First Lord and with Lord Sandwich on a series of naval reforms, which included ending political interference in courts-martial, introducing compulsory retirement, innovations in ship design, and the formation of the Royal Marines under Admiralty control.

In 1751, Anson succeeded Lord Sandwich as First Lord of the Admiralty and served until his death in 1762 (except for one brief interruption in 1756–1757 following the loss of Minorca). The reform programme continued, but his main priority on returning to office (and the Cabinet) in the Pitt-Newcastle coalition was the Seven Years War: its strategic direction, planning operations and preparing naval forces. Although he died shortly before the conflict ended, Pitt later said of Anson: 'to his wisdom, to his experience the nation owes the glorious success of the last war.' Horace Walpole inevitably took a more critical view: 'Lord Anson was reserved and proud, and so ignorant of the world, that Sir Charles Williams said he had been round it, but never in it.'

Anson's earlier biographers have focused on the story of the circumnavigation, which has largely defined his reputation, as well as his victories at sea. However, other aspects of his career, particularly his roles as a naval reformer and wartime strategist, deserve to be given greater weight in reassessing his position as a leading figure in British naval history. As one commentator has pointed out, 'there is an increasing cultural valuation of administrative skills that allows an Anson to be remembered in the same arena with, but still distinctly from, a Nelson. Whereas Horatio Nelson is certainly the most well-known and enduring example of a naval hero, others followed different paths to success during their lifetimes.'

Anthony Bruce was formerly a director at Universities UK and is now a higher education consultant. His first book (based on his doctorate) was on *The Purchase System in the British Army* (1980). It was followed by *An Illustrated Companion to the First World War* (1989) and *The Last Crusade* (2002) on the war in Palestine, 1914-1918. His *Encyclopaedia of Naval History* (1998) covers the period from the sixteenth century to the present day. Revised editions of *The Encyclopaedia* and *The Last Crusade* were published in 2020. He has been a regular contributor to *The Trafalgar Chronicle*, an annual collection of articles on the history of the Georgian navy, since 2016.

Anson

Royal Navy Commander and Statesman, 1697–1762

Anthony Bruce

 Helion & Company

To my wife Sula

Helion & Company Limited
Unit 8 Amherst Business Centre
Budbrooke Road
Warwick
CV34 5WE
England
Tel. 01926 499619
Email: info@helion.co.uk
Website: www.helion.co.uk
Twitter: @helionbooks
Visit our blog at http://blog.helion.co.uk/

Published by Helion & Company 2023
Designed and typeset by Mach 3 Solutions (www.mach3solutions.co.uk)
Cover designed by Paul Hewitt, Battlefield Design (www.battlefield-design.co.uk)

Text © Anthony Bruce 2023
Maps by Mark Thompson © Helion and Company 2023

Cover: 'Capture of the Spanish galleon *Nuestra Señora de Covadonga* by the British ship *Centurion*, commanded by George Anson, June 20, 1743', oil on canvas by Samuel Scott (Royal Museums Greenwich)

Every reasonable effort has been made to trace copyright holders and to obtain their permission for the use of copyright material. The author and publisher apologise for any errors or omissions in this work, and would be grateful if notified of any corrections that should be incorporated in future reprints or editions of this book.

ISBN 978-1-804511-92-3

British Library Cataloguing-in-Publication Data.
A catalogue record for this book is available from the British Library.

All rights reserved. No part of this publication may be reproduced, stored in a retrieval system, or transmitted, in any form, or by any means, electronic, mechanical, photocopying, recording or otherwise, without the express written consent of Helion & Company Limited.

For details of other military history titles published by Helion & Company Limited, contact the above address, or visit our website: http://www.helion.co.uk

We always welcome receiving book proposals from prospective authors.

Contents

List of Plates		vi
List of Maps		vii
Introduction		viii
1	Early Career, 1697–1740	11
2	Around the World, 1740–1743	33
3	Capturing the Treasure Galleon, 1743–1744	54
4	Rising Politician, 1744–1747	72
5	Commanding the Western Squadron, 1746–1747	90
6	Naval Reform, 1748–1751	109
7	First Lord, 1751–1756	133
8	The Minorca Crisis, 1756–1757	157
9	Wartime Cruise, 1757–1758	179
10	Planning for Victory, 1758–1762	199
Conclusion		220
Bibliography		224
General Index		240
Index of Ships		244

List of Plates

Shugborough Hall, Staffordshire. (Ruth Elliott)	12
George Byng, Viscount Torrington, engraving by Jacob Houbraken, after Sir Godfrey Kneller. (Rijksmuseum)	16
Plan of Charleston, South Carolina, c.1780. (Library of Congress, Geography and Map Division)	22
Model of the *Centurion*, by Benjamin Slade, 1747. (Royal Museums, Greenwich)	24
Burning of Payta, November 1741, painting by Samuel Scott. (Royal Museums, Greenwich)	44
George Anson, 1744, engraving by Jan Caspar Philips after Arthur Pond. (Rijksmuseum)	70
Lord Anson's Victory off Cape Finisterre, 3 May 1747, painting by Samuel Scott. (Yale Centre for British Art)	105
Elizabeth, Lady Anson, painting in the style of Sir Godfrey Kneller. (National Trust)	117
Vice Admiral Sir Peter Warren, engraving by William Ridley. (New York Public Library)	128
Moor Park, Hertfordshire. (Peter O'Connor)	141
George, Lord Anson, 1755, mezzotint by J. McArdell after Joshua Reynolds. (Anne S.K. Brown Collection)	151
Philip Yorke, First Earl of Hardwicke, mezzotint by J. McArdell. (Rijksmuseum)	177
Edward, Lord Hawke, mezzotint by J. McArdell. (Yale Centre for British Art)	191
Queen Charlotte's passage to England, painting by Richard Wright. (Royal Collection Trust)	209

List of Maps

Anson's Circumnavigation, 1740-1744. 36
Cape Finisterre, 1747. 100
The Minorca Campaign, 1756. 161
French Atlantic Coast. 185
Cuba, 1762. 214

Introduction

It is now more than 60 years since the most recent biography of George Anson – itself only the third full-length account to appear in the last two centuries – was published, and since his death in 1762 he has languished in relative obscurity.[1] Other prominent eighteenth-century naval leaders who followed more conventional career paths at sea had more opportunities to achieve victory in battle and, as a result, have overshadowed him since then. Only eight years after Anson's death, William Pitt (then the Earl of Chatham) noted in a speech in the House of Lords that he had been quickly forgotten: 'the merits of that great man are not so universally known, nor his memory so universally respected as he deserved'.[2]

Further evidence that he was soon forgotten was provided by Sir John Barrow, the author of the first full biography, who recorded how, in 1835, William IV failed to mention Anson's victory at Cape Finisterre in 1747, when reciting a list of the Royal Navy's past successes.[3] According to Barrow, the King recalled Anson as:

> ...a good man, and knew his business well; though not brilliant, he was an excellent First Lord – improved the build of our ships, made more good officers, and brought others forward, in the Seven Years War, than any of his predecessors had done. Howe, Keppel, Saunders and many others, were of his making.[4]

Despite the King's forgetfulness about the achievements of one of his father's former ministers, during his lifetime Anson was a prominent public figure and a leading member of the Whig establishment. He rose rapidly to prominence, after a long period in obscurity as a long-serving captain of no particular distinction, on his return from circumnavigating the globe in 1744, bringing news of the capture of a Spanish treasure galleon and his acquisition of vast wealth. Despite heavy losses in men and ships, Anson was feted by the public who welcomed his humiliation of the Spanish following several years in which the Royal Navy had failed to make an impact. He was equally fortunate in intercepting and defeating the French in 1747 and adding to his already significant store of wealth. The victory kept him

---

1 Stanley W.C. Pack, *Admiral Lord Anson: The Story of Anson's Voyage and Naval Events of His Day* (London: Cassell, 1960).
2 William Cobbett, *The Parliamentary History of England to the Year 1803* (London: T. C. Hansard, 1813), vol.XVI, p.1100.
3 John Barrow, *The Life of George Lord Anson: Admiral of the Fleet, Vice Admiral of Great Britain and First Lord Commissioner of the Admiralty* (London: John Murray, 1839).
4 Barrow, *The Life of George Lord Anson*, p.374.

in the public eye and his success – the first significant victory against the French in the War of the Austrian Succession (1740–1748) – was widely applauded and recognized by the King who elevated him to the peerage as Baron Anson of Soberton.

After the publication of the official account of the circumnavigation in 1748, which was produced under his close supervision, Lord Anson found wider fame. The book was translated into several European languages and became an international best seller. Anson's reputation still rests largely on his voyage around the world rather than his later achievements at sea and at the Admiralty, where he spent most of the rest of his career. Anson received less welcome public attention when, in 1756, he became the target of widespread public criticism over the loss of Minorca and was forced out of office along with his ministerial colleagues. Following his return to office six months later, Anson's reputation gradually recovered and he was associated in the public mind with the navy's successes against France and Spain in the latter stages of the Seven Years War.

One of the main reasons for Anson's relatively low profile since his death is the fact that his career does not conform to conventional ideas of success at sea, which are based on heroism and victory in battle rather than achievements as the political head of the navy. Anson's earlier biographers have tried to redress the balance by offering 'an increasing cultural valuation of administrative skills that allows an Anson to be remembered in the same arena with, but still distinctly from a Nelson'.[5] But he remains a problematic subject for a biographer because of gaps in our knowledge of his career which are difficult or impossible to fill and to some extent he will always remain in the shadows. This has led his earlier biographers to give more coverage to the circumnavigation than is perhaps justified.

Virtually nothing is known about Anson's early life, including his education and family relationships, or his first 20 years in the navy beyond the formal record of his service. His character was first described in a portrait penned by a resident of Charleston who knew him when he was in command of the station ship in South Carolina in the 1730s. Published in 1747, it is by far the fullest account of his personality to survive but it is difficult to know how accurate it is in the absence of any other contemporary evidence. It is not until the 1740s – more than 30 years after Anson first joined the navy as a volunteer – that more information about him becomes available with the publication of multiple accounts of the circumnavigation. These provide the first insights into Anson's approach to command and throw new light on his character. The official history gives his version of events, but several other independent accounts provide a more critical perspective. His two periods in command of the Western Squadron – in 1746–1747 and 1758 – are also more adequately documented and enable his contribution to be established.

The absence of documentary evidence means that identifying Anson's specific contribution to policy developments during his 17-year Admiralty career is not always straightforward. When Anson was a member of the Admiralty Board under the Duke of Bedford and then Lord Sandwich in the late 1740s, decisions on naval reform were taken collectively and it is often difficult to disentangle their individual roles. This problem is compounded by Anson's distant manner and his distinctive method of working, which was based on a

---

5   Katherine Parker, 'Rewriting Admiral Anson as Naval Hero: Biographical Depictions of George Anson from the Eighteenth Century to the Mid-Twentieth Century', *The Trafalgar Chronicle*, 24 (2014), pp.81–94.

strong aversion to reading and writing and a preference for conducting business in (unrecorded) meetings and bilateral conversations. His surviving correspondence is limited and his letters are typically no more than brief notes, written in a terse style. Even so, they can often be revealing, as the extracts quoted in the book confirm, but provide little information on his work on naval reform.

Despite these obstacles, recent research on the navy has successfully explored Anson's role in planning operations during the Seven Years War when he sometimes came into conflict with William Pitt and other ministers.[6] Anson's role at the head of the peacetime Admiralty has also been illuminated by the increased volume of research on the mid-eighteenth century Georgian navy that has appeared in recent years. Described as 'a golden age of naval history', the period since 1970 has seen the publication of many new studies of naval administration, the organisation of the navy, ship design and other subjects that are relevant to a reassessment of Lord Anson's contribution.[7] Recent work on the circumnavigation has thrown new light on Anson's role as a naval commander and his contribution to the development of tactics and training has been highlighted in several recent studies of naval warfare. A full list of relevant publications is provided in the bibliography.

In the absence of more comprehensive archival sources, these new studies provide a sound basis for a re-evaluation of Anson's career and his place in naval history. Drawing on this material, the book provides as full an account as possible of Anson's personal history and public role and includes a discussion of areas of weakness as well as his achievements. This includes an analysis of instances where his strategic judgement may be questioned, including his role in the Minorca crisis and his failure to support action against Spain when Pitt demanded it in 1761. The biography aims to produce a rounded account of Anson's life rather than emphasising one aspect of his career at the expense of the others.

---

6   For example, Richard Middleton, *The Bells of Victory: The Pitt-Newcastle Ministry and the Conduct of the Seven Years' War, 1757–1762* (Cambridge: Cambridge University Press, 1985).
7   N.A.M. Rodger, 'Recent Books on the Royal Navy of the Eighteenth Century', *The Journal of Military History*, 63 (1999), pp.683–703.

1

Early Career, 1697–1740

Although George Anson was born into a prosperous Staffordshire family, there was nothing in his early life – or in his routine service in the peacetime navy – to suggest that he would rise to national prominence as a naval commander and politician. Anson was born on 23 April 1697 at Oakedge Hall, a mile south-east of Shugborough, near Colwich, Staffordshire. He was the second surviving son of William Anson (1656–1720), a successful provincial lawyer from Dunstan in Staffordshire, where the Ansons had been resident since the fifteenth century. He married Isabella, who was the daughter of Charles Carrier of Wirksworth, Derbyshire, in April 1682, and redeveloped the family estate at Shugborough in the 1690s. George had six sisters and four brothers of whom two died in infancy. He established a close relationship with his elder brother Thomas (*c*.1695–1773) from their early years, which they maintained until he died in 1762, but few details of his other family connections have survived. George's sister Janetta (1690–1771) married Sambrooke Adams of Sambrooke, Shropshire, while his other sisters – Elizabeth (1682–*fl*.1720); Isabella (1685–1769), Mary (1688–1762?), Anna (1693–1782) and Joanna (1699–1786) – were unmarried and lived at Shugborough for most of their lives.

Thomas was educated at St John's College, Oxford, and was called to the Bar in 1719 before inheriting his father's estate at the age of 25. He was a collector, patron of the arts and traveller, who undertook a Grand Tour, 1723–1725, and later visited Egypt and Aleppo. On his return to England, Thomas gave priority to developing the buildings and gardens at Shugborough, with George making a substantial contribution towards the costs from his prize money and other assets. As a result of Thomas's changes to the Shugborough estate from the 1740s, 'the house, its contents, and the park and ornaments are very much a memorial to George and his maritime accomplishments'.[1] In 1747, Thomas was elected as Member of Parliament for Lichfield in his brother's interest.

George Anson's great-grandfather, William (c.1580–1645), who was also a successful lawyer, had purchased the manor house and about 90 acres of freehold land in the riverside village of Shugborough in 1624. According to the deeds, the estate included the 'Manor house houses buildings barnes stables edivises dove house orchard gardens backsides Moates waters'.[2] Anson's father replaced the existing property with a two-story house in red

---

1   Michael Cousins, 'Shugborough: "A Perfect Paradise"', *Garden History*, 43 (2015) p.34.
2   Cousins, 'Shugborough', p.33.

Shugborough Hall, Staffordshire. (Ruth Elliott)

brick between 1693 and 1695 and rented Oakedge Hall as his main home while it was being built. He purchased additional land in Shugborough, a process that was later continued by Thomas Anson, who made much larger acquisitions from the late 1730s, leading to the demolition of several nearby village houses. By the time of Thomas's death in 1773, the Shugborough estate extended for more than 1,000 acres. The new house confirmed the family's position as important members of local society at the beginning of the eighteenth century, but 'neither their place in society nor their house could be compared with that of the overlords of Shugborough, the Pagets of Beaudesert, or of the Ansons' neighbours whose houses were plainly visible from viewpoints in or near the village, the Astons of Tixall and the Chetwynds of Ingestre'.[3] The Anson family's support for the Hanoverian Succession in 1714 (unlike many of their Staffordshire neighbours who backed the Stuarts) helped to ensure that the family prospered during George I's reign.

Unlike his brother Thomas, there is no surviving record of George's childhood or education. He may have received private tuition at home or been sent to a local grammar school in Stafford or Lichfield, but his formal education ended at a young age when he entered the navy. Although the family had longstanding connections with the legal profession and a career at the Bar would have been open to him, more than one of Anson's early biographers suggested that he was destined for the navy at an early age. Many younger sons of the gentry were to make the same career choice – as an alternative to the law, clergy or army – and Anson was fortunate in having influential connections who could help him realise his ambition at a time when access to the patronage system was necessary to secure a naval appointment or promotion.

---

3   F.B. Stitt, 'Shugborough: The End of a Village', *Collections for a History of Staffordshire*, Fourth Series, 6 (1970) p.100.

Anson's mother Isabella's sister Janet Carrier was married to Thomas Parker (later the first Earl of Macclesfield), a prominent barrister whose role in the trial of the High Church divine Henry Sacheverell led to his appointment as Lord Chief Justice in 1710. He was Lord Chancellor from 1718, but his term of office ended abruptly in 1725 when he was impeached and imprisoned for taking bribes. As the most senior member of the legal profession and a member of the Privy Council, Lord Macclesfield was well placed to secure Anson's entry into the navy and to facilitate his progress during the critical first few years of his career. As his career progressed, Anson's connections with senior members of the legal profession were strengthened because of another family link. Macclesfield's nephew, Sir Thomas Parker, Lord Chief Baron of the Exchequer (presiding judge of the Exchequer Court) from 1742, was the uncle of John Jervis, later Admiral of the Fleet Earl St Vincent, who was also born in Staffordshire.

Another distinguished lawyer, Philip Yorke, later the first Earl of Hardwicke, Anson's future father-in-law, was to play a significant role in his political career after his return to England in 1744 when they became close allies. It is not clear when they first met, but Hardwicke is likely to have supported him during the earlier stages of his naval career.[4] Hardwicke was a friend and protégé of Lord Macclesfield, who had helped him secure the post of Solicitor General in 1720. Serving as Lord Chancellor from 1737 to 1756, Hardwicke was a close friend and political ally of Thomas Pelham-Holles, first Duke of Newcastle, Secretary of State for the Southern Department, and then, from 1754, Prime Minister. The dominant influence on the direction of Britain's war policy in the 1740s, Newcastle was directly involved in the decision to dispatch Anson's South Sea expedition at the beginning of the conflict with Spain. Anson was to establish close political links with Newcastle during the late 1740s, which were to continue until Anson's death.

Early in 1712, as the War of the Spanish Succession (1701–1714) was ending, with Britain's naval superiority over its competitors firmly established, Anson entered the navy as a 'volunteer-per-order' at the age of 14. He joined under a system introduced in 1676 'to encourage families of better quality... to breed up their younger sons to the art and practice of navigation'.[5] A volunteer had to be taken on by a serving captain and would normally spend a minimum period of three years at sea acquiring professional skills, with training provided by a schoolmaster if one were present on board. He would then be advanced to the rank of midshipman. Examinations for promotion to lieutenant would follow after a total of six years' service at sea and successful candidates (with a normal minimum age of 20) would then have to wait until a vacancy occurred. Influential patrons could help to accelerate the process as they did in Anson's case, enabling him to obtain his commission at the age of 19 ahead of many of his fellow volunteers.

Anson was first taken on as a volunteer by Peter Chamberlain, the experienced captain of the *Ruby*, a 54-gun fourth-rate ship of the line, joining the ship at Chatham on 2 February 1712. The *Ruby*, which was launched in 1708, had an unremarkable career until 1741 when the captain, Samuel Goodere, murdered his brother on board; Goodere and his accomplices

---

4 Philip C. Yorke (ed.), *The Life and Correspondence of Philip Yorke, Earl of Hardwicke* (Cambridge: Cambridge University Press, 1913), vol.II, p.155.
5 A.B. McLeod, *British Naval Captains of the Seven Years War. The View from the Quarterdeck* (Woodbridge: The Boydell Press, 2012), p.11.

were convicted of the crime and executed. Anson's service on his first ship was brief and after a few weeks on patrol in the Channel the *Ruby* anchored at Spithead – the sheltered anchorage at the entrance to Portsmouth harbour – on 11 March.

A few days later, Chamberlain and his followers (including Anson) transferred to the third-rate *Monmouth* (64) on his appointment as second captain. On 13 April, the *Monmouth* was dispatched to Jamaica but shortly before her arrival 'a hurricane very nearly put an end to Anson and *Monmouth* together. Both pumps were kept going, there was four feet of water on the ballast and the same between decks, the foretopmast went, the main and mizen masts were cut away, and men with buckets worked for their lives "bealing at each hatchway."'[6] On 1 September, the damaged ship arrived at Jamaica, where she served as Sir Hovenden Walker's flagship at Port Royal. After cruising for pirates in the Caribbean, the *Monmouth* returned to Spithead in July 1713, where she was paid off (decommissioned).

It was not until early in 1716 that Anson's name reappeared in the official records when he returned to sea as a midshipman in the fourth-rate *Hampshire* (50), with Peter Chamberlain once more in command. She was one of 16 ships in the Channel fleet that were being sent to the Baltic where the Great Northern War (1700–1721) between a Russian-led coalition and Sweden was in progress. Headed by the veteran Admiral Sir John Norris, who stated in 1744 that he had served 'the Crown longer as an admiral than any man ever did',[7] the squadron was dispatched in response to hostile Swedish action against British merchant ships trading with St Petersburg. The squadron undertook convoy protection duties in cooperation with the Russians and Danes against the Swedes but saw no action.

Before the fleet left England, Norris had intervened on Anson's behalf to secure his promotion to second lieutenant even though he was just below the normal qualifying age of 20. On 17 May, he wrote to the Admiralty Secretary from the Nore – the anchorage in the Thames estuary – to inform him that a lieutenant serving on the *Hampshire* wanted to be put on half-pay and that he intended 'to commission Mr. George Anson, who is cousin [*sic*] to my Lord Parker [later the Earl of Macclesfield]'. Admirals on foreign stations were permitted to make appointments to the rank of lieutenant without reference to seniority and there is little doubt that influence was the determining factor in Anson's rapid promotion: 'in 1716 the most brilliant merit conceivable was all the more brilliant in the nephew of the Lord Chief Justice'.[8] As a junior lieutenant, Anson's principal duties at sea would have included watch-keeping and taking charge of a group of guns during drills and in battle.[9]

On the squadron's return to England, the Admiralty confirmed Anson's appointment as a second lieutenant on 7 December 1716. By this time, he must have completed the qualifying oral examination and received his 'passing certificate', confirming that he had achieved a minimum standard of professional competence. As a gentlemen volunteer Anson had received no pay and would have depended on his parents to meet essential expenses,

---

6 John Masefield (ed.), *A Voyage Round the World in the Years 1740–1744 by Lord Anson* (London: J.M. Dent, [1911]), p.xiii.
7 D.D. Aldridge, 'Admiral Sir John Norris 1670 (or 1671)–1749: His Birth and Early Service, His Marriage and His Death', *The Mariner's Mirror*, 51 (1965), p.173.
8 J.K. Laughton, 'George Anson, Lord Anson (1697–1762)', *The Dictionary of National Biography* (1885), <https://doi.org/10.1093/odnb/9780192683120.013.574.>, accessed on 14 Sept. 2022.
9 Brian Lavery, *Anson's Navy: Building a Fleet for Empire 1744–1763* (Barnsley: Seaforth, 2021), pp.59–60.

including clothing and nautical instruments, but as an officer he would be paid for the first time since joining the service. However, a second lieutenant's salary, which could be paid years in arrears, was low (five shillings a day) and he was only allowed one servant. During periods when he was not on active service, Anson would have been eligible to receive half-pay under a scheme that was first applied to the highest ranks in 1668 and was extended to all commissioned officers in 1713. The Admiralty provided half-pay to officers 'in good standing who could be considered employable and on call', although most recipients regarded it as no more than a reward for past service with no obligation to future service.[10]

In March 1717, Anson returned to the Baltic in the *Hampshire* with the fleet now headed by Sir George Byng, a successful commander who 'left nothing to fortune, that could be accomplished by foresight and application'.[11] At the end of the cruise in November, the *Hampshire* was paid off and Anson did not return to active service until March 1718. He was then appointed as second lieutenant in the fourth-rate *Montagu* (60), under the command of Captain Thomas Beverley (d.1721). By this time, he had parted company with Peter Chamberlain, who was to be lost in a shipwreck off Cuba in 1720. The *Montagu* served in a squadron of 21 warships under Byng's command and Anson was soon to see action for the first time. Two of Byng's sons were present on the cruise and one of them – a young John Byng – was to be the cause of the only real crisis in Anson's career nearly 40 years later. Also present at Cape Passaro were Thomas Mathews and Richard Lestock, whose combined failings at the Battle of Toulon, 1744, were to be an important influence on Anson's work at the Admiralty in the late 1740s.

In May 1718, Byng was dispatched to the Mediterranean in response to Spanish violations of the terms of the Treaty of Utrecht (1713), which had ended the War of the Spanish Succession. By 1717, Spain had reoccupied Sardinia and planned to recover Sicily from the Duke of Savoy as well as other territories on the Italian mainland which had been lost in 1713. In June 1718, 18 warships and 30,000 men were dispatched from Barcelona and soon the whole of Sicily (apart from Messina) would be in Spanish hands. When Byng's squadron approached the Spanish fleet in the Straits of Messina, the latter was taken by surprise and sailed southwards with the British in pursuit.

The decision to flee was explained by the fact that the Spanish fleet only consisted of 14 ships with 50 guns or more, compared to Byng's 21. He made contact with the Spanish off Cape Passaro, the extreme southerly cape of Sicily, on 31 July, ordering his ships to pursue them in a general chase rather than organising a standard battle line formation. They were to advance 'with a loose line ahead, allowing some of his ships to approach on one side, and some on the other side, of the Spanish formation, expecting his captains to engage individual ships of similar size'.[12] By nightfall Byng had secured a decisive victory, capturing 11 enemy ships and destroying three more, and he was raised to the peerage as Viscount Torrington on his return to England.

---

10   Daniel A. Baugh (ed.), *Naval Administration, 1715–1750* (London: Navy Records Society, 1977), pp.38–39.
11   Thomas Corbett, *An Account of the Expedition of the British Fleet to Sicily, in the Years 1718, 1719 and 1720* (London: J. and R. Tonson, 1739), p.89.
12   John B. Hattendorf, 'Byng: Passaro, 1718', in Eric Grove (ed.), *Great Battles of the Royal Navy as Commemorated in the Gunroom, Britannia Royal Naval College* (London: Arms and Armour, 1994), p.68.

George Byng, Viscount Torrington, engraving by Jacob Houbraken, after Sir Godfrey Kneller. (Rijksmuseum)

Following Byng's orders, Anson's ship, the *Montagu*, together with the *Rupert* (60), engaged and captured the Spanish warship *Volante* (44) in an individual action in which Captain Beverley 'very much distinguished himself'.[13] Anson will have noted that Byng was an effective leader who decided to attack the Spanish without first consulting his captains at a council of war. His adoption of a flexible tactical approach, ordering a general chase rather than insisting on a rigid battle line formation, was the main explanation for his success. The battle was to have a lasting impact on the development of Anson's tactical thinking, and he was to demonstrate similar flexibility when he defeated the French at the first Battle of Cape Finisterre almost 30 years later. The *Additional Fighting Instructions* prepared by Anson as commander of the Western Squadron in 1746 were directly influenced by his understanding of Byng's tactics at Cape Passaro.

---

13 John Charnock, *Biographia Navalis; or, Impartial Memoirs of the Lives and Characters of Officers of the Navy of Great Britain, from the Year 1660 to the Present Time* (London: R. Faulder, 1796), vol.IV, p.3.

Early the following year, Byng transferred the well-connected young lieutenant to his flagship, the second-rate *Barfleur* (90) under Captain George Saunders. Anson remained on the *Barfleur* until she was paid off in November 1720. After a further period of shore leave, he was appointed, on 19 June 1722, as master and commander of the sloop *Weazle* (8). At the age of 25, it was Anson's first independent command and an important step in his career. He was dispatched to the North Sea, where his varied responsibilities included fishery protection, convoy duties and the suppression of smuggling between Britain and the Netherlands. For Anson and other rising naval officers, their role in protecting trade,

> …represented a first-class training ground for command in the navy: commanders learned to follow instructions, while interpreting these instructions in unusual circumstances; battling with the weather was a constant factor; local interests had to be accommodated, and local conditions and pilots understood; and once the masters of merchantmen had joined a convoy, they had to be coerced into obedience.[14]

Anson's successful record against North Sea smugglers as commander of the *Weazle* provided ample evidence of his developing professional abilities and soon brought him to the attention of the Admiralty, although his rapid promotion to the rank of post captain (in February 1724) is likely to have been facilitated by Lord Macclesfield. Under a system of naval promotion that was then based on seniority, the date of Anson's promotion to captain would determine when he was likely to be advanced to the rank of rear admiral. Now in command of the sixth-rate frigate *Scarborough* (20), Anson was sent to South Carolina, one of the richest of Britain's 13 American colonies; its wealth was principally built upon slaves and overseas trade in rice.[15] The *Scarborough* was to serve as the station ship at Charleston, the capital of South Carolina and an important commercial and cultural centre with an excellent harbour. The Admiralty had established the 'Carolina Station' in 1720, soon after South Carolina became a royal colony; it was one of a few places – St John's, Boston, New York, Canso (Nova Scotia) and Savannah – on the North American coast where the navy had frigates permanently stationed.

Anson's instructions were to 'protect the trade generally against pirates, who were committing depredations on the coast of that new settlement, to grant convoys to and from the Bahamas, and to prevent all illicit commerce with the young colony'. He was also 'to communicate with the governor, and to assist when necessary in the protection of the settlement, keeping a vigilant look-out on Spanish cruisers'.[16] With piracy in decline by the mid-1720s, his main responsibility was to ensure that the Spanish did not disturb the uneasy peace between Britain and Spain that had existed since the Treaty of The Hague was signed in 1720. In 1725, for example, he was ordered to take the sloop *Shark* (10) under his

---

14 McLeod, *British Naval Captains of the Seven Years War*, p.24.
15 Julian Gwyn, *The Enterprising Admiral. The Personal Fortune of Admiral Sir Peter Warren* (Montreal: McGill-Queen's University Press, 1974), p.120.
16 Barrow, *The Life of George Lord Anson*, p.9.

command when she arrived at Charleston from England and send her on to the Bahamas where the Spanish were taking slaves that belonged to the residents.[17]

Conflict with Spain might also arise because of an unresolved border dispute between Spanish Florida and South Carolina as the boundaries between the two had never been precisely defined. In 1725, a Spanish vessel from St Augustine carrying officials who wished to discuss the border issue with the British governor arrived at Charleston without prior warning. As Anson went to greet the visitors, the guns of Fort Johnson, which was located on the harbour, opened fire even though the ship was showing a flag of truce. Anson needed all the diplomatic skills at his disposal to reassure the Spanish and avoid a diplomatic incident, explaining that the fort commander had ignored the orders issued to him by the colonial authorities.[18] The talks went ahead but the border issue remained unresolved, and relations deteriorated further during the period leading up to the Anglo-Spanish War of 1727–1729. As the war began, Anson was sent orders to burn, sink and destroy all the Spanish ships he encountered, but he does not appear to have had any opportunity to do so.[19]

The *Scarborough* was the first of three similar sixth-rate warships that Anson commanded in succession during his two periods of service in South Carolina (1724–1730; 1732–1735), amounting to some nine years in total. She returned to England when Anson was appointed to the *Garland* (20) in July 1728 on the death of her captain; he held this command for two years before being ordered home. Early in 1732, after a period of service in England, he was appointed to the *Squirrel* (20) and returned to South Carolina. These 20-gun ships, which were ideally suited for their main convoy and patrol duties on the Charleston station, were each about 375 tons burthen, 106 feet in length and 28 feet in the beam, and had a crew of 130. With the help of local pilots, the station ships were able to negotiate the sandbars obstructing the entrance to Charleston harbour that would have posed too great a risk for larger warships.

Anson's principal task as captain of the station ship was to cruise to the Bahamas and along the Carolina coastline several times a year for the protection of the merchant ships sailing in and out of Charleston. These cruises normally lasted for four or five weeks and often involved forming a convoy of merchant ships travelling to New York and other northern ports or to England; he would escort them for the first 300 nautical miles of their journey northwards. Anson's regular patrols succeeded in keeping pirates at bay and he does not seem to have encountered them while on patrol off South Carolina. His presence on the coast 'contributed to the safety and security of [the Charleston] community and facilitated the rising fortunes of the maritime trade flowing in and out of this port'.[20]

Although his responsibilities were largely routine, Anson faced the challenge of maintaining his ships at a remote location without the support of a naval dockyard or its staff.

---

17 Royal Archives: Papers of Frederick, Prince of Wales, GEO/MAIN/54150, George Anson to Josiah Burchett, 15 September 1725.
18 Nic Butler, 'Captain Anson and the Spanish Entourage', Charleston County Public Library (10 November 2017), <https://www.ccpl.org/charleston-time-machine/captain-anson-and-spanish-entourage>, accessed on 23 Aug. 2022.
19 Barrow, *The Life of George Lord Anson*, p.11.
20 'His Majesty's Warships in Charleston Harbor', Charleston County Public Library (6 March 2020), <https://www.ccpl.org/charleston-time-machine/his-majestys-warships-charleston-harbor>, accessed 23 August 2022.

In the absence of a dry dock, the process of careening (tilting a ship on her side to clean or repair the hull) was undertaken in a local creek while repairs above the waterline took place in Charleston harbour. Here 'the crew patched the sails, spliced the cables, fashioned new yards and masts, coated exposed surfaces with tar and rosin, and even scaled the guns to keep them in prime condition'.[21] Managing these essential tasks provided Anson with valuable experience that he would need to draw upon when maintaining and repairing his squadron during the voyage around the world.

Anson's limited official duties, which meant that he was at sea for no more than three months of the year, gave him the opportunity to become an active member of colonial society. He enjoyed drinking and playing cards and like some other naval officers stationed in the colony, he made several astute property investments which laid the foundations of his wealth. Anson seems to have been a popular member of the local community, with one Charleston resident, Mrs Hutchinson, who saw him at balls, plays and concerts, giving a full assessment of his character in a letter, possibly written in 1735, to her sister in London. She paints a much more positive portrait than those offered in later years by the writer and commentator Horace Walpole and other political opponents. The letter was eventually published after his victory at the first Battle of Cape Finisterre, 1747, with the editor commenting that 'when news arrived of [Anson's] late glorious success, I determined no longer to defer the publication of this little essay towards doing honour to his private, which his own conduct has already done to his public character'.[22]

Mrs Hutchinson gives a detailed description of Anson's physical appearance at the age of 38: 'his stature is neither high nor low, his complexion fair and sanguine, his air and mien easy and unaffected, and his address the most agreeable that can be'. His features are 'regular, and… he has what we call blue eyes, and handsome teeth… Though his countenance is rather grave and sedate than otherwise, yet he never accosts one without a smile. Indeed, I don't remember that I ever saw him speak without smiling'. She reports that Anson's 'voice is low and equal, and he is neither noisy nor boisterous, as many gentlemen of the navy are sometimes apt to be'.[23]

The letter-writer provides an equally positive account of Anson's character: he 'is possess'd of every good quality necessary to form a great and good man, as well as a most amiable companion'. She reports that he 'has good sense, good nature, is polite and well-bred… He is generous without profusion, elegant without ostentation; and, above all, of a most tender, humane disposition. His benevolence is extensive, even to his own detriment…'. She also describes him as being 'so old-fashioned as to make some profession of religion; moreover, he neither dances nor swears, nor talks nonsense… As he greatly admires a fine woman, so he is passionately fond of music; which is enough … to recommend him to my esteem'. He was 'one of those few of whom all men speak well', and his popularity may be explained by the fact that amongst 'all the scandalous warfare that is perpetually nourished here, he maintains a strict neutrality, and, attacking no party, is himself attack'd by none'.[24]

---

21 'His Majesty's Warships in Charleston Harbor'. Charleston County Public Library.
22 [J. Hutchinson], *The Private Character of Admiral Anson. By a Lady* (London: J. Oldcastle, [1747]).
23 [Hutchinson], *The Private Character of Admiral Anson*, pp.8–9.
24 [Hutchinson], *The Private Character of Admiral Anson*, pp.9–10, 15–16, 19, 21.

Mrs Hutchinson was a regular visitor to Anson's home and reported that there was nowhere

> I take so much pleasure in going into his house, where, notwithstanding he's a batchelor [sic], the neatness, good order and economy of his servants, gives one the highest satisfaction. How different this from that noisy hurley-burley and confusion, that scolding and storming which I have elsewhere seen, to the great uneasiness of the whole company'[25]

Despite her glowing testimonial, Mrs Hutchinson acknowledged that Anson was not without some minor faults:

> I have nowhere said that he is an Angel. In short, 'tis averred that he loves his bottle and his friend so well, that he will not be very soon tired of their company, especially when they happen to be perfectly to his taste, which is pretty nice as to both. Moreover, if fame says true, he is very far from being a woman-hater, and that now and then his mistress may come in for a share of him.[26]

Anson was an enthusiastic and successful card player who was 'censured for even winning money from his humble midshipman'.[27] He used his winnings to invest in local real estate, ships and slaves. His first significant property purchase was a plot of 64 acres immediately to the north of urban Charleston, which was completed in March 1727. He purchased at least five other properties during his service in South Carolina, including a large tract of wilderness near Hilton Head Island, and some of his acquisitions were only sold years later after he was appointed to the Admiralty.[28] Anson named his first purchase the Bowling Green plantation and he took up residence in a house on the site. The property included a tavern, possibly established by Anson, which he leased to a local vintner, and a recreation ground, which hosted 'public diversions, private challenges, and martial assemblies'.[29] In 1735 Anson, who would be a regular racegoer in later life, hosted the colony's first horse race at the plantation. Four horses ran a one-mile heat and the winner took home a 'handsome sadle [sic] and bridle' valued at nearly £3 sterling.[30] The Bowling Green also hosted cockfights, raffles and swordplay.

---

25 [Hutchinson], *The Private Character of Admiral Anson*, p.10.
26 [Hutchinson], *The Private Character of Admiral Anson*, pp.18–19.
27 Joseph Johnson, *Traditions and Reminiscences, Chiefly of the American Revolution in the South: Including Biographical Sketches, Incidents, and Anecdotes* (Charleston: Walker & James, 1851), p.38.
28 Edgar K. Thompson, 'George Anson in the Province of South Carolina', *The Mariner's Mirror*, 53 (1967), p.279.
29 Nic Butler, 'The Bowling Green: Recreational Space in Colonial Charleston', Charleston County Public Library (26 March 2021), <https://www.ccpl.org/charleston-time-machine/bowling-green-recreational-space-colonial-charleston>, accessed 23 August 2022.
30 Nic Butler, 'George Anson and Charles Codner: Gambling for Real Estate in 1735?', Charleston County Public Library (15 January 2021), <https://www.ccpl.org/charleston-time-machine/george-anson-and-charles-codner-gambling-real-estate-1735>, accessed 23 August 2022.

When Anson returned to England in 1744 after completing his circumnavigation, he instructed his agents in South Carolina to begin selling his property in Charleston. The western part of the Bowling Green plantation was subdivided into 25 lots that were sold in 1745, forming the initial phase of the development of Charleston's first suburb. It was named Ansonburgh and the main route through it was called Anson Street. The remainder of the plantation was subdivided before its sale in 1761 and absorbed into the new development.[31] Anson's long association with America as a landowner and developer was further recognised when Anson County, North Carolina, an area bordering South Carolina, was formed in 1750.

The cost of the property he acquired in Charleston and elsewhere in South Carolina was well beyond the means of a naval captain who depended on his pay alone. He paid £300 for the Bowling Green plantation, which was the equivalent of two years' captain's pay, and he must have relied on success at the card table, loans or family assets to finance the acquisition. There is a story that Anson received property from Thomas Gadsden, Collector of His Majesty's Customs in Charleston, who had previously sold him the Bowling Green, to satisfy a debt incurred in a card game, but no hard evidence has been found to support it.[32] In another card game, his opponent staked substantial property assets and lost, but Anson apparently later returned them and 'the generosity of his host' was never forgotten.[33] He also held mortgages on a further two tracts of land, which may have served as collateral for gambling debts.

Anson was not alone in acquiring a financial interest in the colony and several other naval officers stationed in Charleston invested in real estate, which they retained long after they had returned to England. They included Captain (later Vice Admiral Sir) Peter Warren who was to invest substantial sums in South Carolina (where a street is named after him) and elsewhere in North America. He had married a wealthy heiress and used a substantial dowry to invest in land in New York. In 1728, as he was returning to England from Vera Cruz, where he had negotiated the release of South Sea Company ships seized by the Spanish two years earlier, a hurricane forced him to put his ship, the *Solebay* (24), into Charleston for repairs. He remained there for four months and established a close friendship with Anson, describing the 'evenness of his temper [as] his greatest virtue'.[34] He was to serve as Anson's second in command at the first Battle of Cape Finisterre, 1747, but their lifelong friendship was later severely strained because of his prominent opposition to the controversial half-pay provisions of the 1749 Navy Bill. On Warren's departure from Charleston, Anson agreed to sell his assets, which were valued at £395, apart from a slave who was sold for £28 10s.

Anson remained at Charleston until 1730 and on his departure appointed an agent to manage his property and make further acquisitions. His next purchase was completed on

---

31 Nic Butler, 'The Bowling Green: Recreational Space in Colonial Charleston', Charleston County Public Library.
32 Nic Butler, 'George Anson and Charles Codner: Gambling for Real Estate in 1735?', Charleston County Public Library.
33 Walter V. Anson, *The Life of Admiral Lord Anson: Father of the British Navy, 1697–1762* (London: John Murray, 1912), p.5.
34 Peter Warren to John Norris Jnr., 2 June 1746, in Julian Gwyn (ed.), *The Royal Navy and North America: The Warren Papers 1736–1752* (London: Navy Records Society, 1973), p.249.

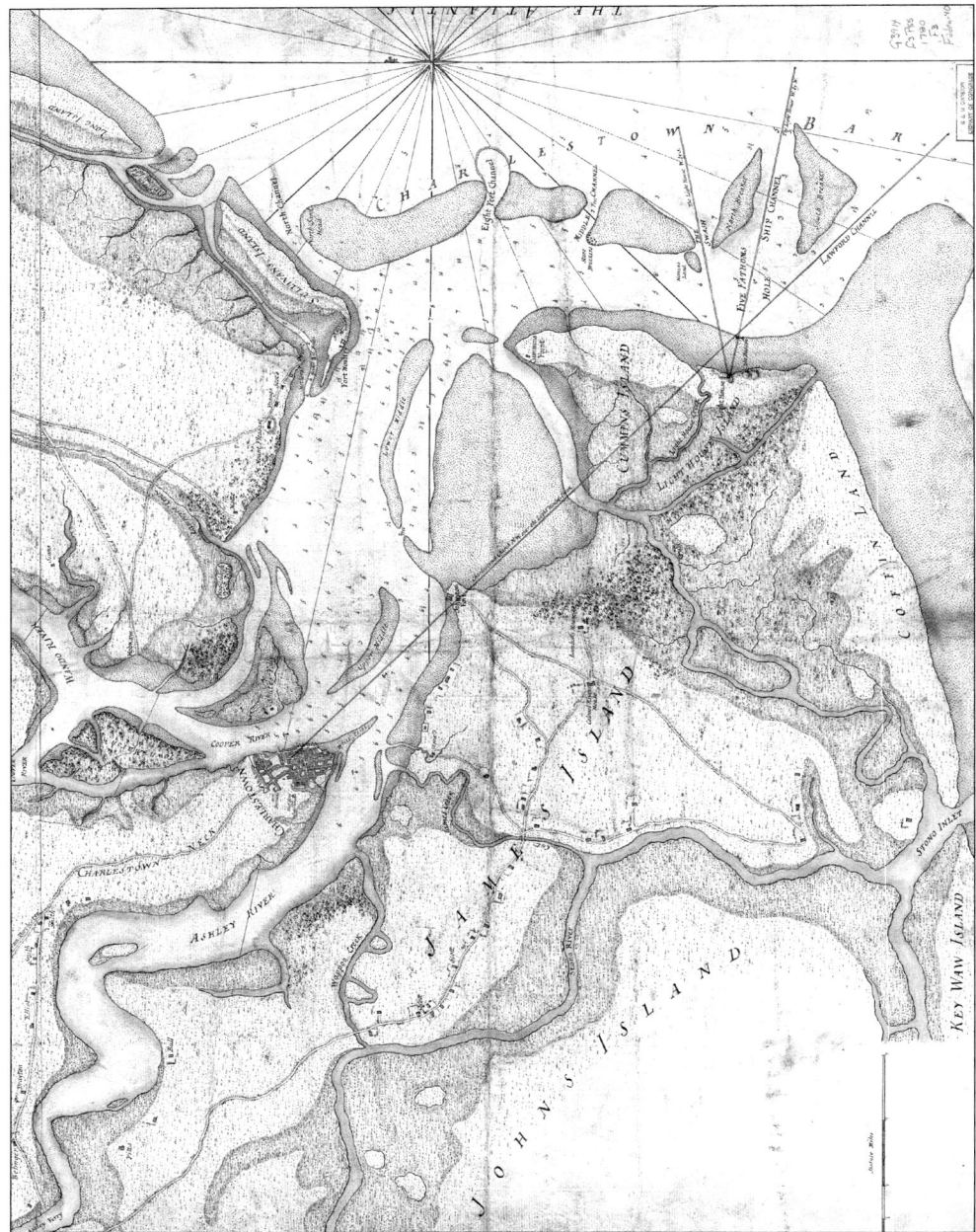

Plan of Charleston, South Carolina, c.1780. (Library of Congress, Geography and Map Division)

29 September 1730, not long after he departed for England: 'to George Anson of the Middle Temple, London, late commander of HMS *Garland*, a certain Barony or tract of land in South Carolina comprising 12,000 acres of land'.[35] On his return to England, the *Garland* was paid off but less than a year later, in May 1731, he was appointed to the command of the fifth-rate *Diamond* (40), which formed part of the Channel Fleet. He went on patrol in the Straits of Dover, where French shipping movements were monitored, but the ship was paid off less than three months later.

On 24 January 1732, Anson was appointed to the command of the *Squirrel* with orders to return to South Carolina, where he arrived on 17 June. By this time Britain's relations with Spain had again deteriorated and, in 1734, he sailed to Georgia to provide the colony with protection from possible Spanish attack. During this second stay in Charleston, Anson continued to manage Peter Warren's financial interests in the colony, sending several payments, in the form of bills drawn on the Navy Board, which were credited to his London account.[36] Early in 1735, during his final weeks in Charleston, he completed further property transactions and provided a loan of £1,000 to a young colonial planter who gave him a tract of 350 acres as collateral. The nature of the planter's obligation is unknown, but it may have represented an earlier gambling debt.

Despite Anson's accumulating property assets, when he was ordered back to England he wrote to his patron Sir John Norris asking if he could delay his return because of financial pressures:

> I hope my orders will come by no other conveyance than the ship that relieves me, as it will be a mutual advantage for us both to meet. As there have been formerly two ships stationed here, and the *Happy* sloop has to be relieved, as *she has seven years' pay due*, if I could be continued a year longer here, it would much contribute to the establishment of *my affairs*, which are yet *pretty much distressed*.[37]

However, his plea went unanswered and in May 1735 the *Squirrel* was relieved by the *Rose* (20) and Anson returned to England the following month. The ship was paid off and Anson was placed on half-pay, remaining on shore in England for more than two years.

There is no record of Anson's activities after his return to England until 9 December 1737 when he was appointed as captain of the *Centurion* (60), a fourth-rate ship of the line. This soon-to-be famous ship would serve as his flagship on the circumnavigation of the globe, 1740–1744, and was the only member of the squadron to return home. She was present at the first Battle of Cape Finisterre 1747 and saw extensive service during the Seven Years War, including the siege of Quebec, 1759, and the Havana expedition, 1762. Built at Portsmouth by the master shipwright Joseph Allin in 1732, the *Centurion* had a complement of 400 men and was armed with twelve 24-pounders on each side on the lower gun deck and smaller guns on the upper gun deck and quarterdeck. Her lower deck was about 140 feet long as specified by the 1719 Establishment but she was one foot wider across the beam than the

---

35 Thompson, 'George Anson', p.279.
36 Gwyn, *The Enterprising Admiral*, p.124.
37 Quoted in Anson, *The Life of Admiral Lord Anson*, p.6.

Model of the *Centurion*, by Benjamin Slade, 1747. (Royal Museums, Greenwich)

regulations prescribed, reflecting concerns about the relative sizes of British ships compared to their European counterparts

Before Anson took command, the *Centurion*'s peacetime service under her first three commanders had been largely uneventful apart from a voyage to Lisbon in 1736 when the horologist John Harrison was on board. He had joined the cruise to test the accuracy of his first sea clock (now known as H1) in his quest to find a method for determining longitude (an east-west measurement of position) at sea. The results were sufficiently promising for Harrison to begin work on a second version of the clock. As chairman of the Board of Longitude in the 1750s, Anson would play an important role in bringing this work to a successful conclusion.

Anson was first sent to the West African coast with orders to protect British merchantmen from the French and later went across the Atlantic to the West Indies, where he repaired the *Centurion* at St Thomas before calling at Barbados.[38] On 5 June 1739, on the return journey to

---

38 A Lieutenant's logbook for the *Centurion*, 1736–1744, is held by the National Maritime Museum, Greenwich, ADM/L/C/83.

England, he called at Charleston (where his friend Peter Warren now commanded the station ship) and stayed for 10 days. On his arrival, he had been unwilling to risk the *Centurion* by attempting to cross the hazardous sandbar at the harbour entrance and used the ship's boats to visit the town. When he reached Spithead on 10 November 1739, he discovered that war with Spain had been declared on 23 October 1739; apart from patrolling the Western Approaches in the latter part of the year, the *Centurion* remained at Portsmouth until it left on the voyage around the world in September 1740.

At this point in his career, Anson had accrued 22 years' service since his appointment as a second lieutenant, with only one significant interruption when he was placed on half-pay following his final return home from South Carolina. Service in these 'profitable but unglamorous posts [suggested] that Anson was a competent professional who preferred a lucrative peacetime side-show to half-pay or occasional fleet service'.[39] His good fortune in being almost continuously employed in the peacetime navy (at a time when the half-pay list was very long) may also be explained by the continuing support of his influential patrons, who now included Sir Charles Wager, First Lord of the Admiralty since 1733, and, according to House of Commons Speaker Arthur Onslow, 'a person of most extraordinary worth'.[40] Despite the routine nature of Anson's service, he ensured that Anson would not have to wait long for news of a significant new appointment following Britain's declaration of war on Spain. Known as the War of Jenkins' Ear, the conflict merged into the War of the Austrian Succession (1740–1748), with France soon joining Spain in the maritime war against Britain.

Tensions with Spain about access to lucrative markets in South America had been developing for several years and there were many reports of Spanish coastguards intercepting British merchantmen, including a notable incident in 1731 when they boarded a ship and assaulted her captain, Robert Jenkins. In 1738, Jenkins produced what he alleged to be his amputated ear in the House of Commons and the incident was exploited by opposition MPs who favoured war. Prime Minister Sir Robert Walpole sought to preserve peace, but public opinion was firmly against Spain and he was eventually forced to go to war. In June 1739, well before the formal British declaration of war, the navy was instructed to seize the Spanish *flota* departing from Cadiz and, in July, Admiral Edward Vernon was dispatched to the Caribbean to attack enemy shipping.

Preparations for a general maritime conflict were soon underway and a variety of proposals for amphibious operations against different parts of the Spanish empire were under discussion, with ministers taking advice from Wager and Norris (by now Admiral of the Fleet). These included a possible large-scale operation against Spanish territory in the Caribbean, which would extend Vernon's limited attacks on enemy shipping. Walpole decided to proceed and, by November, Vernon had captured the Spanish colonial possession of Porto Bello in what is now Panama to national acclaim and held it for three weeks. Although more warships would be dispatched to the Caribbean after this victory, discussions since June had focused on the possibility of sending forces to the Pacific and two proposals were actively considered. The first involved seizing the annual Spanish treasure ship, which sailed from Acapulco to Manila, the principal city of the Philippines, and typically carried silver

---

39 Andrew Lambert, *Admirals: The Naval Commanders Who Made Britain Great* (London: Faber & Faber, 2008), p.124.
40 *Bishop Burnet's History of His Own Time* (Oxford: The Clarendon Press, 1823), vol.V, p.390.

worth some £2,000,000 (about £353 million in 2023 prices). The idea was developed further by James Naish, a former supercargo (commercial agent) of the East India Company, who produced a detailed plan for taking Manila and capturing the galleon. The loss of a major trading centre would be a significant setback for Spain and a British occupation would forestall incursions by the French or Dutch.[41]

In September, an alternative plan, proposed by two former agents of the South Sea Company, Hubert Tassell and Henry Hutchinson, was submitted to Robert Walpole. It involved dispatching a squadron carrying 1,500 troops to the South Sea with orders to attack the coasts of Chile and Peru. The plan included conquering Chile, plundering the Lima treasure house and then attacking Panama; in occupied territory, the Spanish colonial administration would be replaced by indigenous governments allied with Britain. The authors argued that Spanish coastal defences were weak and the arrival of a British squadron could spark a rebellion against the colonial authorities. Although Wager and Norris had reservations about the proposal because it would be difficult to find the necessary troops, they were prepared to support a less ambitious operation that would focus on specific targets on the Pacific coast of South America. They believed that any expedition against Panama should be launched from the Caribbean rather than from the Pacific.

At the end of October senior ministers discussed the options and favoured the Manila proposal. On 1 November, Norris asked Wager whom he believed should command the expedition and he replied that 'he had thought of Captain Anson'; it would prove to be an astute choice. Soon after he arrived at Portsmouth, Anson received a summons from Wager asking him to report to the Admiralty, where he was informed of his appointment to command an ambitious expedition to capture Manila. Although he was an experienced 42-year-old captain who had served in a variety of roles, his combat experience was limited and the opportunity to distinguish himself had not arisen. However, his long and successful service in a remote colony, where his day-to-day decisions were made without reference to the Admiralty, suggested that he was well equipped for the independent command of an expeditionary force and that Wager's recommendation was justified.

As preparations continued, Anson was invited to join meetings of the ministerial group planning the expedition and on 17 November he attended for the first time. However, soon afterwards the project was suddenly cancelled as it became clear that there were not enough soldiers available to capture the colony as priority was to be given to operations in the Caribbean. On 7 December, Walpole decided to replace the Manila project with a smaller expedition to the South Sea, still with Anson in command and decided that it should go ahead as soon as possible. He envisaged sending six ships and 500 soldiers around Cape Horn to raid the costs of Chile and Peru before sailing to Panama, where they would meet up with the British troops who had marched across the isthmus from the Caribbean. With Panama under British control, the export of Spanish silver from both coasts would be disrupted.

Anson's appointment as commander in chief of the expedition with the temporary rank of commodore (the equivalent of brigadier in the army) was confirmed on 10 January 1740,

---

41 *Memorandum* [by James Naish], 2 August 1740, in Glyndwr Williams (ed.), *Documents Relating to Anson's Voyage Round the World 1740–1744* (London: Navy Records Society, 1967), pp.42–44.

but the delivery of his formal instructions was long delayed. Wager had prepared an outline in December and the Duke of Newcastle produced a complete draft, which was approved at a ministerial meeting chaired by Walpole on 7 January. The final version of the instructions, as approved by the King, was dated 31 January, but Anson did not receive it until 19 June. His ambitious orders required him

> …to settle some island in the South Seas; to succeed in a descent on Peru; to take two men-of-war and the Lima fleet; to take Panama and their treasure; to take several valuable towns; to take the Acapulco ship; and to induce the Peruvians to throw off their obedience to the King of Spain.[42]

Anson's squadron was to consist of the flagship *Centurion*, *Gloucester* (50), *Severn* (50), and *Pearl* (40), as well as the *Wager* (24), which had been built as a merchantman and was to serve as a storeship, and the *Tryal* (8), a sloop of war. Two hired victuallers, *Anna* and *Industry*, which were classed as pinks (ships with a very narrow stern), were to accompany the squadron. The *Gloucester* was commanded by Richard Norris; the *Severn* by Edward Legge; the *Pearl* by Matthew Mitchell; the *Wager* by Dandy Kidd; and the *Tryal* by George Murray (later sixth Lord Elibank). The land forces were commanded by Lieutenant Colonel Mordaunt Cracherode. Anson was ordered to proceed to the Pacific via the Cape Verde Islands, Brazil and Cape Horn but was required to interrupt his journey if 'the season is so far advanced that it may not be possible for you to arrive at Cape Horn, or to pass the streights of Magellan before the navigation in those parts may be so dangerous that it cannot be attempted without risk to our squadron'.[43] In these circumstances, he was to proceed to the River Plate and wait there until Cape Horn could be successfully negotiated. However, they were superseded by an additional set of instructions, dated 19 June, which ordered him to avoid the River Plate and sail direct for the Pacific.

When the squadron arrived on the 'Spanish coast of the South Sea', his instructions continued, 'you are to use your best endeavours to annoy and distress the Spaniards either at sea or on land'. He was authorised 'to seize, surprise, or take any of the towns or places belonging to the Spaniards on the coast'. With the instructions referring to the possibility that Anson's arrival might trigger a local rebellion, the expedition was different in character to past privateering raids. According to Anson's instructions, 'there was reason to believe that 'native Indians [on the coast of Chile] may not be adverse [*sic*] to join with you against the Spaniards to recover their freedom'. It was also thought that the Spanish residents of Peru 'have long had an inclination to revolt from their obedience to the King of Spain'. Anson was asked to encourage a rebellion if these reports proved to be correct and consider whether he should launch an attack on Callao (the port of Lima, Peru). He was also to attack any Spanish warships carrying treasure from Lima to Panama that he encountered.[44]

In support of the aim of encouraging a rebellion against Spanish rule in Peru, Anson was handed a draft manifesto, which promised 'British protection, freedom of trade and

---

42 The National Archives (TNA): SP 42/81, ff.293–298; SP 42/88, ff.2–10, 12–13, *Instructions to Commodore Anson*, 1740.
43 Williams (ed.), *Documents*, p.39.
44 Williams (ed.), *Documents*, p.35.

religious liberty to all who rose against the Spanish crown'.[45] This would include providing a 'constant naval force for your protection', as well as establishing garrisons and building fortifications. The British would also 'supply you with all such sorts of merchandise as you shall require… without your being subject to impositions, fatigues and dangers in going to celebrate the fairs at Panama, Portobelo, and Cartagena'.[46]

When he reached Panama, he was to contact British naval forces on the Caribbean coast to assist them 'in making a secure settlement either at Panama or any other place that shall be thought proper'. Anson was given the discretion to decide (in conjunction with his council of war) whether to sail northwards as far as Acapulco or remain longer at Panama, 'in case the place should have been taken by our forces'. The instructions did not specify Anson's homeward route although if he were to sail as far north as Acapulco, it was suggested that he might wish to return westwards across the North Pacific rather than retracing his outward journey, thus raising the possibility that the expedition might involve a circumnavigation of the globe. This route was suggested because there were likely to be difficulties in obtaining provisions in the Spanish-controlled territories along the Pacific coast if he decided to return home by Cape Horn.

There is no record of Anson's reaction to his instructions, which were over-ambitious and seemed likely to lead to failure. Apart from the threat posed by the Spanish navy, there was no evidence that the colonial population of Chile or Peru would welcome the intervention of British forces, which had been instructed to destroy their coastal towns and shipping, and it was much more likely that they would receive a hostile reception. Negotiating their passage around Cape Horn so late in the year would be fraught with difficulty and there would be health problems to contend with as scurvy, for which there was no known treatment, took its toll. (In 1753, James Lind would demonstrate that the consumption of citrus fruit prevented scurvy but it took the Royal Navy another 40 years before it adopted the cure.)

Preparations began shortly after Walpole authorised the expedition at the end of 1739, but it did not depart until the following September. The Navy Board soon issued instructions 'for the victualling of six ships… for 500 soldiers, in addition to their allowed complements, with provisions suitable for hot climates, and with brandy instead of beer'.[47] Tassell and Hutchinson were appointed as Agent-Victuallers and were permitted to travel with the expedition despite Anson's opposition. Apart from their contract to supply victuals, they were authorised to carry trade goods valued at £15,000 (£2.3 million in 2023 prices). Although some merchandise would be needed to exchange for fresh provisions as the voyage progressed, their value was far in excess of what Anson believed to be necessary, suggesting that they were being carried solely for 'the enrichment of the Agents'. The official account records that he 'objected both to the appointment of the Agent-Victuallers, and the allowing them to carry a cargo on board the squadron', but he was overruled by 'some considerable

---

45 Glyn Williams, *The Prize of All the Oceans. The Triumph and Tragedy of Anson's Voyage Round the World* (London: HarperCollins, 1999), p.11.
46 Williams (ed.), *Documents*, p.41.
47 Commissioners of the Navy to the Victualling Commissioners, 29 December 1739, in William A. Shaw (ed.), *Calendar of Treasury Books and Papers, 1739–1741* (London: Her Majesty's Stationery Office, 1901), p.270.

persons' who believed that the agents could establish profitable trading links on the Pacific coast.⁴⁸

Although the victualling arrangements were agreed without undue delay, Anson faced significant difficulties in getting his ships ready and recruiting their crews. With the whole navy being mobilised for war, the ships being prepared for the Caribbean and for patrolling home waters were given higher priority than Anson's small squadron. As a result, the major ship repairs and internal alterations necessary to accommodate the expedition's ground troops were delayed. The *Centurion*, for example, needed her hull and foremast repaired and her mainmast replaced. Discussions about the works continued for several months, and, despite Anson's lobbying efforts, the Admiralty did not approve them until July. Although he was exasperated by the delays, they gave him time to complete his personal preparations for the voyage. He assembled several charts and maps as well as a selection of travellers' accounts of South America, Asia and the Pacific. His acquisitions included books by William Dampier, who was the first person to circumnavigate the globe three times, and Captain George Shelvocke, whose voyage in 1719–1722 was the most recent English circumnavigation.⁴⁹

Anson's greatest difficulty was in recruiting sufficient seamen at a time when other squadrons were being prepared for service overseas. Although he could draw on a nucleus of experienced seamen, volunteers were hard to come by, possibly because they had heard rumours of the likely destination of the expedition. In these circumstances, he was forced to rely on the drafts brought in by his press gang as well as men who had just been discharged from hospital. However, these sources often proved to be unreliable and on one occasion Anson complained to the Admiralty when 20 pressed men were removed from his tender and taken to another ship, but he received no response. Men were also lost through desertion and illness. After the severe winter of 1739–1740, 'the sick lists grew faster than the muster rolls of new recruits, so that in the five months from February to June [1740] the navy received 3,627 additional men but sent 4,875 into the hospitals'.⁵⁰

The recruitment of officers proceeded more smoothly and by mid-year, the *Centurion* had a full complement of lieutenants. They included David Cheap (who was later captain of the ill-fated *Wager*), and third lieutenants Philip Saumarez and Peter Denis, both of whom had significant roles during the voyage and were to become prominent members of Anson's circle after their return to England. Saumarez's later career was cut short by his premature death during the second Battle of Cape Finisterre (October 1747) while Denis, the son of a naval chaplain, rose to the rank of vice admiral and was made a baronet. Denis became one of Anson's political followers and in 1754 was elected as MP for his old constituency of Hedon in Yorkshire.

Apart from the difficulties in recruiting a full complement of seamen, Anson soon learned that his promised landing force – a regiment of regular soldiers and three independent

---

48   Richard Walter and Benjamin Robins, *A Voyage Round the World in the Years MDCCXL, I, II, III, IV by George Anson*. Ed. Glyndwr Williams (London: Oxford University Press, 1974), p.25.
49   William Dampier, *A New Voyage Round the World* (London: James Knapton, 1697); George Shelvocke, *A Voyage Round the World by the Way of the Great South Sea, Perform'd in the Years 1719, 20, 21, 22, in the Speedwell of London* (London: Sennen, 1726).
50   Williams, *The Prize of All the Oceans*, p.18.

companies of 100 men each – would not be provided and that he would have to accept 500 Chelsea Pensioners instead. They were far from ideal replacements as they 'consist of soldiers, who from their age, wounds, or other infirmities, are incapable of service in marching regiments'. According to the authorised account of the voyage, 'Mr Anson was greatly chagrined at having such a decrepid [sic] detachment allotted to him: for he was fully persuaded that the greatest part of them would perish long before they arrived at the scene of action'.[51]

Despite his best efforts more suitable troops were not forthcoming and, on 5 August, the pensioners were ordered on board the squadron but only just over half the expected 500 men turned up, with the most mobile deserting long before they reached Portsmouth. Those who arrived as instructed were the 'most feeble and incapable of effecting their escape from a service which their comrades justly considered as sending them to a certain death'.[52] Many had to be carried on board on stretchers and most were over the age of 60. To those who witnessed it, it was difficult 'to conceive a more moving scene than the imbarkation [sic] of these unhappy veterans. They were themselves extremely averse to the service they were engaged in, and fully apprised of all the disasters they were afterwards exposed to'.[53]

Anson was forced to discharge the weakest but hardly any of those who went on the expedition were alive a year later. On 9 August, the Duke of Newcastle reported that he had seen 'a letter from Commodore Anson, with an account that fourscore of his invalids have deserted, and as many more unfit for service', but he took no action to resolve the problem.[54] To support this reduced complement of invalids, three companies of untrained marines (a total of 300 men) were added to the expedition but they also proved to be of questionable value. They were 'newly raised, consequently totally uninured to the fatigues, even of Channel service, and ignorant of all military discipline'.[55] Like the pensioners, they were prone to sickness and suffered high mortality rates, with few surviving the entire journey.

It was not until 8 August that Anson received the last detachment of marines, and, in total, the squadron now carried 1,939 men (including 174 officers and servants and 1,212 seamen). It may be at this point that Anson's brother Thomas, who was planning to go on a tour of the Mediterranean, came on board the *Centurion*. He sailed with Anson as far as Cape Finisterre, where they would arrive on 29 September, before transferring to another warship headed for Lisbon and Gibraltar. On 10 August, some eight months after he had been appointed to the command of the expedition, Anson sailed from Spithead to the St Helens anchorage in the Solent. Further delays arose because he was ordered to accompany Admiral John Balchen, who was escorting transports carrying 600 troops under Charles Cathcart, eighth Lord Cathcart, on the first stage of his journey to the West Indies. The combined force, which consisted of 21 warships and 124 transports and merchantmen, was

---

51 Walter, *A Voyage Round the World*, p.23.
52 Charnock, *Biographia Navalis*, vol.IV, p.102. See also Philip Saumarez's comments in Thomas Keppel, *The Life of Augustus, Viscount Keppel* (London: Henry Colburn, 1842), vol.I, p.20.
53 Walter, *A Voyage Round the World*, p.23.
54 Duke of Newcastle to the Earl of Hardwicke, 9 August 1740, in Yorke (ed.), *The Life and Correspondence*, vol.I, p.245.
55 Charnock, *Biographia Navalis*, vol.IV, p.102.

held up until 23 August by unfavourable weather, but on their departure they found 'the wind soon returning to its old quarter' and the attempt was abandoned.[56]

Anson made three more abortive attempts to sail before being instructed, on 9 September, to leave St Helens at the first opportunity without waiting to accompany Lord Cathcart if he was not ready. However, Anson's hopes of a rapid departure were not realised as he soon received further orders to escort a large number of merchant ships destined for America and the Mediterranean as far as the Bay of Biscay. Anson finally departed for Madeira, his first port of call, on 18 September, 40 days after he had first arrived at St Helens, together with two warships and the merchantmen they were accompanying. They met the remaining ships in the convoy at Rame Head near Plymouth soon afterwards and the combined fleet under Anson's command now consisted of 11 warships and 151 merchantmen.

At this point, Anson took the opportunity to summon his captains to a meeting on board the *Centurion*, when he briefed them on the squadron's instructions for the voyage. The 50 ships bound for America left him on 25 September, with the remainder departing for the Mediterranean four days later. As Lieutenant Saumarez commented: 'being freed from the incumbrances of so large a convoy was no small relief to us, which joined to the advantage of a fair wind promoted our making a considerable progress in our passage'.[57] However, Saumarez's optimism was misplaced as contrary winds soon caused further delays.

Anson first became aware in August that the Spanish had known about the planned expedition for several months, but was yet to discover that they had also been informed of his recent departure from England. Some two months earlier the Royal Navy had boarded a Dutch merchantman off Cuba, which had been carrying the Viceroy of Mexico and his retinue; they had managed to escape but left behind papers showing that 'the King of Spain had notice of our fitting out six ships... to go round Cape Horn to the South Sea, and expresses have been sent to the Viceroys of Peru and Mexico to be on their guard, and to have all their forces ready to prevent our designs'. The long-drawn-out preparations at Portsmouth meant that 'what was believed to be a well-kept secret soon became common gossip in every southern coastal town'.[58] They gave the French secret service ample time to discover the nature of Anson's instructions and details of the ships under his command. These early intelligence warnings meant that the Spanish would be well prepared to respond when Anson eventually departed.[59] Apart from alerting her colonial governors, Spain prepared a powerful squadron of five warships under the command of *Jefe de Escuadra* (Rear Admiral) José Alfonso Pizarro, which consisted of the flagship *Asia* (64), together with the *Guipuscoa* (66), *Hermonia* (40), *Esperanza* (50), *San Esteban* (40) and a patache (a light sailing vessel with two masts) of 20 guns. When news of Anson's departure reached Spain, Pizarro was dispatched from Santander with instructions to intercept the British squadron as it arrived at Madeira.

As he left the English coast, Anson was as concerned about the impact of his delayed departure on his passage around Cape Horn as he was about the Spanish threat. He now

---

56 Walter, *A Voyage Round the World*, p.26.
57 Williams (ed.), *Documents*, p.60.
58 Leo Heaps, *Log of the Centurion. Based on the Original Papers of Captain Philip Saumarez on Board HMS Centurion, Lord Anson's Flagship during his Circumnavigation, 1740–44* (London: Hart-Davis, MacGibbon, 1973), p.31.
59 There is an account of Pizarro's squadron in Walter, *A Voyage Round the World*, pp.35–46.

expected to reach this point by January 1741, when he would face difficult seasonal weather conditions (the best time to make the journey around the Cape from the east was in June and July). The official history comments that the squadron's late departure 'which in its consequences was the source of all the disasters to which this enterprise was afterwards exposed'.[60] His fears were intensified because the journey to Madeira took much longer than usual – six weeks rather than the normal two – as a result of contrary winds and diversions when unidentified ships appeared. As a result, Anson was unable to make up any of the time lost while he was waiting at St Helens. His supplementary instructions meant that sheltering in the River Plate was no longer an option and he would need to proceed around the Cape regardless of the weather ahead. As we shall see, Anson's growing concerns about the risks facing the squadron would soon be amply justified.

---

60 Walter, *A Voyage Round the World*, p.28.

2

Around the World, 1740–1743

When Anson arrived at Funchal, Madeira, on 25 October 1740, he learnt from the Portuguese governor that a squadron of seven or eight ships of the line and a patache had been sighted to the west of the island during the previous week. They were almost certainly the Spanish ships under the command of Pizarro, which had been sent in search of the British squadron, but Anson could find no trace of them. Before leaving Madeira, he suffered his first significant losses through illness and desertion. These included Captain Richard Norris of the *Gloucester*, who had fallen ill and was permitted to return to England; he was replaced by Captain Matthew Mitchell of the *Pearl*. Consequential moves included the appointment of Captain Dandy Kidd to the *Pearl*, Captain George Murray to the *Wager* and Lieutenant David Cheap to the *Tryal*.

Anson left Madeira on 5 November and headed south across the Atlantic towards the coast of Brazil. Although there was still no sign of the Spanish, Anson soon faced other difficulties. On 20 November, the master of the *Industry*, one of his two victuallers, decided to leave the squadron as he was entitled to do under the terms of his agreement with the Admiralty, but it took three days to transfer her stores to the seven remaining ships. By this time, typhus, dysentery and malaria were spreading rapidly amongst the squadron's crews in the hot and overcrowded conditions on board. As casualties mounted, Anson sought to improve the circulation of air below deck by ordering additional scuttles – small openings in a ship's side – to be cut.

On 21 December, the squadron arrived at Saint Catherine's (Santa Catarina), an island off the southern coast of Brazil, which was part of the Portuguese empire. Anson had planned a short stay to take on water and fresh provisions but he was forced to remain there for a month because the *Tryal* required repairs to her mainmast and foremast. The increasing numbers of sick also needed time to recover; they were sent ashore to live in tents but the island proved to be far from an ideal place to convalesce: 'mosquitoes swarmed on the low-lying, marshy ground where the hospital tents were pitched, and malaria soon appeared'.[1] Illness and death increased as a result: 28 men on the *Centurion* were buried during her stay on the island, with the number of sick increasing from 80 to 96.

Unknown to Anson at the time, the island's Portuguese governor had alerted the Spanish authorities in Buenos Aires to his arrival. After failing to intercept Anson off Madeira,

---

1 Williams, *The Prize of All the Oceans*, p.33.

Pizarro had sailed for the River Plate, where he waited for further news of his movements. In late January 1741, Pizarro set sail for the South Sea, where he planned to intercept the British squadron as it completed its passage around Cape Horn and when it was likely to be in a much-weakened state. Although he sighted and briefly pursued the *Pearl* off the coast of Patagonia, the rest of the British squadron was permanently to elude him. Meanwhile, Anson left Saint Catherine's on 18 January 1741, ordering his captains to rendezvous at Port St Julian (Puerto San Julián) on the coast of Patagonia, some 1,200 miles further south, in what is now southern Argentina. He soon ran into difficulties as he sailed towards a 'hostile, or at best, a desert and inhospitable coast'.[2] During a violent storm four days after his departure, the *Tryal*'s repaired mainmast collapsed again and she was taken in tow by the *Gloucester*. He lost a second captain when Dandy Kidd of the *Pearl* died during the storm and his first lieutenant took temporary command. The latter was soon faced with a major new test when Pizarro's squadron was sighted, but he managed to evade the enemy who abandoned the chase before nightfall.

Although the Spanish squadron was almost certainly still present in the area, Anson had little choice but to stick to his plan to call at Port St Julian because of the need to repair the *Tryal* before attempting the passage around Cape Horn. Arriving on 19 February, Anson was disappointed with the port's bleak setting, which was 'abounding with salt lakes, but destitute of either verdure, shrub, tree or fresh water, and seems the seat of infernal spirits', and was without shelter for the ships.[3] He remained there for nine days while the *Tryal*'s repairs were completed. At this point, Anson made several new appointments following Captain Kidd's death: George Murray replaced Kidd as captain of the *Pearl*, David Cheap was appointed to the command of the *Wager* and Charles Saunders went to the *Tryal*. Anson also moved Peircy Brett, first lieutenant of the *Gloucester*, into the *Centurion*. Brett was an accomplished artist and the drawings he made during the voyage were to be used to illustrate the official account. He became a prominent member of Anson's circle, rose to the rank of admiral and served as a member of the Admiralty Board, 1766–1770.

On 27 February, the squadron left Port St Julian and continued southwards. Once he had passed through the Le Maire Strait, the passage between the Tierra del Fuego archipelago and Staten Island, Anson intended to sail around Cape Horn at a safe distance from the coast before heading north-west into the Pacific, but they soon encountered great difficulties: the Cape had not been accurately charted, they faced severe gales and heavy snow, and there were fresh outbreaks of scurvy. Although he ordered his captains to remain within two miles of the *Centurion* as they sailed around the Cape, it seemed likely that either poor weather or the appearance of the Spanish would cause the squadron to disperse well before it reached the Pacific. In these circumstances, Anson instructed his captains to meet at the island of Nuestra Señora de Socorro (Guamblin) in the Chonos archipelago off the coast of Chile after they had successfully negotiated Cape Horn. After the squadron had reassembled, he planned to launch an attack on the Chilean port of Valdivia, some 360 miles to the north. Capturing the port, which was poorly defended, would enable his ships to be careened and refitted before they moved on to the Juan Fernandez islands, some 370 miles

---

2   Walter, *A Voyage Round the World*, p.67.
3   Philip Saumarez, *Abstract of a Journal*, in Williams (ed.), *Documents*, p.165.

due west of Valparaiso. Juan Fernandez would serve as a final rendezvous point for any ship that had failed to find the squadron at either Socorro or Valdivia.

By 7 March, Anson reached the Le Maire Strait as the squadron began its passage around Cape Horn. At first, the weather was so favourable that Philip Saumarez said they 'began to look on the conquest of the Peruvian mines and principal towns as an amusement which would naturally occur'.[4] However, conditions soon deteriorated rapidly as the squadron 'met with the most intolerable weather… the climate being very cold, and the continual rain, snow or sleet with a constant headwind and a monstrous deep sea made it quite insupportable'.[5] According to Pascoe Thomas, the *Centurion*'s schoolmaster, these 'most terrible and dreadful storms' were to last until 25 May.[6] With storms moving from the south they were in danger of foundering on the rocks of Staten Island.

Although they managed to avoid this danger, the ships were forced back more than 20 miles to the east of Staten Island. It was the beginning of a three-month nightmare as the squadron tried to force its way around Cape Horn in the face of mountainous seas and westerly gales. The huge waves caused significant damage to the ships, while men were 'in perpetual danger of being dashed to pieces against the decks, or sides of the ship', washed overboard or suffering from frostbite as the freezing weather brought snow and sleet.[7] During these continuous storms, the *Anna* disappeared for six days and the *Gloucester* suffered a broken mainyard, a development which Anson later blamed for the delays he faced in rounding Cape Horn.

It was at this point that the first outbreak of scurvy occurred, with many crew members falling ill. Those who had been in poor health from the beginning, particularly the Chelsea pensioners, were the first to be taken ill and among the first to die. The variable symptoms included large spots and ulcers, swollen legs, putrid gums and rotting flesh. According to the official account, the disease was usually accompanied by 'a strange dejection of the spirits, and with shiverings, tremblings and a disposition to be seized with the most dreadful terrors on the slightest accident'.[8] It spread rapidly because of overcrowding and the inadequate food on offer while they waited at Spithead and during the voyage. Without a balanced diet – and in the absence of any effective counter-measures – it was inevitable that, after six months at sea, the disease would make its appearance. Anson and his lieutenants were more fortunate as they had eaten well before their departure and were unaffected by scurvy at this point in the voyage.

By the beginning of April, Anson calculated that they had passed the most westerly point of Tierra del Fuego and he decided to turn northwards in the direction of the Pacific. But if Anson was feeling more optimistic, he would soon have cause to change his mind. On 10 April, the *Severn* and *Pearl* disappeared during a violent storm; they had turned back and the rest of the squadron never saw them again. Three nights later, the remaining ships came close to disaster when they sailed to within two miles of Cape Noir, a promontory on the

---

4   Saumarez, *Abstract of a Journal*, in Williams (ed.), *Documents*, p.165.
5   *Journal of Lawrence Millechamp, September 1740–August 1741*, in Williams (ed.), *Documents*, p.77.
6   Pascoe Thomas, *A True and Impartial Journal of a Voyage to the South-Seas, and Round the Globe* (London: S. Birt, 1745), p.21.
7   Walter, *A Voyage Round the World*, p.85.
8   Walter, *A Voyage Round the World*, pp.105–106.

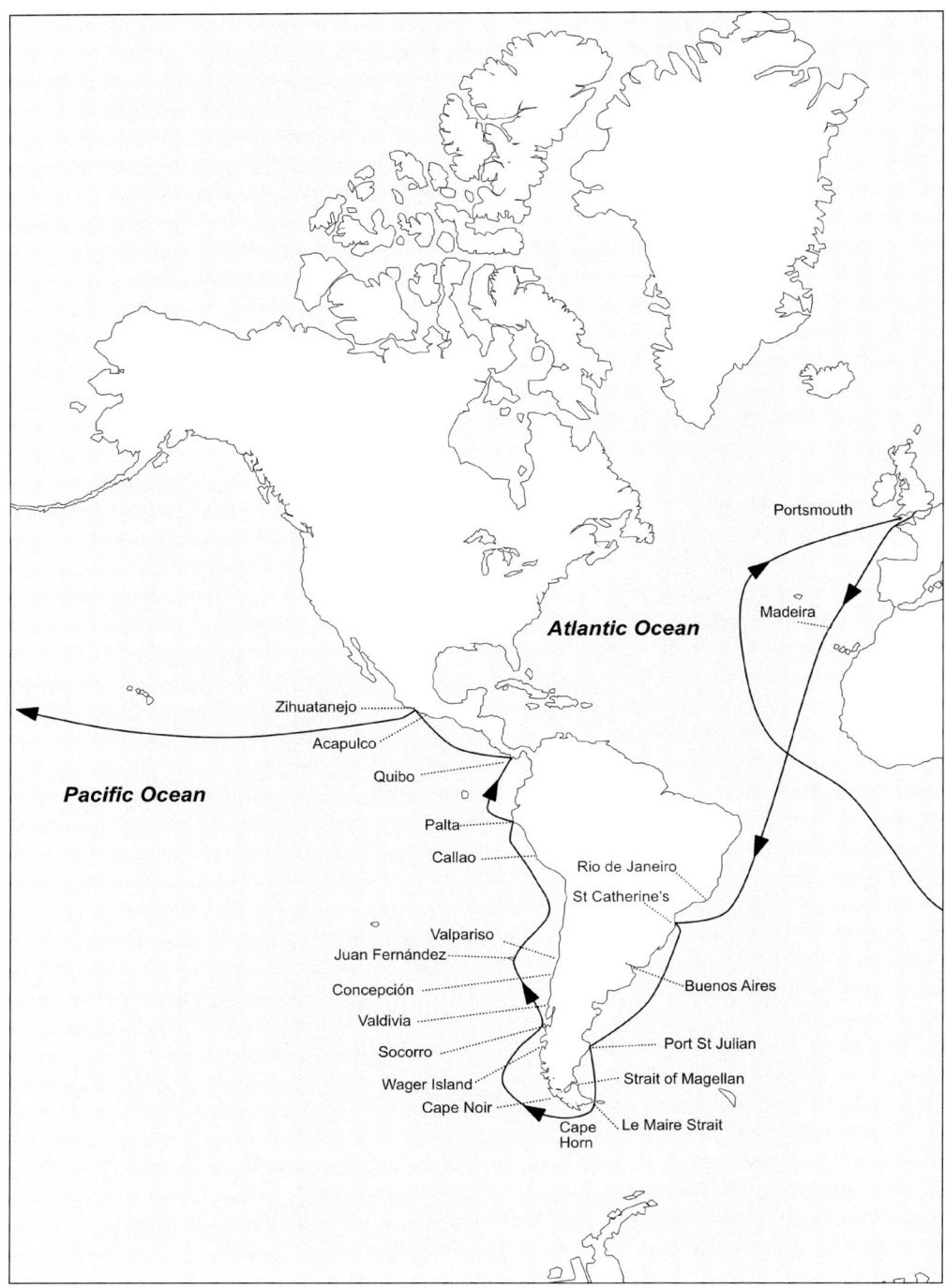

Anson's Circumnavigation, 1740-1744.

AROUND THE WORLD, 1740–1743   37

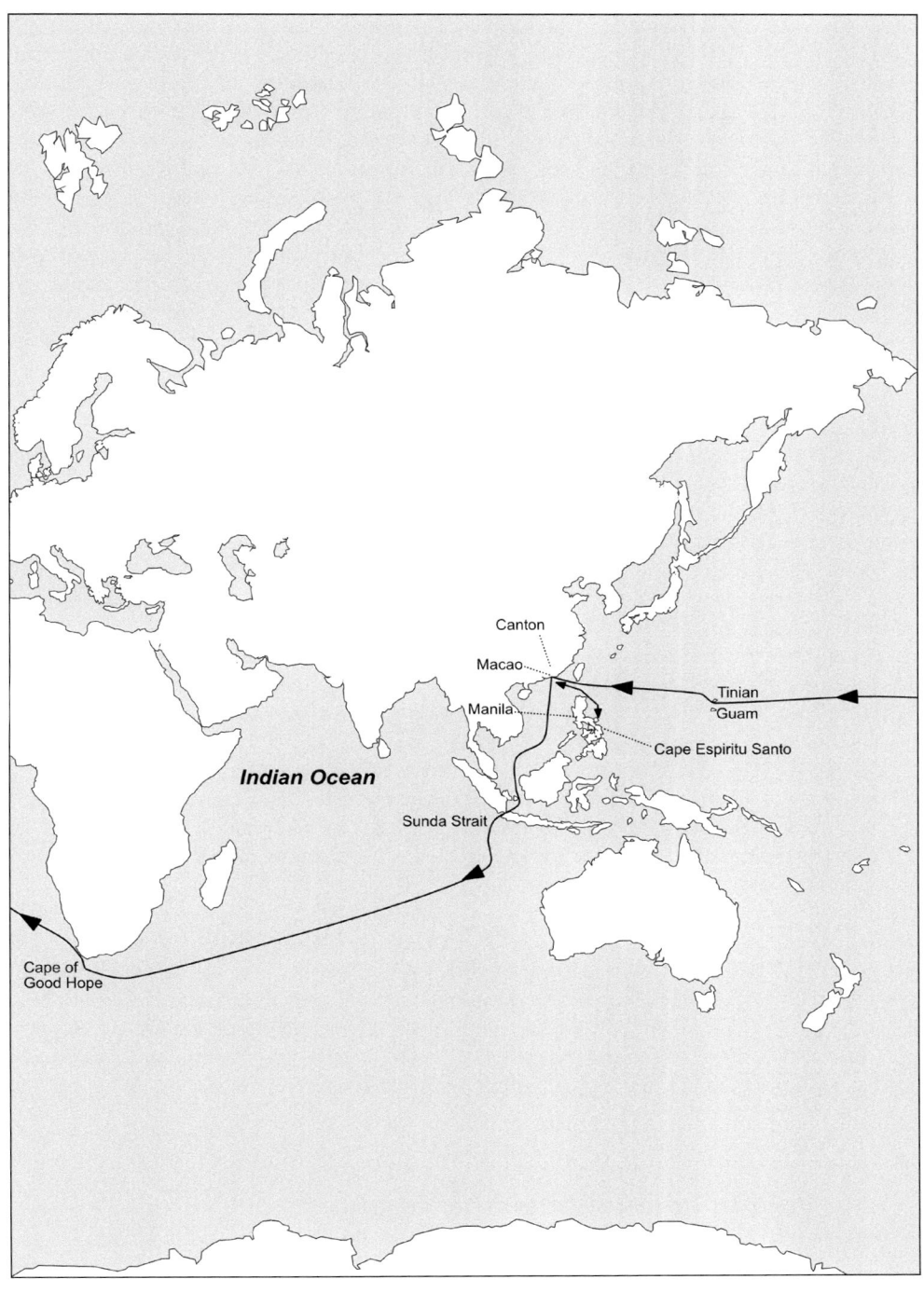

south-west of a small island off Tierra del Fuego, which was some 300 miles east of their estimated position. In calculating their passage, they had failed to take sufficient account of the effects of the strong winds and currents and still not cleared Tierra del Fuego.

To correct this navigational error, Anson first sailed south before turning north-west towards the Pacific once more, losing contact with the *Wager* as he did so. By this point, Lawrence Millechamp, purser of the *Tryal* sloop, reported that 'our seamen now almost all despairing of ever getting on shore voluntarily gave themselves up to their fatal distemper, and only used to envy those whose good fortune it was to die first. Nothing was more frequent than to bury eight or ten men from each ship every morning'.[9] When the remaining four ships turned to the north-west a few days later, they were faced with another major storm and, on 24 April, every sail on the *Centurion* and the *Gloucester* was damaged. During the night, the storm dispersed the squadron and the *Centurion* found herself alone the following morning; she did not see any of them again until after arriving at Juan Fernandez.

As Anson sailed towards the rendezvous point on the coast of Chile, he was faced with an increasing death rate among the *Centurion*'s crew, with 43 dying in April and 'near double that number' in May; the other three ships suffered similar losses. He now barely had sufficient men to operate the flagship and food was in short supply: it 'was generally bread toasted over burning brandy to kill the numerous insects it abounded with'.[10] In view of the persistent storms and heavy losses from scurvy, Anson was lucky to have reached the Pacific. As Admiral Vernon commented, 'it must have been a particular good fortune to Mr Anson to have gained a winter passage around Cape Horn, and to have left Pizarro at Buenos Aires'.[11] On 8 May, he arrived off Socorro Island but there was no sign of the other members of the squadron. At this point, he would have reflected on the damaging consequences of sailing around Cape Horn at the wrong time of year because of his delayed departure from England. As the official history comments, the delay resulted in:

> The separation of our ships, the destruction of our people, the ruin of our project on *Baldivia* [Valdivia]… and the reduction of our squadron from the formidable condition in which it passed Streights *Le Maire*, to a couple of shattered half-manned cruisers and a sloop, so far disabled, that in many climates they scarcely durst have put to sea.[12]

Anson cruised off the island for two weeks in the expectation that his other ships would appear, but his hope that he had now reached calmer waters was not to be realised: 'the *Pacifick* Ocean was to us less hospitable than the turbulent neighbourhood of *Terra del Fuego* and Cape *Horn*'.[13] He reported that he faced 'heavy flaws and dangerous gusts, expecting every moment to have my masts carried away', and he was without the 'men able to keep the deck sufficient to take in a topsail, all being violently afflicted with the scurvy, and every

---

9   *Journal of Lawrence Millechamp* in Williams (ed.), *Documents*, p.78.
10 *Journal of Lawrence Millechamp* in Williams (ed.), *Documents*, p.78.
11 Edward Vernon to the Duke of Newcastle, 15 March 1742, in Williams (ed.), *Documents*, p.171.
12 Walter, *A Voyage Round the World*, p.91.
13 Walter, *A Voyage Round the World*, p.107.

day lessening our number by six, eight or ten'.[14] As she left Socorro, the *Centurion* ran into increasingly violent winds, which seemed to combine 'the fury of all the storms which we had hitherto encountered' and caused further damage to the sails and rigging.[15]

With the plan to attack Valdivia – the second rendezvous – now abandoned, Anson headed directly for the Juan Fernandez islands, some 850 miles further north. First discovered by the Spanish in 1574, the Scottish buccaneer Alexander Selkirk had been marooned there from 1704 to 1709, and his account of the islands provided the basis for Daniel Defoe's *Robinson Crusoe* of 1719. The choice of Juan Fernandez as the final rendezvous was not without its problems because of uncertainty about its longitude.[16] Anson decided to try to find the islands by sailing down its latitude, but his instructions gave the wrong measurement and they were much further offshore than his charts suggested. As a result of these errors, Anson's search took him too far to the north and too far to the east of the islands' actual position. When he realised that he may have sailed too far, he compounded the error by turning east until (on 30 May) the coast of Chile came into view. Anson now realized that he needed to return to the original search area, but, faced with unfavourable winds, it took him nine days to do so. The resulting delay of nearly two weeks cost the lives of up to 80 men who might otherwise have been saved by an earlier arrival at Juan Fernandez.[17]

On 9 June, early in the morning, Anson caught his first sight of Juan Fernandez, which consisted of three uninhabited islands and had served as a refuge for stranded seamen since the late seventeenth century. Like Alexander Selkirk, Anson decided to stay on the second largest island, Más a Tierra, which Philip Saumarez described as 'the most romantic and pleasant place imaginable, abounding with myrtle trees, and covered with turnips and sorrel. Its bays, abounding with all kinds of fish, seem calculated for the reception of distressed seamen'.[18] With a severely depleted crew, the *Centurion*'s arrival in Cumberland Bay on the island's north coast on 10 June was fraught with difficulty, but she eventually anchored with the help of her officers and their servants. Anson's arrival was well timed because a Spanish warship had left the island only three days before, thus avoiding an engagement he was ill-equipped to fight. The *Centurion* was joined a few days later by the *Tryal*, which had also suffered a high death and sickness rate: only 34 men (out of a total of 100) had survived.

Anson's first priority was to evacuate the sick, who were suffering from scurvy, typhus and dysentery, and carry them ashore. All the remaining fit officers and men were employed on the task, which was carried out in heavy seas, but, on 15 June, before everyone had been moved ashore, the *Tryal* was driven out to sea in a storm. By the time she returned four days later, several more seamen had died. For those who were safely landed on the island their prospects of recovery were more promising: 'when we came in again we caught fish for the sick, which with the greens and other refreshments we met with here, together with the smell of the earth, recovered them to a miracle'.[19]

---

14 George Anson to the Duke of Newcastle, 7 December 1742, in Williams (ed.), *Documents*, p.156.
15 Walter, *A Voyage Round the World*, p.108.
16 At the time of Anson's circumnavigation of the globe, it was not possible to calculate longitude accurately at sea.
17 Walter, *A Voyage Round the World*, p.110.
18 Saumarez, *Abstract of a Journal*, in Williams (ed.), *Documents*, p.166.
19 *Journal of Lawrence Millechamp*, in Williams (ed.), *Documents*, p.79.

Despite the availability of fresh food, Anson realised that their survival was still in the balance and it was vital that the rest of his squadron appeared, but it was not until 21 June that another ship was sighted in the distance. Five days later she came close enough to the shore to be identified as the *Gloucester*. Anson dispatched his longboat, which was loaded with fresh fish and water, to meet the badly damaged ship. According to Saumarez, she was 'in a most deplorable condition, nearly two-thirds of her men being dead but very few of the rest able to perform their duty'.[20] The longboat crew was ordered to remain on board the *Gloucester* but even with this additional manpower it proved impossible to bring her into Cumberland Bay because of unfavourable winds.

Attempts to tow the *Gloucester* failed and, on 18 July, she was blown out of sight of land. Five days later she returned and finally anchored in the bay. Since leaving Patagonia the ship had lost 254 men, with only 94 men remaining: most were suffering from scurvy and more were to die after they were brought on land. Despite plentiful provisions, fresh fish and the 'indulgent care of the Commodore, they yet buried three-fourths of their crew, and a very small proportion of the remainder was capable of assisting in the duty of the ship'.[21] Scurvy caused more deaths among the invalids and marines than the seamen, with every invalid and 46 marines (out of a total of 48) dying on the *Gloucester*. Survival rates on the *Centurion* were little better, with only four invalids and 11 marines remaining alive.

During their three-month stay on the island, Anson and about 100 members of the ships' crews lived onshore. His tent was pitched away from his men in an idyllic location, which Pascoe Thomas described as being in a 'small square environ'd by a grove of Myrtle trees, the passage to which was mostly natural, and something like to a labyrinth. Near it ran a fine large rivulet of water, to which a passage was cut through the woods; the whole together forming a pretty romantick scene'.[22] As the crews convalesced, the death rate fell and during August only eight men died. Anson organised the repair and cleaning of the three surviving ships, which were in poor condition, with Anson describing the *Centurion* as 'intolerably loathsome'. He also instructed his officers to survey the harbours and coasts of the islands, 'knowing, from his own experience, of how great consequence these materials might prove to any *British* vessels hereafter employed in those seas'.[23]

On 16 August, the storeship *Anna* pink appeared, the fourth and final member of the squadron to reach Juan Fernandez. Her entire crew of 16 had survived and her stores remained intact; they had missed the Socorro rendezvous because of strong westerly winds but had found a sheltered harbour on the mainland where they spent two months recovering from their passage around the Horn. With the *Anna*'s arrival, Anson was able to restore full rations to his surviving crews. Although this small merchant ship had managed to reach Juan Fernandez, there was still no sign of the *Pearl*, *Severn* or *Wager*. The *Pearl* and *Severn* had not been seen since 10 April and Anson ordered Saunders and Saumarez to go out in the *Tryal* to search for them, but they could not be found, and he was not to discover their fate until he arrived at Macao in 1742.

---

20 Heaps, *Log of the Centurion*, p.114.
21 Walter, *A Voyage Round the World*, p.129.
22 Thomas, *A True and Impartial Journal*, p.42.
23 Walter, *A Voyage Round the World*, p.115.

Both ships had abandoned the attempt to reach the Pacific and turned back, arriving at Rio de Janeiro on 6 June. Captain Murray had wanted to make another attempt to sail around Cape Horn but he was overruled by Legge as the senior officer and the two ships returned home. Both captains recognised that they could be vulnerable to the charge that they had deserted the squadron while on active service and in their reports to the Admiralty they argued that their decision had saved the two ships from almost certain destruction. Anson would later defend their conduct in the official history, referring to the 'great joy' with which news of their survival was received when the *Centurion* reached Canton.[24]

The *Wager*, meanwhile, had lost sight of the squadron at the end of April but continued along the coast of Chile towards the Socorro rendezvous point; she was wrecked on an island now known as Wager Island on 14 May. Mutiny followed and her captain, David Cheap, was unable to regain control despite shooting one of the ringleaders. The surviving mutineers reached England in January 1743, but Cheap and two companions did not return home for another three years. No charges of mutiny were brought by the Admiralty because, under existing law, naval officers' authority came to an end when a ship was lost. Anson was to be involved in producing legislation to close this loophole in 1748.[25]

Anson planned to leave Juan Fernandez as soon as his men had recovered because of the danger that Pizarro's squadron or warships from the mainland might arrive at any moment. Before leaving the island Anson devoted much time to considering his options because he was now in a much weaker position, being reduced to 'three sail of men-of-war, and one storeship, in a most wretched condition, having not more than a fifty-gun ship's complement among us all'.[26] The three surviving warships had left Spithead with a total of 961 men but only 335 had survived, which meant that his crews were unable to sail the ships and operate their guns at the same time. As a result, the squadron's firepower was significantly depleted and his original instructions would need to be significantly modified if they were to survive.

Despite his heavy losses, Anson was determined to continue and there is no evidence that he ever seriously considered abandoning the expedition and returning home. The most difficult part of the journey – the passage around Cape Horn – was over and their stay on Juan Fernandez had improved the health and morale of the survivors. He will have been reassured by the performance of several of his officers – including Saunders, Saumarez and Brett – who had demonstrated their courage and leadership qualities over the past few months. However, he recognised that with fewer men, ships and guns at his disposal, he was no longer in a position to launch an attack on Callao or other major ports on the Pacific coast. Instead, he would be confined to hitting smaller coastal targets and individual Spanish merchant ships. With these objectives in mind, Anson decided to head north to Panama, where he hoped to make contact with Vernon's forces, but he had no means of

---

24   Williams, *The Prize of All the Oceans*, pp.67–76; Arthur C. Murray, *An Episode in the Spanish War, 1739-1744: Admiral Lord Anson and Captain the Hon. George Murray, RN* (London: Seeley Service, 1952).
25   Christopher H. Layman, *The Wager Disaster: Mayhem, Mutiny and Murder in the South Seas* (London: Uniform Press, 2015); Stanley W. Pack, *The Wager Mutiny* (London: Alvin Redman, 1964).
26   *Journal of Lawrence Millechamp,* in Williams (ed.), *Documents*, p.82.

knowing whether this was a possibility since he had received no news since leaving Brazil some nine months before.

On 8 September, as preparations for their departure from Juan Fernandez continued, a Spanish merchant ship was sighted on the horizon and the *Centurion* was sent out in pursuit of her first prize. On the fourth day, just as Anson was about to abandon the search, the ship was sighted again. After an exchange of fire, the *Nuestra Señora del Monte Carmelo*, a 500-ton merchantman bound for Valparaiso, surrendered and was taken back to Juan Fernandez where Anson placed her under the command of Philip Saumarez. Responding to the concerns of the Spanish crew and passengers that they faced brutal treatment at English hands, Saumarez 'assured them that their fears were altogether groundless and that they would find a generous enemy in the Commodore, who was not less remarkable for his lenity and humanity, than for his resolution and courage'.[27]

Coin and silver worth about £17,000 (£2.5 million in 2023 prices) were seized from the *Monte Carmelo*'s passengers and a cache of official letters, which provided mixed news, was found on board. From the letters Anson learnt that Vernon had failed to take Cartagena, ending any hope of a joint operation in Panama. More positively, he discovered that Pizarro's squadron was no longer a threat as he had suffered even more damage and sickness than the English during his attempt to reach the Pacific. With a large proportion of his crew dying from starvation because supplies had virtually run out, Pizarro was forced to abandon the pursuit and return to Buenos Aires. Only the *Esperanza* eventually completed the journey around Cape Horn, while the *Hermonia* was lost at sea. The *San Esteban* was abandoned in Montevideo and the *Guispuscoa* ran aground after a mutiny. Pizarro's flagship *Asia* was the only member of the squadron eventually to return to Spain.[28]

As soon as he arrived in the River Plate, Pizarro sent word to the Viceroy of Peru, advising him of the progress of the British squadron and the need to dispatch warships to intercept him if he succeeded in reaching the South Sea. The Viceroy responded by strengthening Peru's coastal defences and dispatching four warships from Callao: one was sent to Juan Fernandez and the other three were stationed off Concepción. As we have seen, by an accident of timing, the Spanish had left their station off Juan Fernandez early in June, just before the *Centurion*'s arrival, and returned to Callao empty-handed, along with other members of the flotilla. They assumed that the British had failed to reach the South Sea but underestimated Anson's resolve in the face of unrelenting storms and navigational errors.

On 19 September, Anson left Juan Fernandez for the last time. Before he did so he sank the *Anna* pink, whose hull was rotten, and put some of the Spanish prisoners to work on board the *Gloucester*, which like his other ships was significantly under-manned. He distributed his ships along the Pacific coast as they searched for Spanish merchantmen: the *Gloucester* was ordered to cruise off the port of Paita, while the *Centurion* and the Spanish prize joined the *Tryal*, which had already sailed for Valparaiso. The *Tryal* soon encountered the *Nuestra Señora de Aranzazu*, a 600-ton Spanish merchantman, and took her after a chase lasting 36 hours. The ship only yielded £6,000 (£894,000 in 2023 prices) in coin and plate and during the chase in stormy weather, the *Tryal* was dismasted and significant leaks appeared in her

---

27 Walter, *A Voyage Round the World*, p.157.
28 Williams, *The Prize of All the Oceans*, pp.107–108.

hull. On 4 October, Anson scuttled the *Tryal* and her crew and armament were moved to the *Aranzazu*, which was renamed the *Tryal Prize* (20).

Soon after the first two Spanish ships were taken, Anson became aware of discontent among his crews because the prize money had not been immediately divided between them. He responded by ordering the Articles of War to be read and making a speech in which he referred to 'the danger of mutiny, and let them know that he had heard of their murmurings and discontents, but assured them they were entirely groundless, their properties being secured by Act of Parliament as firmly as any one's own inheritance'.[29] According to Pascoe Thomas, the men were reassured by Anson's speech, but within weeks there were to be further disagreements about the division of prize money.

It was not until 5 November that the *Centurion* took a second Spanish ship, the 300-ton *Santa Teresa de Jesus*, which carried cocoa and timber, but she only yielded £170 (more than £25,000 at 2023 prices) in silver. Among her 10 passengers were three women who feared for their lives but, according to the official account, were reassured by Anson's good treatment. He issued orders that they should receive 'no kind of inquietude or molestation whatever', permitted them to retain their own cabins and appointed the ship's pilot to act as their guardian.[30] Under Anson's command his prisoners were 'treated with all manner of humanity [and] they were all as much at their ease as if there had been in their own ships or at their own homes'.[31]

On 10 November, as Anson proceeded northwards, the *Centurion* intercepted a third merchant ship, the *Nuestra Señora de Carmin*. She carried 'steel, iron, wax, pepper, cedar, plank... and other species of merchandize', which were of 'little value to us, yet with respect to the Spaniards, it was the most considerable capture that fell into our hands in this part of the world; for it amounted to upwards of 400,000 dollars prime cost at Panama'.[32] Of more interest to Anson was information from an Irish passenger who informed him that officials in the small coastal town of Paita (in north-west Peru) were aware of the British presence in the South Sea and had organised the removal of the treasure held in the Custom House. Anson decided that the opportunity to seize more treasure – and land a large number of prisoners – should not be missed and made plans to attack Paita without delay. It was to be the only operation he mounted against a Spanish town during the circumnavigation.

On 13 November, at 2:00 a.m., three boats carrying 58 armed men led by Peircy Brett and two other officers landed at Paita and were greeted with a volley of cannon fire from the town fort. The British met light resistance as they advanced towards the town and quickly seized the fort. As described by Peter Denis, 'we march'd up to the fort and attack'd it. After firing one volley we storm'd it, sword in hand, which made the enemy jump over the walls; by which means we became masters of the fort with the loss of one man only kill'd; and three wounded'.[33] The town was virtually deserted when the British arrived as the inhabitants had already fled, concealing themselves in a nearby mountain.

---

29 Thomas, *A True and Impartial Journal*, p.52.
30 Walter, *A Voyage Round the World*, p.169.
31 Thomas, *A True and Impartial Journal*, p.47.
32 Walter, *A Voyage Round the World*, p.176.
33 Peter Denis to his brother, 1 December 1742, in *The Gentleman's Magazine*, XIII (1743), p.325.

Burning of Payta, November 1741, painting by Samuel Scott. (Royal Museums, Greenwich)

During a three-day occupation, the crew looted the abandoned town and transferred the treasure held at the custom house to their ships. On the third day (15 November), when Anson received intelligence from escaped slaves about an imminent Spanish ground attack, he ordered the fort and other buildings (apart from the two churches) to be burnt. Five merchant ships were scuttled and one – the *Solidad* – was spared and taken with the squadron. A Spanish account of Paita's destruction accused Anson of 'ungenerously setting fire to the houses; an action which could reflect but little honour on the arms of their nation, but was rather a malicious transaction, to revenge on the poor inhabitants the coming of the militia whom they did not dare to face'.[34] In England, there were mixed views about the operation, later described as a 'very questionable proceeding', but agreement that Anson's actions were fully justified by his orders.[35] As we have seen, such criticisms were tempered by accounts of his humane conduct towards the prisoners who had been taken from captured merchantmen.

Augustus Keppel. later first Viscount Keppel but then a midshipman on the *Centurion*, concluded that 'Payta was a considerable loss to the Spaniards, though we did not profit so much by it, they having several warehouses full of European goods, which we set on fire,

---

34 George Juan and Antonio de Ulloa, *A Voyage to South America* (third edition, London: L. Davies, 1772), vol.II, p.202.
35 'Sir John Barrow's *Life of Lord Anson*', *The Edinburgh Review*, 139 (1839), p.135.

with other valuable things, which we had not time to take on board'.[36] The Spanish estimated their total losses at 'a million and a half of dollars', which was almost certainly an under-estimate because of the total destruction of the town. The landing party had seized more than £30,000 (nearly £4.5 million in 2023 prices) in gold, dollars and wrought plate, which was the last significant haul of treasure to be taken on the South American coast. It was recorded as official prize money, but a problem arose over the personal booty taken by the landing party, which it was unwilling to share with the rest of the crew. Anson called a meeting in which he pointed out that the entire crew had contributed to the success of the operation, and he ordered all members of the landing party (including the officers) to produce their plunder. It was then divided amongst the whole crew according to their rank. The official account commented that 'this troublesome affair, which if permitted to have gone on, might perhaps have been attended with mischievous consequences, was by the Commodore's prudence soon appeased, to the general satisfaction of the ship's company'.[37]

On his departure from Paita (on 16 November) Anson left the coast of Peru and sailed northwards along the coast of Ecuador and Columbia in the direction of Mexico, where he planned to intercept the Manila galleon, which was due to arrive in Acapulco in December or January. Normally, a single ship made the 8,000-mile journey once a year, carrying spices, silks and teas from the Philippines and returning with a much more valuable cargo of silver coin and plate. On the way, Anson planned to stop at Quibo island in the Bay of Panama to take on water. Apart from the *Centurion* and the *Gloucester*, Anson's squadron now included six Spanish prizes although the three slowest were scuttled before the first sighting of Quibo on 3 December. They spent nine days on the island – a 'delightful, uninhabited place abounding with a great quantity of wild deer and other refreshments' – before departing for Acapulco on 12 December.[38]

A journey that normally took 20 days lasted for 79 as the squadron was faced 'either with tempestuous weather from the western quarter, or with dead calms and heavy rains, attended with a sultry air', and they did not arrive on the Mexican coast until 29 January 1742.[39] They were uncertain about Acapulco's latitude but eventually spotted two hummocks to the north, which, according to a Spanish pilot on the *Centurion*, marked the location of the harbour. They did not know whether they were too late to intercept the treasure galleon before she arrived at Acapulco, but Anson spread his ships along the coast so that she could not pass unobserved. However, there was no sign of the galleon and he suspected that she may already have arrived.

On 6 February, Anson dispatched the *Centurion*'s barge under the command of Lieutenant Denis with orders to establish whether the galleon had reached Acapulco. On his return five days later, Denis reported that they had been unable to find the harbour and sailed further along the coast before being forced to return as they were running out of food and water. However, they had spotted two paps (rounded hilltops) further to the east, which they concluded were probably those in the neighbourhood of Acapulco. Anson decided to sail eastwards and when they arrived, on 12 February, he dispatched Denis for a second time.

---

36   Keppel, *The Life of Augustus, Viscount Keppel*, vol.I, pp.43–44.
37   Walter, *A Voyage Round the World*, p.194.
38   Saumarez, *Abstract of a Journal*, in Williams (ed.), *Documents*, p.167.
39   Walter, *A Voyage Round the World*, p.208.

He returned seven days later to report that they had discovered Acapulco harbour and had intercepted a fishing boat at the entrance. The fishermen informed him that the treasure galleon, the *Pilar*, which carried 58 guns and 400 men, had arrived there on 13 January and was due to return to the Philippines in two weeks (3 March). They also informed him that the Governor of Acapulco had received news of the attack on Paita and had strengthened his defences to prevent Anson from forcing his way into the harbour.

According to the official account, the news that the *Pilar* was preparing to depart 'was most joyfully received by us, as we had no doubt but she must certainly fall into our hands'.[40] Anson planned to take the galleon as she departed by establishing a cordon some 40 miles from the harbour, with his five ships stationed about 10 miles apart. The three remaining prizes would act as lookout vessels, while Anson's two surviving warships, *Centurion* and *Gloucester*, would launch the attack. He positioned two cutters inshore and ordered them to keep a close watch at night in case the treasure galleon tried to leave undetected. However, there was no sign of the ship because, unknown to Anson, the Spanish had spotted the *Centurion*'s barge and decided to cancel the return voyage to Manila until early next year. With the *Pilar* still in port, Anson considered the possibility of a surprise night-time raid on the harbour but quickly ruled it out. Apart from the fact that the town was heavily guarded, Anson learnt that 'nearer inshore there was always a dead calm for the greatest part of the night, and that towards morning, when a gale sprung up, it constantly blew off land; so that the setting sail from our present station in the evening, and arriving at *Acapulco* before daylight, was impossible'.[41]

It is not surprising that, after his unproductive detour to Mexico, Anson became 'tired with this long and fruitless cruise, and [was] now despairing of meeting with the ship he was in quest of'.[42] With water running low he was soon forced to leave the area, leaving one of his cutters behind to monitor the *Pilar*'s movements; if the galleon left for Manila, he would try to intercept her near Cape Espiritu Santo in the Philippines rather than off the coast of Mexico. He now made for Chequetan (Zihuatanejo), some 90 nautical miles west of Acapulco, where Sir Francis Drake had refitted in 1578. Arriving there on 7 April, they anchored in the harbour and obtained water from a lagoon behind the beach. According to Lawrence Millechamp, this water 'was thought good; though in reality I believe the badness of this water proved fatal to many of our people, who were afterwards afflicted with the scurvy.[43]

While anchored at Chequetan, Anson ordered a survey of the surrounding coastline and concluded that it was a place of 'considerable consequence, and the knowledge of it may be of great import to future cruisers'.[44] It was the only secure harbour in the area apart from Acapulco and an ideal base for any future British operations against the Manila galleon, but it was not without risk as Anson's French cook, Louis Leger, was to discover. When he left the immediate area under British guard 'in search of limes for his Master's store', he was captured by Indians and turned over to the Spanish. He was eventually sent to Spain,

---

40 Walter, *A Voyage Round the World*, p.214.
41 Walter, *A Voyage Round the World*, p.234.
42 *Journal of Lawrence Millechamp,* in Williams (ed.), *Documents*, p.115.
43 *Journal of Lawrence Millechamp,* in Williams (ed.), *Documents*, p.115.
44 Walter, *A Voyage Round the World*, p.244.

but when the ship arrived at Lagos in Portugal he managed to escape. The British envoy arranged for George Rodney to bring him to London, where he arrived in the spring of 1743. Although news of the expedition had already reached the capital, Leger was the first member of the crew to return home and provide a first-hand account of the difficulties Anson was facing.

With the Manila galleon apparently out of reach, Anson now needed to decide on the best route home. He quickly ruled out returning southwards because of the difficulty of negotiating a passage around Cape Horn. There was also a risk he could be intercepted by Spanish warships operating from Callao and, as his instructions pointed out, there would be difficulties in replenishing supplies on a hostile coast. In view of these difficulties, he decided to sail westwards across the North Pacific towards the Philippines before heading north-west into the China Sea, a journey that was likely to take about two months. He would aim for the city of Canton (Guangzhou), where the East India Company had a factory, and would refit his ships there before returning home. According to Philip Saumarez, the decision was to lead to 'another series of misfortunes and mortality surpassing the first, in which we were very near having never been heard of more'.[45]

Before he left Chequetan on 28 April, Anson decided to destroy the three remaining Spanish prizes and distribute their men between his two surviving warships, the *Centurion* and *Gloucester*. The warrant officers of the *Tryal Prize* (the former *Aranzazu*), which was still seaworthy, objected strongly to the loss of their replacement ship, fearing (correctly) that they would lose out in any future distribution of prize money. Anson responded that he had no choice as there were not enough men left to operate three ships: the *Centurion* had lost 287 men, the *Gloucester* 296 men and the *Tryal Prize* 40 men, which 'reduced the strength of the three ships to a less number than the complement of one of the fourth-rates. Those remaining being in weak condition, and none of the ships having men sufficient to work them in bad weather'.[46]

Before leaving the Mexican coast, Anson returned to Acapulco to find the crew who were keeping watch on the harbour. At first, their cutter could not be found, and Anson thought it possible that it had been captured and, on this assumption, he sent a boat with some of his prisoners into Acapulco with a demand for the return of his missing crew. However, before a reply arrived from the Spanish authorities, the cutter returned having been driven off course by high winds. These further delays meant that Anson did not leave for China until 6 May and, as Pascoe Thomas pointed out, 'our long stay on the coast of *Mexico* occasioned us to take quite the wrong season of the year for our passage from that coast to *Asia*'.[47]

Anson planned to sail south-west from Mexico until he found the north-east trade winds, but as they 'reached down to equatorial latitudes they found themselves in a region of calms, light winds and blistering heat'.[48] Anson had relied on the narratives of earlier navigators, which suggested that their westbound passage across the Pacific would be relatively easy, but they had made the journey earlier in the year when the north-east trade winds could be picked up by dropping no more than a few degrees of latitude. By early summer when the

---

45 Saumarez, *Abstract of a Journal*, in Williams (ed.), *Documents*, p.168.
46 George Anson, 14 April 1742, *Journal of Lawrence Millechamp*, in Williams (ed.), *Documents*, p.118.
47 Thomas, *A True and Impartial Journal*, p.152.
48 Williams, *The Prize of All the Oceans*, p.134.

Centurion left Mexico, the trade winds were moving north and he later acknowledged that 'he had no apprehension that the season was too far advanced'.[49] It was not until mid-June that Anson realised he had been sailing too far south and changed course. By 23 June, the ships encountered a steady wind from the north-east, but their misreading of the situation meant that their progress was painfully slow.

By this point, Anson was facing a new outbreak of scurvy and the first deaths soon followed. Conditions on board were more favourable than during the first outbreak, but as the seamen

> ...were now too sensible of the fatal consequences of it in coming round Cape Horn, it made a more dreadful impression on them than it had done before. The Indian and Negro prisoners... were the first who were seized by this incurable distemper, and most of them immediately fell victims to its fury. From them it was soon communicated to the Englishmen, who languished and pined away under it a long time.[50]

Men were dying 'like rotten sheep', with up to 12 bodies being thrown overboard every day.[51] With widespread sickness on board, Anson decided to make for Guam, as the 'men must inevitably perish without refreshments'; he issued orders to the captain of the *Gloucester* to head there with 'the utmost dispatch'. Guam, the southernmost of the Mariana Islands in the North Pacific, was defended by a small Spanish garrison but Anson hoped that the appearance of two British warships would persuade them to surrender without a fight.

Anson would soon face even greater difficulties as the condition of his ships deteriorated. Shortly after leaving the Mexican coast, the *Centurion*'s foremast had been damaged and the condition of her sails soon degraded, but a more serious incident occurred in June when the *Gloucester* suffered a sprung mainmast. Although a jury mast (a temporary replacement) was eventually installed, the ship was now very slow-moving. At the end of July, the *Gloucester* sustained further damage when her topmast and associated sails and rigging collapsed, and the *Centurion* took her in tow while repairs were attempted. Anson was soon forced to abandon the work when the *Centurion* started to fill with water in stormy weather and the whole crew was needed to man the pumps. The following days brought further damage to the *Gloucester*, and, by 13 August, there were seven feet of water in her hold and the pumps were unable to cope. Her remaining crew of 94 was either exhausted from continuously working the pumps or weakened by scurvy, but Anson was unable to spare any men to help them.

The captain and officers of the *Gloucester* were convinced that the ship would sink and wrote formally to Anson recommending that she should be abandoned.[52] He agreed that 'it was impossible to save either of the ships without destroying the other, [and] prudently

---

49 National Maritime Museum (NMM): Hartwell Family Papers HAR/4, p.12, *Case heard before the Lords Commissioners for Appeals in Prize Causes*.
50 *Journal of Lawrence Millechamp*, in Williams (ed.), *Documents*, p.124.
51 Peter Denis to his brother, 1 December 1742, in *The Gentleman's Magazine*, XIII (1743), p.326.
52 Matthew Mitchell to George Anson, 15 August 1742, in John Philips, *An Authentic Journal of the Late Expedition under the Command of Commodore Anson* (London: J. Robinson, 1744), pp.128–129.

resolved to destroy the *Gloucester* as being the smallest and most disabled ship of the two'.[53] Orders were issued for the crew and stores to be transferred to the *Centurion* and for the *Gloucester* to be burnt to avoid her falling into enemy hands. On 16 August, she was set on fire and 'burnt all night, making a most grand, horrid appearance. Her guns, which were all loaded, fired so regularly at about the distance of a minute between each as the fire came to them, that they sounded like mourning guns, such as are fired at the funeral of some great officer'.[54] She blew up early the following morning when the fire reached the magazine and ignited some 200 barrels of gunpowder.

Conditions on the *Centurion* were scarcely more favourable with more than 100 members of the crew sick with scurvy and up to 10 men dying every day. She had major leaks and was slowly filling up with water even though the entire crew, including Anson, took turns at the pumps. It was 'perhaps the most critical stage of the journey' and unless an anchorage was found soon, she would almost certainly suffer the same fate as the *Gloucester*.[55] Storms had forced the *Centurion* from Anson's intended route to Guam and the ship was now heading towards the Northern Mariana Islands, which were further to the north. On 23 August, Tinian, one of the three principal islands, was sighted after a passage of 7,000 miles from Mexico. As soon as *Centurion* arrived, the only Spaniard on Tinian came alongside her in a proa (an outrigger sailing vessel) and informed Anson that he had been sent there 'with 22 Indians to jerk beef, which he was to load for Guam on board a small bark of about 15 tun, which lay at anchor near the shore'.[56]

Laurence Millechamp described the island as 'a perfect paradise, for besides a great quantity of coconut and orange trees… we saw large numbers of beautiful cattle grazing on most delightful plains full of herbage, and an agreeable verdure spreading itself over the face of the whole island'.[57] As soon as the *Centurion* anchored, the sick were carried on shore, with Anson and his officers helping in the operation. Of the 128 sick who were moved from the *Centurion*, 21 died during the landing or soon afterwards. Within a few days, the survivors began recovering as Tinian's plentiful supplies of fruit started to have a positive effect. Anson was among those suffering from scurvy and 'had a tent erected for him on shore, where he went with the view of staying a few days for the recovery of his health, being convinced… that no other method but living on the land was to be trusted for the removal of this dreadful malady'.[58] After leaving Tinian, no more cases of scurvy were to be reported for the remainder of the voyage.

As he recovered, Anson focused on the need to repair the *Centurion*'s leak and he ordered her cannon to be shifted astern in order to raise her bow out of the water. The rotten sheathing was replaced but when the cannon were returned to their original position, the leak was still as bad as ever. Her guns and powder barrels were then moved further back so that her stem was raised three feet out of the water, enabling a second repair to be carried

---

53 *Journal of Lawrence Millechamp*, in Williams (ed.), *Documents*, p.126.
54 *Journal of Lawrence Millechamp*, in Williams (ed.), *Documents*, p.128.
55 Williams (ed.), *Documents*, p.128n.
56 Walter, *A Voyage Round the World*, p.277. A bark is a sailing ship with three or more masts.
57 *Journal of Lawrence Millechamp*, in Williams (ed.), *Documents*, p.129.
58 Walter, *A Voyage Round the World*, p.287.

out but the result was the same. Anson concluded that the leak was well below the waterline and could only be repaired in a dockyard.

On 18 September, he was faced with a much more serious problem when a severe storm snapped the *Centurion*'s cables and blew her out to sea. Commanded by Lieutenant Saumarez and manned by a skeleton crew, she fired distress signals that went unheard on the island. It was not until the following morning that Anson discovered that she was missing and he did not know whether she had survived the storm. Even if the ship were still afloat, he believed that the crew would have great difficulty in returning to Tinian in view of the prevailing easterly winds. During the storm, the crew had in fact almost lost control of the ship but they had slowly 'gained the upper hand. After five days they had got up the foreyard and mainyard, and had managed to bring up and secure the sheet anchor'.[59] She drifted close to Guam before changing course back towards Tinian.

The crew still on shore (now reduced to 113) reacted to the news with 'grief, discontent, terror and despair' and after two days they 'had lost even the most distant hope of her'.[60] With the disappearance of the *Centurion*, they were faced with the prospect of remaining on the island indefinitely or being captured by the Spanish forces based in Guam, with 'the most favourable treatment they could hope for would be to be detained prisoners for life'.[61] According to the official account, 'Mr Anson had doubtless his share of disquietude; but he always kept up his usual composure and steadiness'.[62] In an attempt to reassure the crew, Anson said he was confident the ship would return within a few days, but if she did not they would leave the island in the captured bark and try to reach the safety of Macao (a Portuguese trading settlement subject to Chinese sovereignty), nearly 2,000 miles away. As the bark could only house 30 men, the *Centurion*'s carpenters began work on the difficult task of extending her so that she could accommodate more than 100. They were helped by Anson and his officers as well as the crew: 'besides giving necessary directions they all set themselves hard to work, and would be frequently working with an axe, cross-cut saw, or carrying timber with the meanest seamen we had. This raised an emulation in our common people and made everyone endeavour to excel'.[63]

Although good progress was made, there was soon evidence of unrest among the crew, many of whom were unwilling to risk such a precarious journey and were considering deserting and remaining on the island. There is no doubt that the plan was high risk: it was unlikely that their provisions would keep on the long journey; there was a shortage of gunpowder; and the modified bark would only be able to accommodate 50 men below deck, with the remainder being exposed to the elements. Fortunately, on 11 October, with these questions still unresolved, the *Centurion* was sighted in the distance after an absence of 19 days. When Anson first saw the ship, he discarded his axe and ran down to the sea with his men 'in a kind of frenzy', a marked departure from his normally reserved behaviour.[64] But three days after she first reappeared, a sudden gust of wind blew her out to sea again

---

59 Williams, *The Prize of All the Oceans*, p.148.
60 *Journal of Lawrence Millechamp*, in Williams (ed.), *Documents*, pp.132–133.
61 Walter, *A Voyage Round the World*, pp.290–291.
62 Walter, *A Voyage Round the World*, p.291.
63 *Journal of Lawrence Millechamp*, in Williams (ed.), *Documents*, p.133.
64 Walter, *A Voyage Round the World*, p.297.

and she did not return for another five days. She finally managed to anchor off the island and preparations for her final departure were then completed as rapidly as possible as two Spanish proas had been seen off the island. It was likely that the Guam garrison would soon be notified of their presence.

The *Centurion* left Tinian for the last time on 21 October. Once she passed Formosa and entered Chinese coastal waters, which were crammed with a variety of trading vessels and fishing sampans, her progress towards Macao slowed. The official account commented that 'we were surprised to find ourselves in the midst of an incredible number of fishing boats, which seemed to cover the surface of the sea as far as the eye could reach'.[65] On 11 November, as they approached Macao, a local pilot guided them in. Although Anson would be forced to remain there as a guest of the Portuguese for five months and would encounter many difficulties in his dealings with the Chinese, he was relieved that after two years at sea they had 'once more arrived in an amicable port, in a civilized country; where the conveniences of life were in great plenty; where the naval stores, which we now extremely wanted, could in some degree be procured'.[66]

As soon as they arrived, Anson sent an officer ashore to pay his compliments to the governor and to seek his advice on how to approach the Chinese. Merchantmen arriving at Canton would normally be charged duty (measurage) but Anson was unwilling to pay even though he could not repair the *Centurion* without the cooperation of the Chinese authorities. The governor's view was that duty would almost certainly be demanded and he suggested that the work should be carried out at Macao rather than Canton; on his recommendation, the *Centurion* was moved to the safe harbour at Taipa, six miles from Macao. However, he pointed out that with Macao firmly under Chinese control, stores could not be provided without the approval of the Viceroy (chuntuck) at Canton.

The first sign that his relations with the authorities at Canton might run into difficulties came when a Chinese official refused Anson permission to board a junk to take him to the city. Approval was eventually granted but only after Anson threatened to use force and gave a bribe. It took him three days to reach the East India Company's factory at Whampoa, a few miles from Canton, because the journey was frequently interrupted by officials who wished to examine his pass. The Company's supercargoes advised him to work through the Hong (merchants who were authorised to trade with Westerners in porcelain, silk and tea) and to ask them to submit his request for a 'grand chop' (permission to refit and resupply the *Centurion*) to the authorities. While he was waiting to receive their approval, Anson ordered Captain Saunders to take his dispatches to England and he departed on board a Swedish merchantman. Several other officers returned to England on board an East Indiaman, whose passengers also included Richard Walter, the *Centurion*'s chaplain and the named author of the official account of the voyage. Anson was forced to turn down other requests from officers to return home because trained seamen to replace them could not be obtained.

Weeks passed as Anson waited in Canton, a city he described in the following terms: 'Of all the places I was ever in this is the most disagreeable'.[67] On 5 December, with no sign of a response from the Chinese, he expressed his frustration: 'I am cursedly plagued with these

---

65   Walter, *A Voyage Round the World*, p.312.
66   Walter, *A Voyage Round the World*, pp.315–316.
67   George Anson to Philip Saumarez, 24 November 1742, in Williams (ed.), *Documents*, p.149.

people and am afraid all will not come out right at last, though they give me fair words'.[68] Anson concluded that the French and Dutch merchants were obstructing his request because of his action in delaying the return of the treasure galleon from Mexico, which had disrupted the normal pattern of trade between Canton and Manila. Despite these difficulties, Anson did nothing to upset the delicate relations between the East India Company and Chinese officials. In their official correspondence, the supercargoes noted that Anson had

> ...taken all the precaution he could not to hurt our affairs with the ticklish government of this place, and has applied through our means for all the necessaries he wants, notwithstanding which he meets with difficulties almost insuperable, and we heartily wish the Chinese may not force him to quarrel with them before he leaves their country.[69]

The real explanation for the delays may relate to Chinese uncertainty about the status of the *Centurion* as they had 'no notion of a ship commissioned by authority to make war on their enemies'.[70] Their experience was confined to merchant ships and

> ...they look on all others as pirates or *Ladrones*. In this manner they received us, calling us always the Grand Ladrone Ship... the name [Anson] first went by, even among the mandarins and merchants was the Grand Ladrone captain, or the great captain of the thieves. However, he sometime after convinced them of their mistake, and on all occasions insisted on all the ceremonies and respects due to a person of his rank and character.[71]

Anson returned to Macao in mid-December with little to show for his four-week sojourn in Canton beyond a commitment that the Hong merchants would smuggle additional provisions on board departing East India Company ships, which would then transfer them to the *Centurion* when they reached Macao. With the condition of the *Centurion* deteriorating (the leak had worsened and the mainmast was defective), he tried a different approach. On 17 December, shortly after his return to Macao, he wrote directly to the Viceroy requesting permission to repair and provision his ship so that he could leave for Europe as soon as possible. Anson decided against adopting the conciliatory approach recommended by the supercargoes and his letter included a series of demands for supplies and assistance. Within two days there were signs that this direct approach would pay off when a senior mandarin and other officials arrived in a fleet of 18 junks to inspect the condition of the *Centurion*. With music playing and streamers flying, it was evidently a significant ceremonial occasion and Anson reacted quickly to this unexpected development. He ordered 100 members of his crew to change into the uniforms of the dead marines and an improvised guard of honour was formed. While the mandarin was shown around the ship, two Chinese carpenters inspected the leak, which they confirmed was as dangerous as Anson had reported.

---

68 George Anson to Philip Saumarez, 5 December 1742, in Williams (ed.), *Documents*, p.151.
69 *China Diary and Consultation, 1742*, in Williams (ed.), *Documents*, p.146.
70 Thomas, *A True and Impartial Journal*, p.263.
71 *Journal of Lawrence Millechamp*, in Williams (ed.), *Documents*, p.137.

Anson made it clear to the mandarin that he was not willing to pay measurage because

> ...as a King's ship he expected the use of their ports, and such dispatch in their providing him with such things as he wanted... what he demanded was agreeable to the laws of nations, and if they did not immediately comply with his requests, he should forthwith make use of the power he had to compel them to it.[72]

When the Viceroy's council discussed the issue, the question of Anson's reaction in the event of a refusal was raised and it was reported that he had said he 'would consult with my people whether to eat one another or the Chinese'.[73] There were extended debates in the council before the necessary permission was granted on 6 January 1743. They must have been aware from the inspection of the ship, 'that without a refit the *Centurion* might remain indefinitely at Macao, an awkward and threatening presence, a challenge to Chinese sovereignty'.[74] This seems to be a more likely explanation for the Chinese decision than Anson's veiled threats to destroy every vessel in the Pearl River with his 24-pounders.

It was not until early in April that the refitting of the *Centurion* was completed, despite large numbers of local workmen being deployed. The works included repairing the major leak below the waterline, applying new sheathing to the hull and replacing the masts and rigging. As the work was completed, Chinese officials came on board to urge him to depart without further delay. In response, Anson 'answered them in a determined tone, desiring them to give him no further trouble, for he would go when he thought proper, and not before'. In reply, they 'immediately prohibited all provisions from being carried on board him, and took such care that their injunctions should be complied with, that from that time forwards nothing could be purchased at any rate whatever'.[75] Shortly afterwards, Anson left Taipa and headed for Macao Roads in preparation for his departure.

---

72 *Journal of Lawrence Millechamp*, in Williams (ed.), *Documents*, pp.137–138.
73 Heaps, *Log of the Centurion*, p.204.
74 Williams, *The Prize of All the Oceans*, p.157.
75 Walter, *A Voyage Round the World*, pp.330–331.

3

Capturing the Treasure Galleon, 1743–1744

Anson finally left Macao on 19 April 1743 after announcing his intention to sail for England 'with his ship very well refitted, his stores replenished, and an additional stock of provisions on board'.[1] The *Centurion* carried less than half her normal complement, with only some two-thirds of those remaining being part of the original crew; the rest had been recruited or captured at various points during the expedition. At first, Anson headed due south but he had no intention of returning to England without first making another attempt to capture the Manila galleon. If he succeeded, he would follow in the footsteps of the two English privateers who had seized Spanish treasure galleons in 1587 and 1709 respectively. As he sought the elusive ship, he soon changed course, turning eastwards towards Formosa en route for Cape Espiritu Santo. The Cape, a headland on Samar Island in the Philippines, some 1,100 miles from Macao, was the normal landfall of the treasure galleon as she sailed towards Manila.

Anson had been preoccupied with plans to capture the galleon ever since his failure to take the *Pilar* off the coast of Mexico more than a year earlier. By this point, as Anson recalled later, he was 'so ill satisfied with my success, being abandoned by one part of my squadron, and the remainder being either wrecked or reduced to such a condition by the bad treatment we met in passing Cape Horn, that it was not possible for me to keep them above water'.[2] None of his objectives had been achieved and he had lost nearly 1,300 men from disease (out of a total complement of almost 2,000) and five warships in the process. The only positive achievements he could point to were the sacking of Paita and the capture of a few merchant ships, but they did not amount to much compared to the ambitious plans for the expedition which ministers had originally agreed. Unless he could capture the galleon and salvage his reputation, he faced inevitable professional obscurity on his return to England rather than the honours and promotion to flag rank he had always hoped for. Anson did everything he could to avoid this fate and as a result of his resolute leadership and good fortune, a successful outcome was eventually achieved.

Anson worked on the assumption that two treasure galleons – rather than the usual single annual ship – would be making the 8,000-mile journey to the Philippines in 1743. He assumed that the *Pilar*'s return would be delayed until mid-1743 because of his presence

---

1   Walter, *A Voyage Round the World*, p.332.
2   BL: Hardwicke Papers, Add.MS. 35,359, f.360, George Anson to the Earl of Hardwicke, 14 June 1744.

outside Acapulco but in this he was mistaken. The *Pilar* had in fact left for the Philippines as early as the beginning of 1743, and his target was now a single galleon (the *Nuestra Señora de Covadonga*) although he was not yet aware of it. During his stay in Macao, Anson had collected intelligence from an Englishman formerly in Spanish service about the galleons' expected route to Manila, which suggested that the best place to intercept them would be off Cape Espiritu Santo. They were likely to reach the Cape in June and from there they would pass through the San Bernardino Strait as they sailed westwards to Manila.

In an effort to deceive the Spanish, before he left Macao Anson made plans to visit Batavia (Jakarta), the capital of the Dutch East Indies, as his first port of call on the homeward journey. However, his efforts to conceal his plans were far from successful as a Chinese merchant had informed Gaspar de la Torre, Governor of the Philippines, of Anson's presence at Macao and suggested that he might go in search of the treasure galleon rather than make for Batavia. At first, he thought the second possibility was more likely because 'the English are tired of their venture, having accomplished nothing. From what I have learnt of this ship [the *Centurion*] it seems to me so badly damaged and short of crew that I do not think it will attempt anything between here and Manila'.[3] However, he did not rule out the first option and suggested that it would be wise to take precautions. In the light of this advice, the Governor sought the views of his council of war but it decided that no immediate action was necessary.

However, the arrival of a second letter from Canton suggesting that Anson no longer planned to return home immediately, forced de la Torre to change his mind. It gave further information about his plans, 'which show beyond doubt that he has designs of the greatest import. I do not think his intentions go as far as attacking Manila with so few men... but if I am not mistaken he intends to cruise for either the incoming or outgoing galleon'.[4] As the letter suggested that the *Centurion* might leave Macao soon, the Governor was forced to order the dispatch of the *Pilar* and two galeots with orders to patrol the Strait of San Bernardino, where they could either escort the *Covadonga* on the final stage of her journey to Manila or protect the treasure ship *Rosario* as she left for Mexico.[5] But it took so long for the *Pilar* to be fitted out that she did not leave Cavite until 3 June and even then was unable to reach her destination. On 7 July, a week before Anson captured the *Covadonga*, the *Pilar* ran aground off the island of Ticao and was forced to return home. Governor de la Torre later complained that he had faced 'repeated and unexpected misfortunes' in responding to the British threat but, in 1749, the Council of the Indies concluded that he had failed to provide adequate protection to the *Covadonga* in the final stages of her journey.[6]

Before he departed from Macao, Anson had briefed his senior officers on his plans, but he did not then inform the rest of the crew, who were uncertain about whether he would return to Europe or go in search of the galleon. Although they did not know Anson's real intentions, according to Pascoe Thomas, they retained confidence in his leadership: 'as we knew him to be a person of consummate prudence and policy, we did not much doubt but he proceeded on the very best grounds and informations that could possibly be got, and would

---

3 Anonymous to the Governor of Manila, 12 December 1942 (n.s.), in Williams (ed.), *Documents*, p.207.
4 Anonymous to the Governor of Manila, n.d., in Williams, *Documents* (ed.), p.209.
5 Governor of Manila to the King of Spain, 2 July 1743 (n.s.), in Williams (ed.), *Documents*, pp.207–208.
6 Governor of Manila to the King of Spain, 5 July 1744 (n.s.), in Williams (ed.), *Documents*, p.212.

not rashly and unadvisedly undertake a wild goose chace'.[7] As soon as the *Centurion* was on the open sea, he took them into his confidence. Assembling the crew on the quarterdeck, Anson informed them that he was going in search of the two treasure galleons rather than returning home. He was at pains to reassure them about the fight ahead saying that he was certain

> ...that one of them at least could not fail of becoming his prize... many ridiculous tales had been propagated about the strength of the sides of these ships, and their being impregnable to cannon-shot; that these fictions had been principally invented to palliate the cowardice of those who had formerly engaged them.[8]

He assured them that 'whenever he met with them, he would fight them so near, that they should find, his bullets, instead of being stopped by one of their sides, should go through them both'.

Anson's morale-boosting speech 'much reviv'd the spirits of the people, who were really weary of this fatiguing and tedious voyage'. There was now a real possibility of success and the prospect of a share of a large haul of prize money gave them a much stronger incentive to fight than their Spanish opponents. The speech was 'another proof of the Commodore's great capacity, who very well knew that some such method was absolutely necessary to make himself be followed with alacrity and pleasure and to inspire them with that confidence and assurance of success, which scarce ever fails under such conduct'.[9] The *Centurion* arrived off Cape Espiritu Santo on 20 May and her topgallant sails were lowered to reduce the possibility of detection from the island while she lay in wait. The ship's crew was instructed to scan the eastern horizon for a sight of the galleons while looking to the west for any enemy warships that might approach from Cavite. The Governor of Manila later confirmed that 'the enemy had proceeded so cautiously that they were not sighted, nor did they come close to land'.[10]

Anson put the long period of waiting to good use by preparing the crew for the coming engagement, with drills occupying much of the day. Priority was given to instruction in the use of small arms, which was often neglected in the navy because of the 'unskilful methods of teaching it'. The crew 'were constantly trained to fire at a mark, which was usually hung at the yard-arm, and where some little reward was given to the most expert, the whole crew, by this management, were rendered extremely skilful, quick in loading, all of them good marksmen, and some of them extraordinary ones'.[11] With a much-reduced crew of 227 men (of whom nearly 30 were boys), Anson had to decide how to deploy them in battle to the greatest effect and his plans showed a well-developed ability to improvise. He placed 30 of his best marksmen on the tops (the platform at the upper end of each mast), allocating 10 to each mast where they would attack the Spanish with small arms fire. They were ordered to devote the waiting time to continuous musket practice.

---

7   Thomas, *A True and Impartial Journal*, p.277.
8   Walter, *A Voyage Round the World*, p.333.
9   Thomas, *A True and Impartial Journal*, p.279.
10 Governor of Manila to the King of Spain, 5 July 1744 (n.s.), in Williams (ed.), *Documents*, p.210.
11 Walter, *A Voyage Round the World*, p.336.

Although Anson expected two galleons to appear, he assumed that he would engage them one at a time, allowing him to man the guns on one side of the *Centurion* only. These 25 guns (twelve 24-pounders on the lower deck and thirteen 9-pounders on the upper gundeck) would each be allocated two skilled men (rather than the usual 10), who would sponge them out after firing and then reload them. They would be supported by several gangs of up to 12 gunners who were to move from cannon to cannon, where they were to 'run out the gun, fire it, and bring up a new charge of gunpowder and ball for the two-man team to reload with. Then they ran on to the next that was ready'.[12] Although these arrangements meant that the *Centurion* could only fire a single opening broadside, they offered a valuable tactical advantage. After the initial broadside, the guns would be fired independently, maintaining a constant fire which would keep 'the Spaniards fairly "on the jump", not knowing whether to lie down to avoid a ball, or grapeshot, or to be standing up and firing their own gun. Nor could they tell from which end of the ship the next shot would come'.[13]

Anson's intended target, which was commanded by Don Gerónimo Montero, an experienced Portuguese officer in Spanish service, had left Acapulco on 15 April, 72 days earlier. When Montero put into Guam for supplies, he learnt from prisoners released at Tinian that the *Centurion* had sailed through the area in the autumn of the previous year and that her crew had shrunk to no more than 130 men. Despite this promising news, Montero remained cautious and wanted either to stay in Guam for the coming winter or make a long detour to avoid the high-risk route via Cape Espiritu Santo. However, when he consulted his council of officers he was overruled, with a majority agreeing that the *Covadonga* should maintain her normal direct course towards Manila. They did not believe that the *Centurion* would pose a threat in her present condition, but even if she had managed to reach the Cape it was likely that warships from Manila would have captured her.

Despite the views of his officers, Montero had good reason to be cautious. The *Covadonga* was built as a merchant vessel rather than a warship and 'her low bulwarks gave little protection to the men on deck, and the narrow gun ports made it difficult to slew the cannon round at any kind of angle'.[14] Her lower gun ports could not, in any case, be used as they were too near the waterline. At 700 tons, she was significantly smaller than the 1,000-ton *Centurion* and her gundeck (124 feet long) was 20 feet shorter. While the ship had 550 men on board compared to 227 on the *Centurion*, of these only 266 were listed as crew (about half of them Filipinos). Most of the remainder were servants (as many as 177) together with 20 passengers and 24 convicts, who had been 'condemned for their crimes to their galleys at Manila... and who of consequence would rather be taken by an enemy than continue where they were in slavery'.[15] Montero's *plan de guerra* assumed that 423 men would be available to him during the engagement, but many of them had no training or experience for their designated roles. The *Covadonga* could accommodate 64 guns but there were only 44 on board and only 32 were available to fire (the remaining 12 were stored); the heaviest guns were 12-pounders, with the rest being 6- or 8-pounders. She also carried 28 swivel guns,

---

12 Boyle Somerville, *Commodore Anson's Voyage into the South Seas and Around the World* (London: William Heineman, 1934), p.221.
13 Somerville, *Commodore Anson's Voyage*, p.222.
14 Williams, *The Prize of All the Oceans*, p.172.
15 Thomas, *A True and Impartial Journal*, p.286.

mounted on the gunwales and tops, whose impact would have been devastating had Anson tried to board the ship during the action.

On 19 June, after cruising for a month, Philip Saumarez commented that 'all hands began to look very melancholy… it being rare that the galleons arrive so late; but still hoped'.[16] But at sunrise (5:40 a.m.) on the next day, Charles Proby, a midshipman, sighted a Spanish ship some 18 miles to the south-east, ending a long period of uncertainty when they had not seen a single vessel: 'a general joy spread through the whole ship; for they had no doubt but this was one of the galleons, and they expected soon to see the other'.[17] As the galleon approached, she made no effort to change course and headed straight towards the *Centurion* in a light wind. At first, the captain of the *Covadonga* may have thought that the approaching vessel was a Spanish warship as he could not have known that there was no prospect of any assistance arriving from Manila after the *Pilar* had run aground. However, Montero soon concluded that the ship was likely to be the *Centurion* and by 7:30 a.m. she was clearly visible. Although she was still far out of range, the *Covadonga* soon took in her top-gallant sails and fired a gun, clearly indicating Montero's intention to fight. Anson was 'surprised to find, that in all this time the galleon did not change her course, but continued to bear down upon him; for he hardly believed, what afterwards appeared to be the case, that she knew his ship to be the *Centurion*, and resolved to fight him'.[18] In response, Anson 'fired a gun to leeward in order to amuse and distract them', but he was still far out of range.[19]

As the two ships slowly converged in light wind and rain, Anson completed his preparations, deploying his marksmen and gunners according to the plan he had drawn up. At about 11:30 a.m., the *Centurion*, which was faster and more manoeuvrable than her opponent, altered course and passed the stern of the *Covadonga*. She came up slowly on the galleon's port side, thus preventing her from escaping to Palapag, the nearest port on Samar, some 30 miles away. In response, the galleon hove-to, raised Spanish colours and began clearing her decks, and by 12:30 p.m. the ships were about half a mile apart. The *Centurion* also hoisted her colours and, to disrupt Spanish preparations, opened fire with a few rounds from her bow guns, although Anson's 'general directions had been not to engage till they were within pistol shot'.[20] As there was insufficient wind for the galleon to manoeuvre, she replied with two of her 12-pounder stern-chasers (a gun used to fire at a pursuing vessel) and her chain-shot damaged the *Centurion*'s sails and rigging.

There was still no sign of the expected second galleon and Anson concluded that the two ships had separated. He ran out the lower deck guns and prepared for boarding, with 'the *Centurion* getting her sprit-sail-yard fore and aft', while 'the Spaniards in a bravado rigged their sprit-sail-yard fore and aft likewise'.[21] In this unequal fight, boarding the *Centurion* and overpowering her smaller crew offered the Spanish their only real hope of success, with Saumarez commenting: 'as he [Montero] had no lower tier of guns we were amazed to think

---

16 Philip Saumarez, *Capture of the Acapulco Galleon*, in Williams (ed.), *Documents*, p.197.
17 Walter, *A Voyage Round the World*, p.338.
18 Walter, *A Voyage Round the World*, p.338.
19 Saumarez, *Capture of the Acapulco Galleon*, in Williams (ed.), *Documents*, p.198.
20 Walter, *A Voyage Round the World*, p.339.
21 Walter, *A Voyage Round the World*, p.339.

what he could propose against our weight of metal and a ship of our appearance; we learnt afterwards that they depended on their superior number of men'.[22]

By 1:00 p.m., the *Centurion* came within pistol shot and the 'engagement began on both sides with great briskness'.[23] Throughout the fight, Anson would stand 'upon the deck, with his sword drawn, in the thickest of the fire, and the smoke of the powder almost smothered him'.[24] As soon as the close action began, 'the mats, with which the galleon had stuffed her netting, took fire, and burnt violently, blazing up half as high as the mizentop'. The accident '…threw the enemy into great confusion, and at the same time alarmed the Commodore, for he feared least the galeon should be burnt, and least he himself too might suffer by her driving on board him'. But the Spaniards 'at last freed themselves from the fire, by cutting away the netting, and tumbling the whole mass, which was in flames, into the sea'.[25]

The *Centurion*'s first (starboard) broadside had 'good effect, both with [the galleon's] men and rigging', while the Spanish made effective use of their small 4-pounder guns, which were loaded with stones, iron nails and musket ball fragments. They caused damage to the *Centurion*'s sails and rigging but few casualties among her crew who were mainly working on the guns below deck. The *Centurion*'s 30 marksmen, under the command of Peter Denis, were deployed to great effect. Operating from the tops they fired at the enemy who manned the guns and *pedereros* in the *Covadonga*'s tops for no more than 10 minutes before they were cleared.[26] As Lawrence Millechamp commented, this 'greatly contributed to the preservation of our men, who otherwise must have been greatly annoyed by them'.[27] They then fired down on the galleon's decks, with her officers and gun crews being the priority targets. This fire wounded or killed all but one of the officers on the quarterdeck.

As the exchange continued, the *Centurion* moved ahead until she took position off the galleon's port bow, which meant that Anson could deploy all of his starboard cannon, while the Spanish could only respond with their bow guns. By 1:30 p.m. the *Centurion* had lost this position and moved alongside the *Covadonga*, battering her sides and firing grapeshot onto the deck. The *Centurion*'s fire continued 'without any intermission; nothing was to be seen but fire and smoke, nor heard but the thunder of the cannon, which was fired so quick that it made one continued sound'. The crew manning the ship's guns fired the small arms that Anson had ordered to be loaded, 'laid along on the gratings', and picked up when they had the opportunity. He made 'so good a disposition of the small arms that the want of men to be quartered to them was not felt'.[28]

The Spanish responded with grapeshot and small arms fire but casualties on the *Centurion* were light because her high bulwarks protected the crew. As the battle continued, the volume of enemy fire gradually diminished as the crew, who faced a mounting death toll, 'began to run from their quarters, and to tumble down the hatchways and scuttles in heaps, regardless

---

22 Saumarez, *Capture of the Acapulco Galleon*, in Williams (ed.), *Documents*, p.198.
23 Philip Saumarez, *Journal*, in Keppel, *The Life of Augustus, Viscount Keppel*, vol.I, p.62.
24 Philips, *An Authentic Journal*, p.175.
25 Walter, *A Voyage Round the World*, p.339.
26 A *pederero* was short piece of chambered ordnance that was used to fire stones and pieces of iron.
27 *Journal of Lawrence Millechamp*, in Williams (ed.), *Documents*, p.187.
28 *Journal of Lawrence Millechamp*, in Williams (ed.), *Documents*, p.187.

of their defence, and only seeing their safety in hiding their heads'.[29] Under the weight of the *Centurion*'s fire, Montero's officers were unable to prevent the men from deserting their posts. Evidence of the disorder on the *Covadonga* was later provided by Pascoe Thomas when he went on board the captured ship to secure the abandoned small arms lying on deck: 'I took care in particular of those which I found on the poop, consisting of about 50 or 60 swords, and near as many muskets, all thrown down in a confused manner without any order, and scarce one of the muskets discharged'.[30]

By 2:00 p.m., Spanish resistance began to collapse as heavy casualties took their toll; they included the Spanish commander, who was hit in the chest by a musket ball from a marksman in the *Centurion*'s tops and was taken below. He was replaced by his second in command at a time when Spanish resistance was faltering and he soon abandoned the fight. When informed that they were facing defeat, Montero ordered his deputy to set fire to the powder magazine but was told that it was too late: at 2:30 p.m., after a final discharge from six of her largest guns, the Spanish galleon had struck her colours, bringing this unequal 90-minute action to an end. It was marked by a small fire on the *Centurion*, which was caused by a cartridge accidentally igniting due to a seaman's carelessness; it set fire to a quantity of oakum near the after powder room but was soon put out.

As we have seen, Anson remained on deck throughout the action and his coolness in the face of Spanish fire was noted by more than one observer, with a fellow officer referring to 'the serenity he preserved in his countenance'.[31] Pascoe Thomas commented:

> During the fight the Commodore behaved in the most gallant manner; he gave his orders with coolness and calmness, and, though his piercing eyes were everywhere, he seemed as perfectly unconcerned, and present to himself, as if he had nothing to mind. This calmness of behaviour caused the whole engagement to be carried on in the same manner: every man knew his duty, and performed it without the least confusion, noise, or disorder.[32]

The official account describes the Spanish galleon as being much larger than the *Centurion*, with Anson having to overcome unfavourable odds to secure victory, but the claim is obviously misleading. It reflects the fact that Anson, who closely supervised the preparation of the text, was 'anxious to make the most of one of the few successes of an expedition scarred by disappointment and failure'.[33] In truth there was little real doubt about the final outcome: the *Centurion* was a more powerful warship and although she was undermanned, her crew were highly trained and well-motivated.

The Spanish, on the other hand, lacked the skills to overcome a more powerful enemy and their sole advantage – superior numbers – had little impact because Anson deployed his limited manpower effectively to maintain the *Centurion*'s volume of fire. He was fortunate

---

29   Somerville, *Commodore Anson's Voyage*, p.228.
30   Thomas, *A True and Impartial Journal*, p.286.
31   *The Universal Spectator and Weekly Journal*, no. 829, 25 August 1744.
32   Thomas, *A True and Impartial Journal*, p.284. See also John Entick, *A New Naval History, or, Compleat View of the British Marine* (London: R. Manby, 1757), p.785.
33   Glyndwr Williams, 'Commodore Anson and the Acapulco Galleon', *History Today*, 17 (1967), p.530.

that Montero, who, according to Pascoe Thomas, had 'extraordinary confidence in his own force and our weakness', had decided to fight rather than 'endeavouring to get away from us at first, which he had the greatest probability of effecting, if he had only hauled close on a wind'.[34] It has been suggested that Anson's achievement was not in defeating the galleon but 'in preserving his ship and enough of his crew intact to be able to intercept the *Covadonga* in the third year of one of the most gruelling voyages in British naval annals'.[35] Even if the galleon's capture were not a remarkable feat of arms, Anson's leadership skills and courage were much in evidence during the action and in the weeks leading up to it. He was prepared to take a calculated risk by going against one or two Spanish ships of uncertain strength, he motivated a crew that had suffered many hardships and trained them to fight effectively with reduced numbers.

The *Centurion*'s superior fire meant that the *Covadonga* suffered far heavier casualties than her opponent: 56 Spanish seamen were killed and 83 wounded (of whom eight later died) compared to two British dead and 16 wounded (of whom one later died). Anson reported that the Spanish ship's 'mast and rigging were shot to pieces, and 150 shot passed through her hull, many of which were between wind and water, which occasioned her to be very leaky'. This outcome refuted the view widely held by seamen that the hulls of Spanish galleons were shot-proof. By contrast, according to Anson, the *Centurion*'s damage was much more limited: 'the greatest damage I received was by my foremast, mainmast, and bowsprit being wounded. And my rigging shot to pieces, having only fifteen shots through my hull'.[36]

Anson dispatched Saumarez and 10 men in the *Centurion*'s cutter to take possession of the galleon: once on board, he confirmed that they had captured one of the largest hauls of treasure ever seized by a British ship. On the first day, 112 bags and six chests of treasure were removed but, in unfavourable weather, it took until 29 June for the rest of the haul to be transferred to the *Centurion*. When they reached Canton, the crew conducted a thorough search of the galleon and discovered a large quantity of concealed silver. Saumarez reported to Anson on the scene of devastation he witnessed when he went on board:

> The decks were promiscuously covered with carcasses, entrails and dismembered limbs. The main hatchway contained likewise several of their dead which had been thrown down it during the action, though as I learnt afterwards, they had been industriously employed in throwing the slain overboard since their first striking their colours to my coming on board.[37]

Anson soon sent a further 50 men to the *Covadonga* to undertake immediate repairs and two surgeons to attend to the wounded. This second party included Pascoe Thomas, who learnt that during the engagement the Spanish had 10 men on deck who were employed to 'swab up the blood, and throw the dead men immediately over-board, and remove the wounded out of the way'. This was necessary because 'the blood about the decks makes

---

34 Thomas, *A True and Impartial Journal*, p.290.
35 Williams, 'Commodore Anson', p.532.
36 BL: Hardwicke Papers, Add. MS. 35,359, f.360, George Anson to the Earl of Hardwicke, 14 June 1744.
37 Saumarez, *Capture of the Acapulco Galleon*, in Williams (ed.), *Documents*, p.199.

them so slippery that the living can scarcely stand on their feet... and the sight of so many dead men and their blood is a very great discouragement to the survivors'.[38] Saumarez transferred 300 prisoners to the *Centurion*, leaving less than 200 on board the galleon. Anson renamed the *Covadonga* the *Centurion Prize* and appointed Saumarez to the command. Brett replaced Saumarez as first lieutenant on the *Centurion*, with Denis and Keppel being appointed to the consequential vacancies as second and third lieutenants respectively.

Anson soon recognised that he was in 'great danger in navigating two such large ships in a dangerous and unknown sea, and to guard 492 prisoners'.[39] Both vessels had been damaged and there was a real risk of being intercepted by Spanish warships as they sailed towards China. He had no alternative but to return there to carry out repairs and replenish his supplies before leaving for England even though he did not expect a warm welcome after his first troublesome visit. He commented that there were 'no ports where I could harbour the ships, but those on the coast of China, where I had before met with great difficulties, and could not expect that my treatment would be better for bringing in a prize, a great part of whose wealth would have centred in that kingdom'.[40]

After completing essential repairs to the ships' rigging, they sailed slowly northwards while the silver was still being transferred from the *Covadonga*. Apart from securing the prisoners, the security of the treasure was Anson's top priority: 'it was of great consequence that the treasure should be sent on board the *Centurion*, which ship, by the presence of the Commander in Chief, the greater number of her hands, and her other advantages, was doubtless much safer against all the casualties of winds and seas than the galleon'.[41] The *Covadonga*'s 18 officers were transferred to the *Centurion*, where they were held under armed guard in the first lieutenant's cabin, while Montero, who 'acted with great bravery', was placed in Anson's quarters when he came on board on 25 June. On his arrival, he had apparently 'almost wept for shame when he discovered the insignificant force that had subdued him'.[42]

Anson soon decided to move 100 prisoners back to the prize where they could be accommodated more securely but those remaining on the *Centurion* still outnumbered their captors and were strictly controlled. They were held on the orlop deck (the lowest in the ship), where they would remain for five weeks during the hottest period of the year. Escape attempts were deterred by the removal of access ladders and by mounting swivel guns on the two hatchways leading down to the deck, which were kept open to give the prisoners as much air as possible. Their guards were ordered to open fire in the event of any disturbance but no such action was necessary despite

> ... the sufferings of the poor prisoners... [which] were much to be commiserated; for the weather was extremely hot, the stench of the hold loathsome beyond all conception, and their allowance of water but just sufficient to keep them alive, it not

---

38 Thomas, *A True and Impartial Journal*, pp.285–286.
39 BL: Hardwicke Papers, Add. MS. 35,359, f.360, George Anson to the Earl of Hardwicke, 14 June 1744.
40 TNA: SP 42/88, ff. 87–88, George Anson to the Duke of Newcastle, 14 June 1744.
41 Walter, *A Voyage Round the World*, p.342.
42 Entick, *A New Naval History*, p.785.

being practicable to spare them more than at the rate of a pint a day for each, the crew themselves having only an allowance of a pint and a half.[43]

On 8 July, as Anson approached Chinese waters, he sighted a French vessel of uncertain status 'and gave chase to her, there being very little wind'. He was aware of tensions between Britain and France from conversations with the officers of the *Covadonga* but he did not know whether war had begun (Louis XV did not formally declare it until 15 March 1744 (n.s.)). As he prepared for possible action, Anson cast off the *Centurion Prize* and ordered Saumarez and most of his crew to return to the *Centurion* in the event of an engagement as they would be needed to man her guns. Early the following morning they came within four miles of the ship, which then hoisted French colours, 'on which we hoisted ours, and fired a gun to leeward; but she taking no notice of it, but keeping on our course, about noon we quitted the chace'.[44] As the French ship continued to sail eastwards, Anson took the prize in tow once more and sailed for Macao, where he arrived on 11 July.

At Macao, he organised pilots and boats to tow him towards Canton and managed to disembark 72 prisoners before he was prevented from landing the remainder. On 14 July, as he approached the Bocca Tigris (the Tiger Gate), the narrow channel which protects the mouth of the Pearl River (Zhujiang River), he anchored the two ships. They faced two forts (one on each side of the channel) armed with a total of twenty-two 4- and 6-pounders. Shortly after their arrival, the mandarin commanding the forts came on board and learnt that the *Centurion* was a British warship, which sought shelter at Canton during the typhoon season. But he remained uncertain as to her status because the Chinese, 'had no notion of a ship commissioned by authority to make war on their enemies, any farther than their own coasts, [and] looked on us only as thieves and robbers'.[45]

Anson was ordered to remain in position until he received permission (in the form of a permit from the Viceroy) to sail further upstream. The mandarin demanded payment of measurage but Anson refused as he believed that a man-of-war should be treated differently from a merchant ship. However, as a percentage of the duties earmarked for Peking (Beijing) was listed as the 'emperor's present', Anson's refusal to pay was likely to damage the East India Company's relationship with the Chinese merchants authorised to trade with Europeans. To prevent the *Centurion* sailing, the mandarin ordered the pilots not to guide her through the Bocca Tigris, but Anson was more concerned about approaching bad weather than complying with official instructions and, on 15 July, he decided to press ahead.

Anson ordered 'the pilot to carry him by the forts, which were outgunned by the *Centurion* and offered no resistance, threatening him that, if the ship ran aground, he would instantly hang him up at the yardarm. The pilot, awed by these threats, carried the ship through safely, the forts not attempting to dispute the passage'.[46] The mandarin was subsequently held responsible for failing to stop the ship and, although Anson intervened on his behalf, he was taken away as a prisoner. He was also unable to prevent the pilot from being 'rigorously disciplined with the bamboo' for his alleged failures, but, on his return,

---

43 Walter, *A Voyage Round the World*, p.343.
44 John Philips, *An Authentic Journal of the Late Expedition*, p.294.
45 Thomas, *A True and Impartial Journal*, p.263.
46 Walter, *A Voyage Round the World*, p.347.

Anson gave him 'such a such a sum of money, as would at any time have enticed a Chinese to have undergone a dozen bastinadings [a beating on the soles of the feet using a stick or cudgel]'.[47] While waiting at anchor just beyond the forts, two heavily armed French East Indiamen passed the *Centurion* without incident although Anson regarded their failure to lower their topsails (the customary courtesy paid by a foreign merchant ship to a warship) as an insult. An armed confrontation could have occurred, underlining the risks he faced while waiting at a location where 'he might be trapped, far from open water, by warships sent from Manila, and his efforts to fight would be hindered by the hundreds of prisoners sweltering below deck'.[48]

On 16 July, in an effort to speed up the process of obtaining a permit, Anson dispatched Peter Denis to Canton, some 27 miles upriver, with a letter addressed to the Viceroy. There are differing accounts of how he was received, but the Chinese promised that Anson would receive a reply the following day. While he was in the city, he heard the concerns of Chinese merchants about the likely impact of Anson's presence on their trade, which was reflected in their reluctance to mix with the *Centurion*'s officers. Denis's boat also carried several Spanish officers who had been invited to go to the Viceroy's palace and were temporarily released from imprisonment. On their arrival, they were questioned about the reasons for their defeat. The Chinese expressed surprise that they had not been put to death but the Spanish explained that this was not customary in European warfare and commented 'that the Commodore, from the natural bias of his temper, had treated both them and their countrymen, who had formerly been in his power, with very unusual courtesy, much beyond what they could have expected'.[49] The dialogue helped to modify official attitudes to Anson, who was no longer seen as a 'lawless freebooter', but increasingly as an 'important and powerful personage', who was also immensely rich.

While Anson waited for a response, he increased pressure on the Chinese by preventing the *Harrington*, an East India Company ship, which had just arrived from the Malabar coast, from proceeding upriver past the *Centurion*. Shortly afterwards, on 20 July, three mandarins came on board the *Centurion* to give Anson the necessary permit to proceed towards Canton. They authorised him to sail to a point some four miles from Whampoa, where the East Indiamen were anchored because the river was too shallow beyond this point. Anson refused further demands to pay measurage but reached an agreement on the removal of many of his remaining prisoners, who left for Macao in two large junks on 28 July and were later sent to the Philippines. Anson wanted to be rid of the prisoners while the Chinese were concerned that the emperor 'might be displeased… that persons, who were his allies, and carried on a great commerce with his subjects, were under confinement in his dominions'.[50]

Anson reached his new anchorage off Whampoa on 27 July and was to remain there until 7 December. While they were detained there, the crew were forbidden to land or send letters ashore and two guard ships were moored nearby to enforce the restrictions. Anson used the time to complete the search of the *Centurion Prize* for concealed silver and repair

---

47   Walter, *A Voyage Round the World*, p.347.
48   Williams, *The Prize of All the Oceans*, p.178.
49   Walter, *A Voyage Round the World*, p.349.
50   Walter, *A Voyage Round the World*, p.350.

and repaint the *Centurion*. A thorough search uncovered a great deal of hidden treasure, including

> ...some cast into large lumps like cheeses, and so artfully covered in the rind of cheese, that 'twas by the weight only we could discover them. Some parcels of money we found hid between the beams and timbers of the ship, and in all places where there was any possibility of concealment we were sure to find money.[51]

The total haul recovered from the *Covadonga* amounted to 1,313,843 pieces of eight (a silver coin worth eight Spanish *reales*) and 35,682 ounces of virgin silver and plate; it was the final prize to be taken by the *Centurion* on the voyage around the world. When the search was completed, Anson decided to distribute part of the prize money; he received 10,000 dollars while 26,667 dollars were allocated to the crew.

Although supplies were delivered to the *Centurion* on a daily basis, Anson could not complete the preparations for his departure because he was unable to obtain the large quantities needed for the voyage to England. Chinese merchants had agreed to supply him, but nothing had been delivered and he was unable to secure the Viceroy's agreement to the move. Anson assumed that his efforts to move supplies on board were being obstructed because officials were waiting for authorisation from Peking. However, according to Pascoe Thomas, the delay in granting a meeting stemmed primarily

> ... from the opinion that their Emperor is the greatest prince in the world, and that as all the rest are his inferiors, the Chantucks, his representatives in the respective provinces, could not without diminution of his grandeur, receive the representative of any other prince without such marks of submission as he had been satisfied from enquiry our Commodore would never consent to.[52]

Anson, who seemed to be unaware of these sensitivities, decided to see the Viceroy in person to secure the necessary permit and announced that he would be arriving in Canton on 1 October. On the previous day, he had appointed Peircy Brett as acting captain in his absence and instructed him, if he was detained, to destroy the *Centurion Prize* and sail the *Centurion* towards Macao. His main priority was ensuring the security of the treasure while he was away, although the circumstances he planned for did not arise. As we shall see, when the *Centurion* returned home, the Admiralty refused to backdate Brett's promotion as a captain to 30 September 1743, and Anson temporarily left the navy as a consequence.

On 1 October, as Anson was about to set off in the *Centurion*'s barge, a message arrived from Canton asking for the meeting to be postponed for two or three days and he delayed his departure. However, later the same evening he received a further message informing him that the Viceroy (or rather his temporary replacement, the chuncoon, the acting Viceroy) had waited for him all day and was 'highly offended' that he had not appeared. There was a risk that this confusion would damage relations between the Chinese and the English

---

51 *Journal of Lawrence Millechamp*, in Williams (ed.), *Documents*, p.190.
52 Thomas, *A True and Impartial Journal*, p.305.

supercargoes, who wrote to Anson to convey their concerns; they were shared by Edward Page, the chief supercargo and Anson's main contact. Relations with the Chinese had always been fraught with difficulty, but the presence of a British warship with a Commodore who was reluctant to acknowledge their sovereignty, had little understanding of their culture and might threaten to use force could make it more difficult for Page to 'stave off any fatal mischief'.[53] He was concerned that their trading advantages might be 'sacrificed about a trifling punctillo in a foreign port, to which the Commodore had no credentials'.

Anson, in turn, was increasingly irritated by the difficulties in contacting senior Chinese officials and he decided to move to the Company factory on the city waterfront in the hope that he would have better access to them. At these offices, the supercargoes transacted business with the Hong merchants and his stay would allow him to apply more pressure on them. Anson made the move on 13 October in a blaze of publicity to announce his arrival in the city with the intention of impressing the Chinese. He was accompanied by Saumarez and Keppel in the *Centurion*'s barge, which was manned by a crew of 19 dressed in an impromptu uniform. They bore a strong resemblance to 'the watermen on the *Thames*; they were in number 18 and a coxswain; they had scarlet jackets and blue silk waistcoats, the whole trimmed with silver buttons, and with silver badges on their jackets and caps'.[54] Anson's party included Page and several foreign supercargoes and at Whampoa he was saluted by all the European merchant ships except for the French. A contingent of musketeers acted as a guard of honour on his arrival at the factory, where he was to stay for seven weeks. Page later noted Anson's outrage at the behaviour of the French and that generally he 'was pretty hard of belief, & strongly fix'd to his own opinions'.[55]

During his stay at the factory, the leading Chinese merchants came to pay their respects and it is likely that 'this degree of attention helped to change the attitude of at least some of the Chinese'.[56] He was able to make arrangements for the delivery of stores to the factory but the Hong merchants were still unable to secure the Viceroy's agreement for them to be shipped to the *Centurion*. An unsatisfactory meeting with the senior Hong merchant, Seuqua, convinced Anson that his problems would only be resolved if he could meet the Viceroy in person. The official account suggests that he also held Company officers partly responsible for his difficulties: 'the *Chinese* merchants had so far prepossessed the supercargoes of our ships with chimerical fears, that they (the supercargoes) were extremely apprehensive of being embroiled with the Government, and of suffering in their interest'.[57] On 24 November, Anson sent the Viceroy a letter but, according to Edward Page, when it was returned unopened he reacted with fury and threatened to blockade the river. Although this proved to be an empty threat, Page was concerned that the Chinese could respond by attacking the Company's ships at Whampoa.

Two days after the letter was sent a fire broke out in the suburbs, which threatened to destroy the city, and Anson and about 40 of his people helped to bring it under control:

---

53   Quoted in Williams, *The Prize of All the Oceans*, p.195.
54   Walter, *A Voyage Round the World*, p.356.
55   Oregon Historical Society (OHS): MS.2,894, Edward Page, *A Little Secret History of Affairs at Canton in the Year 1743 when the Centurion, Commodore Anson was Lying in the River* (1765), p.21.
56   Williams, *The Prize of All the Oceans*, p.190.
57   Walter, *A Voyage Round the World*, p.359.

'they were rather animated than deterred by the flames and falling buildings… [and] by their boldness and activity the fire was soon extinguished to the amazement of the *Chinese*'.[58] In the end, the damage seems to have been confined to a few streets and warehouses on the waterfront. Several leading Chinese merchants thanked Anson in person and the European supercargoes presented him with a porcelain dinner service (which is now at Shugborough). Anson's efforts were also recognised by the Viceroy who contacted him shortly afterwards to offer a meeting on 30 November, nearly four months after he had first arrived in Macao.

On the appointed day, Anson left for the city in a sedan chair carried by eight seamen. He was accompanied by Saumarez and Keppel, James Flint, his interpreter, and members of his crew, who wore scarlet and blue uniforms. They were also joined by Chinese merchants and East India Company captains. When he arrived at the South Gate, he was received by a guard of 200 soldiers who led the way to the emperor's palace. In a 'great parade' outside the palace, 'a body of troops, to the number of ten thousand, were drawn up under arms, and made a very fine appearance, being all of them new cloathed for this ceremony'.[59] When he first entered the palace Anson was kept waiting in an antechamber, and he later complained that it was a place in 'no ways proper for the reception of the representative of the King of Great Britain'. Despite his private anger, in public Anson 'appeared as cool and dignified as circumstances allowed' and did nothing to offend Chinese conventions or sensitivities.[60]

Anson was eventually ushered into the great hall of audience where the Viceroy and two mandarins were seated; a fourth chair was provided for Anson. During the meeting, he recited the various difficulties he had encountered in seeking a meeting and raised several grievances on behalf of the East India Company before turning to the main item of business: the shipping of his provisions. It was now the right season for him to return to Europe and he wanted to depart as soon as he received a licence to transfer his stores from the Company factory to his ship. In response, after an awkward silence, the Viceroy agreed 'that the licence should be immediately issued, and that everything should be ordered on board the following day'.[61] There was no demand to pay measurage and Anson later claimed this as an important precedent, although this did not stop the Chinese from imposing dues on British warships in the future. Despite this positive outcome, tensions between the two sides remained, with the Viceroy refusing to accept Anson's gift and then sending him 'two ordinary pieces of Taffaty' later in the day. Anson was offered 'an entertainment' after the meeting but declined when he discovered that the Viceroy would not be present.

The Chinese poet and painter, Yuan Mei (1716–1797), provided a completely different account of the meeting from that recorded in the official history. He reported that Anson, as the 'commander of the red-haired people', had been subject to the 'most ferocious curses' and fell to his knees in the presence of the Viceroy. He agreed to Chinese demands to offer his 500 Spanish prisoners as tribute and asked that provisions for his homeward journey be made available in return. Anson was unaware of the symbolic significance of handing over

---

58   Walter, *A Voyage Round the World*, p.362.
59   Walter, *A Voyage Round the World*, p.363.
60   Williams, *The Prize of All the Oceans*, p.197.
61   Walter, *A Voyage Round the World*, p.365.

his prisoners as tribute, thus acknowledging China's sovereignty over Britain.[62] The official account does not refer to this, simply reporting that Anson had been anxious to remove the remaining Spanish prisoners who 'were a great incumbrance [sic] to him'.[63]

On 3 December, Anson returned to the *Centurion*, where fresh supplies had already been loaded and, according to Millechamp, 'we were now in a better condition than we had ever before been. We were finely recruited and refreshed in China… Mr Anson had the decks filled with live cattle and sheep, [so] that we lived nobly for almost all our homeward bound passage'.[64] Before he departed, Anson wrote to Page apologising for 'the trouble I have given you and all the gentlemen at the factory'. On 7 December, the *Centurion* and the *Centurion Prize* left their anchorage, passing through the Bocca Tigris three days later. The forts were filled with men and arms and the display was 'doubtless intended to induce Mr *Anson* to think more reverently than he had hitherto done of the *Chinese* military power'.[65]

Before his departure, Anson had decided that the *Centurion Prize* was unseaworthy and when he arrived at Macao, on 12 December, he negotiated the sale of the ship (and her goods) to local merchants. They paid 6,000 dollars, which was far less than the galleon's true value, but also agreed to take most of the remaining Spanish prisoners (with a small number still being required for the homeward journey). Anson had been in no mood to haggle as he was impatient to get to sea and left Macao on 15 December 1743. He assumed that the war with Spain continued, possibly with French support, and he wanted to reach England before merchant ships returning to Europe brought news of the capture of the *Covadonga*: 'he was resolved to make all possible expedition in getting back, that he might be himself the first messenger of his own good fortune, and might therefore prevent the enemy from forming any projects to intercept him'.[66]

As he sailed through the South China Sea, Anson could not have known that the Spanish warships based in the Philippines posed no further threat as the Governor of Manila did not start the search for him until March 1744. When the Spanish finally reached Canton, they discovered that Anson had left several months earlier having freed his prisoners and sold the *Covadonga*. They were able to buy the galleon back but at first struggled to find any reliable intelligence about Anson's movements after his departure. There were suggestions that he had gone in search of another treasure galleon, but more accurate information was obtained from a merchant captain who had recently arrived from Java; he informed them that Anson was on his way to Europe having made a stop in Batavia early in January. In the light of this news, the Spanish decided to wait for the expected arrival of English merchant ships in June and July, in order (according to the Governor of Manila) to 'avenge the humiliation suffered through the loss of the *Covadonga*'.[67]

Anson left the South China Sea on 1 January 1744, passing through the Sunda Strait, which separates the islands of Java and Sumatra, and into the Indian Ocean. As they sailed

---

62 Arthur Waley, *Yuan Mei: Eighteenth Century Chinese Poet* (Stanford: Stanford University Press, 1970), p.208.
63 Walter, *A Voyage Round the World*, p.350.
64 *Journal of Lawrence Millechamp*, in Williams (ed.), *Documents*, p.193.
65 Walter, *A Voyage Round the World*, p.366.
66 Walter, *A Voyage Round the World*, p.370.
67 Governor of Manila to the King of Spain, 5 July 1744 (n.s.), in Williams (ed.), *Documents*, pp.211–212.

westwards, Anson and his officers had an opportunity to reflect on their frustrating experiences in Canton and the negative views they had formed of the Chinese people and their culture. The official history acknowledged that they were 'a very ingenious and industrious people', but otherwise had little positive to say about them. Anson's contacts with Chinese officials confirmed his view that 'their magistrates are corrupt, their people thievish, and their tribunals crafty and venal'.[68] On 11 March, the *Centurion* reached the Cape of Good Hope where they were to remain until the beginning of April. The settlement was then ruled by the Dutch East India Company and Anson was

> ...highly delighted with the place, which by its extraordinary accommodations, the healthiness of its air, and the picturesque appearance of the country, all enlivened by the addition of a civilized colony, was not disgraced in an imaginary comparison with the valleys of Juan Fernandez, and the lawns of Tinian.[69]

During their stay, Anson recruited 40 seamen: apart from the English, there were now 18 nationalities on board, including Europeans, Malays, Persians, Indians of Manila, Negroes of Guinea and Creoles of Mexico.

On leaving the Cape, Anson made straight for England, and, on 10 June, he learnt from a passing ship that Britain and France were now at war and that there were many warships and privateers, both English and French, at sea. When the *Centurion* passed through a French squadron in the English Channel, Anson's good fortune did not desert him as he went undetected because of thick fog. On 14 June 1744, he arrived at Spithead, three years and nine months after his departure, completing the first official British circumnavigation of the globe since Francis Drake's voyage of 1577–1580. On the day of his return, Anson wrote to the Duke of Newcastle to inform him of his safe arrival and sent Peter Denis to London to deliver the letter. It brought the first news of the capture of the *Covadonga*, details of the captured treasure and an account of his subsequent experiences in Canton. Although Anson had expected problems with the Chinese authorities after the difficulties encountered during his first visit, he reported that the Viceroy had received him with 'great civility and politeness... and granted me everything I desired'. His main aim had been to establish a precedent 'upon record that the emperor's duty and measurage had not been demanded from me, by which means his Majesty's ships will be under no difficulties in entering into any of the Emperor of China's ports for the future'.[70]

Anson's letter also defended his record in command of the expedition: he had carried out his instructions of 31 January 1740 'in the best manner I was able', pointing out that by the time he had reached the Juan Fernandez Islands, he was reduced to three ships and 340 men, all of whom were 'violently affected with the scurvy'. He recognized that while the expedition had not achieved all of its original objectives, he was 'not conscious that the failure can be imputed to any misconduct of mine as commander in chief'. He might

---

68   Walter, *A Voyage Round the World*, p.369.
69   Walter, *A Voyage Round the World*, p.371.
70   TNA: SP 42/88, ff.87–88, George Anson to the Duke of Newcastle, 14 June 1744. Anson had submitted earlier reports to the Admiralty from Madeira, 3 November 1740; from Saint Catherine's, 16 January 1741; and from Canton, 7 December 1742.

George Anson, 1744, engraving by Jan Caspar Philips after Arthur Pond. (Rijksmuseum)

have added that by all accounts his treatment of the prisoners taken during the voyage was exemplary and, as he later explained, 'I think it is barbarous and brutal not to treat prisoners with all possible kindness and civility, and shall never have an opinion of any man that acts otherwise'.[71] Anson sought Newcastle's permission to return to London 'for the recovery of my health, which is greatly impaired by the fatigues and hardships of this long voyage'.

On the same day, Anson wrote in similar terms to his patron the Earl of Hardwicke, acknowledging that 'the expedition had not had all the success the nation expected from it, which is a great misfortune to me', while also denying any personal failings. He explained

---

71 George Anson to the Duke of Bedford, 10 October 1747, in John Russell, *Correspondence of John, Fourth Duke of Bedford, Selected from the Originals at Woburn Abbey* (London: Longman, Green, Brown and Longmans, 1842), vol.I, p.271.

that he 'should have great pain in returning to my country after all the fatigues and hazards I have undergone in endeavouring to serve it, if I thought I had forfeited either your Lordship's favour and protection or the esteem of the public'.[72] Anson also mentioned that he had recommended Peter Denis for promotion in his letter to Newcastle as 'he well deserves it' and it was, in any case, customary for the officer sent to report victory in battle by his commander in chief to be rewarded in this way. Denis had in turn made a brief assessment of Anson in a letter to his brother while he was waiting in Macao: 'to give you a character of him would require a more masterly pen; but his favours to me as well as all the other officers, are sufficient proofs of his inclinations to serve us all'.[73]

When the *Centurion* came into Portsmouth dockyard, the remaining Spanish prisoners were released and sent directly to Spain. In total, there were 195 men on board, excluding prisoners, with only 145 members of the original crews and some 50 replacements recruited or taken during the voyage surviving. The voyage around the world had cost the lives of more than 1,415 men, with scurvy (997) and fevers and dysentery (320) causing by far the greatest number of deaths. Only four seamen died in action during the voyage, with fatalities occurring when Paita was raided and during the engagement with the *Covadonga*.[74]

---

72   BL: Hardwicke Papers, Add. MS. 35,359, f.360, George Anson to the Earl of Hardwicke, 14 June 1744.
73   Peter Denis to his brother, 1 December 1742, in *The Gentleman's Magazine*, XIII (1743), p.326.
74   Christopher C. Lloyd, 'Victualling of the Fleet in the Eighteenth and Nineteenth Centuries', in J. Watt, E. J. Freeman and W. F. Bynum (eds.), *Starving Sailors. The Influence of Nutrition upon Naval and Maritime History* (London: National Maritime Museum, 1981), p.57.

4

Rising Politician, 1744–1747

On 15 June, Anson came on shore at Portsmouth for the first time in nearly four years, escorted by Captain John Byng (whose failure to save Minorca in 1756 would lead to his execution). Byng's sister, the letter-writer Sarah Osborn, who saw Anson – together with Augustus Keppel – soon after he arrived, commented: 'Anson looks well, but much thinner; Keppel as brown as a mahogany table'.[1] Anson arrived in London shortly afterwards and if he had any concerns about his reception in the capital they were soon put to rest. The King and leading members of the Government received him as a national hero at a time when England had little to show for five years of war. He was feted by the Pelham administration, with the Duke of Newcastle acknowledging his 'success in taking the great Acapulco ship… the honour you have acquired for yourself, and the service you have done your country' and reporting that George II had expressed his 'great approbation of your conduct'.[2] Anson was received by the King shortly afterwards and, on 19 June, he was appointed rear admiral of the blue. The following day he dined with Newcastle at Claremont, his country house in Surrey.

Although Anson's expedition had been highly lucrative, contemporary estimates of the sterling value of the *Centurion's* treasure varied widely, with the *Gentleman's Magazine* reporting that it included '2,600,000 pieces of eight and 150,000 ounces of plate, 10 bars of gold and a large quantity of gold and silver dust; in the whole to the amount of £1,250,000 sterling'.[3] However, the official account provided a much lower figure, which valued it at 'not much short of 400,000*l*' [nearly £80 million in 2023 prices] independent of the ships and merchandise, which she either burnt or destroyed, and which… could not amount to so little as 600,000*l*. more; so that the whole loss of the enemy, by our squadron, did doubtless exceed a million sterling'.[4]

The value of the bullion brought to Britain represented no more than a small proportion of the total losses Spain had incurred because of Anson's expedition: 'an estimated 8 to 10 million dollars were taken or destroyed, and a similar amount attributable to lost trade, delays and the deterioration of cargoes. Above all, he had crippled the flow of specie from

---

1 Sarah Osborn to Danvers Osborn, 20 June 1744, in John McClelland (ed.), *Letters of Sarah Byng Osborn 1721–1773* (Stanford: Stanford University Press, 1930), p.57.
2 TNA: SP 42/88, f. 89, Duke of Newcastle to George Anson, 15 June 1744.
3 *The Gentleman's Magazine*, XIV (1744), p.336.
4 Walter, *A Voyage Round the World*, p.344.

Peru to Spain'.⁵ Spain also incurred significant costs in fitting out Pizarro's squadron and suffered heavy losses in men and warships during the failed pursuit of the British squadron. The net amount available for distribution to the *Centurion's* officers and men was estimated at £243,360 (£47.8 million in 2023 prices) after legal fees and other expenses had been deducted. Anson gained a 'vast fortune, substantial and lucky'⁶ and his share – three-eighths of the total – was estimated at £91,000 (nearly £18 million in 2023 prices). In 1745, a new silver shilling, called a 'Lima', was minted from the hoard of Peruvian silver that he had brought home. Anson hoped that his success could be repeated, and, in September, he wrote to his friend Commodore Curtis Barnett, commander of a small squadron in the East Indies, giving him guidance on how to intercept next year's treasure galleon off Cape Spiritu Santo.⁷ But although Barnett would capture three French East Indiamen, which he sold to the governor of Batavia for £92,000, the Manila galleon eluded him.

When the treasure was unloaded, it was transferred to 32 wagons and on 2 July, guarded by 139 officers and seamen, the convoy left for London. On its arrival two days later, *The Daily Post* reported that 'the people are to breakfast at Mr Parry's, the bowling green house on Putney Common, between nine and ten in the morning, after which they will come over Fulham Bridge, pass through Piccadilly, St James's Street, Pall Mall, the Strand, and so to the Bank [of England] at about twelve'. At the head of the procession were the ship's officers, who were 'richly dressed' with their swords drawn and they were followed 'by a kettle-drum, trumpets, and French horns'. On the first wagon 'was the English colours, with the Spanish ensign under it, and every third or fourth wagon carried some trophy of honour, which had been taken from the Spanish in the South Sea, as well as from the Acapulco ship'.⁸

Ann Donnellan, the Irish literary critic, 'saw two and thirty dirty waggons pass by, guarded by a number of tanned sailors, but we had the pleasure of knowing or thinking those dirty waggons contained what make all the pursuits of this world'.⁹ Anson viewed the procession from a house in Pall Mall in company with the Prince and Princess of Wales, while Horace Walpole, who 'saw it in profile from my window', was inevitably much more critical: 'a trumpery sight it was – I don't conceive anybody's being pleased with it'.¹⁰ However, the London historian and editor Thomas Birch more accurately reflected the public mood: 'The procession of Anson's people... was a sight more rare and not less agreeable to an Englishman than the secular games to a Roman'.¹¹

Samuel Johnson, the poet and lexicographer, was one of the few contemporary critics of the expedition and, in a pamphlet published in 1756, he was dismissive: it 'miscarried by the

---

5   Andrew Lambert, *Crusoe's Island: A Rich and Curious History of Pirates, Castaways and Madness* (London: Faber & Faber, 2016), p.100.
6   Horace Walpole to Horace Mann, 18 June 1744, in W.S. Lewis, *The Yale Edition of the Correspondence of Horace Walpole* (New Haven: Yale University Press, 1977), vol.18, p.463.
7   George Anson to Curtis Barnett, 14 September 1744, quoted in Robert Beatson, *Naval and Military Memoirs of Great Britain from 1727 to 1783* (London: Longman, 1804), vol.III, pp.54–55.
8   *The Daily Post*, 2 July 1744; *The Gentleman's Magazine*, XIV (1744), p.392.
9   Emily J. Climenson (ed.), *Elizabeth Montagu, the Queen of the Bluestockings, Her Correspondence from 1720 to 1761* (London: John Murray, 1906), vol.I, p.186.
10 Horace Walpole to Charles Hanbury Williams, 7 July 1744, in Lewis (ed.), *The Yale Edition of the Correspondence of Horace Walpole*, vol.30, p.53.
11 Thomas Birch to Philip Yorke, 7 July 1744, in Yorke (ed.), *The Life and Correspondence*, vol.I, p.349.

lateness of the season, and our ignorance of the coasts, on which we were to act. We returned with loss, and only exerted our enemies to greater vigilance, and perhaps to stronger fortifications'.[12] Other dissenting voices pointed out that the human cost of the expedition was high and that its impact on the course of the war had been virtually non-existent, but the overwhelming popular response was positive. Anson's achievements were widely celebrated in poems and songs as well as in the national press. On 6 July, many of the *Centurion*'s crew were present at the New Wells, a rival to Sadler's Wells, when a new song 'in honour of their glorious commander taking the Acapulco ship from the Spaniards' was performed.[13]

The celebrations were soon to be overshadowed by a damaging dispute between Anson and the Admiralty about the promotion of one of his officers on the *Centurion*. The Admiralty Board was headed by Daniel Finch, eighth Earl of Winchilsea, a weak and unsuccessful First Lord in the administration led by Henry Pelham and his brother the Duke of Newcastle. Although the Board had responded quickly to Anson's recommendation in favour of Peter Denis, who was appointed as master and commander of the *Swift* (8) sloop before the end of June, it was not so accommodating when deciding on the date of Peircy Brett's promotion to captain. Although it agreed to advance him in rank, it would not backdate the promotion to the date Anson had appointed him as acting captain of the *Centurion* (30 September 1743) during their stay in China while Anson was visiting Canton. Anson argued that Brett's appointment (and pay) should start from that point, but the Admiralty refused to recognize the earlier date because Anson did not have the power to make such an appointment.

The Admiralty's decision is likely to have been unexpected, particularly as Anson's brother Thomas had previously commented on the positive official attitude to the expedition. In a letter to his brother in November 1743, he noted that the Admiralty had 'graciously received' Captain Saunders and the other officers on their return from Macao and they 'had been promised what ships they would ask for. Lord Winchilsea... declaring that they would confirm whatever Anson did'.[14] He continued: 'This I mention in case you have a mind to make any new officers, or advance any that are made, the least pretence may probably suffice'. However, his prediction proved to be wide of the mark as Winchilsea's attitude had changed by the time Anson returned and, on this occasion, he was determined not to give way.

Anson was equally intransigent and, on 24 June, as soon as he was notified of Winchilsea's decision, he resigned and returned his commission as rear admiral to the Admiralty. In his letter, he argued that the date of Brett's original appointment should be honoured even if he had technically exceeded his formal powers of promotion:

> It has ever been my opinion that a person entrusted with a command may, and ought to, exceed his orders, and dispense with the common rule of proceedings when extraordinary occasions require it. In what I have acted I have had no other views than the honour and advantage of his Majesty's service.[15]

---

12 Samuel Johnson, 'An Introduction to the Political State of Great-Britain (1756)', in J.P. Hardy (ed.), *The Political Writings of Samuel Johnson* (New York: Barnes & Noble, 1968), p.13.
13 Glyndwr Williams, *The Great South Sea: English Voyages and Encounters 1570–1750* (New Haven: Yale University Press, 1997), p.248.
14 Thomas Anson to George Anson, 30 November 1743, in Williams (ed.), *Documents*, p.180.
15 Quoted in Anson, *The Life of Admiral Lord Anson*, pp.64–65.

In response the Admiralty cancelled his commission and Anson reverted to the rank of captain (on half-pay). He sought no further naval employment while Winchilsea remained in office and, as he was now independently wealthy, he could afford to wait until political circumstances changed. Anson's unexpected departure was widely regretted: 'People are sorry because a commodore, so successful and otherwise so good a character, promised to make a successful admiral'.[16]

Thomas Corbett, Secretary to the Admiralty and Anson's friend, subsequently wrote to him at length justifying the Board's decision. He acknowledged that a commander may exceed his orders when extreme circumstances require it but argued that the rule was not relevant in this case. Although the measures 'you took to secure the King's ship and the treasure *in case* any accident happened to your person were prudent and necessary measures, but the trust was conditional, and to take place upon an inability to act yourself, which did not happen'. Creating a precedent would mean that the Admiralty 'is no longer master of any rule or order; but every commander who goes abroad without a captain may appoint one as soon as he is clear of the land of England, and insist upon it, from the precedent'.[17] Despite his lengthy explanation, Corbett was unable to persuade Anson to change his firm view that because of the exceptional circumstances that prevailed in Canton, the Admiralty should have backdated the promotion.

Anson was soon drawn into another acrimonious dispute between the officers of the *Centurion* and the officers of the *Gloucester* and *Tryal Prize* about the distribution of prize money taken from the *Covadonga*. The disagreement could not be resolved informally and led to protracted legal proceedings over a period of three years. As Lawrence Millechamp explained, 'as we had nothing else to encounter or make us unhappy [now that the voyage had ended] we must fall out one among another concerning the distribution of the money we had taken. By which means we had more terrible engagements in the courts of law, than ever we had in the South Seas, or even in taking the galleon'.[18] Anson gave evidence in court on four occasions but was not directly involved in the dispute or a party to the proceedings. He maintained his distance from it and did not attempt to bring his former colleagues together to try to settle the issue before it went to court. Philip Saumarez, as an established officer on the *Centurion*, appeared to be more concerned about the impact of the action on his relationships with those on the opposing side than in winning the case at all costs: 'This fatal lawsuit lays me under, and all my friends by restraining and preventing my assisting them in the manner I could wish is a most scandalous thing'.[19]

The legal battle was fought between 10 officers of the *Centurion* (the appellants) and 11 officers of the *Gloucester* and *Tryal Prize* (the respondents) whose ships had been scuttled during the circumnavigation.[20] It began with a hearing in the High Court of Admiralty in August 1744. Prize money was divided into eight parts and distributed according to rank. Anson, as captain of the *Centurion*, received by far the largest share – three-eighths of the total – with lieutenants and other officers, and midshipmen each receiving one part equally

---

16   Bakers to Peter Warren, 27 July 1744, in Gwyn (ed.), *The Royal Navy and North America*, p.34.
17   BL: Anson Papers, Add. MS. 15,955, ff.249–251, Thomas Corbett to George Anson, 25 June 1744.
18   *Journal of Lawrence Millechamp*, in Williams (ed.), *Documents*, p.194.
19   Heaps, *Log of the Centurion*, p.255
20   The respective 'Allegations' of the two parties are included in Williams (ed.), *Documents*, pp.249–267.

divided. Seamen and other ordinary crew members received two parts divided equally between them. The dispute concerned the status of the officers of the *Gloucester* and *Tryal Prize* after their transfer to the *Centurion*, which affected the share of the prize money due to them. If they were regarded as serving as officers on the *Centurion*, they would be entitled to share one-eighth of the officers' prize money, but if they were classed as supernumeraries they would only be entitled to share the two-eighths allocated to ordinary seamen. This would be distributed to some 200 crew members, giving them a much smaller sum.

The *Centurion*'s officers, including Philip Saumarez who appeared as their senior representative, argued in court that the officers of the *Gloucester* and the *Tryal Prize* should be classed as supernumeraries who were only entitled to a seamen's share of the prize money. Their argument was based on the claim that the complement of the *Centurion* was fixed before the start of the voyage and Anson did not have the power to increase it. The respondents, on the other hand, claimed that the *Tryal Prize* had been in good condition and was only destroyed because Anson needed to supplement the crews of the *Centurion* and *Gloucester*, which were both undermanned. He had promised to maintain their status after they were transferred from the *Tryal Prize*, but the *Centurion*'s officers rejected this claim and asserted that the ship was in a poor state of repair. However, definitive evidence, confirmed by Anson himself, was produced that showed that he had ordered the ship's destruction because he needed to redeploy the men rather than because of any concerns about her condition.

In his evidence, Anson said he had decided that the officers of the *Tryal Prize* – and the *Gloucester* after it was scuttled – should be listed as supernumeraries rather than officers on the *Centurion*. They had played a useful role but had not served as officers even though he had continued to pay them at that level for the rest of the voyage because of the circumstances in which their ships were destroyed. The Court also heard evidence on the duties undertaken by the respondents who asserted that 'in the several emergencies of this stage of the voyage they pitched in at every conceivable level to help work, fight and at times save the *Centurion*'.[21] However, the appellants disputed the claim that they had served as officers, arguing that their duties were voluntary and without legal standing. The respondents strongly disputed Anson's evidence, asserting that 'in every one of his orders [he] constantly requires the duty of officers from us, and directs every one of his orders to us as officers'. Despite Anson's intervention, in March 1745, the High Court of Admiralty ruled in favour of the respondents, concluding that they 'were officers in His Majesty's service on board the *Centurion* at the time of capture [of the *Nuestra Señora de Covadonga*]' and were entitled to a share 'according to their ranks with the officers of the *Centurion*'.

The *Centurion*'s officers then appealed and, in May 1747, after a four-day hearing, the Lords Commissioners of Appeals in Prize Causes reversed the judgement of the Admiralty Court. In a majority decision, they decreed that the officers of the *Gloucester* and the *Tryal Prize* were not commissioned officers of the *Centurion* and therefore had no right to share in the distribution of the prize money with the officers; they were only entitled to an ordinary seaman's share. Even if the ruling were strictly correct in law, it not take account of the extreme difficulties that Anson faced in crossing the Pacific. Without the support of the

---

21   Williams, *The Prize of All the Oceans*, p.214.

officers of the other two ships it is unlikely that the *Centurion* would have reached China or later captured the *Covadonga*.

Following his return home to public acclaim and confirmation of his status as a national hero, Anson's priorities were to enter London society, use his newfound wealth to acquire property, and launch a political career. At first, he was based at Thomas Anson's house in Spring Gardens, Westminster, but within months of his return, he had acquired a small country estate: Holywell Farm, to the north-west of Soberton Heath in the Lower Meon Valley in Hampshire. He combined and extended the two existing cottages, with Thomas Anson reporting that it was 'much improved upon the scheme you proposed of decency and convenience'.[22] Situated some nine miles north of Portsmouth, where Anson would also acquire a house, Holywell Farm (now Holywell House) was conveniently located for the dockyard when Anson returned to the sea. This purchase was the first of several property acquisitions he was to make in London and elsewhere in England over the next few years.

As he established himself in the capital, Anson was elected as a member of White's and other London clubs where he was to lose large sums at cards and roulette. Despite rapidly becoming a prominent member of London society Anson soon gained a reputation for being unclubbable, but his brother-in-law Philip Yorke, second Earl of Hardwicke, had an explanation for this apparent inconsistency: 'he was in himself shy and reserved, but when he was once free or admitted others to be so with him, no man could be more agreeable or communicative'.[23] He later joined the Society of Dilettanti, where he was elected as a member in 1750. Thomas Anson was a founder member of the Society, which was established to sponsor the study of ancient Greek and Roman art and the creation of new work in the same style. Walpole described it as 'a club, for which the nominal qualification is having been in Italy, and the real one, being drunk'.[24] A letter from the Society's treasurer about Anson's election, seems to confirm Walpole's assessment:

> Ld Anson was balloted for, and unanimously chosen as a member. I won't steal an old joke and talk of shewing him more of the world than he saw in the circumnavigating it: but we shall, I fancy, make him drink and subscribe very liberally, which will be two quite new and surprising discoveries in his Ldship's character.[25]

Both brothers were patrons of James 'Athenian' Stuart, the Scottish architect and artist, who designed the Tower of the Winds and other neoclassical garden buildings at Shugborough. He was a member of the Dilettanti Club and nominated them for membership of the Society for the Encouragement of Arts, Manufactures and Commerce (later the Royal Society of Arts). They were also fellows of the Royal Society, with Anson being elected to Europe's leading scientific society in May 1745. The Society's fellows included distinguished scientists

---

22 BL: Anson Papers, Add. MS. 15,955, f.31, Thomas Anson to George Anson, n.d.
23 BL: Hardwicke Papers, Add. MS. 35,428, f.4, 'Memorial of Family Occurrences from 1760 to 1770 inclusive'.
24 Horace Walpole to Horace Mann, 14 April 1743, in Lewis (ed.), *The Yale Edition of the Correspondence of Horace Walpole*, vol.18, p.211.
25 Henry Harris to Henry Fox, 4 December 1750, in Giles Fox-Strangways, Earl of Ilchester (ed.), *Letters to Henry Fox, Lord Holland* (London: Roxburghe Club, 2015), p.54.

and mathematicians as well as the French writer Voltaire. William Pitt was already a fellow and Anson's political allies – Newcastle and Hardwicke – would soon follow him.

Freed of his naval responsibilities, Anson made an early decision to seek election to the House of Commons and used his existing contacts to join a group of opposition Whigs and secure his nomination as a Parliamentary candidate. His political connections included Lord Hardwicke and his cousin George Parker, second Earl of Macclesfield. A fellow Staffordshire resident John Leveson-Gower, first Earl Gower, the first Tory to enter the Government since the accession of George I, may have provided Anson with an introduction to his son-in-law John Russell, fourth Duke of Bedford, a leading member of the opposition and one of the wealthiest men in England. Bedford's group included John Montagu, Earl of Sandwich, an able young politician who was to become one of Anson's closest political allies. Anson joined the group and would work closely with both men when all three were appointed to the Admiralty Board later in the year.

Another prominent opposition Whig, William Pulteney, first Earl of Bath, provided Anson with the opportunity to stand for election to the Commons. Lord Bath had controlled the constituency of Hedon in the East Riding of Yorkshire for many years, and he put Anson forward in a by-election, held on 8 December 1744, when he defeated Luke Robinson, a Walpole Whig. When the King asked him how the election had gone, Lord Bath said that Anson 'had let fly an Acapulco ship at 'em and that was powerful'.[26] The constituency, which had about 130 voters, was later described 'as to be bought' and it is perhaps not surprising that the unsuccessful candidate petitioned against the return, alleging that Anson was 'guilty of the most notorious bribery and corruption'.[27] Although he attended Parliament regularly and exercised his vote, there is no record that the 'shy and reserved' Anson ever spoke in a debate in either House. He remained as MP for Hedon until his elevation to the peerage in July 1747.

Anson was fortunate that the reconstruction of the coalition led by Pelham and his brother shortly before his election gave him an early opportunity to advance his political career. When John Carteret, second Earl Granville, was dismissed as Secretary of State for the Northern Department after only a few months in office, several opposition Whigs – and some Tories – were invited by the Pelhams to join a 'broad-bottom ministry'. They included the Duke of Bedford who was appointed as First Lord of the Admiralty and Lord Sandwich who also joined the Admiralty Board. Bedford and his followers had a shared concern about the problems of decay in British society and believed that they could be addressed by 'standardisation, reassertion of central authority and hierarchical obedience to that authority'.[28] Bedford and Sandwich had a strong interest in naval issues and thought that similar remedies should be applied to the navy, which had achieved little success since the beginning of the war. These included strengthening the service, improving its discipline and performance,

---

26 Quoted in Romney Sedgwick, 'George Anson', *History of Parliament Online*, <https://www.historyofparliamentonline.org/volume/1715-1754/member/anson-george-1697-1762>, accessed 18 September 2022.
27 Godfrey R. Park, *The History of the Ancient Borough of Hedon in the Seigniory of Holderness, and East Riding of the County of York* (Hull: W.G.B. Page, 1895), p.172.
28 Sarah Kinkel, 'The Kings Pirates? Naval Enforcement of Imperial Authority, 1740–76', *The William and Mary Quarterly*, 71 (2014), p. 9.

and deploying it more aggressively so that it could defeat the French and enable Britain to take control of Canada.

The Royal Navy had not performed well since Vernon's capture of Porto Bello in November 1739 at the beginning of the war against Spain. A succession of wartime failures followed, but the outcome of the opening engagement of the war with France – the Battle of Toulon, 11 February 1744, when Vice Admiral Thomas Mathews fought a combined Franco-Spanish fleet – was the most damaging. The British failed to prevent the enemy's escape or to capture a single ship during the action and Mathews sent his second-in-command, Richard Lestock, who headed the rear division, home for failing to come up quickly in support. A Parliamentary enquiry into the battle, which was held early in 1745, led to all those involved being court-martialled and eventually to Mathews' dismissal. The apparent cowardice displayed by Lestock and other officers at Toulon was not an isolated event and there had been several examples of warships surrendering to the enemy without a fight during the war. Apparently guilty officers were taken to court but often acquitted by their peers and it is not surprising that Anson was soon complaining that 'this Admiralty is cursed with court-martials'.[29] They were a reminder of why the priority the new Admiralty intended to give to improving discipline was justified.

There were also unresolved questions about the relationship between naval courts-martial and the civil law courts that needed to be addressed. They had been raised most recently in the trial of George Frye, a lieutenant of marines, for disobedience and disrespect in Jamaica in March 1744. The court-martial found Frye guilty and sentenced him to be cashiered and imprisoned for 15 years. When his sentence was declared illegal, Frye obtained a verdict of false imprisonment in a civil action in the Court of Common Pleas and won damages of £1,000 against the president, Admiral Sir Chaloner Ogle, and other members of the court-martial. Ogle was then serving as president of the court trying Richard Lestock, sitting with Rear Admiral Perry Mayne, who had also been a member of the Frye court-martial. In Ogle's absence, Mayne, who served as his deputy, and fellow members of the court, complained that the verdict was a direct infringement of the Admiralty's authority, and they passed a vote of censure on the Lord Chief Justice, Sir John Willes, who in turn threatened to arrest them. When faced with the prospect of arrest, Mayne backed down and members of the court-martial issued an apology, bringing the immediate dispute to an end but leaving the wider issue unresolved.

Bedford and his followers believed that such disorder and disobedience could only be addressed by radical new policies which emphasised discipline, obedience and hierarchy, reflecting their wider political beliefs. As the Admiralty later informed George II, 'Nothing but discipline will effectually answer and make good every expectation which Your Majesty and the public can found upon the behaviour of the fleet of Great Britain'.[30] Their programme of reform, which included some changes that were to prove controversial, helped to transform the navy's fortunes, leading to its two victories against the French in 1747 under Anson and Edward Hawke respectively. One of their most significant changes – a revised disciplinary code that would help to restore discipline and revise the powers of courts-martial

---

29 George Anson to the Duke of Bedford, 10 October 1747, in Russell, *Correspondence of John, Fourth Duke of Bedford*, vol.I, p.271.
30 The Admiralty to George II, 31 January 1746, quoted in Kinkel, 'The King's Pirates?', p.16.

– required legislation and would generate significant public debate; it would not be enacted until after the end of the war. In the meantime, the Bedford Admiralty initiated earlier legislation to strengthen specific aspects of naval discipline, and Bills were passed in 1744 and 1748.

When Bedford and Sandwich (who served as his deputy) joined the new coalition, they had 'insisted on choosing the Admiralty in spite of opposition from the outgoing ministry', replacing the Earl of Winchilsea, who had presided over a weak and divided Board since 1742. Despite their interest in the navy, Bedford and Sandwich had no experience of naval policymaking and quickly concluded that they needed to strengthen the professional advice available to them. Two naval members of previous boards – Lord Archibald Hamilton and Lord Vere Beauclerk (later first Lord Vere), who were both sons of Whig dukes – were reappointed but neither was likely to provide the fresh perspectives that Bedford wanted and he had no hesitation in sidelining them whenever necessary. Hamilton, who was appointed as first naval lord, had been a member of the Board since 1729 apart from one short interval. Now in his early seventies, his naval career was over but he continued to serve as MP for Dartmouth. Beauclerk, a long-serving MP and naval captain, was to rise through the flag ranks but never returned to a sea command.

If Bedford and Sandwich needed new naval blood, the newly elected MP for Hedon – and a new member of their group – was an obvious choice. Anson's high professional reputation, fame and popularity were undiminished since his return to England earlier in the year despite his dispute with Lord Winchilsea. Untouched by the naval failures of the past few years and tested to the limit during the circumnavigation, Bedford had no doubt that Anson would be a real asset to the new board. As the second Earl of Hardwicke later commented: 'He had very extensive knowledge, acquired more by practice than study of his own profession; he could explain it to others clearly and pointedly without parade or affectation'.[31] The Duke of Newcastle, who recognised Anson's abilities and potential, endorsed his nomination to the Admiralty Board. He 'had shared the enthusiasm of the public over the romantic story of the voyage around the world, and Anson eagerly accepted him as his political patron'.[32] Anson joined the Board along with Bedford and Sandwich in December 1744.

Nothing is known of Anson's political beliefs at this time although he was clearly in sympathy with Bedford's views on the need to reinforce hierarchy and discipline as they applied to the navy. His approach to naval reform is also unrecorded but there is little doubt that he was willing to jettison traditional methods when these were no longer useful. At the same time, he recognised that there would be significant barriers to change, including:

> Custom, or the practice of those who have preceded us. This is usually a power too mighty for reason to grapple with; and is the most terrible to those who oppose it, as it has much of superstition in its nature, and pursues all those who question its authority with unrelenting vehemence.[33]

---

31 BL: Hardwicke Papers, Add. MS. 35,428, f.4, 'Memorial of Family Occurrences from 1760 to 1770 inclusive'.
32 Oswyn A. R. Murray, 'The Admiralty', *The Mariner's Mirror*, 24 (1938), p.216.
33 Walter, *A Voyage Round the World*, pp.335–336.

Despite these constraints, at least one senior officer, his like-minded friend Commodore Curtis Barnett, had high expectations of his appointment:

> You have nothing to ask and less to fear; I therefore expect a great deal from you… our young men get wrong notions early, and are led to imagine that he is the greatest officer who has the least blocks in his rigging. I hope you will give another turn to our affairs and form a society for the propagation of sea military knowledge. I think you had formerly such a scheme.[34]

Anson did not pursue the idea of a naval society at a time when 'standards of education and politeness in the navy were rising considerably in the years before and during the Seven Years War', but he was to give high priority to training when he was in command at sea.[35]

When the new board was formally constituted on 27 December, Anson was still a half-pay captain but was restored to flag rank in April 1745, when he was promoted two steps as rear admiral of the white. The first act of the new Board was to backdate Peircy Brett's promotion to captain to 30 September 1743, reversing Lord Winchilsea's earlier decision. Anson joined the Admiralty as the junior naval member – he did not become the senior naval lord until November 1749 – with only one (civilian) member below him in the pecking order. However, his formal position belied his actual role as the Admiralty's principal professional adviser, a position he held for seven years until he was appointed First Lord in 1751. Anson worked closely and harmoniously with the Duke of Bedford until his resignation in 1748, even though he may not have been an ideal superior as he had a 'keen sense of his own importance, and his pride and arrogance frequently caused offence'.[36] According to Hugh Hume-Campbell, third Earl of Marchmont, a Tory peer, 'the Duke of Bedford governed the Admiralty absolutely, was very obstinate, and would not be spoke to; and that the ministers knew no more of what was doing there, than I now did'.[37]

Apart from Bedford and Sandwich, Anson's other civilian colleagues on the Board were Lord Baltimore, an Irish peer who sat in the Commons, and George Grenville, MP, a future Treasurer of the Navy, Chancellor of the Exchequer, and Prime Minister; neither was knowledgeable about naval affairs. They were soon joined by the young Henry Bilson-Legge MP, Anson's friend and brother of Edward, who had served as captain of the *Severn* during the voyage around the world. Henry Legge was to serve as Chancellor of the Exchequer on three occasions and supported the need for naval reform.

As members of the Admiralty, Anson and his colleagues had overall responsibility for the navy and for deciding on the issues that should be referred to one of the two Secretaries of State or to the Cabinet Council, which determined wartime strategy and how the navy should be used to support it. In practice, these decisions were taken by an 'inner committee' of senior ministers (who included the First Lord of the Admiralty) while the Admiralty had

---

34 BL: Anson Papers, Add. MS. 15,955, ff.113–114, Curtis Barnett to George Anson, 16 September 1745.
35 N.A.M. Rodger, *The Wooden World: An Anatomy of the Georgian Navy* (London: Collins, 1986), p. 261.
36 Martyn J. Powell, 'John Russell, fourth Duke of Bedford (1710–1771)', *Oxford Dictionary of National Biography*, <https://doi.org/10.1093/ref:odnb/24320>, accessed 3 January 2023.
37 George H. Rose (ed.), *A Selection from the Papers of the Earl of Marchmont* (London: John Murray, 1831), vol.I, p.213.

responsibility for preparing the fleets and selecting their commanders (subject to approval by the King and his ministers). It would normally issue operational orders, but these were often prepared by one of the Secretaries of State, who sometimes sent them direct to fleet commanders. The Admiralty's specific responsibilities included the movement of ships, the personnel of the fleet (except for paying them) and their discipline. Its personnel functions included the 'promotion and assignment of commissioned and warrant officers, leaves, discharges, regulation of impressment, transfers of seamen and petty officers from one ship to another'.[38]

The Board was supported by Thomas Corbett, Secretary to the Admiralty since 1742, who was responsible for deciding whether incoming letters should be discussed by the Board or by an individual member. He replied directly to most of the letters that were not considered by the Board itself. Corbett was supported by John Clevland, who served as second secretary from 1746; he is likely to have secured his appointment as a result of Anson's intervention on his behalf. On Corbett's retirement in 1751, Clevland replaced him as Admiralty Secretary, shortly before Anson succeeded Sandwich as First Lord.

Apart from the Admiralty's specific responsibilities, all other aspects of naval administration were handled by its subordinate bodies – the Navy, Victualling, and Sick and Hurt Boards – and by the independent Ordnance Board. The long-established Navy Board was responsible for constructing and maintaining the fleet, purchasing stores (apart from victuals) and administering the six royal dockyards and the navy's overseas bases. Its long-serving Commissioners (the principal officers), who were responsible for up to 9,000 employees, were elderly civilians who had jobs for life unless they could be persuaded to retire. The Victualling Board managed the purchase, manufacture and distribution of food and drink to the navy, while the Sick and Hurt Board was responsible for the navy's sick and wounded. The Ordnance Board was responsible for issuing guns and warlike stores to the army and navy but was independent of both. The division of naval administration into several different boards had worked well in the past but the appointment of the new board under Bedford with wide-ranging plans for reform was bound to lead to tensions with the conservative Commissioners of the Navy Board.

This complex division of administrative responsibilities was not the only constraint on the powers of the Admiralty. As First Lord, the Duke of Bedford played a leading role in Cabinet discussions on naval strategy and the deployment of fleets, but he could not determine the outcome. The Duke of Newcastle, who took a great interest in naval issues, was also highly influential. The Admiralty also had no control over the size of the naval budget, which was determined by the Cabinet Council and the House of Commons, or the administration of naval funds, which was the responsibility of the Treasurer of the Navy. Despite these limitations on the Admiralty's role, boundaries with other parts of government were not always clearly defined. For example, Anson's professional advice on strategic issues was regularly sought informally by the Duke of Newcastle and other senior ministers despite his position as the junior naval lord.

As a member of the Admiralty, Anson would be expected to attend daily meetings of the Board and handle a large volume of papers and correspondence. His presence was required

---

38 Baugh (ed.), *Naval Administration*, pp.11–12.

to sign the multiple orders that were issued daily to admirals and captains at sea and required the signature of three members of the Board. There was no formal division of policy responsibilities between Board members and Anson worked closely with Bedford and Sandwich on all aspects of Admiralty business, based on their shared view of the changes that were needed. Their working arrangements meant that it is difficult to determine their individual contributions to specific policy developments, although, as we shall see, Anson would make significant contributions in several professional areas. The First Lord and his deputy relied on Anson as their trusted adviser, with key decisions being taken by Bedford in consultation with the other two members of his team. However, their regular absences from the office meant that on occasion it was necessary to share power with other Board members even though Sandwich had advised Bedford to be wary of everyone except Anson.[39]

Their collective decisions were often reached by correspondence rather than in person as all three were often absent from London for long periods. Within months of his appointment, Bedford began spending most of his time at Woburn, his family seat in Bedfordshire, only appearing at the Admiralty for two days a week; when he was absent, he was consulted by post on important issues, including appointments. More routine matters were left to Sandwich or, in his absence, to Anson to handle and Bedford maintained these arrangements until his departure from office in February 1748. Sandwich was also often away from the Admiralty. In the autumn of 1745, he took a leave of absence to serve in a regiment raised by the Duke of Bedford to fight the Jacobites as they advanced on London. From August 1746, he was based in the Netherlands as the British representative at the peace talks at the Congress of Breda and, in 1748, at Aix-la-Chapelle (Aachen). Anson was away at sea during the summer of 1745 before assuming command of the enlarged Western Squadron in 1746 and 1747. During the remainder of his Admiralty career, he was only to return to active service on one further occasion, in 1758, during the Seven Years War, although he was also absent from the office when escorting the royal family on their travels to the Continent.

When he was in London, Anson assumed charge of the Admiralty in the absence of Bedford and Sandwich, while remaining in regular contact with them. Sandwich, with whom he worked closely, retained his interest in naval issues when he was away, as he explained to Anson in a letter from the Hague: 'You see tho' I am at this distance I cannot help meddling in sea affairs, and indeed I must own that these are my inclinations, & that that is my favourite object'.[40] While these remote communications must have added to the complexity of the Admiralty's business, they do not seem to have undermined its efficiency. Anson's responsibilities covered all aspects of the Board's work, but he played a key role in establishing the Western Squadron, professionalising the officer corps, giving greater priority to training, improving ship design, and reforming the marines. He would also make a major contribution to revising the navy's disciplinary code.

Anson's increasingly influential position at the Admiralty gave him the opportunity to advance the careers of his friends – particularly those who had served with him on the *Centurion* – to positions where they could demonstrate their abilities. As his fellow commissioner Henry Legge pointed out to the Duke of Bedford: 'Is it not very remarkable that

---

39   Lord Sandwich to the Duke of Bedford, 4 April 1747, in Russell, *Correspondence of John, Fourth Duke of Bedford*, vol.I, p.207.
40   BL: Anson Papers, BL Add. MS. 15,957, f.29, Lord Sandwich to George Anson, 14 November 1747 (n.s.).

almost all the glory we have got this war had fallen to the share of Mr Anson's pupils – Brett, Stephens and Saumarez?'[41] As well as his secretary, Philip Stephens, Anson promoted the careers of other administrators whose abilities he valued, including John Rule, the former purser of the *Centurion*. Rule received rapid promotion after Anson's appointment to the Admiralty and, following a succession of moves, was appointed as Clerk of the Survey at Deptford in December 1746, even though Jacob Acworth, the influential Surveyor, had sponsored other candidates. In a letter to the Duke of Bedford recommending the appointment, Lord Vere Beauclerk said that he believed 'Mr Rule (who is Mr Anson's man) would be extreamely glad to be remov'd from Woolwich to Deptford'. Anson's patronage explained why 'he was promoted just as fast as vacancies appeared'.[42]

The immediate priorities of the new Board were dealing with the Jacobite rebellion, fighting the naval war against France and Spain more effectively, and addressing the problems with the navy's wartime performance that had been evident since 1739. Hopes of a quick victory had soon faded and although Spanish trade had been disrupted, Britain had failed to make any territorial gains and her opponent had not been forced to the negotiating table. Britain was initially not directly involved in the wider European conflict (the War of the Austrian Succession), but France had been acting in concert with Spain since 1740. She joined Spain in the fight against Austria, Britain's ally, in 1743 before declaring war the following year.

In the months before Anson joined the Admiralty, the navy had missed the opportunity to intercept the Brest squadron as it sailed towards Dunkirk to cover a planned invasion of Britain and, as we have seen, it had failed to prevent the escape of the French fleet at the Battle of Toulon later in the year. By 1745, French successes in Flanders were intensifying fears that a second attempt to invade England would soon be made and the new Admiralty produced a more vigorous response than had been evident in the past. On 4 July 1745, Anson attended a meeting at the Duke of Newcastle's house together with Sandwich and Lord Vere following the arrival of news that Ghent had been taken by the French. With the fall of Ostend soon expected, it was agreed urgently to assemble a fleet in the Downs and send frigates into the Channel to intercept an invasion from Flanders.[43] Admiral Vernon was appointed as commander in chief of the naval forces in home waters to coordinate Britain's response, but his tenure was to be short-lived.

The most immediate threat to Britain came from the Jacobites, with Prince Charles Edward Stuart sailing to Scotland in July in the French privateer *Du Teillay*, accompanied by the warship *Elizabeth* (64). They were intercepted by the *Lion*, commanded by Captain Peircy Brett, 100 miles west of Lizard Point, and an intense five-hour duel followed. Both warships were badly damaged, but Prince Charles Edward was able to continue his journey in the *Du Teillay*. He landed in Scotland early in August and had advanced as far as Derby

---

41   Henry B. Legge to the Duke of Bedford, 25 October 1746, in Russell, *Correspondence of John, Fourth Duke of Bedford*, vol.I, p.164.
42   Woburn MSS: vol.XV, f.54, Lord Vere Beauclerk to the Duke of Bedford, 28 November 1746; Daniel A. Baugh, *British Naval Administration in the Age of Walpole* (Princeton: Princeton University Press, 1965), pp.302–203.
43   Lord Sandwich to the Duke of Bedford, 4 July 1745, in Russell, *Correspondence of John, Fourth Duke of Bedford*, vol.I, pp.23–24.

by December before being forced to retreat. During the rebellion, the navy transported troops to the front line and intercepted several French ships sent to aid the rebels before the Jacobites were finally defeated at the Battle of Culloden in April 1746.

Vernon continued to keep a close watch on the Flanders coast during the summer and autumn of 1745 to prevent the French from providing support to the Jacobites. During this period, he became involved in an increasingly acrimonious dispute with the Admiralty, which focused on his right to appoint warrant officers and the size of his squadron. By the end of December, the Admiralty's patience had been exhausted, and he was ordered to hand over his command to Vice Admiral William Martin. When copies of his correspondence with the Admiralty were published anonymously in two pamphlets, he was summoned to a meeting at the Admiralty on 9 April to explain himself. In the presence of Bedford, Anson and other members of the Board, he refused to confirm or deny whether he was responsible for the publications and complained about his treatment by the Admiralty. Unwilling to accept the authority of the Lord Admiral, Vernon was dismissed from the service; it was an early example of the Board's determination to reinforce discipline and strengthen the naval hierarchy.[44]

In 1746, as the French invasion threat receded, British naval efforts focused on Canada, which produced the first significant operational success against France since the reinvigorated Admiralty took office. On 19 June, Peter Warren notified Anson that he had captured the fortress at Louisbourg and made a plea for the 'dispatch of a number of troops to keep possession of this valuable acquisition'. He asked for instructions as to 'how I am to conduct myself with regard to the safety of this garrison, if anything should be intended against Canada in the spring'.[45] In London caution prevailed and a planned expedition against Quebec was abandoned in August 1746, a decision Anson fully supported. On 23 August, he wrote:

> There is no man in this kingdom who thinks that the putting the American [expedition] in[to] execution will be a righter measure or have more good consequence to the country than I do. But the season being so far advanced made it dangerous to attempt it... I own I said a great deal against it going now, because I felt a great deal from [my knowledge of] the coast of America after the month of October.[46]

The campaign to recover Louisbourg had 'effectively [broken] the capability of the French navy to operate extensive oceanic campaigns', while an expanded Royal Navy soon had significantly greater strength than France and Spain combined, leading to Anson's and Hawke's victories off Cape Finisterre in 1747.[47]

---

44 Sarah Kinkel, *Disciplining the Empire: Politics, Governance, and the Rise of the British Navy* (Cambridge: Harvard University Press, 2018), p.104.
45 Peter Warren to George Anson, 19 June 1745, in Gwyn (ed.), *The Royal Navy and North America*, pp.127–128.
46 Woburn MSS: vol.XIII, f.29, George Anson to the Duke of Bedford, 24 August 1746.
47 Richard Harding, '"Neglect or Treason": Leadership Failure in the Mid-Eighteenth Century Royal Navy', in Helen Doe and R. Harding (eds.), *Naval Leadership and Management 1650–1950* (Woodbridge: The Boydell Press, 2012), p.56.

The Board's ability to progress its reform agenda effectively was affected by its relations with the Navy Board, which had deteriorated quickly from 1744 as the cooperation which had previously existed between the two organisations came to an end. Conflict between the relatively youthful senior members of the Board – Bedford was 35 years old, Sandwich was only 27 – and the ageing leaders of the Navy Board, whose conservative views had been formed in a different era, was almost inevitable. The reform-minded Anson was, of course, older than his new colleagues – he was 48 at the time of his appointment – but he also had little in common with the elderly men of the Navy Board. In its first weeks, the new Admiralty sent the Navy Board a flurry of requests for information and ordered them to undertake a variety of investigations as they began work on their reforms.[48] They started several new projects, including the construction of three naval hospitals, which were approved in 1745; the first, Haslar Hospital at Gosport near Portsmouth, was opened in 1754.

By 1746, tensions between the two boards had come to a head as they argued about the performance of the dockyards, following continual complaints about delays in loading stores on warships after they had been cleaned. The Admiralty ordered the Navy Board not to dock any ships unless it could guarantee that their stores would be loaded promptly. When it became clear that this instruction had not been followed at Portsmouth, the Navy Board was ordered to ensure that the dockyard officers took orders directly from Vice Admiral James Steuart, the port admiral, rather than from the Navy Board's resident commissioner, as was the established practice. The Navy Board refused to comply with the request and argued that precedent indicated that the Admiralty had 'always consulted this Board with regard to the civil economy of it; and there is no instance of any alteration having been made in its rules or establishment but by the advice and opinion of this Board, who have always been treated as counsel to their Lordships in such matters'.[49]

Neither Bedford nor Anson seems to have considered addressing the Admiralty's troubled relationship with the Navy Board by seeking changes to the administrative structure of the navy. They confined themselves to using their power to appoint more suitable candidates to the subordinate boards when vacancies arose. The Admiralty's first new appointment to the Navy Board was made in 1746 following a series of disagreements about ship design, which had begun soon after Anson's appointment. The Navy Board's Surveyor, Sir Jacob Acworth, who was in post from 1715 to 1749, had primary responsibility for the design of new ships but had been an obstacle to progress for much of his career, with Edward Vernon describing him as a 'half judicious and half experienced surveyor', who had 'half ruined the navy'.[50] At a time when Anson and his colleagues gave high priority to making improvements in British warship design, it was necessary to try to dilute his negative influence.

Anson was aware of the shortcomings of British designs from his past service and wanted the navy to build larger ships. He played a leading role in briefing the Board on the weaknesses in warship design and the need to make improvements. As his thinking developed, he maintained close contact with John Goodwin and Benjamin Slade, Master Shipwrights

---

48 N.A.M. Rodger, *The Command of the Ocean: A Naval History of Britain, 1649–1815* (London: Allen Lane, 2004), p.299.
49 Navy Board to Admiralty Secretary, 23 May 1746, in Baugh (ed.), *Naval Administration*, p.32.
50 Quoted in Baugh (ed.), *Naval Administration*, p.224.

at Plymouth and Deptford respectively. He was also briefed by serving sea officers, including Commodore (later Admiral Sir) Charles Knowles, about the superior performance of French and Spanish ships of the line.[51] He noted that they were generally faster and had greater firepower than their British equivalents, which did not sail as well. British ships were thought to be too small to bear the weight of their armament and could not use their lower tier of guns in adverse weather conditions. British frigates were also outclassed by their faster French opponents. Anson's own experience on the voyage around the world confirmed that the *Centurion* and the other ships under his command were not large enough for the duties that they were expected to perform.

Since 1719, the dimensions and armament of each rated ship (down to sixth rates of 20 guns) had been laid down in considerable detail in a shipbuilding 'establishment', which made innovation in design virtually impossible except for the smaller craft that were designed in the dockyards rather than by the Navy Board. The Bedford Admiralty wanted to adopt a new establishment that would address the shortcomings it had identified as well as providing for greater standardisation with interchangeable spares. It appointed a committee of sea officers under Sir John Norris to make recommendations and, in the meantime, made some modest changes to the dimensions of ships under construction where this was possible and also commissioned new standard designs. The Navy Board was ordered to forward its surveys of captured French ships so that they could be inspected by the Admiralty but it soon became clear that these initiatives would not produce the progress that Anson had hoped for.

The Norris Committee proved to be a disappointment. It did not address the underlying weaknesses of British warship design satisfactorily, failed to specify larger dimensions that matched the size of foreign ships and would not replace the bulky three-deck 80-gun ship with a more powerful two-deck 74-gun ship.[52] All Anson and his colleagues achieved when the Committee reported was an average increase in the length of gun decks of four feet and a foot in breadth, but this did not match the dimensions of comparable French or Spanish ships. The outcome reflected the pervasive influence of Jacob Acworth, who regularly attended the committee's meetings, and ensured that the new 1745 Establishment ruled out a significant increase in the capacity of the largest ships. The Committee's recommendations were ratified by an Order-in-Council, which meant that future changes would need to be approved by the Privy Council rather than by the Admiralty alone, introducing another barrier to innovation.

It was clear to Anson that there could only be limited progress in updating warship design, with the introduction of the 74-gun ship he favoured being ruled out, while Acworth remained in post. Henry Legge reported Anson's views as well as his own in a letter to the Duke of Bedford of 6 March 1746:

> We are then extreamly of opinion & agree in wishing that Sr. Jacob should retire with every circumstance that can make his old age easy & happy, but retain no

---

51 BL: Anson Papers, Add. MS. 15,956, ff.119–122, Charles Knowles to the Duke of Bedford, 6 January 1744/45.
52 Baugh (ed.), *Naval Administration*, p.200.

influence in naval architecture. For it is high time ships began to have bottoms to them, & more expedition as well as better economy prevail'd in dockyards.[53]

However, they had no power to force Acworth's retirement and the surveyorship only became vacant on his death in 1749. In the meantime, they could do no more than appoint a joint surveyor to try to dilute his influence. Joseph Allin, Master Shipwright at Deptford, who had built the *Centurion* in 1732, was appointed, but Legge foresaw difficulties with a joint arrangement:

> We know Sr. Jacob to have so much of the nature of Pompey the Great in him that he cannot be an equal & if Mr Allen [Joseph Allin] should have so much of the temper of Julius Caesar about him that he cannot brook a superior – what must ensue but civil war added to the many indecorums & distresses the dock yards at present labour under?[54]

Despite its concerns about the joint appointment, the Admiralty made limited progress in introducing a new 74-gun ship design soon after Allin's arrival. Following the capture of the French warship *Invincible* at the first Battle of Cape Finisterre in May 1747, the Admiralty instructed the Navy Board to produce a draught similar to the captured ship, and two 74-gun ships based on it were ordered. However, the project was cancelled at the end of the war because of a lack of funds and progress on Anson's preferred design was to be stalled for more than six years. One reason for these additional delays was that Allin, who was appointed Surveyor on Acworth's death in 1749, did not live up to Anson's expectations and proved to be almost as conservative as his predecessor. He was eventually dismissed at the beginning of the Seven Years War. By that time, it had long been evident that 'the ships of 1745 were badly designed and could not be rectified merely by a few small amendments'.[55] It must have soon become clear to Anson that the 1745 review had been placed in the wrong hands, but the beginning of the Seven Years War would give him the opportunity to make the changes he had long wanted.

Anson was able to make more progress in developing new frigate designs even though the 1745 Establishment had increased the dimensions of sixth-rate warships by no more than 10 tons. This small improvement was not sufficient to improve their sailing qualities at a time when the weight of their armament and upperworks (the parts above the waterline when fully laden) was increasing. With the naval war at its height, the Admiralty bypassed the Navy Board and took direct action to produce a new small cruiser. It turned for inspiration to the frigates deployed by the French, which were faster than their British equivalents and were responsible for an increase in merchant shipping losses. The Admiralty had access to several frigates captured during the war, including the *Tygre* (26), a St Malo privateer, which had been carried into Plymouth and was found to have fine sailing qualities. Like other

---

53 Woburn MSS: vol.XI, f.34, Henry B. Legge to the Duke of Bedford, 6 March 1746.
54 Woburn MSS: vol.XI, f.34, Henry B. Legge to the Duke of Bedford, 6 March 1746.
55 Brian Lavery, *The Ship of the Line* (London: Conway Maritime Press, 1983), vol.I, pp.94–95.

French frigates of the period, the *Tygre* had a single gun deck with a low quarterdeck and forecastle; her lower deck was unarmed.[56]

The Master Shipwright at Plymouth, Benjamin Slade, was asked to work on new designs and, on 6 March 1747, the Admiralty Board formally agreed that the *Tygre* should be surveyed. Anson, who had recently returned from an extended winter cruise off Brest, supported the decision, as it was not unlikely that he 'felt the urgent need of a better all-weather cruiser for his newly developed strategy of year-round blockade, and was prepared to step outside the confines of the Establishment types to achieve it'.[57] He had a high opinion of Slade and later in the year commissioned him to make a model of the *Centurion*, which is now in the National Maritime Museum, Greenwich. Just over a month later Anson was asking Bedford to issue an order to the Navy Board 'to direct Mr Slade the Builder at Plymouth to take off the body of the French *Tyger* with the utmost exactness, and that two frigates may be order'd to be built with all possible dispatch'.[58]

Slade asked his nephew, Thomas Slade, Assistant Master Shipwright at Woolwich, to deliver his plans of the *Tygre* and other French prizes to Anson with the message that the French design was superior to English 24-gun ships.[59] Thomas later became Anson's principal adviser on ship design (Benjamin died in 1750) and, in 1755, he appointed him as joint surveyor of the navy. The two 28-gun ships – *Lyme* and *Unicorn* – that were built to the *Tygre's* draught were launched in December 1748, having been delayed by the end of the war. Described as 'the first true frigates', their excellent sailing qualities meant that the construction of conventional 24-gun ships of the 1745 Establishment ended in 1749. They were to be used as a model for the 28-gun frigates which Anson's Admiralty was to order in 1755.

By the summer of 1746, Anson had completed a successful 18-month stint as a member of the Admiralty Board. He had been Bedford's right-hand man on professional matters since his appointment and had established a firm friendship with Lord Sandwich. Although they had concentrated on the French and Jacobite threat, the first steps in the reform programme, focused on ship design, were taken with Anson in the lead. With the naval war intensifying, he was now called to the command of the Western Squadron and would remain at sea for the next nine months. In his absence progress on naval reform slowed and would not pick up until his return.

---

56 Robert Gardiner, *The First Frigates. Nine-Pounder & Twelve-Pounder Frigates, 1748–1815* (London: Conway Maritime Press, 1992), p.10.
57 Gardiner, *The First Frigates*, p.13.
58 Woburn MSS: Vol XVI, f.73, George Anson to the Duke of Bedford, 17 April 1747.
59 Staffordshire Record Office (SRO): Anson Family Papers: D615/P(S)1/9/22, Benjamin Slade to George Anson, 21 July 1747.

5

Commanding the Western Squadron, 1746–1747

On 9 August 1746, Anson, now vice admiral of the blue, left his desk at the Admiralty and returned to the sea for the second time since completing the voyage around the world (he had been at sea for a short period the previous summer). He had been appointed to the command of the newly formed Western Squadron in succession to Vice Admiral William Martin, who had resigned due to ill health. It was now much larger than the small squadron commanded by Martin, which had been unable to intercept several departing French squadrons including the expedition to recapture Louisbourg, led by Jean-Baptiste de La Rochefoucauld de Roye, Duc d'Anville, which had left the Île-d'Aix in June 1746.

The creation of the squadron – by combining the navy's previously dispersed forces in home waters – has been described as 'one of the most valuable and enduring legacies of Bedford's Admiralty, and in one shape or another it formed the core of Britain's naval strategy for a century and more'.[1] It would cruise off the Western Approaches (the area to the west of the English Channel and the French Atlantic coast) for as long as possible, with several objectives in mind. These included the protection of British merchant shipping, providing a defence against invasion, and monitoring the movements of the French fleet at its main Atlantic naval bases – Brest, Lorient and Rochefort – with the aim of intercepting convoy departures for North America or the Indies as well as fleets returning from overseas.

The idea of deploying the main fleet in the Western Approaches to the windward of the English Channel and the French Atlantic ports was first adopted at the time of the Spanish Armada in 1588 although the concept of a Western Squadron may have originated when Captain William Penn was appointed as 'commander in chief of the western squadron' in 1650. By the end of the seventeenth century, the Admiralty recognised that the French fleet would concentrate its activities in the Western Approaches rather than the Channel and the development of Plymouth dockyard 'made it easier to operate the traditional type of Western Squadron on a somewhat larger scale'.[2] The instructions given to successive commanders in the Western Approaches helped to define the squadron's role, but, in 1745, Admiral Vernon was the first clearly to articulate the idea, which was then developed by Bedford, Sandwich and Anson.

---

1   N.A.M. Rodger, *The Insatiable Earl: A Life of John Montagu, Fourth Earl of Sandwich 1718–1792* (London: HarperCollins, 1993), p.35.
2   Michael Duffy, 'The Establishment of the Western Squadron as the Linchpin of British Naval Strategy', in M. Duffy (ed.), *Parameters of British Naval Power 1650–1850* (Exeter: University of Exeter Press, 1992), p.63.

In September 1745, Vernon wrote to the Admiralty expressing his concern that Vice Admiral Martin did not have sufficient ships to meet the French threat, while cruising 'within the Channel between the Lizard and the coast of France may prove ineffectual, as that will leave all Ireland, the western coasts of this island, and even the Bristol Channel, and all our East and West India trade expected home, open to them to do what they please'. The French would prioritise operations in the Western Approaches rather than in the Channel and this threat should be met by an enlarged Western Squadron. Vernon argued that it should be 'formed as strong as we can make it by the junction of these five great ships [being prepared for service] to those Vice Admiral Martin has to the westward, and what others can be spared, and got speedily out into Soundings [the Western Approaches]'. Once on station, it 'might face their united force, cover both England and Ireland, and be in condition to pursue them wherever they went, and be at hand to secure the safe return of our homeward bound trade from the East and West Indies'.[3]

The strategy was based on the prevailing westerly winds and the need for the French to move up from the west to cover an invasion force as they had no naval bases in the English Channel. If the main squadron cruised to the westward, it would be in a good position to block the French from entering the Channel, intercept their warships entering or leaving Brest and protect arriving and departing English convoys. Supplies to their colonies in North America and India could be disrupted while the security of Britain's overseas possessions could be enhanced. Its main weakness was the fact that it was unable to monitor the French fleet based at Toulon and the failure to address this gap was to lead to the loss of Minorca in 1756. At a time when England faced the combined threat of a French and Jacobite invasion, the Admiralty Board unanimously agreed that an expanded Western Squadron was needed to meet the threat, but there was less agreement about how it should operate.

Anson, who was always concerned about the risk of naval inferiority in home waters, believed that a combined Western Squadron should be concentrated as a single, powerful force, while Lord Sandwich was prepared to take more risks. He argued that it should be divided so that smaller detachments could be deployed for offensive operations against merchant convoys but this approach had the disadvantage that none of these units would be strong enough individually to deal with a significant enemy force.[4] Vernon, on the other hand, believed that the whole fleet should be kept cruising off the French Atlantic coast as he had

> ...always looked upon squadrons in port, as neither a defence for the kingdom, nor a security for our commerce, and that the surest means for the prevention of both, was keeping a strong squadron in the Soundings, which may answer to both purposes, as covering both Channels and Ireland, and at the same time secure our commerce.[5]

---

3   Edward Vernon to the Secretary of the Admiralty (draft), 6 September 1745, in Brian Ranft (ed.), *The Vernon Papers* (London: Navy Records Society, 1958), p.459.
4   BL: Anson Papers, Add. MS. 15,957, f.4, Lord Sandwich to George Anson, 20 July [1746] (n.s.).
5   Edward Vernon to the Duke of Bedford, 5 August 1745, in Ranft (ed.), *The Vernon Papers*, pp.445–446.

It would thus be in the best position to engage the enemy although remaining at sea for extended periods in bad weather would inevitably take its toll on ships and men.

Anson's view – which was to prevail – was slightly different as he believed the main fleet should remain in port until intelligence confirming that the French were ready to sail – or expected to return home – was received. As he explained to Bedford, 'The French can never be so much annoy'd nor this Kingdom so well secured, as by keeping a strong squadron at home, sufficient to make detachments, whenever we have good intelligence that the French are sending ships either to the East or West Indies'.[6] As discussions on the role of the Western Squadron came to an end, Anson and Bedford exchanged letters, with the First Lord confirming his support for a single squadron in home waters that would be sufficiently strong to deal with the combined naval forces of France and Spain:

> You know my opinion has long been that we ought to unite all the ships cruising to the Westward… into one squadron, and I am the more strongly confirmed in that opinion at present because, by the sending away so great a force to America … we are incapacitated from dividing our force to the westward, which, when collected together is not more than sufficient to withstand the Brest or Rochefort fleets, if united with that of Ferrol.[7]

As head of the newly enlarged Western Squadron, Anson helped to refine its role in two separate cruises in 1746 and 1747. On his arrival in Portsmouth early in August 1746, Anson took command of 17 ships of the line, six 50-gun ships, four frigates and two sloops. He flew his flag in the third-rate *Yarmouth* (64), launched in 1745, which had been built to an enlarged design as an Admiralty experiment, and arranged for Peircy Brett to be transferred to the ship as his captain and for John Campbell, who had also served on the *Centurion* during the circumnavigation, to serve as his first lieutenant. Anson's priority was to focus on the French fleet rather than enemy merchantmen and his main objective was to intercept the French squadron, commanded by the Duc d'Anville, which was expected to return from Chebucto (now Halifax) in the autumn.

Anson's orders, which were issued on 6 August, gave him much greater freedom than his predecessor Martin had enjoyed:

> You are to cruise on such station or stations as you shall judge proper (according to the intelligence you may receive) for intercepting and destroying the ships of the enemy, their convoys outward and homeward bound, and for suppressing their privateers and annoying their trade and for protecting the trade of his Majesty's subjects.

He was given the discretion 'to send detachments from you, whenever you may judge it necessary, to cruise on separate stations for the better meeting with the ships of the enemy'. Anson was also authorised 'to send such ships of your squadron as shall be foul or sickly

---

6   Woburn MSS: vol.XVII, f.65, George Anson to the Duke of Bedford, 2 August [1747].
7   Woburn MSS: vol.XII, f.72, George Anson to the Duke of Bedford, 17 July 1746; BL: Anson Papers, Add. MS. 15,955, f.133, Duke of Bedford to George Anson, 18 July 1745.

into port, and to order their captains to return to you or otherwise as you shall judge best for the service'. He was ordered 'to continue this service so long as you shall judge yourself able to put this order into execution'.[8]

Anson was soon complaining about the difficulties he faced in preparing the squadron for sea and he was unable to leave for Plymouth until the end of August. The fleet was short of men because large numbers had died on Martin's last cruise as a result of scurvy, smallpox and bad provisions and they could not easily be replaced. On 11 August, he informed Bedford that:

> The equipment of my squadron goes on but slowly. Admiral Lestock's expedition [to Lorient], while it continues here, will clog every other service at this port… Admiral Lestock had not left the face of a seaman at Spithead… I don't blame him, because it is the custom of all admirals; but I feel a good deal upon the occasion, because all the ships of my squadron are greatly under complement.[9]

He was critical of shortages in the dockyard and of failings in the Ordnance Office, which had 'allowed their channel to be blocked up'. He also complained that 'the supply of beer is not to be had at Portsmouth: as the captains all agree that the men's health depends chiefly upon it, I have ordered Plymouth to supply'. The squadron's leisurely preparations were interrupted by news that a French convoy of 75 merchant ships had put into Corunna and was due to be escorted through the Bay of Biscay by a squadron of 12 warships based at Rochefort. In response, Anson dispatched an advance squadron of 11 ships, under the command of Captain the Hon. Edward Boscawen, with instructions to sail to Cape Finisterre, where he was to intercept the convoy.

On 4 September, Anson left Plymouth and sailed to join Boscawen, arriving off Cape Finisterre on 18 September. On arrival, he deployed his ships of the line about a mile apart to cover as much of the surrounding area as possible, but was 'greatly in want of some clean frigates and one or two 50-gun ships'. As discussed earlier, his experiences in command of the Western Squadron subsequently led him to advocate new frigate designs and a frigate building programme. Before he arrived at Cape Finisterre, Anson had begun drilling the squadron and his command is notable for the 'diligence in which day after day he exercised it in forming line of battle, bearing down together, and the evolutions of the attack. The care taken by Anson on all occasions of his command afloat to practise his captains tactically is very marked'. On 15 September, for example, he recorded in the *Yarmouth*'s log that he had 'made the signal for the line of battle abreast. 3:00 p.m. Hauled down the signal for the line of battle abreast and made the signal for the ships that lead on the starboard tack to lead large'.[10]

Anson remained at Cape Finisterre until 5 October when he received intelligence that a Spanish convoy was due to arrive at Cadiz. He sailed south to intercept it, leaving Boscawen

---

8   Herbert W. Richmond, *The Navy in the War of 1739–48* (Cambridge: Cambridge University Press, 1920), vol.III, pp.38–39.
9   George Anson to the Duke of Bedford, 11 August 1746, in Russell, *Correspondence of John, Fourth Duke of Bedford*, vol.I, pp.136–137.
10 Richmond, *The Navy in the War of 1739–48*, vol.III, p.40.

in position in the hope of meeting the French convoy and arrived off Cape St Vincent on 14 October. As there was no sign of the Spanish ships and with widespread sickness among his crews and a shortage of water, he was soon forced to return to Plymouth. As he sailed north, he instructed Boscawen to continue cruising to the west of Finisterre until he re-joined him. Shortly after he arrived at Plymouth on 28 October, he learnt that the Duc d'Anville's squadron was returning home after its abortive expedition to recapture Louisbourg. Anson sent orders to Boscawen to leave Cape Finisterre and set sail for Ushant, where he was to await the arrival of the French squadron. Boscawen was already aware of d'Anville's movements from information discovered on a French prize and he had moved northwards well before his instructions arrived, taking position off Brest with 10 ships on 28 October, the same day that Anson returned to Plymouth.

On Anson's arrival at Plymouth, his ships were short of water, his 'men begin to be sickly, and most of the ships very foul'.[11] He was far from happy with the performance of the dockyard, which did not keep a ready stock of masts and would not clean a ship without written authorisation from the Admiralty. In response, the master shipwright wrote to the Navy Board to report that 'Mr Anson was pleased to take notice how expedient it would be if a main and foremast were kept ready-made at this place to be supplied on any emergency for a ship of each class from 74-guns downwards, and would be of great consequence for the service, particularly with regards to ships of the Western Squadron'.[12] Anson expected to stay for at least a fortnight but, as he explained to the Duke of Bedford, he would leave sooner if at all possible: 'the hopes of destroying some of the enemy's fleet will make me risk health and everything else'.[13] While he was at Plymouth, Anson questioned George Grenville's decision (as a fellow member of the Admiralty Board) to permit his brother Thomas and another captain to leave the Western Squadron to go to the Canaries in search of prizes. Although he did not try to overturn it, he believed that a powerful squadron, which deployed all available ships, was needed to meet the French threat and none should be released for service elsewhere: 'I differ in opinion with you, for, by the scheme the enemy pursues, they will not put it in the power of two or four ships to part them, for their convoys are strong, and no French or Spanish trade permitted to sail unprotected'.[14]

Anson did not leave Plymouth until 9 November when it was too late to intercept the convoy under Hubert de Brienne, Comte de Conflans, which had arrived at Brest from the West Indies three days earlier. He made for Ushant where he planned to join Boscawen and cruise while waiting for the Duc d'Anville to arrive. By combining his forces with Boscawen's 'and continually relieving ships, not allowing them to spend one hour longer in harbour than was necessary for watering and making ready, he managed to keep about 15 ships

---

11 George Anson to the Duke of Bedford, 28 October 1747, in Russell, *Correspondence of John, Fourth Duke of Bedford*, vol.I, p.167.
12 Plymouth Master Shipwright to the Navy Board, 31 October 1747, in Baugh (ed.), *Naval Administration*, p.259.
13 George Anson to the Duke of Bedford, 28 October 1747, in Russell, *Correspondence of John, Fourth Duke of Bedford*, vol.I, p.167.
14 George Anson to George Grenville, 4 November 1746, in W. J. Smith (ed.), *The Grenville Papers: Being the Correspondence of Richard Grenville, Earl Temple, and the Right Hon. George Grenville, Their Friends and Contemporaries* (London: John Murray, 1852), vol.I, p.53.

together'.¹⁵ Despite this strong presence, as he commented to Bedford on 4 November, there was no guarantee of success even though he commanded a more powerful squadron than d'Anville: 'all schemes at sea are very uncertain. The nights are long, the winter gales blow hard, and, unless fortune favours, a good look out will not always succeed'. Even though he was generally pessimistic, he thought Admiral Lestock had a much better chance of success but was critical of his efforts: 'I am surprised that Mr Lestock, who had such certain intelligence, from the French ships burnt in the bay, of the shattered condition of d'Anville's ships, should not cruise off Ushant for them, as his squadron was not in want of anything'.¹⁶

On 25 November, Anson captured the *Mercure*, a French hospital ship returning from Louisbourg, which gave him hope that the rest of d'Anville's squadron was on its way. However, he was unable to capture two privateers because he lacked the frigates and clean ships he needed and his chances of success were fading. He also faced deteriorating conditions off Ushant as winter approached:

> The winds of these last three or four days have blown so extraordinarily hard at S.W. that... I have not been able to keep my station; but am driven ten leagues to the north of it, and indeed the winter gales blow so excessively hard there is no possibility of keeping long on any station.¹⁷

Anson had originally intended to move south to Cape Finisterre on 7 December to intercept the French warships returning from Martinique as well as Louisbourg, but he decided to remain off Brest in view of d'Anville's likely arrival. He maintained his position in poor weather conditions and with increasing sickness on board, but with no sign of the French he sailed southwards on 22 December. As Anson feared, d'Anville had entered Rochefort (on 20 December) rather than sailing north for Brest as he had been forewarned of the British presence there by a Dutch merchant ship. Anson later discovered what had happened when Jacques-Pierre de Taffanel, Marquis de la Jonquière, was taken prisoner at the Battle of Cape Finisterre in May the following year:

> How heartily have I cursed the Dutch who, I find (by their French general Jonquière) prevented his whole fleet falling into my hands the last winter when he came from Chibatou by one of their vessels informing him he was within twenty leagues of me and must see me the next morning, upon which he altered his course for Rochefort.¹⁸

From Cape Finisterre, Anson sailed to Lisbon intending to cruise off Cadiz, but with his crews coming down with scurvy in increasing numbers he was forced to abandon the plan and return to England. He arrived in the Downs on 6 February 1747, poor weather having prevented him from entering either Plymouth or Portsmouth. By this time, he had persuaded

---

15 Richmond, *The Navy in the War of 1739–48*, vol.III, p.47.
16 George Anson to the Duke of Bedford, 4 November 1746, in Russell, *Correspondence of John, Fourth Duke of Bedford*, vol.I, p.174.
17 Quoted in Anson, *The Life of Admiral Lord Anson*, p.94.
18 Quoted in Richmond, *The Navy in the War of 1739–48*, vol.III, p.47.

the Admiralty to agree to double the allowance of fresh meat (previously issued twice a week) for crews who had been afflicted by scurvy or any other disease: 'The ships companys of cruising ships should be supply'd with fresh meat and greens four days in a week when they come into port afflicted with the scurvy or other illnesses'.[19] Like many of his contemporaries, Anson believed that beer was also beneficial to seamen's health, pointing out that 'as soon as our beer is expended the ships soon become hospitals'.[20]

In a letter of 6 February to Bedford, Anson acknowledged that the cruise had not been a success, explaining that 'he had not been able to move in response to intelligence as effectively as he hoped and the damage his squadron had received being at sea for so long in the winter was far greater than he anticipated, but he learned a great deal'.[21] Later in the month, he wrote again to Bedford to describe how his lack of success had affected him:

> From what I have felt this last fortnight I think whoever happens to have success at sea cannot be too well rewarded, for I would not suffer the same anguish of mind that I have done upon this disappointment for all the honours, riches and pleasures this world can afford.[22]

Anson's failure did not go unnoticed in the City of London, as John Le Keux, a Treasury official, reported to Vice Admiral Henry Medley early in 1747:

> I can with pleasure tell you that you are a favourite flag with the voice of the people; Mr Warren, another; all the others seem in no great vogue with the city. The lawyers are angry with those of the late court-martial, and the City with Mr Anson, who they say has done nothing since he has been out, but gone from the Channel and let the French take their ships.[23]

Despite his lack of success in capturing the returning French ships, Anson's first cruise had established the value of an enlarged Western Squadron that was able to stay on station for extended periods. Success would follow his return to sea two months later when he defeated the French and ensured that the squadron would become 'the pivot of our naval strategy'.[24]

When ministers learnt that the French were planning to send two convoys, one to Canada, the other to India, it was decided at a meeting on 30 March at the Duke of Bedford's house to assemble 'all the force that can be got should go to sea under the command of Vice Admiral Anson'.[25] His old friend Peter Warren was appointed second in command after plans to send his squadron to the Gulf of St Lawrence were abandoned so that the Western Squadron could be strengthened, although it was also agreed that if any part of the Brest

---

19 Quoted in Christian Buchet, *The British Navy, Economy and Society in the Seven Years War* (Woodbridge: The Boydell Press, 2013), p.53.
20 Woburn MSS: vol.XIII, f.23, George Anson to Duke of Bedford, 21 August 1746.
21 Woburn MSS: vol.XVI, f.30, George Anson to Duke of Bedford, 6 February 1746/47.
22 Woburn MSS: vol.XV, f.83, George Anson to the Duke of Bedford, 26 December 1746.
23 John Le Keux to Henry Medley, 19 January 1746/47, in Historical Manuscripts Commission (HMC), *Report on the Manuscripts of Lady Du Cane* (London: H.M. Stationery Office,1905), p.162.
24 Richmond, *The Navy in the War of 1739–48*, vol.III, p.50.
25 Richmond, *The Navy in the War of 1739–48*, vol.III, p.82.

squadron were to escape into the Atlantic en route for Canada, Warren was to go in pursuit. Horace Walpole described Warren as 'richer than Anson and as absurd as Vernon',[26] but he was to play a leading role in the forthcoming engagement with the French and was to assume command of the Western Squadron after Anson returned to the Admiralty in May. Anson's instructions, dated 30 March, reflected these decisions and gave him a considerable degree of discretion in the deployment of his squadron: 'you are to cruise on such station or stations as you shall judge proper… You are at liberty to send detachments from you, whenever you judge it necessary, to cruise on separate stations, for the better meeting with ships of the enemy'.[27]

Among Anson's captains, were three friends who had served with him on the voyage around the world: Peter Denis who was in command of the *Centurion*, together with captains Peircy Brett (*Yarmouth*) and Philip Saumarez (*Nottingham*). Edward Boscawen in the *Namur* was to play a prominent role in the coming engagement, but his wife Fanny, the bluestocking, predicted that he was unlikely to receive any public recognition for his efforts:

> Though you should do great things now (which God grant!) will it be Mr Boscawen? Not at all! Mr Anson will have the great crack; a little echo for Mr Warren, and you will have no more share in the applause and thanks of the public than Captain Mostyn, whom they hate.[28]

Anson did not know when the French convoys would sail and he wanted to leave Portsmouth without delay, but on his arrival found that his frigates' hulls had not been cleaned. He held their captains responsible for failing to carry out his previous orders to clean their ships and to be prepared to leave at a moment's notice. He also encountered difficulties with the dockyard administration and wrote several letters to the Admiralty complaining of delays. Early in April, for example, he wrote to the Duke of Bedford: 'Tho' Mr Warren and I are working from daylight till it is dark, the delays are such from the bad regulation of the dockyards, and the people that are worn out in office there that it is impossible to do things with the dispatch I could wish'.[29] He also complained about shortages of stores in the docks, for which he held the Navy Board responsible. He suggested to Thomas Corbett that the Board 'should have directions to keep an extraordinary magazine of all kinds of stores at that port, during the war'.[30] He also sought to avoid the need to seek the Admiralty's approval to clean his ships when he needed to send them into Plymouth during the cruise: 'to remedy the inconvenience of its being so great a distance from London, I wish their Lordships would please give me a standing order for all the ships of my squadron to be cleaned and refitted as often as I shall send them'.[31]

---

26   Horace Walpole to Horace Mann, 4 March 1749, in Lewis (ed.), *The Yale Edition of the Correspondence of Horace Walpole*, vol.20, p.33.
27   Richmond, *The Navy in the War of 1739–48*, vol.III, pp.82–83.
28   Fanny Boscawen to Edward Boscawen, 14 April 1747, in Cecil F. Aspinall-Oglander, *Admiral's Wife: Being the Life and Letters of the Hon. Mrs. Edward Boscawen from 1719 to 1761* (London: Longmans & Co, 1940), p.40.
29   Woburn MSS: vol.XVI, f.53, George Anson to the Duke of Bedford, 3 April 1747.
30   George Anson to Thomas Corbett, 2 May 1747, in Pack, *Admiral Lord Anson*, p.158.
31   TNA: ADM 1/87, George Anson to the Admiralty, 2 May 1747.

As well as these logistical difficulties, Anson also had to deal with two captains – Thomas Grenville of the *Defiance* and William 'Mad' Montagu of the *Bristol* – who wanted to leave the Western Squadron to go on a second independent cruise in search of prizes (following their previous expedition to the Canary Islands in 1747). Both had brothers on the Admiralty Board and George Grenville (with the support of his colleague William Wildman, second Viscount Barrington) used his influence on Thomas's behalf (as he had done for other serving relatives since his appointment in 1744) to secure his colleagues' agreement to the cruise. But now that circumstances had changed – the French fleet was expected to go sea – Anson was not prepared to reduce the squadron's strength and refused to release them until the threat had receded. Grenville, who was angry that the promise was not kept, refused to sign the original order putting the ships under Anson's command and tried to obtain Bedford's signature to a revised instruction that would have required his brother to remain with the fleet for only seven days after it had sailed.

Bedford treated Grenville's action with 'the contempt it deserved', the original order was duly signed, and professional standards were maintained.[32] Unlike Grenville, Sandwich objected to his brother's request and gave priority to Anson's requirements. Soon afterwards, Anson wrote to Bedford saying he was 'sorry Your Grace has so much trouble at the Board', while sending a conciliatory letter to Grenville, explaining that Montagu and Grenville 'shall be detained from putting the Board's orders in execution as short a time as possible; if there should be any service, I know they would both of them be glad to be in it'.[33] However, Thomas Grenville, denied the opportunity to leave the Western Squadron in search of prizes, was killed at the Battle of Cape Finisterre soon afterwards.

Anson, who transferred his flag from the *Yarmouth* to the second-rate *Prince George* (90), finally left Spithead on 6 April with Warren in the *Devonshire* (66); they were joined by six ships of the line and a bomb vessel.[34] Five other ships – the *Yarmouth, Kent* and three fireships – which were not ready to depart, were ordered to join Anson at a rendezvous point off the southern coast of Brittany, 60 miles west of Belle Isle. He sailed for Plymouth where he was joined by a further 11 ships with others expected to leave later.[35] In total, Anson's squadron consisted of 18 ships of the line, five frigates, three sloops and two bomb vessels. As he approached the French coast, he dispatched the *Falkland* (50) and the cutter *Tavistock* (10) to cruise off Brest with orders to gather information about the presence of the French convoys and report to him as soon as possible at the rendezvous point. But after three weeks at sea, poor weather meant that the two ships had been unable to obtain any useful intelligence about the Brest squadron. Anson had also been unsuccessful in obtaining information from ships passing close to his station off Belle Isle but, on 20 April, the *Nottingham* learnt that a convoy bound for Canada was anchored in Aix Roads off Rochefort. It was

---

32   BL: Anson Papers, Add. MS. 15,955, f.137, Gertrude, Duchess of Bedford to George Anson, April 1747. See also Philip Lawson, *George Grenville. A Political Life* (Oxford: Clarendon Press, 1984), pp.48–50.
33   George Anson to George Grenville, 3 April 1747, in Smith (ed.), *The Grenville Papers*, vol.I, p.60.
34   *Lyon* (60), *Defiance* (60), *Prince Louisa* (60), *Chester* (60), *Pembroke* (60), *Bristol* (50) and the bomb vessel *Terror*.
35   *Namur* (74), *Hampton Court* (70), *Monmouth* (64), *Prince Frederick* (64), *Nottingham* (60), *Eagle* (60), *Windsor* (60), *Centurion* (50) *Falkland* (50), the sloop *Otter* and the cutter *Tavistock*.

likely that the warships waiting there had been sent from Brest and Anson switched his attention to Rochefort.

After consulting with Warren and his captains, Anson concluded that the French convoy was likely to pass the coast of Galicia in north-west Spain and that Cape Ortegal would be the most likely location to intercept it. But it was no more than their best guess and they were aware that the French might take a different route. As Warren commented to Anson, if they encountered a southerly wind it was 'likely they may not be able to hold their course off Spain nor you to get there, in short 'tis all chance to which we must submit, and content ourselves with the merit of deserving success by our diligence whether we meet with it or not'.[36] Anson left his Belle Isle station without delay, leaving the newly arrived frigate *Inverness* (22) and sloop *Viper* (10) there with instructions to send any additional ships arriving from England on to the new location.

As he sailed south across the Bay of Biscay, Anson ensured that the squadron was kept in readiness for battle, taking the opportunity to hold daily exercises 'in forming line and in manoeuvres of battle till then absolutely unknown'.[37] He ordered his captains to cruise in extended order in line ahead and line abreast formations while instructing his 50- and 60-gun ships 'to extend the front as look-outs, taking station at daylight as far in advance, when in line ahead, or as wide upon the beam when in line abreast, as signals could be seen'.[38] His preparations included moving his heaviest ships to the centre of his line, which reflected his view of how the French were likely to form their own line of battle, and priming his fireships so that they were ready for action. As discussed below, during these exercises Anson made use of the new signals he had prepared a few months earlier, which gave him much greater flexibility when issuing orders.[39]

When he reached his new station off Cape Ortegal, Anson deployed his ships in line abreast about a mile apart so that the French would find them difficult to avoid. He waited for several days with no intelligence and became increasingly concerned that they had taken a different route. On 2 May, he dispatched the *Inverness* and *Falcon* to Rochefort in search of news, while sending newly arrived frigates to monitor movements in the other French Atlantic ports. The *Falcon* sloop returned before 8:00 a.m. on the following day with news that the previous afternoon she had sighted a convoy of 38 ships sailing westwards at a distance of some 15 miles. By this point, it was calculated that the French were south-west of the squadron and Anson issued orders to intercept them; within 30 minutes Edward Boscawen in the *Namur* had sighted them. A general chase was signalled and the ships were cleared for action.

By 11:00 a.m. the fleet that Anson had been trying to find for nearly a month came clearly into view and he followed them in loose formation (as was permitted by the *Fighting Instructions* when pursuing an enemy). The French convoy had left Aix Roads on 30 April and consisted of two squadrons, which in total had fewer ships and guns than the British. The first, under the command of the Marquis de la Jonquière, consisted of his flagship

---

36 BL: Anson Papers, Add. MS. 15,957, f.172, Peter Warren to George Anson, 23 April 1747.
37 Julian S. Corbett, (ed.), *Fighting Instructions, 1530–1816* (London: Navy Records Society 1905), p.142.
38 Richmond, *The Navy in the War of 1739–48*, vol.III, p.85.
39 Laughton, 'George Anson, Lord Anson', in *The Dictionary of National Biography*.

Cape Finisterre, 1747.

Sérieux (64), four other warships,[40] and 24 merchant vessels. It was bound for Canada where La Jonquière was due to take up the post of governor-general of New France with orders to retake Cape Breton Island. The second squadron, under the command of Jacques-François Grout, Seigneur de Saint Georges, carried reinforcements destined for India, where the French sought to extend their territorial gains following the capture of Madras in September 1746. It consisted of the flagship *Invincible* (74), *Jason* (52), six converted warships operated by the Compagnie des Indies,[41] and 18 merchantmen. The combined squadrons were due to sail south-west across the Bay of Biscay for the north-west coast of Spain, where they would pass Cape Ortegal and Cape Finisterre.

---

40 *Diamant* (56), *Rubis* (52), *Gloire* (46), *Emeraude* (24).
41 *Apollon* (30), *Philibert* (30), *Vigilante* (22), *Modeste* (22), *Thétis* (20), *Dartmouth* (18).

By 1:00 p.m. the British, who were now some 72 miles west of Cape Ortegal, had closed to within three miles of the French. La Jonquière ordered his nine largest ships (including his East Indiamen) to turn into the wind with shortened sail and adopt a line ahead formation, while the rest of the convoy was to sail away to the westward as quickly as possible. Anson responded by forming his squadron in line abreast but soon afterwards he made a signal to form a line of battle ahead, with Boscawen in the *Namur* leading. As the *Devonshire* came alongside the *Prince George*, Warren discussed the position with Anson. Suspecting that the French manoeuvre was designed to allow the convoy to escape overnight, he suggested an immediate pursuit without forming a line. However, despite his overwhelming superiority, Anson cautiously decided to continue forming a line of battle ahead in accordance with the *Fighting Instructions* before mounting a concentrated attack. He was almost certainly alert to the risks of authorising individual attacks on the French line even if had numerical superiority as the combined firepower of the British line gave Anson an advantage that he would be reluctant to cast aside.[42] However, Anson's decision meant that offensive action was delayed, allowing the French merchant ships time to escape. It has been argued that Anson's caution meant that his 'performance on the day fell short of what it should have been'.[43]

It took some two hours for the British line to form, and it was not until 3:00 p.m. that Anson signalled for his leading ships to head for the centre of the French line. When Warren saw the signal, he bore away in chase rather than in succession (as Anson had intended) and several members of his van division followed. Anson immediately signalled Warren to re-form the line, enabling them to strike the French centre followed by an attack on their rear. Although the reasons for these decisions were not recorded, it is likely that 'after months of practising his fleet in bearing up and attacking in good order, he may well have determined that his attack should be orderly, his squadron well in hand, and its effect as conclusive as possible'.[44]

When La Jonquière saw the British heading for his centre in great strength, he ordered a fighting retreat and sailed away to the south-west. At about 3:15 p.m., when the French had broken their line, Anson hoisted the signal for a general chase for the first time, abandoning the line, which had been 'sacrosanct since the time of James, Duke of York [Lord High Admiral, 1660–73]'.[45] At about 4:00 p.m., the *Centurion*, commanded by Peter Denis, was the first ship to engage the French, opening fire on the enemy's rear with her chase guns. She attacked La Jonquière's flagship *Sérieux* and *Invincible* for 15 minutes alone at close range before three other members of the van division – *Namur*, *Defiance* and *Windsor* – entered the fight. At first, the British were outnumbered as 'they came into action in a rough line ahead and were met with a heavy fire from the more closely grouped French main body, each British ship as she arrived receiving the broadsides of two ships and the shot from

---

42 Patricia K. Crimmin, 'Anson: Cape Finisterre, 1747', in Eric Grove (ed.), *Great Battles of the Royal Navy as Commemorated in the Gunroom, Britannia Royal Naval College, Dartmouth* (London: Arms and Armour, 1994), p.76.
43 Ruddock F. Mackay and Michael Duffy, *Nelson and British Naval Leadership 1747–1805* (Woodbridge: The Boydell Press, 2009), p.101.
44 Richmond, *The Navy in the War of 1739–48*, vol.III, p.90.
45 Lambert, *Admirals*, p.133.

the chase guns of others'.⁴⁶ As the remaining members of the van division – *Nottingham*, *Yarmouth* and *Devonshire* – arrived, the balance began to shift in favour of the British. At this point, Anson sent the *Falcon* to shadow the convoy, with orders to send signals indicating the course it was taking, and she later captured the Indiaman *Dartmouth*.

The French fought with courage and determination, inflicting significant damage on the British ships that were able to join the fight in the first hour. By 5:00 p.m., the majority of the British squadron had engaged the French rear and were now able to bring their greater force to bear upon them. The *Devonshire*, Warren's flagship, played a leading role in the battle, fighting the *Sérieux* at close quarters until the latter surrendered with significant damage and 140 crew killed or wounded. He then opened fire on the *Invincible*, the largest ship in the French fleet, which surrendered after a second broadside from the *Bristol*, commanded by William Montagu. When the *Pembroke* had attempted to get between the *Bristol* and *Invincible*, 'Mad' Montagu shouted at her commander: 'Run foul of me and be damned; neither you, nor any other man in the world, shall come between me and my enemy'.⁴⁷

By 6:00 p.m., when the first French ships surrendered, Anson had come up in the slow-moving *Prince George* but, along with five other ships, he played no part in the battle. The engagement continued until 7:00 p.m. when the French surrendered after all hope of resistance was at an end. Both La Jonquière and Saint Georges were taken prisoner and remained in British captivity until the peace of Aix-la-Chapelle (1748). When Saint Georges presented his sword to Anson, he was unable to resist a pun even as he surrendered: 'Monsieur, vous avez vaincu *l'Invincible*, et *la Gloire* vous fuit', pointing to the two ships he had named. Anson now turned his attention to the rest of the convoy which had slipped away and sent three more ships (*Monmouth*, *Yarmouth* and *Nottingham*) in pursuit. They were now some 15 miles away and vanished as night fell, but 18 merchant ships were captured the following day together with the warships *Vigilante* and *Modeste*. The surviving merchant ships, accompanied by the frigate *Emeraude*, reached Quebec safely towards the end of June.

The four-hour engagement had resulted in heavy casualties on both sides, with the French losing 700 men killed and wounded; British losses were some 520 men killed and wounded. The dead included Captain Thomas Grenville of the *Defiance*, whom Anson described as 'by much the cleverest officer I ever saw'.⁴⁸ They took 18 French ships (including six ships of the line, several frigates and part of the convoy) and prize money valued at £755,896 (nearly £132 million at 2023 prices). Anson thought that the *Invincible* (which was commissioned as HMS *Invincible* in the Royal Navy) was a 'prodigious fine ship, and vastly large; I think she is longer than any ship in our fleet, and quite new, having made only one voyage'.⁴⁹

The French had fought a British squadron that was significantly stronger and had been deployed skilfully, engaging at close range as Anson had demanded. In a letter to the Duke

---

46   Richmond, *The Navy in the War of 1739–48*, vol.III, p.92.
47   Quoted in *The Naval Chronicle: Or, Voyages, Travels, Expeditions, Remarkable Exploits and Achievements, of the Most Celebrated English Navigators, Travellers, and Sea-Commanders, From the Earliest Accounts to the End of the Year 1759* (London: J. Fuller, 1760), vol.III, p.166.
48   George Anson to the Duke of Bedford, 11 May 1747, in Russell, *Correspondence of John, Fourth Duke of Bedford*, vol.I, p.214.
49   George Anson to the Duke of Bedford, 11 May 1747, in Russell, *Correspondence of John, Fourth Duke of Bedford*, vol.I, p.215.

of Bedford, Anson said he 'ought to be satisfied but wish he [La Jonquière] had had a little more strength, though this is the best stroke that has been made upon the French since La Hogue', referencing Admiral Edward Russell's victory of 1692. In explaining his success, Anson pointed to the benefit of superior British gunnery: 'my ships made a much hotter fire, and much more regular than theirs, when they had a superior number, which they had in the beginning'.[50] He might also have mentioned that, unlike the French, the English were able to fire their large cannon from the lowest gun deck.[51] Although Anson did not lead his squadron in battle, he directed it effectively from a distance and his well-trained captains followed his orders. In a letter to Bedford, Warren reported on his experience of serving with Anson:

> In my life I never served with more pleasure, nor saw half such pains to discipline the fleet. While I have the honour to continue in it [as Anson's successor], I will endeavour to follow his example, however short I may fall of it, and could wish to be commanded by him rather than command myself.[52]

As soon as Anson had completed his official account of the battle, he ordered Peter Denis to take it to Portsmouth, where he arrived in the *Centurion* on 16 May.[53] George II awarded Denis £500 for delivering the news and Bedford reported that 'the King told me …this morning that I had given him the best breakfast he had had this long time; and I think I never saw him more pleased in my life'.[54] Henry Pelham described the 'total defeat of their projects in both India and America, [as] an event which no one could have expected, and seems reserved for the fortunate and able hand of our friend Anson'.[55] It was the navy's first decisive victory after seven years of war and was widely welcomed.

Apart from their heavy losses in ships, men, guns and money, the French incurred £1.5 million (£268 million in 2023 prices) in abortive costs in equipping the two expeditions. Their defeat would also affect 'the course of affairs both in Canada and India. The operations in [Canada] would have taken a different turn if M. de la Jonquière had reached Quebec and had been able to support the expedition then in progress against Annapolis, while in the East Indies, the precarious condition to which the French settlements had been brought would have been mitigated'.[56] Lady Elizabeth Yorke, who was to marry Anson less than a year later, described it as 'the greatest blow that has been given the French marine since the Battle of La Hogue'.[57] Even Horace Walpole, one of Anson's fiercest critics, commented that 'it is a very big event, and by far one of the most

---

50 George Anson to the Duke of Bedford, 11 May 1747, in Russell, *Correspondence of John, Fourth Duke of Bedford*, vol.I, pp.214–215.
51 Julian Gwyn, *An Admiral for America: Sir Peter Warren, Vice Admiral of the Red, 1703–1752* (Gainesville: University Press of Florida, 2004), p.130.
52 Woburn MSS: vol.XVI, f.105, Peter Warren to the Duke of Bedford, 18 May 1747.
53 Reprinted in *The London Magazine*, vol.16 (May 1747), pp.203–205.
54 BL: Anson Papers, Add. MS. 15,955, f.139, the Duke of Bedford to George Anson, 16 May 1747.
55 Henry Pelham to the Duke of Bedford, 16 May 1747, in Russell, *Correspondence of John, Fourth Duke of Bedford*, vol.I, p.217.
56 Richmond, *The Navy in the War of 1739–48*, vol.III, p.94.
57 Elizabeth Yorke to Joseph Yorke, 25 May 1747, in Yorke (ed.), *The Life and Correspondence*, vol.I, p.639.

considerable that has happened during this war. By it he has defeated two expeditions at once… He has always been most remarkably fortunate'.[58] One of Walpole's correspondents, the army commander Henry Seymour Conway, suggested, a little less seriously, that the victory meant 'the Ansons will soon beat the Cumberlands… as a water-hero in the eyes of true Britons is superior to a land one'.[59]

Despite this chorus of approval, there were some dissenting voices in the press and elsewhere who questioned Anson's achievement mainly because of his overwhelming superiority, with personal and political motives also being in evidence. Captain Augustus Hervey (later the third Earl of Bristol), who was no friend of Anson, had more serious criticisms, claiming that the victory

> …was more owing to Admiral Warren's courage and conduct than to that of Admiral Anson, who might have taken them all [the French ships] had he not chased in a line so long, and who would not have taken one had he not agreed to Admiral Warren's intercessions of pursuing the enemy without the line.[60]

According to Elizabeth Yorke, some negative comments were politically inspired, with the Prince of Wales and his protégé Admiral Vernon leading the charge. She reported that Anson had been 'very coldly received' by the Prince and Princess of Wales.[61]

After Anson's return to Portsmouth on 16 May, the prize money was loaded onto 20 wagons and taken to London where it 'went, in grand military procession, quite through the city, amidst the acclamations of many thousand people to the Bank [of England], where it was lodged'.[62] The streets were filled with illuminations and bonfires as the people celebrated this rare victory. Anson added significantly to his wealth as a result of the battle, receiving £62,991 (almost £11 million in 2023 prices) in prize money, which represented two-thirds of the flag's eighth share; Warren received the balance of £31,496. Both admirals received their funds in Navy Bills, which were orders to the Treasurer of the Navy to pay an individual for goods or services supplied. They were available at a two per cent discount and paid five per cent interest a year, which was payable quarterly.

Anson was received by the King who said he had 'done a great service. I thank you and desire you to thank, in my name, all the officers and private men for their bravery and conduct, with which I am well pleased'. On 3 June, he was created Lord Anson of Soberton (the location of his Hampshire estate) and adopted the motto *Nil Desperandum* (never despair), which had first been used in Horace's *Odes*. On 15 July, he was appointed vice admiral of the red. Peter Warren was awarded a knighthood and promoted to the rank of vice admiral of the white shortly afterwards.

---

58 Horace Walpole to Horace Mann, 19 May 1747, in Lewis (ed.), *The Yale Edition of the Correspondence of Horace Walpole*, vol.19, p.402.
59 Henry Seymour Conway to Horace Walpole, 12 June 1747, in Lewis (ed.), *The Yale Edition of the Correspondence of Horace Walpole*, vol.37, p.273.
60 David Erskine (ed.), *Augustus Hervey's Journal. Being the Intimate Account of the Life of a Captain in the Royal Navy Ashore and Afloat, 1746–1759* (London: William Kimber, 1953), p.48.
61 Elizabeth Yorke to Joseph Yorke, 25 May 1747, in Yorke (ed.), *The Life and Correspondence*, vol.I, p.639.
62 Beatson, *Naval and Military Memoirs*, vol.I, p.342.

Lord Anson's Victory off Cape Finisterre, 3 May 1747, painting by Samuel Scott. (Yale Centre for British Art)

Anson helped to secure the promotion of Edward Boscawen, who had been a captain for just over 10 years, by recommending him to Bedford shortly after the battle: 'Boscawen got a shot in the shoulder but is almost well; his behaviour in the action pleased me, and I hope your Grace will make him a rear admiral'.[63] Shortly afterwards, Boscawen was advanced to rear admiral of the blue at the age of 36, and later in the year, Anson appointed him to the command of an expedition to capture Mauritius and Pondicherry. The operation was unsuccessful but there is no evidence to support Walpole's malicious claim that Anson 'projected this business on purpose to ruin Boscawen'.[64] In fact, they worked in unison from the time Boscawen became a member of Anson's Admiralty Board in 1751 until his untimely death in 1761.

Anson commissioned Samuel Scott, the leading British marine painter of the period, to produce a painting commemorating his victory, which is now in the National Maritime Museum, Greenwich. According to Horace Walpole, who could never resist the opportunity to make a critical comment, the painting originally depicted:

> Anson's own ship in a cloud of cannon… boarding the French admiral. This circumstance, which was as true as if Mademoiselle Scudéry had written his life (for he was scarce in sight when the Frenchman struck to Boscawen) has been so ridiculed by

---

63 George Anson to the Duke of Bedford, 11 May 1747, in Russell, *Correspondence of John, Fourth Duke of Bedford*, vol.I, p.214.
64 Horace Walpole to Horace Mann, 31 January 1750, in Lewis (ed.), *The Yale Edition of the Correspondence of Horace Walpole* vol.20, p.113.

the whole tar-hood, that the romantic part has been forced to be cancelled, and one only gun remains firing at Anson's ship.⁶⁵

Anson's success was also celebrated in a medal produced by Thomas Pingo, which his brother Thomas would commission some six years after his death. The obverse shows a bust of Anson being crowned by Winged Victory, above the date 3 May 1747. The reverse, which celebrates the circumnavigation, shows Winged Victory standing on a sea monster above a globe. A circle of laurel wreaths encloses the names of six officers of the *Centurion* – Keppel, Saumarez, Saunders, Brett, Denis, and Campbell. The medal was struck in large numbers, but gold versions were produced only for Anson, the six named officers, and the captains of Anson's ships at Cape Finisterre.

With Anson's reputation (and wealth) significantly enhanced, Timothy Brett could comment that he 'certainly is the most rising man we have; and don't be surprised if, within a twelvemonth, you see him at the head of the fleet'.⁶⁶ With Anson now back at the Admiralty, Peter Warren replaced him in command of the Western Squadron and was determined to follow his successful example, although ill-health meant that he was soon superseded by his deputy Edward Hawke. Both Warren and Hawke adopted Anson's approach to command, which emphasised intensive training and flexibility during an engagement. In June 1747, Warren had described his experiences as second in command to Anson:

> No service had ever been so agreeable to him as this cruize under Anson, & that with respect to action he had learned more from him than in all the time he had been at sea before; adding that tho' the ship-captains in their squadron were very good officers, yet he did not think they would have done so well under any other commander, Mr Anson having called them all on board him the morning before the action, & given them directions on what he believed would be right for them to do, supposing they should not be able to see, or he to change his signals.⁶⁷

One of Hawke's first acts after he succeeded Peter Warren was to issue the additional fighting instructions that Anson had prepared when he assumed command of the Western Squadron in 1746. The rigid official *Fighting Instructions* – a code of tactical signals at sea which had first been issued by Robert Blake in 1653 – were designed to produce a well-ordered line of battle against equally matched fleets, while Anson wanted greater flexibility and more aggressive action. He followed other admirals, including Vernon, Mathews and Rowley, who had also issued their own additional instructions as tactics at sea evolved.

Anson's instructions, which were officially adopted at the beginning of the Seven Years War, 'envisaged the maximum degree of offensive effort' and were designed for use against a weaker or retreating enemy and gave individual captains much greater autonomy. Article

---

65 Horace Walpole to Horace Mann, 23 March 1749, in Lewis (ed.), *The Yale Edition of the Correspondence of Horace Walpole*, vol.20, p.38.
66 Timothy Brett to Philip Saumarez, 12 August 1747, in Keppel, *The Life of Augustus, Viscount Keppel*, vol.I, p.104.
67 Quoted in N.A.M. Rodger, 'Image and Reality in Eighteenth Century Naval Tactics', *The Mariner's Mirror*, 89 (2003), p.293.

8, for example, pointed to a significant difference between Anson's instructions and the official version:

> If engaged with an inferior enemy, the overlapping ships either ahead or astern were to leave the line without waiting for a signal and to rake the enemy's van or rear ships as the case may be, notwithstanding the first part of the 24th Article of the *Fighting Instructions* to the contrary.[68]

He may also have been responsible for issuing separate instructions for a significant tactical innovation – the 'bow and quarter line' (or line of bearing) – which was based on forming a line on a prearranged compass bearing. The main advantage of the line of bearing was that 'a fleet could process under easy sail, making the most of a fresh breeze... but at the same time be in a position to form a close-hauled line of battle quickly at the first sign of danger'.[69]

Hawke used Anson's methods at the Second Battle of Cape Finisterre (25 October 1747) when he defeated the French, capturing six warships and damaging two more. The course of the battle closely resembled Anson's victory in May in the 'tactical sequence of chase, then line, then chase again, followed by the signal for a close engagement'.[70] Anson commented that Hawke's victory had 'raised the reputation of our fleet to the highest pitch', but the navy's revival had begun with the first victory in May. Lord Sandwich, who was still in the Netherlands, commented on the 'credit and reputation it will give to our marine' of which Anson is 'so deservedly the chief director and to whose knowledge and ability the world is very ready to attribute the different figure that the English fleet has made in the last years from what did at the beginning of the war'.[71]

Following their defeats at the hands of Anson and Hawke, the French did not attempt to launch a naval counterattack in 1748. Anson's assessment of the position in February was that 'our fleets have had pretty good success and are in excellent condition, for which reason the French will never think of trying their strength at sea nor carry on more trade than is absolutely necessary to supply their colonies'.[72] In these unfavourable circumstances, the French focused on land operations in the Austrian Netherlands before peace preliminaries were agreed in April 1748.

The Treaty of Aix la Chapelle ended the war in October 1748 but Anson had already expressed regrets at the impact of the peace on the Admiralty. In May, he wrote to Sandwich complaining that his success in the peace negotiations had 'almost brought the office of the Admiralty to be a sinecure for all our last orders are sent so that there remains nothing but to dismantle our ships, a grievous affair to me for I shall never live to see so well disciplined

---

68 Brian Tunstall, *Naval Warfare in the Age of Sail: The Evolution of Fighting Tactics 1650–1815* (London: Conway Maritime Press, 1990), p.97; BL: Add. MS. 62,936, *Naval Signal Book, circa 1747–1748*.
69 Sam Willis, *Fighting at Sea in the Eighteenth Century: The Art of Sailing Warfare* (Woodbridge: The Boydell Press, 2008), p.64.
70 Ruddock F. Mackay (ed.), *The Hawke Papers: A Selection 1743–1771*, Navy Records Society, vol.129 (Aldershot: Scolar Press, 1990), p.22.
71 BL: Anson Papers, Add. MS. 15,957, f.28, Lord Sandwich to George Anson, 14 November 1747 (n.s.).
72 NMM: Sandwich Papers, SAN/V/50, p.96, George Anson to Lord Sandwich, 23 February 1748.

and complete a squadron as we have to the westward'.[73] If Anson had reservations about working in the post-war Admiralty, his brother Thomas was quick to reassure him:

> Nothing surely remains to be added to your fame in commanding squadrons: a discipline unknown before, a new manner of cruising, and a decisive way of engaging the enemy... have already secur'd you all merit of that kind in its largest extent. Then to frame and direct the whole plan is much more glorious to yourself as well as more beneficial to the public, that to execute with all the ability and success imaginable only a part of it.[74]

---

73 NMM: Sandwich Papers, SAN/V/50, p.109, George Anson to Lord Sandwich, 10 May 1748.
74 SRO: Anson Family Papers, D615/P(S)/1/10/24, Thomas Anson to George Anson, 24 July [1748].

6

Naval Reform, 1748–1751

One of Anson's first priorities after he relinquished the command of the Western Squadron and returned to London in May 1747 was the forthcoming General Election, which began on 26 June and concluded on 4 August. Anson's tenure as an MP had ended on his elevation to the House of Lords, but he maintained a close connection with his former constituency as Lord Bath had transferred his interest in Hedon to him. Anson entered his friend Captain Charles Saunders as one of the candidates but was unwilling to enter into an electoral pact with one of the other candidates and Saunders was defeated. He was eventually elected as MP for the constituency at the 1754 General Election when Anson's associate Peter Denis was nominated as the second candidate and also won.

In 1747, Anson also consolidated his political influence in the Staffordshire constituency of Lichfield, where he had used some of his prize money to buy up freeholds and burgages, joining forces with Lord Gower, the former Jacobite who now supported the Government. From this point, Anson and Gower each nominated one candidate for Lichfield, with Anson's brother Thomas and one of Lord Gower's sons both being elected in 1747 against strong Jacobite opposition. According to Horace Walpole, 'Anson spent great sums at the Staffordshire elections', with the victory at Lichfield costing him and Gower £20,000 between them, leading Elizabeth Anson to describe it as the 'borough of Guzzledown'.[1] The following year she helped him secure a continuing electoral agreement with Lord Gower that gave one Lichfield seat to the Ansons, which meant that Thomas would remain as the MP until 1770 although he did not serve continuously.[2]

Anson invested more time and money in the constituency over the next few years to maintain the family's political presence in the county. Anson's continuing interest in Staffordshire is shown when, in 1758, he (and Lord Gower) asked the engineer James Brindley to investigate the feasibility of building a canal between Lichfield and Burton on Trent as part of a larger scheme to link the Trent and Mersey rivers. Brindley concluded that the scheme was feasible but would be prohibitively expensive and it was not pursued further at the time.[3]

---

1 Quoted in Lewis (ed.), *The Yale Edition of the Correspondence of Horace Walpole*, vol.19, p.418.
2 Eveline Cruickshanks, 'Thomas Anson', *History of Parliament Online*, <https://www.historyofparliamentonline.org/volume/1715-1754/member/anson-thomas-1695-1773>, accessed 20 September 2022.
3 Nick Corble, *James Brindley. The First Canal Builder* (Stroud: The History Press, 2005), p.50.

Anson was also active on the Duke of Bedford's behalf in the 1747 General Election and gave him advice on how to manage his political interests in his local constituency:

> I am sorry you are apprehensive of a farther opposition at Bedford, if the breach you lately made there is not sufficient to carry the place by storm you must do as Louendalk [Count Löwendal] did at Bergen op Zoom and proceed by sapping and bribing, the latter you have been so little used too that I think you should try your hand now, as you may probably have some occasion for it upon another election.[4]

Anson's return to the Admiralty brought a new impetus to the work on reforming the officer corps, which had made little progress in his absence. The plans included improvements to the status and discipline of officers as well as a move to a modified system of promotion that was not based entirely on seniority. The first change – a compulsory retirement scheme for underperforming captains – which was introduced earlier in the year, was intended to give the Admiralty greater flexibility in the choice of candidates for flag rank. Before Anson's reform, admirals were normally appointed from amongst the most senior captains, based on seniority, and if more able junior candidates were promoted it produced complaints and damaged morale. To overcome this problem, a compulsory retirement scheme for senior captains who were considered unsuitable for promotion to an active flag command was developed.

Under Anson's scheme, captains who were selected for retirement would be advanced to the rank of rear admiral 'without distinction of squadron' and their active service would thus be brought permanently to an end. Known as 'yellow admirals', they would be given the half-pay of a rear admiral for the rest of their lives without the possibility of resuming their careers. In July 1747, the first batch of 20 of the most undistinguished senior captains was promoted as 'yellow admirals' and, at the beginning of the Seven Years War, Anson removed several more senior captains using the same mechanism. The reform gave the Admiralty much greater freedom to promote more able and energetic officers to flag rank while still giving due weight to the principle of seniority. The new mechanism meant that unfit captains who were much lower down the list could also be removed, diluting the seniority principle still further.

Anson further loosened the constraints imposed by the seniority rule by using the Admiralty's power of appoipntment to the temporary rank of commodore (the position he had held during the circumnavigation) more frequently. It was one step below the rank of rear admiral and allowed 'any captain to be appointed to command a squadron without affecting his permanent seniority'.[5] He used the rank to promote his young friend and protégé Augustus Keppel as a commodore commanding in the Mediterranean in 1749 and on three further occasions before he was appointed as a rear admiral in 1770. It did not prove possible to extend the principle of compulsory retirement to admirals (as Anson had wished) but the number of flag officers was significantly increased during the 1740s,

---

4   Woburn MSS: vol.XVIII, f.12, George Anson to the Duke of Bedford, 17 September 1747. During the siege of Bergen op Zoom (July–September 1747) the French used mines and covered trenches as they overcame the Dutch defences.
5   Rodger, *The Wooden World*, p.299.

giving further opportunities to promote the most able captains. At the beginning of the decade, there were nine admirals, with one each in the following ranks: admiral of the fleet; admirals of the blue and white; vice admirals and rear admirals of the red, white, and blue. By the end of 1747, this had increased to a total of 21 flag officers (one admiral of the fleet; six admirals; six vice admirals; and eight rear admirals) giving the Admiralty many more options.

The third major change to officers' conditions – the regular payment of captains' and lieutenants' wages – was adopted shortly after Anson's return from the Western Squadron. It was decided that captains should be paid once a year rather than at the time their ships were paid off when large arrears of pay were likely to be due to them. As the Admiralty pointed out in a memorial to the King, it was

> ...customary for your Majesty's ships to be many years in commission before they are paid off and laid up, until which time the said officers receive no part of their pay; and as most of them have only their said pay to live upon, and many of them have large families, which necessitates them to take up money at exorbitant usury for their support.[6]

It was hoped that a system of regular payment would reduce corruption as well as the need for officers to borrow money although the reform did not address the longstanding problem of low pay.

Anson's most significant change to the status of naval officers – associating officers' ranks with their military equivalents for the first time – soon followed. Naval ranks had never been legally defined and were linked to specific employment at sea rather than to a permanent service-wide appointment. Anson was aware that 'the experience of this as well as of former wars [had] long shown the inconveniences arising from the want of an establishment of rank and precedence between your Majesty's sea and land officers'.[7] Establishing the military equivalents for naval ranks would help to increase the standing of sea officers at home and overseas.

In progressing this reform, Anson received helpful reinforcement from a group of 80 naval officers led by Chaloner Ogle, Edward Boscawen and Peter Warren. In a submission to the Admiralty, they explained some of the problems that the absence of military equivalents to naval ranks had caused, particularly when they were serving overseas:

> Naval captains and inferior officers are treated with an unbecoming want of regard, and in a manner different from that shown to commanders and other officers of foreign ships of war. And as the cause of this distinction we presume arises from a rank being given them with the officers of their army and for want of that rank being given to officers of equal trust in his Majesty's navy.[8]

---

6   Admiralty Memorial to the King in Council, 10 April 1747, in Baugh (ed.), *Naval Administration*, p.79.
7   TNA: SP 42/32, f.306, Admiralty Memorial to the King in Council, 13 November 1747.
8   Enclosed with Admiralty Memorial to the King in Council, 13 November 1747, in Baugh (ed.), *Naval Administration*, p.83.

Anson's proposals addressed these problems by specifying the naval ranks from lieutenant to admiral and commander in chief of the fleet and their army equivalents. For example, he decided that rear admirals should rank with major generals, captains of three years' experience commanding post ships with army colonels, and naval lieutenants with army captains. Anson's proposals ran into some opposition in the Privy Council, but they were approved by George II and announced in February 1748.[9]

Although Anson's proposals did not refer to the question of naval uniform, the officers' submission on naval ranks made the case for its introduction. They argued that it should be adopted to 'distinguish the rank of each officer from the other; and with regard to petty officers, if no rank should be thought proper to be given them with the army, yet every person acting in quality of mate or midshipman may carry that appearance which is necessary to distinguish it as the post of a gentleman'. The need for a naval uniform had first been raised with the Admiralty early in 1746 by a group of officers, known as the 'Navy Club', who met in London and decided 'that a uniform dress is useful and necessary for the commissioned officers, agreeable to the practice of other nations'.[10]

Anson supported the officers' view and recognised that a uniform would differentiate naval officers by rank, establish their identity in society and ensure that they gained the respect they were due. It would reinforce hierarchy and discipline among them, in line with the political principles that had determined Admiralty policy since 1744. Anson had recognised the value of a uniform on two previous occasions (at Macao in 1742 and Canton in 1743) during his visits to China on the voyage around the world. On the second occasion, he dressed the crew of his barge in an impromptu uniform – scarlet jackets and blue silk waistcoats, trimmed with silver – as he was taken to meet the Viceroy in Canton. In this case, Anson used the uniform to emphasise his official standing as the representative of a foreign power.

In July 1747, he circulated a proposal about rank and uniform prepared by Peter Warren, which ran into opposition from some senior officers. Despite their reservations, Anson pressed ahead and, in August, issued a general invitation to officers to create their own uniforms, with a preferred design being submitted to George II for his approval. As Augustus Keppel explained to Philip Saumarez, 'My Lord Anson is desirous that many of us should make coats after our own taste, and then a choice to be made of one to be general; and if you will appear in yours, he says he will be answerable your taste will not be amongst the worst'.[11] A blue and white uniform created by Saumarez was selected as Anson's preferred design and it was quickly approved by the King. Although he may have agreed to it on its own merits, Anson suggested that there was another reason for the King's preference for blue and white, reporting that he had 'seen my Duchess [of Bedford] riding in the park a few days ago in a habit of blue faced with white, the dress took the fancy of his Majesty, who had appointed

---

9 Sarah Kinkel, 'Disorder, Discipline, and Naval Reform in Mid-Eighteenth-Century Britain', *The English Historical Review*, 128 (2013), p.1470.
10 Quoted in Amy Miller, *Dressed to Kill: British Naval Uniform, Masculinity and Contemporary Fashions, 1748–1857* (London: National Maritime Museum, 2007), p.19.
11 Augustus Keppel to Philip Saumarez, 20 August 1747, in Keppel, *The Life of Augustus, Viscount Keppel*, vol.I, p.107.

it for the uniform of the Royal Navy'.[12] The adoption of this design, which consisted of two suits – dress and undress – both of blue wool with white facings, was announced in regulations, issued on 13 April 1748, which required officers to replace their civilian clothes with the new uniforms. The announcement said that a uniform was necessary 'in order the better to distinguish the rank of sea officers', who were 'required and directed to conform yourself to the said establishment, by wearing clothing accordingly at all proper times'. Officers were also ordered 'not to wear any other uniform than that which properly belongs to his rank'.[13]

The final – and most significant – of Anson's reforms aimed to improve naval discipline by applying martial law to half-pay officers and enhancing the sentencing powers of courts-martial. Work began on this major reform soon after Anson's return from the sea, but Parliamentary approval to revised Articles of War was not sought until 1749. In the meantime, the Admiralty promoted legislation to extend the scope of courts-martial to resolve an issue which had arisen in 1746, when it was unable to prosecute the former crew of the *Wager*, who had mutinied following the loss of their ship in 1741 during the circumnavigation. The mutineers successfully argued that as the mutiny occurred after the ship had been wrecked, they were no longer on active service or being paid, and were therefore no longer subject to the provisions of the Articles of War. The 1748 Act closed this loophole by establishing that the Articles should remain in force 'with respect to the crews of such of his Majesty's ships as shall be wrecked, or be otherwise lost or destroyed, and all the command, power and authority given to the officers of the said ship or ships, shall remain and be in full force'.[14]

At a time when work on the reform programme was intensifying, Anson also had to deal with the consequences of a change in the leadership of the Admiralty. He first became aware that Bedford was considering resigning as First Lord as early as 1746 when he (Bedford) had discussed the possibility with Lord Sandwich. Sandwich, who had seen himself as Bedford's successor since joining the Board in 1744, said that if he were appointed, he would want Anson to act as First Lord when he was absent in Europe. In a letter to Bedford in November, he described his close relationship with Anson, saying that there could 'never subsist any jealousy between us, but, on the contrary, a perfect union both in our private and public designs'. He would have 'as much of the power of the office while I am at the head of it as he can ever desire, and will be certain, on any accident that should happen to me... to step into the post without the least difficulty'.[15]

In a letter to Bedford in December 1746, Anson explained his position on the question of his successor, acknowledging that he was 'no great politician' himself and that Sandwich was:

> The only person after your Grace that I would act with and cannot help declaring that ever since your Grace made me acquainted with him I have the greatest esteem

---

12 Quoted in Havilland de Sausmarez, *Captain Philip Saumarez, 1710–1747, and His Contemporaries. From Letters and Portraits at Sausmarez Manor, Guernsey. And an Account of the Origin of the Naval Uniform as Designed by Him* (Guernsey: Guernsey Press Company, 1936), p.14.
13 TNA: ADM 2/71, *Uniform Regulations*, 13 April 1748.
14 *An Act for Further Regulating the Proceedings Upon Courts Martial* (1748; 21 George II, c.1).
15 Lord Sandwich to the Duke of Bedford, 24 November 1746 (n.s.), in Russell, *Correspondence of John, Fourth Duke of Bedford*, vol.I, p.192.

and friendship for him, not so much for his parts which are equalled by very few but from a thorough conviction that he will upon all occasions act upon the same honest principles for the good of his country that Your Grace has ever acted.[16]

However, the rumours about Bedford's departure did not prove accurate and he remained in office for another year, an outcome that suited both Anson and Sandwich. With Anson away at sea for months at a time and Sandwich involved in the protracted peace talks in the Netherlands, both feared that Bedford's early departure would give other contenders on the Board a greater opportunity to make a bid for the vacancy. Even after his triumphant return in May 1747, Anson remained concerned that Bedford would resign, a prospect which 'I never think of without uneasiness'. In a letter to the First Lord, he reaffirmed his loyalty to Sandwich as 'the only person in the kingdom, after Your Grace, that I will serve under: if he continues there seven years, and I live as long, I will never quit him, for I esteem him much'.[17]

Despite Bedford's continuation in office, there was continuing uncertainty over the future leadership of the Board and, in mid-1747, Anson's hopes of working with Sandwich as the next First Lord were briefly thrown into doubt. Sandwich's diplomatic successes overseas had led Newcastle to consider him as a possible successor to Philip Stanhope, fourth Earl of Chesterfield, Secretary of State for the Northern Department, rather than as a future head of the Admiralty. However, Newcastle was unable to secure the agreement of his colleagues to the move because 'they did not care to advance the Duke's power by installing at his behest so young and so ambitious a client, one who might easily become a rival to any one of them'.[18] When Chesterfield suddenly resigned in February 1748, a further effort was made to promote Sandwich's claims to the Secretaryship but the outcome was the same. In a letter to Sandwich, Anson explained the reason for his rejection: 'it was not pretended that any part of the opposition was from a dislike to Ld Sandwich but to the warlike measures he had pursued in which nobody else is embarked upon but the D of Newcastle'.[19]

When it became clear that Newcastle would not succeed in appointing Sandwich, Lord Anson suggested a way forward to him: Bedford should take the post of Southern Secretary and Sandwich should replace him as First Lord, with the Duke going to the Northern Department.[20] Newcastle and his colleagues adopted Anson's solution even though Sandwich would continue to be based in Europe for the rest of the year. Despite suggesting these changes, Anson found the outcome unwelcome, writing to Newcastle on hearing the news of Bedford's departure to complain 'that you have taken from us the main support of our Board, and I am afraid we resemble a ship without a commander as Lord Sandwich is absent, which I look upon as a very unfortunate circumstance for me who wish his Lordship much reputation in everything he undertakes'.[21]

---

16 Woburn MSS: vol.XV, f.74, George Anson to the Duke of Bedford, 13 December 1746.
17 George Anson to the Duke of Bedford, 11 May 1747, in Russell, *Correspondence of John, Fourth Duke of Bedford*, vol.I, p.215.
18 Rodger, *Insatiable Earl*, p.58.
19 NMM: Sandwich Papers, SAN/V/50, p.94, George Anson to Lord Sandwich, 23 February 1747/48.
20 NMM: Sandwich Papers, SAN/V/50, pp.88–89, George Anson to Lord Sandwich, 15 February 1747/48.
21 George Anson to the Duke of Newcastle, 15 February 1748, in Anson, *The Life of Admiral Lord Anson*, p.111.

In supporting Sandwich's appointment, Anson recognised that his own claims to succeed Bedford were not yet sufficiently strong, but he remained highly ambitious and, with ever closer political and personal links to the ruling Pelhams, he was likely to receive preferment before too long. Although he was still the junior naval lord, he had served as Bedford's principal naval adviser and had quickly established himself as the professional head of the navy. His successful term of office had coincided with a revival in the navy's fortunes as the balance of power began to change in England's favour.[22] He was fortunate that potential rivals, including, most notably, Admiral Vernon had fallen by the wayside while he enjoyed the friendship and support of two of England's most successful admirals – Hawke and Boscawen – as well as the rising group of officers who had served with him on the circumnavigation.

Despite his strong endorsement of Sandwich, Anson remained concerned about how the Board would operate in his absence in the Netherlands. In a letter to Anson sent soon after his appointment, Sandwich reiterated the high degree of trust that he had in his friend, who was to be given a free hand while consulting him as necessary:

> I would not lose a moment to desire that you consider yourself as in effect at the head of the Admiralty; that you would not only write to me your sentiments, as to any measures you would wish to have executed, and where my assistance is necessary, but that you would always make use of my name wherever it is necessary… I shall beg you would suffer everything I do to go through your hands, as it is my meaning to throw my share of the power, and the direction of the whole as much as possible into your hands.[23]

Sandwich advised him that he had written in similar terms to the Duke of Newcastle informing him that 'in Admiralty business he must consider you as one as the same thing with me, and that I intend to depend entirely upon your Lordship'.[24]

Despite Sandwich's reassuring words, Anson was concerned that Lord Vere Beauclerk might cause him problems and sought his advice on how to handle him. Lord Vere, who had once seen himself as Bedford's successor and had threatened to resign when he failed to secure the appointment, continued as a member of the Board in the hope that Sandwich might soon leave office.[25] Anson had always had a strong personal antipathy to Lord Vere and he feared that, as the senior naval member, he would try to dominate the Board while the new First Lord was overseas. On 15 February, he wrote to Sandwich expressing his fear that:

> In your absence Lord Vere may make as much a cipher [sic] of me as he pleases, which you will easily imagine must be very disagreeable to me after the share the

---

22 Richard Harding, 'Leadership Networks and the Effectiveness of the British Royal Navy in the Mid-Eighteenth Century', in R. Harding and Agustín Guimerá (eds.), *Naval Leadership in the Atlantic World. The Age of Reform and Revolution, 1700–1850* (London: University of Westminster Press, 2017), pp.21–34.
23 BL: Anson Papers, Add. MS. 15,957, f.51, Lord Sandwich to George Anson, 5 March 1748.
24 BL: Anson Papers, Add. MS. 15,957, f.83, Lord Sandwich to George Anson, 19 March 1748.
25 NMM: Sandwich Papers, SAN/V/50, p.83, George Anson to Lord Sandwich, 14 February 1747/48.

Duke of Bedford has allowed me in the direction of affairs afloat... He has been in my way ever since I came into the world. Two years ago I endeavoured to shove him before me, but there was no moving him from the earth to his proper element; and to continue now in his rear, both at land and sea, I own I cannot well endure.[26]

In his reply, Sandwich sought to reassure him:

I'm sorry Ld Vere remains at the Board if that is in any way disagreeable to you, but I think that so far from his being able to make a cipher of you that you must put him absolutely in that situation himself. I always told you that whenever I got to the head of the Admiralty, it should, except in the name and show of it, be the same thing as if you were there yourself.[27]

He then explained how he intended to reinforce Anson's preferential position:

As to Lord Vere taking advantage of my absence to forward any of his purposes; if they are such as are disagreeable to you, it is very easy to prevent them, by desiring first to know my opinion... You may be assured I will do no act whatever but directly through your hands, which will plainly show where the power centres.

It is evident from his regular correspondence with Anson that Sandwich was as good as his word and did not seek to constrain him as the effective head of the Board. His surviving letters from the Netherlands were dominated by his accounts of the peace negotiations rather than naval issues, with only occasional references to political developments in England, including a request to Anson to intervene in a troubling disagreement between Bedford and Newcastle.[28] A rare exception was a reminder Sandwich sent to Anson in November 1747 about one of the reforms he had taken a close interest in: 'I have heard nothing since I left England about the regulation of the rank of our sea officers. I hope that the matter does not sleep. As I am sure it will do great good to the service'.[29]

With Anson now running the Admiralty in Sandwich's absence, his timely marriage to Lady Elizabeth Yorke (1725–1760), the eldest daughter of the Earl of Hardwicke, on 25 April 1748, helped to consolidate his position at the centre of political power. However, it soon became clear that it was far more than a marriage of convenience and a strong relationship developed between the couple, which only ended with Elizabeth's premature death in 1760. It is not clear when they first met, but, at an earlier point, Anson had mentioned her to Peircy Brett, who commented: 'Tho' I never had the pleasure of seeing her Ladyship, yet I am not a stranger to her perfections, which I remember well to have had from your Lordship at a time when I believe you had no thoughts of marrying'.[30] Edward Boscawen's wife Fanny also voiced her approval in a letter to her husband:

---

26   Barrow, *The Life of George Lord Anson*, p.201.
27   BL: Add. MS. 15,957, f.53, Lord Sandwich to George Anson, 19 March 1748 (n.s.).
28   BL: Anson Papers, Add. MS. 15,957, f.41, Lord Sandwich to George Anson, 30 January 1748.
29   BL: Anson Papers, Add. MS. 15,957, f.28, Lord Sandwich to George Anson, 14 November 1747.
30   BL: Anson Papers, Add. MS. 15,955, f.81, Peircy Brett to George Anson, 3 May 1748.

Elizabeth, Lady Anson, painting in the style of Sir Godfrey Kneller. (National Trust)

He has escaped all the trammels and snares that were laid for him and, flying the traps of the Levesons, he has voluntarily surrendered to Miss Yorke… she is extremely sensible and good-natured and that sort of stuff… that will make a good wife. Her father and mother are remarkably happy together and have bred her up with all the care imaginable, so I believe you'll approve of your friend's choice.[31]

The ceremony was conducted by the Archbishop of Canterbury at Hardwicke's London residence, Powis House in Great Ormond Street, and the bride received a dowry of £12,000. Despite her privileged background, Elizabeth expressed her concerns about marrying such a prominent public figure in a letter to her friend Catherine Talbot: 'when one had moved in one small sphere, one cannot help feeling as many alarms upon stepping out of it, as if it

---

31 Fanny Boscawen to Edward Boscawen, 11 January 1748, in Aspinall-Oglander, *Admiral's Wife*, p.71.

were a magic circle'.³² Lord Hardwicke, who described his new son-in-law as a 'man of strict probity and honour', welcomed him warmly to the family and they remained close political allies until Anson died in 1762. He helped to maintain Anson's close links with the Pelhams, advising the Duke of Newcastle that 'with a little cultivating, you may keep him thoroughly connected with you'.³³

Elizabeth was raised in a political family that also had a great enthusiasm for literature, philosophy and the arts, and her wide-ranging interests are evident in her relationship with her brothers. Her lifelong correspondence with her favourite brother, Joseph Yorke, first Lord Dover, British ambassador to the Hague, was dominated by news of the war in Europe and well-informed political gossip. Another brother, Philip Yorke (Lord Royston, later the second Earl of Hardwicke) was married to Jemima, Marchioness Grey, and the couple had shared interests in literature, the classics and gardens. Jemima became Elizabeth's closest friend and later said that she was her 'most constant companion ever since she married. I have passed few days without seeing her in town and very short time in the country without hearing'.³⁴ Elizabeth was a member of Jemima's and Philip's literary circle (the Wrest Coterie), which was drawn from friends and family who visited them at Wrest Park, their country estate in Bedfordshire. Other members of the circle included Elizabeth's friends Catherine Talbot and Thomas Birch. At Wrest, they held lively discussions 'over the follies of courts many centuries since buried or debated the politics of a hundred years ago. Sometimes on matters of literature, the style or merit of authors'.³⁵ Apart from her literary interests, Elizabeth was also a noted pastellist, with Horace Walpole commenting that she 'painted remarkably well in crayons', an assessment endorsed by the artist and bluestocking Mary Delany.³⁶

Soon after their marriage, Fanny Boscawen had heard a rumour that 'Lord Anson is excessive fond of his wife and, moreover, that she is pregnant', but it proved to be false.³⁷ The marriage was to be childless, but despite an age difference of 28 years and Anson's more reserved character, there is little doubt that they were happy. As Mary Delany commented, 'If you hear of any reports of a disagreement between Lord Anson and his Lady, you may contradict them – *there have never been any*'.³⁸ Anson's only cause for concern was Elizabeth's indifferent health: although she was 'lively & sprightly in nature', she was frequently ill and was to die prematurely. Only a few months after her marriage Lord Hardwicke expressed concern that her 'feverish disorder' might return and asked Anson 'to make use of your

---

32 Bedfordshire Archives: Wrest Park Archive, L30/21/1/3, Elizabeth Anson to Catherine Talbot, [1748].
33 Earl of Hardwicke to the Duke of Newcastle, 4 October 1748, in Yorke (ed.), *The Life and Correspondence*, vol.I, p.678.
34 Quoted in Joyce Godber, *The Marchioness Grey of Wrest Park*, Publications of the Bedfordshire Historical Record Society, vol.XLVII (Bedford: Bedfordshire Historical Record Society, 1968), p.66.
35 Catherine Talbot, *Journal* (1751) quoted in Jemima Hubberstey, '"The only place that can heighten my enjoyment of my friends": The literary coterie at Wrest Park', *The History of Parliament*, https://thehistoryofparliament.wordpress.com/2020/03/05/the-only-place-that-can-heighten-my-enjoyment-of-my-friends-the-literary-coterie-at-wrest-park>, accessed 10 October 2022.
36 Lewis (ed.), *The Yale Edition of the Correspondence of Horace Walpole*, vol.41, p.240, fn.1.
37 Fanny Boscawen to Edward Boscawen, 21 June 1748, in Aspinall-Oglander, *Admiral's Wife*, p.86.
38 Mary Delany to Mrs Dewes, 26 November 1749, in Lady Llanover (ed.), *The Autobiography and Correspondence of Mary Granville, Mrs Delany* (London: Richard Bentley, 1861), vol.II, p.524.

authority with her'. He commented: 'she has great spirits, rather superior to her strength, and is always inclined to make the best of her case. It is therefore necessary, on such occasions, to look a little beyond her own representations'.[39]

Despite his increasing workload as a rising politician, the Ansons made regular visits to Shugborough, Wimpole (Lord Hardwicke's estate near Cambridge) and Wrest, went on holiday to Yorkshire and enjoyed family trips up the Thames in the Admiralty barge. His visits to Shugborough were often combined with attendance at the Lichfield Races, one of the leading meetings in the Midlands, and on one occasion Thomas advised him that his presence there during the first week in September was 'absolutely necessary upon public and political considerations'.[40] Elizabeth often visited Shugborough alone, establishing a close relationship with Thomas, for whom she had a high regard. They made several journeys together exploring the landscapes and country houses of Staffordshire, Derbyshire and Yorkshire.

During her marriage, Elizabeth became a prominent society figure who moved in leading political and intellectual circles. The novelist Henry Fielding referred to her 'humanity' but Mary Delany had some reservations about her character: 'she is a little coxcombical, and affects to be learned, which may sometimes put him out of countenance; but Lord Anson is a most generous, good natured, amiable man, and he deserved a wife of more dignity'.[41] Such criticisms seem wide of the mark and, as we shall see, she gave invaluable support to her husband, providing him with political intelligence and frequently acting informally as his private secretary, particularly after he was appointed as First Lord. According to Thomas Anson, Elizabeth was 'the best correspondent in the world' and also claimed, rather unconvincingly, that she was to turn her husband into a 'very good one'.[42] Anson in fact was a notoriously unreliable correspondent who disliked writing letters or dealing with paper, as he admitted to George Rodney: 'I find you have dropped me as a correspondent because I have not been punctual in answering your letters; don't ascribe it to anything but the real cause, indolence and an aversion to writing'.[43] His lack of enthusiasm is confirmed by his relatively few surviving letters, which were concise and to the point, often consisting of little more than a few scrawled notes.

When she died prematurely, Walpole was to describe Elizabeth as 'exceedingly good-humoured, and did a thousand good-natured and generous actions',[44] but he had previously been unable to resist spreading scurrilous rumours about the state of her marriage because of his intense hostility to Lord Anson as a leading member of the Newcastle administration. His correspondence includes several references to Anson's alleged impotence, including a story that Lord Hardwicke had been warned that if he 'gave his daughter to the Admiral,

---

39 BL: Anson Papers, Add. MS. 15,956, f.13, Lord Hardwicke to George Anson, 30 August 1748.
40 BL: Anson Papers, Add. MS. 15,955, f.66, Thomas Anson to George Anson, [1747].
41 Mary Delany to Mrs Dewes, 26 November 1749, in Llanover (ed.), *The Autobiography and Correspondence of Mary Granville*, vol.II, p.524.
42 BL: Anson Papers, Add. MS. 15,955, f.93, Thomas Anson to George Anson, 26 August 1749.
43 George Anson to George Rodney, 10 November 1747, in David Syrett (ed.), *The Rodney Papers: Selections from the Correspondence of Admiral Lord Rodney* (Aldershot: Ashgate, 2005), vol.I, p.119.
44 Horace Walpole to the Earl of Stafford, 7 June 1760, in Lewis (ed.), *The Yale Edition of the Correspondence of Horace Walpole*, vol.35, p.302.

he would be obliged hereafter to pronounce a sentence of dissolution to the marriage'.[45] He maintained that the marriage was never consummated and, in December 1748, he quoted the diplomat Sir Charles Williams as saying that '"my Lord Anson has been around the world but never in it". My Lady T[ownshend] says, "It is just his case with his wife". It is imagined that he is as little made for a tête-à-tête as for society'.[46]

Before his marriage, the Admiralty had been his principal residence in the capital but in 1748 he purchased a substantial townhouse, 15 St James's Square (later Lichfield House), from Henry Hyde, fourth Earl of Clarendon. Three years later he employed the architect Matthew Brettingham the Elder, one the leading architects of his generation, to survey the house but little work seems to have been done and it is not known how much time the Ansons spent there. Anson left the house to Thomas who rebuilt it between 1763 and 1766. Anson continued to use his Admiralty accommodation throughout his tenure as First Lord except for a brief period following his dismissal in 1756 when he lived at 14 Downing Street.

Early in 1749, the Ansons leased Carshalton House near Croydon in Surrey as their country retreat, where they lived for the first few years of their marriage.[47] Some 12 miles from the Admiralty in Whitehall, it was 'a handsome country residence, comprising a mansion and pleasure grounds'.[48] The property had been owned by the Earl of Hardwicke between 1731 and 1740 and this family connection persuaded Lord Anson to take up residence there. According to Joseph Yorke, who visited the estate shortly before the Ansons moved in, his sister had fond childhood memories of the place: 'I wish you joy of Carshalton, which, I am sure, gives you great pleasure & I am persuaded Lord Anson will like it as much as you do when he comes to know the beauties of it'.[49] Joseph referred to a letter from Elizabeth which described her early life at Carshalton: 'I enjoyed excessively the ideas which struck you upon inhabiting the same place as mistress of it, where formerly one was constrained by the looks of Papa and Mama. I dare say you were much surprised to find you could go out when you pleased, and I question whether you had half the inclination to go out you had then'.[50] Anson terminated the lease in 1752 when he acquired Moor Park in Hertfordshire as his new country estate.

Shortly after his marriage, in May 1748, Anson was promoted to admiral of the blue and the authorised history of his circumnavigation – *A Voyage Round the World by George Anson* by Richard Walter – was published.[51] The book included 42 engravings, most of

---

45 Horace Walpole to the Earl of Montagu, 18 May 1748, in Lewis (ed.), *The Yale Edition of the Correspondence of Horace Walpole*, vol.9, p.54.
46 Horace Walpole to Horace Mann, 15 December 1748, in Lewis (ed.), *The Yale Edition of the Correspondence of Horace Walpole*, vol.20, p.13.
47 A.E. Jones, *The Story of Carshalton House* (Sutton: London Borough of Sutton Library and Arts Services, 1980).
48 George Harris, *The Life of Lord Chancellor Hardwicke: With Selections from his Correspondence, Diaries, Speeches, and Judgments* (London: E. Moxon, 1847), vol.I, p.263.
49 Quoted in Jones, *The Story of Carshalton House*, p.59.
50 Joseph Yorke to Elizabeth Anson, 12 July 1749, in Yorke (ed.), *The Life and Correspondence*, vol.II, p.168.
51 *A Voyage Round the World, in the Years MDCCXL, I, II, III, IV. By George Anson, Esq; Commander in Chief of a Squadron of His Majesty's Ships, Sent upon an Expedition to the South-Seas. Compiled from Papers and other Materials of the Right Honourable George Lord Anson, and Published under his Direction, by Richard Walter, M.A. Chaplain of his Majesty's Ship the Centurion, in that Expedition* (London: J. and P. Knapton, 1748).

which were based on drawings by Peircy Brett. There were 1,800 advance subscribers to the first edition and three more editions appeared before the end of the year. It was serialised in *The Gentleman's Magazine*, extracts were widely published in the national press, and it was soon translated into French, German and Dutch. The book remained in constant demand and, by 1781, 16 editions and numerous reprints had appeared.

The first account of the voyage had been published as early as 1743 and Anson announced his intention to produce his own history in September 1744, but the project was delayed. At some point Anson commissioned Richard Walter, former chaplain of the *Centurion*, to prepare a draft and, although the book would appear in his sole name, he was not the only author. According to Thomas Birch, Anson soon became unhappy with Walter's lack of progress and he turned to Benjamin Robins for help. Robins was a mathematician, engineer and pamphleteer who had been elected as a fellow of the Royal Society in 1727 when he was only 20 years of age. In 1742, he published *New Principles of Gunnery*, which reported the results of his experiments to improve the accuracy and effectiveness of cannon shot. In August 1746, Anson met Robins at Portsmouth to discuss the book and offered him a fee of £1,000 to finalise the draft.

Although the division of labour between Walter and Robins cannot be established with any certainty, there is no doubt that the book was produced in close consultation with Anson and was not, in any sense, an independent history.[52] Walter's wife, who was to assert her late husband's claim to be the principal author, reported that she had 'frequently heard him say how closely he had been engaged in writing for some hours to prepare for his constant attendance upon Lord Anson at six every morning for his approbation as his Lordship overlooked every sheet that was written'.[53] In view of his close involvement, it is not surprising that he was at the centre of the narrative and always 'appeared in the third person as Mr Anson… detached, serene, judicious and wise. Although this was a deliberate literary construction, other accounts confirm that Anson wore the "mask of command", a potent blend of authority and detachment'.[54] In Anson's hands, the book was far more than a detailed travelogue and devoted much space to discussing the circumnavigation from several different perspectives, including navigation, natural history, Spanish trade and future strategic opportunities.

According to Thomas Birch, the official history was received 'with general applause and admiration' and went on to become the best-selling travel book of the century; it was widely read in Europe, making 'Anson famous across the literate world'. The book stimulated a growing interest in the Pacific, which led to further exploration later in the century, and Charles Darwin would read it during his voyage on the *Beagle*, 1831–1836. However, Birch did also acknowledge that there was some criticism of the book for personal or political reasons. These included 'Lord Bath and his friends' who dismissed it as 'a gross panegyric upon him', while Horace Walpole, who found the book 'very silly and contradictory', ridiculed Anson's account of 'what they would have done if they had set out two months sooner; and that was no less than conquering Peru and Mexico with this disabled

---

52 See Williams, *The Prize of All the Oceans*, pp.237–241, for a discussion of the authorship of *Anson's Voyage*.
53 Jane Walter to John Walter, 16 June 1789, in Williams (ed.), *Documents*, p. 284.
54 Lambert, *Crusoe's Island*, p.92.

army'.⁵⁵ Birch also reported that 'divines complain of the total absence of piety and religion throughout the work'.

The official account of Anson's two difficult visits to China was widely commented upon. In particular, the accuracy of the report of his meeting with the Viceroy in Canton was questioned as some readers did not believe that he could have played such a prominent role in the proceedings. The book's criticisms of the Chinese also came as a surprise as they were in sharp contrast to 'two centuries of European writing that depicted China as an incredibly wealthy, well-ordered, peaceful and powerful empire'.⁵⁶ Criticisms of the East India Company may well have been less of a surprise to the book's readers, but the supercargo Edward Page, who was flattered when Anson visited him at his London house, was very disappointed by what he read. He commented that he was:

> Greatly surprised at the gloss he had put upon the transactions at Canton. We had lived in perfect harmony and friendship all the time. The little debates we had about his visit, and the mischiefs that might follow if he should go to resent the Vice Roy's not seeing him, were when we were by ourselves, and never in publick company.⁵⁷

In response, Page gave his version of the events in the autumn of 1743 in *A Little Secret History of Affairs at Canton in the Year 1743* (1765), but the manuscript was never published. He claimed that the arrival of the *Centurion* had 'given disgust' and it proved impossible for Company officers 'to remove all the prejudices the Chinese had conceived against a ship coming into their river, who had taken the money that was bringing to their port, and a ship that refused to pay measurage, of which there had never been any precedent'.⁵⁸ His comments reflected the need for Company officials to proceed cautiously in their dealings with the Chinese to avoid losing their valuable trading concessions.

There was less public interest in Anson's varied policy recommendations, which were discussed at length in the book, but his proposal to establish British bases in the South Atlantic and the South Pacific based on a new exploration of those seas attracted support from within Government. He drew attention to the importance of the Falkland Islands, which were then uninhabited, and recommended that Britain should colonise them. This would enable English warships and merchantmen to be resupplied before sailing around Cape Horn. He also proposed that the Juan Fernandez Islands should be developed as a second permanent base, which would enable warships to resupply and, as a result, a voyage could be 'made from *Falkland's* Isles to *Juan Fernandez* and back again, in little more than two months. This, even in time of peace, might be of great consequence to this nation, and, in time of war, would make us masters of those seas'.⁵⁹

---

55   Horace Walpole to the Earl of Montagu, 18 May 1760, in Lewis (ed.), *The Yale Edition of the Correspondence of Horace Walpole*, vol.9, p.55.
56   Robert Markley, 'Anson at Canton, 1743: Obligation, Exchange, and Ritual in Edward Page's "Secret History"', in Linda Zionkowski and Cynthia Klekar (eds.), *The Culture of the Gift in Eighteenth-Century England* (Basingstoke: Palgrave Macmillan, 2009), p.218.
57   OHS: MS. 2,894, pp.47–48.
58   OHS: MS. 2,894, p.61.
59   Walter, *A Voyage Round the World*, p.97.

Eager to progress these recommendations, Anson developed plans for a voyage to survey the Falklands, Patagonia and Tierra del Fuego before sailing to Juan Fernandez. He secured the King's agreement that 'two sloops should be forthwith fitted to be sent on discoverys in the southern latitude' and reported the decision to members of the Admiralty Board in January 1749.[60] Under the approved plan, they would call at Juan Fernandez before heading west across the Southern Pacific in the direction of New Holland (now Australia). Captain John Campbell (who had served on the *Centurion*) was appointed to command the expedition, which would consist of two sloops – *Porcupine* and *Raven* – and work on fitting them out progressed in March and April. But within months the expedition was abandoned in the face of strong opposition from Spain, which continued to believe that it had exclusive territorial rights in the Pacific. Britain had every reason to avoid antagonising Spain at a time when the two countries were negotiating a new commercial treaty, which she hoped would give her 'most-favoured-nation' status and other concessions.

Forced to abandon his original plan, Anson examined an alternative – a search for a northern passage to the Pacific – and the fitting out of the two sloops continued during the summer. He worked on proposals for an expedition from the north-east into the Arctic Ocean and also sought information about the costs of a voyage in search of the north-west passage.[61] Anson's interest in the north-east passage was later confirmed by a merchant who had proposed sending an expedition:

> I had a visit from Lord Anson... his Lordship approv'd very much of my plan – but was of opinion that it ought to be executed by government. Said that he had two ships which had been intended to be sent to the South Seas and that he would get Capt Dennis [sic] and Captain Campbell to take command of them.[62]

The proposal came to nothing and other priorities prevented Anson from pursuing his ideas for further explorations. Despite these setbacks, Anson had succeeded in focusing attention on the strategic importance of the South Sea and it has been argued that his plans for an expedition to the Falkland Islands and Juan Fernandez 'should be seen as the real beginning of the British exploration of the Pacific Ocean in the second half of the eighteenth century'.[63]

The next Pacific expedition, which did not sail from England until 1764, was based on a modified version of Anson's 1749 plan. Commanded by Commodore John Byron ('Foul-Weather Jack'), who had served as a midshipman on the *Wager* during the voyage around the world, the expedition annexed the Falkland Islands in January 1765 before entering the South Pacific. Soon after receiving Byron's report on the islands, John Perceval, second Earl of Egmont, First Lord of the Admiralty, 1763–1766, commented that they were 'the key to

---

60 TNA: ADM 3/60, Minutes of the Board of Admiralty, 19 January 1749.
61 SRO: Anson Family Papers, D615/P(S)/1/9/37A, John Holland to George Anson, 5 December 1748.
62 Cramond to G.L. Scott, 24 December 1772, in J.C. Beaglehole (ed.), *The Journals of Captain Cook: The Voyage of the Resolution and Discovery 1776–1780*, The Hakluyt Society (Cambridge: Cambridge University Press, 1967), p.li.
63 Alan Frost and Glyndwr Williams, 'The Beginnings of Britain's Exploration of the Pacific Ocean in the Eighteenth Century', *The Mariner's Mirror*, 83 (1997), p.411.

the whole Pacifick Ocean',⁶⁴ confirming Anson's judgement of their significance. Although he expressed regrets that he had not been able to establish a settlement on the Falklands, there is little doubt that Anson 'did more than any other person either before or since to draw attention to their importance; in fact, had it not been for Lord Anson's recommendations it is doubtful whether the Union Jack would now be flying over the colony'.⁶⁵

Anson also wanted to contribute to the 'safety and success of future navigators' and in the introduction to the official history made the case for the 'pursuit of all kinds of geographical and nautical observations and of every species of mechanical and commercial information'.⁶⁶ He recommended that every officer should take nautical measurements as part of his normal duties, while specialists with an engineering background who were skilled in drawing and surveying should be responsible for preparing charts and views of the coast. Without them, navigation would be at a 'full stand', but no action to implement these recommendations was taken during Anson's time at the Admiralty. It was not until 1795 that the post of Hydrographer of the Navy, who was responsible for the production of charts, was established, replacing previous arrangements where this duty fell to individual captains.

Surprisingly, Anson did not refer to the threat posed by scurvy in the introduction despite the frequent references to the devastation it had caused in the main narrative. However, his experiences did not throw any new light on the causes of scurvy or suggest any possible cures and, in 1746, he had informed Bedford of his mistaken belief that 'wort' – unfermented beer – was a healthy drink that could act as a remedy.⁶⁷ Soon after his return to England, Anson met Richard Mead, a leading physician, who wanted a first-hand account of his experience of scurvy during the voyage. As a result of this briefing, Mead concluded, quite incorrectly, that scurvy was caused by putrid air at sea and he became an advocate of one of the mechanical devices then being developed to improve ventilation below deck, an initiative which Anson supported.⁶⁸

In a more promising development, the huge loss of life on the circumnavigation prompted Dr James Lind, a naval surgeon, to start investigating the disease. He conducted clinical trials on board the *Salisbury*, which suggested that a daily allowance of oranges and lemons had a beneficial effect, and he published the results of his trials in *A Treatise of the Scurvy* (1753), which was dedicated to Lord Anson. His proposals included an antiscorbutic diet based on preserved lemon juice (a process which destroyed the beneficial vitamin C it contained) together with cleanliness and fresh air as effective preventative measures. Despite the results of the trials, Lind attributed the disease to multiple causes, which included the salt used to preserve meat and the absence of fresh fruit in the seamen's diet, and he failed to make a specific recommendation to the Admiralty on the supply of citrus fruit to the fleet.⁶⁹

---

64 TNA: SP 94/253, f.238: Earl of Egmont to the Duke of Grafton, 20 July 1765.
65 William L. Allardyce, *The Story of the Falkland Islands. An Account of their Discovery and Early History, 1500–1843* (Falkland Islands: Government Printing Office, 1909), p.9.
66 Walter, *A Voyage Round the World*, p.14.
67 Woburn MSS: vol.XIII, f.23, George Anson to the Duke of Bedford, 21 August 1746.
68 Kevin Brown, *Poxed and Scurvied: The Story of Sickness and Health at Sea* (Barnsley: Seaforth, 2011), p.65.
69 U. Tröhler, 'Lind and Scurvy: 1747 to 1795', *Journal of the Royal Society of Medicine*, 98 (2005), pp.519–522.

Without clearer scientific evidence, the navy's preferred treatments for scurvy continued to be an elixir of vitriol (a mixture of sulfuric acid and alcohol) and vinegar. Lind's proposals were not taken up by Anson's Admiralty and official scepticism of the value of citrus fruits as antiscorbutics continued until 1795 when lemon and lime juice were first regularly distributed to the fleet. By this time, a method of preserving the juice without destroying its beneficial properties had been found. Although Anson did not authorise the distribution of citrus fruits, he acknowledged that 'sickness has been a sore enemy to us' and acted to improve the seaman's diet.[70] He had previously recognised the health benefits of ensuring a regular supply of fresh meat and green vegetables for some seamen although his belief that they were a treatment for scurvy was incorrect. He also supported the plan to establish naval hospitals rather than relying on hospital ships or rented accommodation. As mentioned above, the first naval hospital opened at Haslar, near Portsmouth, in 1753 and five years later Anson appointed James Lind as its chief physician.

Encouraged by the great success of the official account, Anson commissioned Robins to produce a second volume of 'nautical observations' which, in August 1749, Elizabeth Anson had expected to appear imminently.[71] When Robins was appointed as Engineer General of the East India Company, Anson wrote to him, on 22 October, asking whether 'you intended to publish the second volume of my "Voyage" before you leave us, which, I confess, I am very sorry for. If you should have laid aside all thoughts of favouring the world with more of your works, it will be much disappointed'.[72] There is no record of Robins' reply but a second volume never appeared. He died prematurely at Fort St David near Cuddalore in India in 1751 and no trace of the manuscript could be found amongst his papers.

Since 1747, Anson had supported Robins' career by facilitating his employment as an engineer in the Netherlands, describing him as the 'perfect master of all the theory of that science… He has an excellent understanding, and great firmness of temper'.[73] He could see the potential of Robins' experimental work on naval gunnery in the late 1740s, which built on the findings he had reported in *New Principles of Gunnery*, and actively supported him.[74] Anson's patronage was of 'great benefit to him, not only in securing for him the means of varied experiment with all types of gun in use in the Royal Navy, but by the encouragement which his Lordship gave him to publish his opinions even when they were in conflict with the orthodox opinion of the day'.[75] For example, in a letter to Lord Anson, read at the Royal Society in October 1749, Robins reported on his extensive experiments with an 18-pounder cannon at Chatham. He explained that the subject of his experiments 'relates to a matter about which I have formerly troubled your Lordship; I mean, the diminishing allotment

---

70 BL: Newcastle Papers, Add. MS. 32,865, f.208, George Anson to the Duke of Newcastle, 5 June 1756.
71 Elizabeth Anson to Thomas Birch, 2 August 1749, in *The Oriental Herald and Journal of General Literature*, 10 (1826), p.290.
72 George Anson to Benjamin Robins, 22 October 1749, in John Nichols, *Literary Anecdotes of the Eighteenth Century* (London: Nichols, Son, and Bentley, 1812), vol.II, p.206.
73 George Anson to the Duke of Bedford, 25 August 1747, in Russell, *Correspondence of John, Fourth Duke of Bedford*, vol.I, p.241.
74 Anthony Bruce, 'Benjamin Robins and the Science of Naval Gunnery', *The Trafalgar Chronicle*, New Series, 7 (2022), pp.37–47.
75 Frederick L. Robertson, *The Evolution of Naval Armament* (London: Constable, 1914), p.121.

of powder for heavy cannon, and thereby facilitating the reduction in the weight of these pieces.[76]

Despite Anson's support and some expressions of interest in the navy, it was not until the 1770s that a practical design – the carronade – derived from Robins' ideas would appear although new long guns based on his findings were produced much earlier. During the time he benefited from Anson's patronage, he also produced papers on the benefits of rifling in small arms and ordnance and on the use of rockets for naval purposes. Robins also collaborated with Anson in efforts to speed up the process of loading naval guns, which included plans to fit gunlocks (a modified version of the flintlock musket's firing mechanism) and to use flannel instead of paper for making cartridges.[77]

Anson's role as acting First Lord came to an end when Lord Sandwich returned to London following the conclusion of the peace negotiations which brought the war to an end in 1748. During his final two years in office, Sandwich continued the programme of reform that had begun in 1744 and he focused on two priority areas – naval discipline and the performance of the dockyards. While Sandwich led on dockyard reform, Anson played a key role in developing comprehensive proposals to strengthen naval discipline by updating the Articles of War – the navy's disciplinary code.[78] Developed in conjunction with fellow Admiralty Commissioner Lord Barrington, they were embodied in a Bill 'for amending, explaining, and reducing into one act of Parliament the laws relating to the government of his Majesty's ships' that was submitted to the House of Commons in February 1749.

The new articles, which were perhaps the most significant naval reform of the 1740s, were intended to replace the existing disciplinary code, which had been issued by Charles II in 1661. This was later supplemented by the *Fighting Instructions* and by the *Regulations and Instructions relating to His Majesty's Service at Sea* (first issued in 1731) as well as by individual laws passed by Parliament since then. In contrast to civil law, which was based on individual laws and precedents created over many years, Anson's legislation established a single naval penal code, which gave the Articles their 'special character' as a parallel jurisdiction.[79] Apart from consolidating existing laws, the main purpose of the legislation was to strengthen discipline among naval officers, encourage them to perform more effectively in combat and impose severe penalties for cowardice. It included clauses which would render half-pay officers liable to naval discipline, bringing them under much closer Admiralty control. The legislation also defined the boundaries between the army and navy by limiting officers' authority to their own services. The legislation included clauses which increased the severity of punishments for some offences, removed the ability of courts-martial to vary such sentences and made several other changes.[80]

---

76   Benjamin Robins, 'A Letter to Lord Anson. Read 26th of October 1749', in *Mathematical Tracts of the Late Benjamin Robins Esq* (London: J. Nourse, 1761), vol.I, p.306.
77   Peter Padfield, *Guns at Sea* (New York: St Martin's Press, 1974), p.102.
78   N.A.M. Rodger, *Articles of War: The Statutes which Governed our Fighting Navies 1661, 1749 and 1866* (Havant: Kenneth Mason, 1982).
79   Marcus Eder, *Crime and Punishment in the Royal Navy of the Seven Years War, 1755–1763* (Aldershot: Ashgate, 2004), p.151.
80   Reginald Acland, 'The Naval Articles of War', *Journal of Comparative Legislation and International Law*, Third Series, 3 (1921), pp.190–201.

The articles of 1661 gave courts-martial the power to sentence those convicted of serious offences to death 'or in such other way as the court shall decide', but this discretion – which had been frequently misused during the last war – was significantly reduced in Anson's revised articles. Death was now the only possible sentence for officers 'who shall treacherously or cowardly yield or cry for quarter' (Article 10); for those who hold back in action (Article 12); fail to pursue an enemy or 'relieve a known friend in sight' (Article 13); and for making mutinous assemblies (Article 19). It was under Article 12 that Admiral Byng was to be charged and convicted following the loss of Minorca in 1756, with the result that his court-martial had no choice but to sentence him to death on finding him guilty.

For some other offences, the discretion to impose lesser punishments as an alternative to death was introduced for the first time. These included simple desertion, deliberate destruction of naval ships, and spying and supporting the enemy. Courts-martial were not able to impose the death penalty in cases of embezzlement or the waste of naval stores. The revised Articles also included a strengthened clause (Article 9), which was designed to prevent the ill-treatment of prisoners of war, with a court-martial being given the discretion to impose an appropriate punishment. This measure was a direct reflection of Anson's views and past conduct, with his humane treatment of prisoners during the circumnavigation being widely praised.

The legislation included a significant new measure which required officers on half-pay to obey orders to return to active duty and made them subject to a court-martial if they refused. Under clause 34 of the Bill, 'all half-pay officers belonging to his Majesty's navy, when ordered upon service… shall, in case of their disobedience to such commands, be liable to be tried and punished by a court-martial'. This replaced the existing penalties for refusing to serve, which included stopping half-pay and preventing a future return to the service. Anson believed that under the existing rules half-pay officers could escape their obligations too easily by resigning their commissions and more effective penalties were needed. The new clause would place all officers on an equal footing but, despite the clear justification for the change, it soon came under heavy attack, with Horace Walpole, reporting that it was 'vehemently opposed by half the fleet, headed by Sir Peter Warren'.[81]

Anson developed the half-pay proposals in consultation with Prince William, Duke of Cumberland, captain general of the army, who introduced a similar measure affecting army officers in the 1749 Mutiny Bill. It passed through Parliament at the same time as the Navy Bill and was equally unpopular. In writing about the navy legislation, Walpole wrote that:

> My Lord Anson, who governed at the Admiralty Board, was struck with so amiable a pattern, and would have chained down his tars to a like oar; but it raised such a ferment in that boisterous profession, that the Ministry were forced to drop several of the strongest articles, to quiet the tempest that this innovation had caused.[82]

Opponents of the Bill included the Prince of Wales and his political allies as well as a large group of naval officers, whose objections focused on the half-pay proposals. The patriot

---

81   Horace Walpole to Horace Mann, 4 March 1749, in Lewis (ed.), *The Yale Edition of the Correspondence of Horace Walpole*, vol.20, p.33.
82   Horace Walpole, *Memoirs of the Reign of King George II* (London: H. Colburn, 1846), vol.I, p.38.

Vice Admiral Sir Peter Warren, engraving by William Ridley.
(New York Public Library)

press disliked other aspects of the legislation, claiming that it gave the Admiralty excessive power and elevated martial law over common law. The Bill's opponents argued that half-pay was a reward for past service rather than a retainer for the future and the change would force these officers to accept whatever service they were offered, however dangerous or unattractive it might be. In the wrong hands, the legislation would give the Admiralty the power 'to persecute political and service rivals by appointing them to posts unacceptable by reason of rank and seniority, and then have them broken by court-martial for refusing to assume them'.[83]

Captain Augustus Hervey, who played a leading role in the campaign against the Bill, explained the arguments against clause 34 in a pamphlet published anonymously.[84] On 19

---

83 Erskine (ed.), *Augustus Hervey's Journal*, p.78.
84 [Augustus Hervey], *A Letter from a Friend in the Country to a Friend at Will's Coffee-House; in Relation to Three Additional Articles of War* (London: J. Bromage, 1749).

February, he discussed the Bill with the Prince of Wales, who 'spoke of the hardship of it' and said it was shameful for Lord Anson to make 'so many brave men slaves'.[85] A petition against the clause, which was signed by 50 officers, was submitted to Lord Sandwich in advance of a meeting with members of the Admiralty Board on 21 February. It claimed that the offending clause would 'lessen the ardour of the truly gallant & faithful officer in taking away that liberty which must ever animate him in defence of his king and country'.[86] In responding to the petition, Sandwich justified the proposal and complained that recent meetings on the Bill had been 'mutinous, seditious, and not to be paralleled in a civilised country' before bringing the meeting to an end. His arguments may have persuaded some officers to sign a counter-petition in support of the Bill, which was submitted to the Admiralty shortly afterwards.[87] It was signed by 96 officers, including some of Anson's closest associates – Keppel, Saunders, Brett and Denis – and several flag officers, including Hawke, Byng and Ogle.

On 24 February, a petition against the Bill was presented to the House of Commons by John Norris and with naval opposition to the measure increasing, Anson, as the principal architect of the measure, 'grows every day into new unpopularity', according to Horace Walpole.[88] Anson lobbied MPs in support of the Bill, including his brother Thomas, who received a letter which Elizabeth sent on his behalf: 'I am commissioned by my Lord to desire Mr Anson will be so good as not to forget how material his presence must be to the poor Navy Bill, for want of which, like an exposed foundling, it was very near being thrown out of the House the day of the adjournment'.[89] However, with ministers divided and Parliamentary opposition increasing, the Admiralty abandoned hopes of a compromise and backed down. It amended clause 34 at report stage in the Commons so that only those on 'actual service and full pay, and part of the crew in or belonging to any of His Majesty's ships or vessels of war who shall be guilty of mutiny, desertion or disobedience to any lawful command... shall be liable to be tried by a court-martial'.[90] In this revised form, Anson's Articles were to remain in force for more than a century, until they were replaced by the Naval Discipline Act, 1866. Despite the defeat of his half-pay proposals, Anson had made considerable progress in addressing the discipline problems that the Bedford Admiralty faced when it came to office in 1744. The enactment of the 1749 legislation meant that the Admiralty 'now had some, though not all, of the means it had sought to impose courage and discipline, and during the Seven Years War the example of Byng, and the leadership of Anson, visibly strengthened the sea officers' professional standards'.[91]

In his second pamphlet on the Bill, Hervey had described the Admiralty Board as 'a medley of Court nobility, broken squires, and now and then a solitary, nominal sea-officer or two,

---

85   Erskine (ed.), *Augustus Hervey's Journal*, p.81.
86   TNA: ADM 3/60, *Admiralty Board minutes*, 20 February 1749.
87   TNA: ADM 1/578.
88   Horace Walpole to Horace Mann, 23 March 1749, in Lewis (ed.), *The Yale Edition of the Correspondence of Horace Walpole*, vol.20, p.38.
89   Elizabeth Anson to Thomas Anson, 28 March 1749, in Josiah C. Wedgwood, *Staffordshire Parliamentary History from the Earliest Times to the Present Day* (London: Harrison and Sons, 1920), vol.II, p.262.
90   *An Act for Amending, Explaining and Reducing into one Act of Parliament, the Laws Relating to the Government of His Majesty's Ships, Vessels and Forces by Sea* (1749; 22 George II c.33).
91   Rodger, *The Command of the Ocean*, p.326.

who sit there and sleep for their salaries'.[92] It is perhaps not surprising that Hervey's hostile attitudes provoked a response and he acknowledged that both 'the Duke of Cumberland and Lord Anson was [sic] very angry with me', but this did not prevent Hervey being reappointed as captain of the *Phoenix* (20) in 1752.[93] Anson's anger also extended to other naval officers who had been involved in the protests. His friendship with Peter Warren was severely tested as a result of his campaign against the Bill, although he never acted against him. George Rodney also had reason to regret voting in the Commons contrary to Anson's wishes as he claimed it still apparently affected his attitudes towards him nearly 10 years later. In a letter to George Grenville, he said: 'You know him; you remember the Navy Bill, you know his resentment, and in case a squadron should be ordered to winter in that part of the world [America], if he thinks it will be disagreeable to me, I know if left to him my ship will be the one that stays'.[94]

With the Navy Act on the statute books, Anson and Sandwich turned their attention to the six royal dockyards, the largest employer in the mid-eighteenth-century British economy, with a labour force of about 7,000 men in 1749. They recognised that there was a longstanding need to increase the efficiency of the dockyards, whose failings had become increasingly apparent during the last war. The navy was also faced with the need to make peacetime economies as the Government sought to reduce the national debt by cutting expenditure across the board. Although the Navy Board had reduced the dockyard labour force at the end of the war, numbers were still high compared to earlier periods and the Admiralty believed there was scope for further reductions. It increasingly questioned the effectiveness of the Navy Board's management of the dockyards because it was reluctant to make further cuts to the labour force or to address concerns about excessive costs and delays in completing ship repairs. It was also unwilling to deal with a conservative workforce that was resistant to change. By 1749, the death of Jacob Acworth and the retirement of the elderly Comptroller Richard Haddock raised hopes that at least one barrier to innovation had been removed and that Admiralty intervention in the dockyards might produce much-needed changes.

On 9 June, the Admiralty Board decided on its next steps. With the Navy Board reluctant to answer its repeated requests for information, Sandwich, Anson and other members of the Board decided that they would visit every yard themselves.[95] A visit would be unprecedented but was essential if the Admiralty were to make an independent assessment of the yards' performance, which would then place it in a much stronger position in future dealings with the Navy Board. It is not clear who first proposed the idea of an Admiralty visitation, but there is no evidence that Anson had any particular interest in dockyard management or reform and during his eleven-year tenure as First Lord, he never made another inspection of the yards. Sandwich, on the other hand, introduced annual dockyard inspections when he returned to the Admiralty as First Lord in 1771.

The Admiralty visitations in the summer of 1749 were intended:

---

92 [Augustus Hervey], *A Detection of the Considerations on the Navy-Bill*. By a Seaman (London: W. Owen, 1749), p.9.
93 Erskine (ed.), *Augustus Hervey's Journal*, p.83.
94 George Rodney to George Grenville, 15 March 1758, in Smith (ed.), *The Grenville Papers*, vol.I, p.232.
95 TNA: ADM 7/658, *Minutes of Visitation to the Dock Yards*, 1749.

> To examine into & become acquainted with the abilities and conduct of the officers, the sufficiency of the workmen, the condition of the ships and magazines, together with what works were carrying on, that such reformations might be made as should be found needful to prevent any unnecessary expense.[96]

Inspections were expected to lead to greater productivity as they hoped to ensure:

> That the officers paid due obedience to their instructions, that the several rules & orders for the government of the yards were punctually carried into execution, that the ships of the Royal Navy were kept in condition for service, and the money granted [by Parliament] was frugally expended.[97]

Anson was present at the visits to all six yards, which began with an inspection of the Woolwich yard towards the end of June.[98] Although examples of good practice and a trial of piece work ('task work') – payment according to the work produced as a means of increasing productivity – were found, the visiting party soon uncovered numerous problems and abuses: standing orders were largely ignored, buildings had been neglected, the men were poorly supervised and accounts were often in arrears. The was evidence of over-manning, while the ships in Ordinary (out of service for repairs or maintenance) were not being properly maintained. There were too many old and underperforming workmen who could not be removed and for whom there was no pension provision. The dockyard workers' right to take 'chips' – timber offcuts which they could use to heat their homes – was widely abused and large quantities of valuable wood were routinely stolen and resold. Another common abuse was the payment of overtime for hours that had not been worked so that dockyard managers could match the significantly higher wages paid to shipwrights in private yards, particularly in wartime.

The inspections were completed by mid-August and a list of 14 recommendations was agreed upon and sent to the Navy Board in November. The Admiralty believed that the management of the yards would be strengthened if standing orders were complied with, the men mustered frequently, and accounts submitted on time. There was scope for reducing the number of artificers and their servants. Ships should be inspected four times a year and ships in Ordinary should be better maintained, but vessels that were beyond useful service were not to have money spent on them. A programme to repair the fleet should be undertaken. Finally, the Admiralty supported the introduction of piecework in order to increase productivity.

When the inspection tour was completed, Anson hoped that the 'public will reap some benefit' from the Admiralty's efforts, but in this he was to be disappointed.[99] The Navy Board did not write to yard officers about the outcome of the visitation until March 1750, when it

---

96 James M. Haas, *A Management Odyessy. The Royal Dockyards, 1714–1914* (Lanham: University Press of America, 1994), p.17.
97 James M. Haas, 'The Royal Dockyards: The Earliest Visitations and Reform, 1749–78', *Historical Journal*, 13 (1970), p.196.
98 Richard Middleton, 'The Visitation of the Royal Dockyards, 1749', *The Mariner's Mirror*, 77 (1991), p.22.
99 BL: Anson Papers, Add. MS. 15,955, f.93, Thomas Anson to George Anson, 26 August 1749.

reported that the Admiralty had 'found several irregularities were become so general as to want a thorough reformation'. It issued 15 new regulations based on the Admiralty Board's recommendations, which it judged to be 'necessary to enforce a more strict observance of the standing orders of the navy', but they were to have little impact on the ground.[100] Some progress was made in reducing the size of the labour force – which had fallen to just over 6,000 men by the end of 1750 – but the Admiralty believed that further cuts were needed. By the time Sandwich fell from office, it was clear that the Navy Board had not acted to reduce costs and had failed to improve the efficiency of the yards, and it would be for Anson as his successor to decide how much priority to give to this issue in the future.

In July 1749, while the dockyard visits were still in progress, Lord Anson was made 'Vice Admiral of Great Britain and Lieutenant of the Admiralty thereof, and also lieutenant of the navies and seas'. The sinecure, which became vacant on the death of Sir John Norris, paid 20s a day as well as monthly allowances for 16 men at 10s each. It was awarded on merit rather than seniority but this did not prevent Lord Vere Beauclerk from resigning from the Admiralty Board and as a flag officer in protest at the promotion of his old adversary, complaining to Newcastle that 'as his Majesty has thought proper to give a junior officer a superior commission over my head, I must conclude he thinks me unfit for his service'.[101] Lord Vere's departure meant that Anson now became formally the senior naval lord although in practice he had held the position ever since he joined the Board.

According to Walpole, 'what heightened the disgust, was Lord Vere's going a party to visit the docks with Sandwich and Anson, after this was done, and yet they never mentioned it to him. It was not possible to converse with them upon good terms every day afterwards'.[102] In a letter to Thomas Birch, Elizabeth Anson said she differed from him in his opinion of Lord Vere's resignation 'not being *at all regretted*, for I, who see him every day here [at Tunbridge Wells], think it is a good deal regretted *by himself*; and though his place may be filled with *as much satisfaction to the public*, I very much doubt whether it can be with so much satisfaction to himself'.[103] When Lord Vere was created Baron Vere of Hanworth nearly a year later, Walpole recalled that he had resigned 'upon a pique with Lord Sandwich' and claimed that Anson was 'treading in the same path, and leaving the Bedfords to follow his father-in-law the Chancellor'.[104]

At about the same time, in March 1750, his increasingly close links to the Pelhams were demonstrated when Anson was made a privy councillor at Lord Hardwicke's suggestion; Hardwicke had asked Newcastle to add him to the Council because there was 'at present no seaman there'.[105] The value of his strong connections with the ruling party would soon be demonstrated again when he was selected to succeed Lord Sandwich as First Lord of the Admiralty and as a member of the Cabinet.

---

100 *Navy Board Order to All Yard Officers,* 13 March 1750, in Baugh (ed.), *Naval Administration*, p.323; Haas, 'The Royal Dockyards', p.198.
101 BL: Newcastle Papers, Add. MS. 32,718, f.315, Lord Vere Beauclerk to the Duke of Newcastle, 18 July 1749.
102 Horace Walpole to Horace Mann, 24 July 1749, in Lewis (ed.), *The Yale Edition of the Correspondence of Horace Walpole*, vol.20, p.80.
103 Elizabeth Anson to Thomas Birch, 2 August 1749, in *The Oriental Herald*, p.289.
104 Horace Walpole to Horace Mann, 2 April 1750, in Lewis (ed.), *The Yale Edition of the Correspondence of Horace Walpole*, vol.20, p.135.
105 BL: Newcastle Papers, Add. MS, 32,720, f.133, Earl of Hardwicke to the Duke of Newcastle, 9 March 1750.

7

First Lord, 1751–1756

On 12 June 1751, Sandwich was dismissed as First Lord of the Admiralty as Henry Pelham and the Duke of Newcastle moved against their opponents in the administration. Sandwich's relations with Pelham had deteriorated because he resisted expenditure cuts to the peacetime navy in line with those that had been made to the army. He had wanted to keep the navy at wartime strength so that it could respond to the continuing French threat in North America, but lost the battle. Sandwich had also fallen out with the King, who treated him 'ill, particularly by talking to Lord Anson before him on all matters relating to the fleet'.[1] However, the main reason for his removal was to provoke the resignation of the Duke of Bedford as Secretary of State for the Southern Department. The Pelhams had been unable to dismiss him because of the King's opposition but they were certain that Bedford would resign as a gesture of support for his friend and protégé. They lined up Anson to replace Sandwich. Anson, for his part, was more than willing to sever his close connections to Sandwich and Bedford if it smoothed his path to the top job he had long wanted.

Anson had already indicated that he would be willing to accept the significant reductions to the manning of the navy that his predecessor had resisted. The peacetime naval establishment had fallen to 8,000 men – a number he had previously viewed as inadequate – but he did not attempt to question it openly after his appointment and, as a result, the navy would face manpower shortages during the initial stages of the Seven Years War. Despite his acceptance of Pelham's policies of retrenchment, Anson was aware that changes to the manning system were needed if the navy were to expand rapidly in the event of another war. He had worked with Lord Barrington on the legislation, introduced in the House of Commons in 1749, to create a naval reserve of 3,000 men, who would be called up in the event of an emergency and would be paid a retainer of £10 a year. The proposal failed because of Parliamentary opposition to the cost and concerns that it might infringe civil liberties, but it would have reduced dependence on the press and increased the number of seamen who were immediately available.[2]

Anson was the first naval First Lord to be appointed since Charles Wager's resignation in 1742. He headed a Board which had overall responsibility for the navy, including its ships,

---

1   Walpole, *Memoirs of the Reign of King George II*, vol.I, p.187.
2   John S. Bromley, 'Away from Impressment: The Idea of a Royal Naval Reserve, 1696–1859', in A.C. Duke and C.A. Tamse (eds), *Britain and the Netherlands.* Anglo-Dutch Historical Conference, War & Society Series, vol.6 (The Hague: Nijhoff, 1977), pp.168–188.

officers and men, and infrastructure; as we have seen, it was the largest and most complex organisation in Europe, which at the height of the Seven Years War would have over 300 ships in commission and employ more than 100,000 men. Apart from the six royal dockyards in England, the navy had overseas bases in Minorca, Gibraltar, Antigua, Jamaica, and Halifax and associated victualling yards. As described in 1746:

> The First Lord or Commissioner of the Admiralty is in effect Lord High Admiral, having the supreme direction of the Board, and disposes affairs at his pleasure, except that no orders or commissions are valid sign'd by him alone, it being necessary for two or more to sign with him; notwithstanding which he is not to be controuled by them.[3]

Anson's 'unparalleled authority' as First Lord derived from his political standing as a close ally of Pelham, Newcastle and Hardwicke and from his professional reputation rather than from the formal powers of his office.[4] His high standing in the maritime world was recognised when he was elected in 1752 as Master of Trinity House, London, a corporation established in 1513 '"to treat and conclude upon all and singular articles anywise concerning the science or art of Mariners," and, particularly, to aid and encourage navigation, to provide for the pilotage of ships (especially the Royal Navy) into and out of port, and to relieve poor and aged mariners'.[5] His term of office as Master ended in 1756 but he remained an Elder Brother of Trinity House until his death.

Despite being the dominant voice on the Board from the outset, Anson faced similar limits to his power to those experienced by his predecessors. The Cabinet Council rather than the Admiralty decided on the funding of the navy (subject to Parliamentary approval), naval and military strategy, the deployment of fleets and the oversight of operations. Operational orders were normally issued by the Admiralty, but on some occasions they were sent directly by the relevant Secretary of State without prior consultation with the Board (as was the case during the Seven Years War when William Pitt was Secretary of State for the Southern Department). Anson could not make appointments to senior commands on his own authority but was required to put his recommendations forward to leading ministers and the King.

Despite these constraints, as a member of the Cabinet – and the inner committee – Anson was an influential voice on naval issues and he also had the opportunity to influence decisions on issues outside his direct control. His close ties to the Newcastle Whigs, his achievements at sea and his long experience at the centre of power meant that he spoke with authority when naval matters were discussed in Cabinet. His seniority was acknowledged with his appointment as one of the Lords Justices, who were responsible for running the country when the King was absent in Hanover. His views on national policy issues outside his sphere of interest have largely gone unrecorded, but he had a wider political role as a

---

3   *The Laws, Ordinances and Institutions of the Admiralty of Great Britain, Civil and Military* (London: A Millar, 1746), vol.II, p.329.
4   N.A.M. Rodger, *The Admiralty* (Lavenham: Terence Dalton, 1979), p.59.
5   Frederick Arrow, *An Account of the Corporation of Trinity House of Deptford Strond: A Memoir of its Origin, History, and Functions* (London: Smith and Ebbs, 1868), p.20.

useful intermediary when Newcastle or Hardwicke needed disagreements between Cabinet colleagues resolved informally, confirming that they had confidence in his political and diplomatic skills.

As we have seen, the fact that the administration of the navy was mostly handled by subordinate boards was another significant constraint on Anson's power. The organisational structure was complex and inefficient, with an underlying division between the sea service under the Admiralty and the civilian administrators who ran the boards. Anson had longstanding concerns about the performance of the Navy Board, which he saw as inefficient and a barrier to progress, but he made no proposals to reform the structure of naval administration during his time as First Lord. He continued to facilitate change by exercising his power of appointment to the civil departments, but without the power to fire staff or a compulsory retirement age, it was a protracted process. Jacob Acworth had retired in extreme old age in 1749, but other long-serving officials whom Anson wished to move on would not leave until advanced old age or illness made their departure inevitable. These delays meant that important reforms – particularly those relating to ship design and the dockyards – were to be stalled for years.

On his appointment as First Lord, Anson retained all the civilian members of the Sandwich's Board except for Granville Leveson-Gower, Viscount Trentham (later Marquess of Stafford), a follower of the Duke of Bedford, while adding two serving naval officers. He selected Admiral William Rowley and Rear Admiral Edward Boscawen. Rowley was a competent officer who had commanded the van at the Battle of Toulon before shortly afterwards being appointed commander in chief of the Mediterranean fleet. However, less than a year later, he had been recalled on Newcastle's orders for presiding over a court-martial that was condemned by the House of Commons as 'arbitrary, partial, and illegal', when an officer accused of cowardice was permitted to go on half-pay thus avoiding judgement.[6] Anson's friend Boscawen, who had been promoted to flag rank in 1748 following the first Battle of Cape Finisterre, served as a member of the Board until his premature death in 1761. He has been described as 'one of the faithful who helped to make Anson the autocrat he was'.[7]

Anson was ably supported by John Clevland, the recently appointed Admiralty Secretary, who had replaced Thomas Corbett. An experienced administrator who was previously Second Secretary, Clevland was MP for the Cinque Ports, an Admiralty seat. As Secretary, he was the permanent head of the administration and, and as we have seen, was responsible for deciding whether incoming letters were considered by the Board or the Admiralty office.[8] He recorded the Board's decisions and was responsible for their execution. He managed a small staff of clerks, who were responsible for 'copying orders and letters, issuing passes and protections, making out commissions and warrants, organising convoys, dealing with the endless appeals for employment or promotion'.[9]

---

6   Quoted in Robert McGregor, 'Sir William Rowley (c.1690–1768)', *Oxford Dictionary of National Biography*, <https://doi.org/10.1093/ref:odnb/24228>, accessed 21 September 2022.
7   Julian S. Corbett, *England in the Seven Years War. A Study in Combined Strategy* (London: Longmans, Green & Co, 1907), vol.I, p.44.
8   Ann V. Coats, 'John Clevland (1706–1763)', *Oxford Dictionary of National Biography*, <https://doi.org/10.1093/ref:odnb/64851>, accessed 21 September 2022.
9   Rodger, *The Admiralty*, p.62.

Clevland, who remained in office until he died in 1763, has been described as 'a hard-working hungry Scot who acquired unrivalled knowledge of Admiralty matters, and thereby rose to a position of considerable importance'.[10] He became Anson's most trusted adviser as well as his chief administrator, providing timely advice on naval tactics and producing political briefings defending Admiralty policy, particularly during the difficult period following the loss of Minorca in 1756. He also handled the large volume of formal correspondence from commanders in chief about appointments and promotions, although they would often also write privately to Lord Anson as they sought Admiralty confirmation of their recommendations. Replies would normally be sent on Anson's behalf by his private secretary, who also dealt with requests from civilian patrons who sought appointments for their friends and followers. As a letter from Lord Sandwich in 1756 suggests, direct application to Lord Anson was the preferred route except when his credit was exhausted: 'I have been so often troublesome to Lord Anson that I don't choose upon this occasion to apply through his channel, though I know it would be the most expeditious method'.[11]

An indication of Clevland's influence with the First Lord is provided by several incidents which Fanny Boscawen described in her letters. In the first case, she had been annoyed by the Admiralty's failure to order her husband Edward home while he was at sea in the Channel, with Clevland being the particular focus of her criticism. In the second instance, on 4 October 1756, she wrote to Edward, referring to his objections to an unspecified Admiralty policy and commenting 'that Cleveland [sic] is angry at your anger is very likely, but that his Lordship [Anson] should adopt his secretary's resentment – that is surely very unworthy and would tend to confirm a vulgar opinion that Clevland is Lord High Admiral'. The third example concerns Anson's decision, in November 1756, to promote Clevland's second son Archibald as captain of the *Gibraltar* (20) at the early age of 18 at a time when the minimum age for the appointment was 20. Fanny Boscawen criticised the promotion in a letter to her husband: 'T'other day his son Archibald was made a captain and John Cleveland told me Lord Anson had done it unasked by his father… The boy is but 18, I believe. This looks as if Clevland really had that influence which people give him over our superior'.[12]

On his appointment as First Lord, Anson promoted his trusted secretary, Philip Stephens, as the first clerk of the Admiralty over the heads of the other six clerks who had up to 26 years' service in the office.[13] Anson had first come across Stephens on his return to England in 1744 when he was a ticket office clerk in the Navy Office. He was involved in sorting out the pay of Anson's seamen on their arrival and became his secretary soon afterwards. In 1748, Stephens acted as the joint prize agent for the Western Squadron, when he handled the distribution of prize money after the first Battle of Cape Finisterre, including the large sum due to Anson. His career continued to flourish with Anson's support: he accompanied him to sea on at least two occasions before being appointed as Admiralty Second Secretary in 1759, succeeding John Clevland as Secretary on his death in 1763. He remained in office until 1795 and on his retirement was created a baronet and appointed to the Admiralty Board.

---

10   Lewis B. Namier, *The Structure of Politics at the Accession of George III* (London: Macmillan, 1963), p.39.
11   Quoted in Rodger, *The Wooden World*, p.283.
12   Fanny Boscawen to Edward Boscawen, 4 October 1756, in Aspinall-Oglander, *Admiral's Wife*, p.209.
13   William Allix to John Russell, 14 May 1751, in Mary E. Matcham (ed.), *A Forgotten John Russell: Being Letters to a Man of Business 1724–1751* (London: Edward Arnold, 1905), p.323.

Apart from the Admiralty's small permanent staff of less than 40, which was temporarily expanded in the latter stages of the Seven Years War, Anson was ably supported by Elizabeth, who served as his unofficial adviser and political secretary. As we have seen, she dealt with some of his correspondence and, more important, provided him (and other members of her family) with political news gleaned from visitors to the Admiralty, political contacts, attendance in Parliament and political pamphlets. She was also assumed to have some influence over naval appointments and 'like other patronage brokers, she supported those that she felt were most worthy… and secured a number of successes'.[14] Her ability to write fluently was put to good public use in 1756 as Lord Anson came under attack for the loss of Minorca, when she published a defence of the Admiralty's conduct anonymously in the *Public Advertiser* on 27 August.[15]

Anson relied heavily on Clevland and Stephens as well as Lady Anson in the conduct of routine Admiralty business. He managed his responsibilities largely through meetings and conversations rather than by correspondence or policy papers, but this method of working had its disadvantages. As his brother-in-law Philip Yorke (later the Second Earl of Hardwicke) commented:

> He loved reading little and writing or dictating his own letters less; and that seeming negligence in an office, which must be attended with frequent applications to the First Lord in person, to which answers are always expected and are often proper, drew upon him the ill-will of many.

Despite these shortcomings, he quickly established a reputation as an effective First Lord who had:

> A remarkable quickness in making dispositions of ships and appointing them to the services, for which they were fittest, and, without making a bustle or raising the daily newspaper or coffee house puffs, conducted the business of a very complicated department with uncommon vigour and dispatch.[16]

Apart from his role as a senior member of the Pelham administration, as First Lord Anson had a direct influence on national politics through the six Parliamentary boroughs controlled by the Admiralty, which amounted to 10 Commons seats in total. Awarded for distinguished service at sea, members of the Admiralty boroughs during Anson's tenure as First Lord included Peircy Brett, Edward Hawke and George Pocock. His influence extended to other seats occupied by naval officers who had been nominated by the Government or by Anson himself. These included at least five of the officers who had served with him on the circumnavigation. At the 1761 General Election, for example, 21 naval officers were returned and of these Anson controlled 15, the largest group in

---

14 Elaine Chalus, 'Elizabeth Anson [née Yorke], Lady Anson (1725–1760)', *Oxford Dictionary of National Biography*, <https://doi.org/10.1093/ref:odnb/68350>, accessed 21 September 2022.
15 Elaine Chalus, *Elite Women in English Political Life c.1754–1790* (Oxford: Clarendon Press, 2005), p.66.
16 BL: Hardwicke Papers, Add. MS. 35,428, f.4, 'Memorial of Family Occurrences from 1760 to 1770 inclusive'.

the Commons.[17] The group was expected to vote with the Government on major political issues as well as on legislation relating to the navy, but there were always limits to Admiralty influence as the strong opposition to the Navy Bill in 1749 demonstrated.

Maintaining Admiralty control of its boroughs depended on satisfying the interests of important local electors through the award of naval contracts and by granting requests for officers' appointments and promotions. As will be seen, Anson was to be largely successful in managing these demands without compromising the navy's professional requirements. As the second Lord Hardwicke noted in 1771, 'He withstood recommendations of interest or favour more than any First Lord of the Admiralty was ever known to do'.[18] Anson was not, of course, simply a passive recipient of requests for favours, but, as a member of the Government and the House of Lords, he often made political nominations himself.[19]

Anson received numerous requests for appointments from the Duke of Newcastle and other ministerial colleagues. Newcastle, as First Lord of the Treasury with ready access to the King, was the principal figure in the distribution of patronage in England as he sought to maintain the Government's position in Parliament. However, he had no control over appointments in the navy (except for nominations to the Admiralty Board itself) and his successful use of naval patronage depended on the First Lord's cooperation, which was not always forthcoming and led to several disputes between them. In February 1755, for example, Newcastle asked Anson to appoint an individual who had no relevant experience as a member of the Victualling Board, which he had no hesitation in rejecting:

> I had the honour of Your Grace's letter, with an enclosure from my Lord Powis, recommending Mr Whitmore to be a Commissioner of the Victualling… His Lordship might as properly have asked to have him made a capt. of a man of war that branch having always been filled with a seaman… This giving me the opportunity of observing to your Grace, that instead of adding to the useless people that are already in that office (if we should have a war with France) more people of business must be brought into it.[20]

This direct snub did not prevent Newcastle from making similar demands throughout the Seven Years War, but they met with mixed success. Anson was alert to the danger of undermining the efficiency of the navy by making questionable appointments and the strength of his position meant that he could reject those requests which he thought had no merit. Before the outbreak of the Seven Years War, turning down such applications was relatively straightforward because he could point to the lack of vacancies in peacetime. As he noted in a letter to Lord Hardwicke in 1753: 'we must be very sparing in making officers in time of peace as we have already so many on our lists that cannot be employed'.[21]

---

17 Rodger, *The Wooden World*, p.328.
18 BL: Hardwicke Papers, Add. MS. 35,428, f.4, 'Memorial of Family Occurrences from 1760 to 1770 inclusive'.
19 See Rodger, *The Wooden World*, pp.331–343, for a discussion of naval patronage during Anson's tenure at the Admiralty.
20 BL: Newcastle Papers, Add. MS. 32,852, f.485, George Anson to the Duke of Newcastle, 15 February 1755.
21 BL: Hardwicke Papers, Add. MS. 35,359, f.376, George Anson to the Earl of Hardwicke, 23 August, 1753.

Anson was much more likely to respond favourably to political nominations if they were supported by an admiral rather than recommended by a politician alone, which he often rejected out of hand.[22] In 1759, for example, Newcastle made more than one request on behalf of a lieutenant seeking promotion, which met with a robust response from the First Lord:

> I must now beg your Grace will consider seriously what must be the condition of your fleet if these Borough recommendations, which must be frequent, are to be complied with. I wish it did not at this instance bring to my mind the misery poor Pocock (that excellent officer) suffered from the misbehaviour of captains of that cast; which has done more mischief to the public (which I know is the most favourite point with you) than the loss of a vote in the House of Commons.

Anson then explained to Newcastle how he decided which candidates should be promoted from lieutenant to captain:

> My constant method has been to promote the lieutenants to command whose ships have been successfully engaged on equal terms with the enemy, without having any friend or recommendation, and in preference to all others – and this I would recommend to my successors, if they would have a fleet to be depended upon.[23]

Although success in action and professional commitment were Anson's most important criteria, personal preferences inevitably played a part in his appointment decisions as well. He advanced the careers of his followers – and attended to their own patronage recommendations – as he was expected to do, but there is little evidence to support contemporary criticisms that he also placed his enemies at a disadvantage. A more serious weakness in the system of promotion as operated by Anson was his lack of personal knowledge of some of the prospective candidates for flag rank. In 1756, when he needed to make a list of captains who ought to be promoted to rear admiral, he admitted to the Duke of Newcastle that 'he knew few of them, and yet several must be recommended'.[24] His recommendations for promotion to rear admiral were always subject to approval by the King and were sometimes rejected without any specific reason being given.[25]

On his appointment as First Lord, Anson joined the Board of Longitude as ex officio chairman. The Board had been established in 1714 and offered a reward of £20,000 for the discovery of an accurate method for determining discovering longitude – a measurement of location east or west of the prime meridian at Greenwich – at sea within certain limits of accuracy. As every 15 degrees of longitude corresponds to a time difference of an hour, it can be calculated by comparing local time with the time at Greenwich. It was a subject in which Anson retained a strong personal interest because of the navigational problems he had experienced during the circumnavigation. He attended every meeting

---

22 Rodger, *The Wooden World*, p.333.
23 BL: Newcastle Papers, Add. MS. 32,892, ff.96–97, George Anson to the Duke of Newcastle, 15 June 1759.
24 BL: Newcastle Papers, Add. MS. 32,865, f.222, George Anson to the Duke of Newcastle, 6 June 1756.
25 BL: Newcastle Papers, Add. MS. 32865, f.251, George Anson to the Duke of Newcastle, 10 June 1756.

of the Board during his term of office except for the last, which was held shortly before his death.[26]

During Anson's leadership of the Board, two practicable methods for establishing longitude were developed and the marine sextant was invented. The trials he sponsored were to have 'a profound influence on marine navigation in the next 250 years'.[27] The first method depended on the invention of an accurate chronometer, a task to which John Harrison would devote much of his working life before eventually winning the prize with his fourth watch, which is now known as H4. Completed in 1760, Anson ordered a test of H4, which was undertaken on a ship travelling to Jamaica in 1761, but the Board was not entirely satisfied with the results and a second trial took place in 1764. Harrison was eventually awarded the full prize in 1772 and his chronometers were subsequently made available to warships sailing overseas.[28]

Anson also supported an investigation into a second method of establishing longitude, which used the position of the moon in relation to fixed stars as a means of finding Greenwich time. In 1755, the Board of Longitude received accurate lunar tables from the German mathematician Tobias Meyer, who had used Hadley's octant to produce them. A later version of the tables made it possible to calculate the position of the Moon several years in advance and allowed longitude to be established within a few nautical miles. In 1757, Anson ordered his friend Captain John Campbell to undertake a sea trial of Meyer's lunar tables. Carried out successfully when he was in command of the third-rate ship of the line *Essex* (70), it led to the Board recommending the publication of an annual almanack giving the position of the Moon every three years. Campbell also suggested several modifications to the Hadley octant and the result was a prototype of the marine sextant, commissioned by the Board of Longitude in 1759, which is still in use today.

Anson was now at the pinnacle of his profession and his enhanced status was underlined by the purchase of estates in Hertfordshire, Staffordshire and Norfolk, drawing on his prize money and other resources. His acquisitions included country houses in Hertfordshire and Staffordshire, with Moor Park, near Rickmansworth, an estate of some 4,000 acres, being by far the more substantial of the two. Later described as the 'grandest eighteenth-century mansion' in Hertfordshire, it was comparable to the estates of other Whig grandees. Anson purchased it for £14,000 (nearly £2.5 million in 2023 prices) from Benjamin Styles, a merchant and speculator, who had acquired it for £86,000 in 1720, using a fortune made from the South Sea Bubble. Rebuilding the house and remodelling the gardens at a cost of £130,000, Styles created a 'white Palladian palace', consisting of a three-storey rectangular building with a four-column portico on the entrance side. It stood on a spur with views to Cassiobury Park and Watford to the north, and southwards towards Uxbridge.

Moor Park was in a poor state when the Ansons moved in 1752 and Elizabeth had already sought Thomas's advice in renovating it: 'Moor Park waits for you to *Comb* it, as the genteel

---

26 The papers of the Board of Longitude are held by the Cambridge Digital Library: https://cudl.lib.cam.ac.uk/collections/rgo14/1.
27 Derek Howse, 'John Campbell (b. in or before 1720, d. 1790)', *Oxford Dictionary of National Biography*, <https://doi.org/10.1093/ref:odnb/4518>, accessed 21 September 2022.
28 Dava Sobel, *Longitude: The True Story of a Lone Genius Who Solved the Greatest Scientific Problem of His Time* (New York: Walker, 1995).

Moor Park, Hertfordshire. (Peter O'Connor)

phrase for opening & improving has it'.[29] They employed the architect Matthew Brettingham the Elder, who had previously worked on their London townhouse in St James's Square, to carry out internal repairs and alterations. Anson decided to remodel the grounds and was introduced to Lancelot 'Capability' Brown, the fashionable landscape gardener, by Charles Wyndham, second Earl of Egremont, who was later Secretary of State for the Southern Department, 1761–1763. Anson wrote to Brown in September 1753:

> I am sorry to hear of your indisposition by Lord Egremont. I am going to Moor Park today and shall be there till Sunday. The next week I shall go down on Thursday and shall not return till Monday by which time I hope and wish you may think yourself well enough to let me see you.[30]

Elizabeth Anson described one of Brown's first visits to Moor Park when Lord Anson and William Pitt accompanied him on a four-hour tour of the grounds, which consisted of

---

29 SRO: D615/P(S)/1/3/16B, Elizabeth Anson to Thomas Anson, 15 October 1751.
30 Jane Brown, *The Omnipotent Magician: Lancelot 'Capability' Brown, 1716–1783* (London: Chatto & Windus, 2011), p.97.

formal gardens and the 'old pleasure grounds', surrounded by a park. She described the tour to her sister-in-law, Jemima Yorke, which she said

> …would have given you great entertainment. I walked on horseback & was attended by the gentlemen on foot, whilst we surveyed the garden, as it is called; afterwards they mounted too, to view the park: – My Lord acted the part of owner – Mr. Anson of a good cousin… to shew and puff – Pitt of an enthusiastic admirer, & Brown of an artist who scorned to find difficulties in raising or levelling any spot to the height desired.[31]

Brown was commissioned to make extensive changes to the gardens and, according to Horace Walpole, they were to cost a total of £6,000.[32] The works, which began in 1754 and continued until 1759, included removing earth from the front of the house and creating artificial hillocks on either side, thus giving the surroundings greater variety. He laid out the old pleasure grounds, which lay beyond the formal gardens to the south-east, in the naturalistic form that was fashionable at the time. A lake created in the pleasure grounds was overlooked by an Ionic Temple, possibly designed by Brettingham and erected by Brown, which was dedicated to The Winds. Anson was sufficiently impressed with the results of his labours to support a petition, organised by William Pitt, for Brown to be awarded a royal appointment and pension.

Anson's close interest in the gardens at Moor Park, which he shared with Elizabeth, extended to the cultivation of new plants from hotter climates. It was an enthusiasm they had in common with other landowners in the mid-eighteenth century. The Ansons successfully introduced the *Lathyrus nervosus* (Lord Anson's Blue Pea), which had been discovered in Patagonia during the circumnavigation, using seeds that were brought back to England in 1744. He also succeeded in introducing the apricot at Moor Park, where it was first grown in 1760. Efforts to grow the fruit in England had been made since the sixteenth century, but Anson's attempt was the first to succeed. The variety was known as the Moor Park apricot (*Prunus armeniaca*) and is still cultivated today.

Samuel Johnson was one of the distinguished figures who visited Lord Anson at Moor Park, where he reported he was 'well received and kindly treated and with the true gratitude of a wit ridiculed the master of the house before I had left it an hour'. He composed an epigram after seeing the newly erected Temple of the Winds in the gardens: 'A grateful mind I praise! All to the winds he owed / And so upon the Winds a Temple he bestowed'.[33] Horace Walpole visited Moor Park in July 1760 and left a brief record of his visit in his journal. He commented favourably on the magnificent entrance hall, which had been 'painted by Amiconi [Jacopo Amigoni], one of his best performances', but was otherwise less impressed: 'Few places have so much laid out on them, & yet there is little real beauty in it'.[34] He elaborated his views in a letter to George Montagu:

---

31   Kate Felus, *The Secret Life of the Georgian Garden. Beautiful Objects and Agreeable Retreats* (London: I.B. Tauris, 2016), p.41.
32   Paget Toynbee, 'Horace Walpole's Journals of Visits to Country Seats', *The Volume of the Walpole Society,* 16 (1927–1928), p.24.
33   George B. Hill (ed.), *Johnsonian Miscellanies* (New York: Harper & Brothers, 1897), vol.I, pp.195-196.
34   Toynbee, 'Horace Walpole's Journals of Visits to Country Seats', p.24.

We went to see More-park, but I was not much struck with it, after all the miracles I had heard that Brown had performed there. He has undulated the horizon in so many artificial molehills, that it is full as unnatural as if it was drawn with a rule and compasses. Nothing is done to the house; there are not even chairs in the great apartment. My Lord Anson is more slatternly than the Churchills, and does not even finish children.[35]

Anson purchased Orgreave Hall, a much smaller estate at Alrewas in Staffordshire, in the same year as he acquired Moor Park. It was a 'smallish L-shaped house, built probably in 1668… in a local version of the Baroque'.[36] Conveniently located some 15 miles from Shugborough, it provided Anson with a local base that enabled him to maintain his Staffordshire connections and his close links to Thomas as he transformed the family estate in the 1740s and 1750s. At about the same time, he bought an estate at Knightley, west of Stafford, from Thomas Coke, first Earl of Leicester, who used the proceeds to complete the construction of Holkham Hall in Norfolk. Anson later acquired estates in Norfolk from Coke, establishing a close connection between the two families.

Thomas Anson had worked on a plan for developing Shugborough even before his brother set out on the voyage of circumnavigation, which was to make the family fortunes. Admiral Anson's success, however, 'transformed the scale of his brother's thinking and the years following his return in 1744 saw a great flurry of activity at Shugborough'.[37] His programme of improvements included developing the gardens and park as well as extending the house. In the late 1740s, it is likely that he employed Thomas Wright as the architect, possibly on the recommendation of Jemima Yorke, to remodel the house. Wright added a third storey and a pair of two-storey neo-classical pavilions, which were connected to the original seventeenth-century house by single-storey links, creating an impressive Georgian mansion.

The remodelled interior included several items commemorating Anson's naval victories and Thomas fully involved his brother in developing his plans. In a letter to Jemima Yorke, Elizabeth Anson described the naval paintings which had been added to the entrance hall:

The Action of Cape Finisterre [by Samuel Scott] is already up and looks finely; the burning of Patya is to be over the chimney, and the actions between the *Centurion* and the galleon, and the *Lyon* and *Elizabeth* on each side of the door into the room you dined in, and the two other actions of captains of my Lords in the war over the other doors, so that the whole will be a kind of history.[38]

The anteroom to the dining room (formerly the gallery) was fitted with an arched recess, which housed a model of the *Centurion* until it was sold in 1842.[39] Since the early years

---

35 Horace Walpole to George Montagu, 4 July 1760, in Lewis (ed.), *The Yale Edition of the Correspondence of Horace Walpole*, vol.9, p.285.
36 Nicholas Pevsner, *The Buildings of England: Staffordshire* (London: Yale University Press, 1974), p.54.
37 John M. Robinson, *Shugborough* (London: The National Trust, 1989), p.19.
38 Quoted in Stephanie Barczewski, *Country Houses and the British Empire, 1700–1930* (Manchester: Manchester University Press, 2014), p.199.
39 Now in the National Maritime Museum, Greenwich. A photograph of the model is reproduced on page 24.

of the twentieth century, a surviving remnant of the *Centurion's* figurehead (a lion's leg mounted on a mahogany shield) has been on display at Shugborough.

In the redeveloped gardens and park, Thomas built the Chinese House, completed in 1748, which may have been 'a wedding token, to the recently married Admiral Anson and Elizabeth Yorke'.[40] Based on pencil sketches drawn by Peircy Brett in Canton, the house was built in the real Chinese style on an island in the middle of a medieval moat; it was reached by a pair of bridges also of Chinese design. The house contained furniture, porcelain and painted mirrors that Anson had brought back from China. In 1752, Thomas built a second major Chinese monument – a timber pagoda – in the park, but it was destroyed in a flood before the end of the eighteenth century. Nearby, the Cat's Monument, constructed in 1749, may have commemorated a cat which travelled around the world with Anson in the *Centurion*.

Thomas employed James 'Athenian' Stuart to build several neo-Classical garden monuments, including the Tower of the Winds, commemorating his brother's life. Work started on the Triumphal Arch (a copy of the Arch of Hadrian in Athens) at the end of 1761 and Jemima Yorke describes seeing the arch under construction on a hill 'that commands a very fine prospect… A most beautiful structure'.[41] Following his brother's death, Thomas decided that the monument would honour the memory of Lord and Lady Anson as well as celebrating his naval achievements. The sculptor Peter Scheemakers was commissioned to produce busts of Anson and his wife, which were added to the arch in 1764.

Although Anson devoted considerable energy to his new estates, his first priority remained Admiralty business and one of the most important issues he faced as First Lord was the condition of the fleet and the declining number of ships of the line that were fit for service. By 1750, the fleet consisted of 93 ships of 60 to 100 guns, but only 33 were ready for service, with the remainder being under repair or needing repair; this compared with the 69 ships that had been available for service in 1745.[42] The large numbers needing repair is variously explained by the effects of wartime service, the fact that the dockyards had more work than they could handle, and a succession of milder winters which allowed dry rot to flourish and significantly reduced ships' longevity. As we have seen, the dockyard problem was first tackled by Lord Sandwich's Board but little progress was made in enhancing capacity through productivity improvements. Anson had even less success than Sandwich in obtaining additional funding through the extraordinary estimate, with the allocation granted by Parliament for shipbuilding and repairs in 1751 showing a 29 per cent decrease on the previous year, as Henry Pelham sought to cut public expenditure.

Although Anson was unwilling to challenge Pelham's fiscal policies, he recognised that more money would be needed if the fleet was to be properly maintained. He requested additional funding for shipbuilding and repairs in the period before the outbreak of the Seven Years War, but it continued to fall short of his requirements. In 1752, for example, Anson's extraordinary estimate sought £108,000 but he was granted a total of £100,000

---

40   Cousins, 'Shugborough, p.38.
41   Quoted in Susan Weber Soros, *James "Athenian" Stuart, 1713–1788: The Rediscovery of Antiquity* (New Haven: Yale University Press, 2006), p.331.
42   Clive Wilkinson, *The British Navy and the State in the Eighteenth Century* (Woodbridge: The Boydell Press, 2004), p.68.

(£17.5 million in 2023 prices), which was little more than half the amount allocated in 1750. Despite this reduction, the allocation was significantly underspent and, in 1753, his request for more than £121,000 was rejected. Anson's requests in the next two years were reduced by Parliament, with the amount allocated being capped at £100,000 a year before it was increased to £200,000 in 1756 following the declaration of war with France. Expenditure on shipbuilding and repairs then continued at this level until the end of the war.[43] These funding pressures meant that a significant reduction in the backlog of ships needing repair could only be achieved by improving the productivity and infrastructure of the dockyards, but he did not give these issues any great priority. Building new docks could be ruled out because the funds were simply not available in a period of peacetime retrenchment, and it was not until 1765 that a large programme of dockyard expansion began.

Anson did not return to the issue of dockyard reform until the end of 1751 when the Admiralty expressed concern about the Navy Board's limited progress in implementing its recommendations and correcting abuses following the inspections in 1749. However, it did no more than ask for information on the inspection of ships in Ordinary and other issues but took no further action. With the Navy Board announcing that it was 'against any innovation, more especially the attempting to build anything whatever by task', it is not surprising that little had changed since 1749. It has been suggested that Anson 'was content to allow disruptive reforms to sleep' and he never returned to the dockyards for a formal inspection during his tenure as First Lord. The next visitation, which did not take place until 1764 when Lord Egmont was First Lord, concluded that 'the malaise which afflicted the yards 18 years before was but little abated'.[44]

Despite the lack of progress, Anson continued discussions with the Navy Board on two dockyard issues – piecework and manpower reductions. In 1749, the Navy Board had been asked to produce a plan for the introduction of piecework but it failed to do so. In 1752, when Anson raised the subject again, the Navy Board made it clear that its position had not changed, arguing that 'it was simply unsuitable… especially in wartime when the labour force had to be switched rapidly from job to job. In addition, task work led to shoddy results'.[45] The Navy Board also resisted pressure to make further cuts in the number of shipwrights, justifying its position on the grounds that the number of ships that were fit for service had increased significantly since 1749. However, with the debt of the navy rising rapidly, Anson needed to save money and he also had to ensure 'that the financial credit of the government and the navy was kept strong. Effective mobilisation meant that the navy's suppliers had to have confidence in the creditworthiness of the state'.[46]

In March 1753, even though it conflicted with his aim of restoring the fleet, Anson was compelled to issue orders for the dismissal of 890 dockyard workmen, including 442 shipwrights, reducing the workforce to a total of 4,834 men. Numbers rose again during the Seven Years War but remained below those in the previous war even though more ships were in service, suggesting 'that during the Anson era the nation did get better value for

---

43 Wilkinson, *The British Navy*, p.213.
44 Haas, 'The Royal Dockyards', p.202.
45 Middleton, 'The Visitation', p.26.
46 Wilkinson, *The British Navy*, p.93.

its money'.⁴⁷ With continuing resistance from the Navy Board, Anson abandoned further attempts at dockyard reform and nothing of significance was done until Lord Sandwich returned as First Lord in 1771. Despite these obstacles, five new ships of the line were built between 1751 and 1754 and progress was made in tackling the large backlog of repair work, with 17 ships of the line being repaired and only four declared unserviceable.

By 1753, 46 ships of the line (and nineteen 50-gun ships) were declared fit for service, a figure that had increased to at least 50 by 1755. This record proved to be more than a match for the French navy, which was also affected by financial constraints.⁴⁸ Further expansion of the fleet would need to await increased funding following a declaration of war and, in the meantime, Anson worked on plans as to how this could be achieved by making much greater use of private shipyards. It was a plan that would rapidly bring the fleet up to strength by the end of 1756 while avoiding the cost of expanding the infrastructure and labour force of the royal dockyards beyond what was normally required. Making use of the private sector to build new ships was a significant part of Anson's plan to use the navy's limited resources more efficiently and it amounted to 'the introduction of task work by the back door' after the failure to implement it in the royal yards.⁴⁹

The year 1754 marked the beginning of the armed conflict between Britain and France in America that was to lead to the Seven Years War and the most difficult period of Anson's career. The initial mobilisation of the fleet proceeded without difficulty (with George II approving of the 'wise measures' taken under Anson's direction), but Britain would have little success during the first three years of war, with the Royal Navy receiving much of the blame for a succession of costly failures.⁵⁰ The loss of Minorca in 1756 led to Anson's departure from office, and, although he returned as First Lord within six months, his reputation took longer to recover. That process was well underway by 1758 when Louisbourg, the French naval base on Cape Breton Island, was captured. It was the first stage in William Pitt's plan to win control of North America, which was Britain's principal war aim. In Europe, Britain adopted a defensive strategy and its first priority was protecting George II's electorate of Hanover from France, partly to avoid it being used as a bargaining counter in future peace talks. She supported Ferdinand of Brunswick and Frederick the Great in their land operations against France and her allies. In European waters, Britain used the Western Squadron and the Mediterranean fleet to deter French invasion attempts, prevent them from sending reinforcements overseas and disrupting their trade.

The longstanding tensions between Britain and France in North America had their origins in the Treaty of Aix-la-Chapelle, 1748, which ended the War of the Austrian Succession, but did not settle their colonial disputes. British possessions in North America were concentrated on the Atlantic coast, while French-controlled territory was located around Montreal and Quebec in the north-east and New Orleans in the south, with a link between them being provided by the Mississippi and Ohio rivers. The journey between Montreal and New Orleans required travel overland through Ohio and this area became a source of conflict between the two powers. In 1754, the French successfully resisted British attempts to expand

---

47 Middleton, 'The Visitation', p.29.
48 Wilkinson, *The British Navy*, p.93.
49 Wilkinson, *The British Navy*, p.101.
50 BL: Anson Papers, Add. MS. 15,956, f.61, Earl of Holderness to George Anson, 3 August 1755.

westwards and completed the construction of Fort Duquesne in the Ohio valley, at the Forks of the Ohio where the Allegheny and Monongahela rivers join. The Duke of Newcastle, who had succeeded his brother Henry Pelham as Prime Minister in March 1754, was keen to respond to French advances in North America without provoking a war in Europe, but as the conflict developed the French threatened to extend it to home waters.

In response to the growing French threat, the Government decided to reinforce its North American garrisons with the aim of removing the French from Fort Duquesne and other forts in the Ohio valley. It was a decision that Anson, who had supported proposals to raise additional men in America, strongly endorsed.[51] In January 1755, two infantry regiments under the command of Major General Edward Braddock left Cork escorted by the *Centurion* and the *Norwich* (50) under the command of Commodore Augustus Keppel. The French responded to the news of the British expedition by preparing a squadron at Brest to transport reinforcements to their Canadian garrisons but, as we shall see, it did not leave until May. On 21 January, when the French plan became known in London, Newcastle organised a meeting of the inner committee of the Cabinet, which was to be responsible for military strategy throughout the war. Apart from Lord Anson, its core members included Newcastle, Hardwicke, Granville and Fox, and the two principal secretaries of state, Robert Darcy, fourth Earl of Holderness, and Sir Thomas Robinson. Cumberland was present as army commander-in-chief together with Sir John Ligonier, Lieutenant General of the Ordnance, who served as de facto chief of staff. But, as James Waldegrave, second Earl Waldegrave noted, detailed planning at this early stage of the conflict took place elsewhere: 'the preparations for war and all military operations were chiefly conducted by the Duke [of Cumberland], Fox, and Lord Anson.[52]

Ligonier had a personality that made him easy to work with and he established an effective working relationship with Lord Anson, which was to continue throughout the war. Ligonier's long military career included distinguished service during the War of the Austrian Succession before his capture at the Battle of Laffeldt in 1747. When Cumberland resigned following his surrender at Klosterzeven in September 1757, Ligonier succeeded him as commander-in-chief and was later raised to the peerage and promoted to the rank of field marshal. It was fortunate that 'never perhaps did England start a war with two more competent men at the helm' and their harmonious partnership was to make a major contribution – as Pitt's principal professional advisers – to the eventual defeat of France and Spain.[53]

Based on their joint advice, the inner committee concluded that steps should be taken to ensure that French reinforcements did not reach Canada and from this point Anson began to mobilise the navy for war. It is perhaps not surprising that at a time when war with France threatened, Anson thought of returning to sea. Since mid-1747, he had been confined to his desk at the Admiralty apart from a few journeys across the North Sea when he escorted George II on his regular visits to the Continent. Such thoughts may have been stimulated by a visit to Hawke's squadron at Spithead, which reminded him of the high cost of remaining

---

51 J.C.D. Clark, *The Dynamics of Change. The Crisis of the 1750s and English Party Systems* (Cambridge: Cambridge University Press, 1982), p.101.
52 J.C.D. Clark (ed.), *The Memoirs and Speeches of James, 2nd Earl Waldegrave 1742–1763* (Cambridge: Cambridge University Press, 2002), p.168.
53 Corbett, *England in the Seven Years War*, vol.I, p.33.

at the Admiralty, as he admitted to Lord Holderness in May 1755: 'I am certain I sacrifice the one thing that would give me the greatest pleasure'.[54] But Anson was a highly effective administrator who would have been very difficult to replace at this point and he was not able to return to the sea until 1758 when exceptional circumstances compelled him to take command of the Western Squadron for the last time.

The process of expanding British land forces had begun in the autumn of 1754 as the rivalry between the English and French in North America intensified. Parliament voted additional funds in November, but the mobilisation of the navy did not start until January 1755, when preparations to send 17 ships to North America began. Ministers approved Anson's request to begin recruiting and the Admiralty was authorised to pay bounties to volunteers (30s for seamen between the ages of 20 and 55 who had a minimum of three years' experience) and to start the press. Anson proposed recalling British seamen serving in foreign ships and a proclamation to this effect was issued early in February. He also supported attempts to enlist foreign seamen and non-French prisoners of war in the navy. Anson took a much less favourable view of English prisoners of war who were serving on French ships and thought that they 'ought to be hanged if they happen to be taken, and some of them in that case certainly will, as examples to deter others from the same practice'.[55]

At first, there were few difficulties in recruiting seamen but this did not remain the case for long. In the first six months of 1755, 20,175 men joined the service but between July and November, only 5,802 were mustered, which was far fewer than the number lost through death and disease. At the beginning of 1756, there were 168 ships in commission with a combined complement of 49,565 men, but only 35,955 had been mustered (and of these some 6,000 were too ill for immediate service).[56] Anson's Board soon took action to address the slowdown in recruitment and early in 1756 press warrants were renewed, the scope of the impress service was extended and bounties for volunteers were increased. At a meeting of the inner committee on 3 February, Anson sought a rise in the recruitment bounty to 60s to encourage more volunteers to enlist and ministers agreed. However, with private shipowners offering higher wages than the navy – an issue that Anson did not pursue – the supply of volunteers would continue to be restricted.[57]

As a result of these difficulties, impressment at sea and on land continued to be the principal method of raising seamen during the war. The Admiralty ordered press gangs to operate over a wider area ashore and afloat and offered them greater incentives to bring in more seamen. Despite these efforts, the number of recruits they obtained in the first few months of 1756 remained low. As we shall see, the manning crisis was to delay the departure of Byng's squadron to Minorca and was to affect the fleet's capabilities for at least another year. Recruitment increased from the summer of 1756 but did not keep pace with the number of ships being commissioned during the same period. Desertion remained a significant problem even though the Admiralty had employed established measures – such as restricting shore leave and confining seamen on hospital ships – to prevent it.

---

54 BL: Holderness Papers, Egerton MS. 2444, ff.42–43, George Anson to Lord Holderness, 9 May 1755.
55 TNA: ADM 1/634, undated letter, probably written in 1757.
56 Stephen F. Gradish, *The Manning of the British Navy during the Seven Years' War* (London: Royal Historical Society, 1980), pp. 33–34.
57 Gradish, *The Manning of the British Navy*, p. 72.

The limited changes introduced to the recruitment system while Anson was First Lord were the responsibility of his colleagues Grenville and Pitt rather than the Admiralty. His reluctance to intervene may simply reflect his recognition of Parliament's unwillingness to address two of the major barriers – low pay and the absence of a time limit on naval service – to easier recruiting. In 1758, Grenville, the Treasurer of the Navy, tackled the longstanding problem of delays to the disbursement of seamen's wages with legislation that provided for payments to be made regularly. It also made it easier for a proportion of seamen's earnings to be sent to their families although it did not address the issue of low pay. Grenville believed that seamen would be less likely to desert if their conditions of service were more beneficial, but Anson, who did not support the proposals, took a different view arguing that making regular payments would make the problem worse.

At a meeting between the Admiralty and Treasury officials to discuss the expenditure implications of Grenville's legislation, which was held at the end of 1758, Anson expressed his reservations about its impact. According to James Grenville, a Lord of the Treasury, most of the Admiralty Lords attending the meeting

> …were more able and not less cordial friends. In short, the only vivacities that made their sallies from the enemy, were certain blunt thrusts and hints from Lord Anson about desertion and unmanning the fleet, seconded by a gruff brightness or two from Admiral Boscawen on the same topic.[58]

Despite his reservations, Anson worked to ensure that the funds allocated for wages were paid out in accordance with the legislation. Desertion continued to be a problem for the rest of the war, but it is not clear whether Anson's reservations about the impact of the legislation were correct. It has been suggested that the failure to enact a further measure – the Registry Bill – was a more likely explanation.[59] This Bill would have imposed a maximum three-year period of service and seamen who continued beyond this point would be entitled to a higher rate of pay. The seafaring population would have been required to register with the navy, which could then call up as many of them as it needed during wartime, but it was defeated in the Commons because of opposition from the merchant community. There is no record of Anson's views but he may have believed that the registration requirement was unenforceable if the shipowners had been unwilling to cooperate.

When the fleet was mobilised early in 1755, one of Anson's major priorities was re-establishing a marine force, as had been the case at the outbreak of every previous war since the Restoration. He had first been involved in discussions about the future organisation of the marine regiments soon after joining the Admiralty Board some 10 years earlier, but they were halted at the end of the war in 1748 when the marines were disbanded. Under the arrangements then in place, the infantry regiments raised during wartime to serve as marines at sea were responsible to the army rather than the Admiralty, resulting in divided control, administrative complexity and financial chaos. The marines' regimental structure 'was quite unsuitable for forces which seldom served together as regiments, but went to sea

---

58 James Grenville to George Grenville, 20 December 1758, in Smith (ed.), *The Grenville Papers*, vol.I, p.281.
59 Gradish, *The Manning of the British Navy*, p.119.

in small detachments borne on the books of ships'.[60] Following a Parliamentary investigation into their financial affairs in 1746, the marines were transferred to Admiralty control but for the moment they retained their existing structure and colonels still owned their regiments.

In August 1748, Lord Sandwich raised the question of the future of the marines with Anson following a discussion with the Duke of Cumberland, who thought they would be disbanded at the end of the war, as had been the case in the past. He reported Cumberland's view that it would be right to do so because 'they were upon a bad footing, and neither land or sea forces; that whenever they were appointed again the establishment should be changed, and the marines be entirely in our jurisdiction'.[61] Anson subsequently discussed the issue with Henry Pelham and Henry Fox (who was then Secretary of War), with Fox confirming in October that he had not the 'least objection either in form or substance' to the Admiralty assuming responsibility for 'the preparing and signing of the warrants to break the marines' at the end of the war, but no decisions were taken at that point about replacing their regimental structure.[62]

The proposals to re-establish the marines in 1755 directly addressed the questions of Admiralty control and regimental structure which Anson and Sandwich had been unable fully to resolve in the late 1740s. In March, Anson and other members of the Board agreed to a proposal for the creation of the marines 'as a separate corps, entirely distinct from the army, to act with the navy, when afloat, and to be regulated by a Marines Mutiny Act, when on shore'.[63] It was submitted to the Council at the end of March and the new Marine Corps was formed on 3 April. The Admiralty decided on appointments to the senior ranks and it would consult these officers on the structure, recruitment and uniforms of the corps in the following months. These 'discussions eventually formed the Marines into something truly new and distinct from their previous formations'.[64]

While there is no doubt that Anson was 'a prime mover' in the creation of the marines in 1755, he received professional advice on the structure and administration of the new organisation from Lieutenant Colonel James Patterson, who was to be appointed as commander of the new corps at the end of the year.[65] His advice was based on the adoption of a new divisional structure, which replaced the regimental organisation employed in earlier wars. Three new divisions, located at Chatham, Portsmouth and Plymouth dockyards respectively, were to be subdivided into independent companies, offering much greater operational flexibility than the previous regimental structure. The creation of the first modern marine service under full Admiralty control has been described as 'the single major innovation in the manpower and social life of the navy in the mid-eighteenth century'.[66]

At the time mobilisation began, the Royal Navy was much larger than the French navy, which only had 57 ships of the line in commission. It was estimated in August 1756 that 346

---

60   Rodger, *Insatiable Earl*, p.35.
61   BL: Anson Papers, Add. MS. 15,957, f.77, Lord Sandwich to George Anson, 7 August 1748 (n.s.).
62   BL: Anson Papers, Add. MS. 15,955, f.270, Henry Fox to George Anson, 25 October 1748.
63   Britt Zerbe, *The Birth of the Royal Marines 1664–1802* (Woodbridge: The Boydell Press, 2013), p.57.
64   Zerbe, *The Birth of the Royal Marines*, p.45.
65   Zerbe, *The Birth of the Royal Marines*, p.57.
66   Rodger, *The Command of the Ocean*, p.406.

George, Lord Anson, 1755, mezzotint by J. McArdell after Joshua Reynolds. (Anne S.K. Brown Collection)

ships of all rates would eventually be needed to ensure 'the total stagnation and extirpation of the French trade upon the seas and the general protection of that of Great Britain upon the seas'.[67] When peace was signed on 3 November 1762 the navy had attained a total strength of 305 ships and 85,665 seamen and marines.[68] By the end of 1755, there were 88 ships of the line in service, together with 112 other warships, which was close to the total achieved in the last war, but new ships were now urgently needed. As we have seen, Anson turned to commercial builders to increase shipbuilding capacity and they were to make an

---

67 Quoted in Basil Williams, *The Life of William Pitt, Earl of Chatham* (London: Longmans, Green & Co, 1915), vol.I, p.295.
68 TNA: SP 42/43, pp.33–36.

increasingly important contribution as the war progressed. In 1755, Anson ordered nine ships of the line, of which three were to be built in private yards; six were ordered in 1756, five of them in private yards. A total of 22 ships of the line were built between 1755 and 1758 and a further 11 were repaired.[69] In total, more than 80 ships of the line were ordered between 1754 and 1762 at a cost of £1,893,221 (about £268 million in 2023 prices).

Anson's wartime building programme, which, as mentioned above, was supported by additional funding of £200,000 a year from 1756, included orders for the construction of two new designs – the 74-gun ship of the line and the 32-gun frigate – with the former being described as 'the greatest breakthrough of British naval shipbuilding in the eighteenth century, not just because the individual ships… were better than anything that had gone before, but because the way was open for further improvements'.[70] This breakthrough was the direct result of Anson's decision to remove the elderly Sir Thomas Allin as Surveyor of the Navy in mid-1755 when he became 'disordered in his senses'.[71] He was also able to remove the aged Comptroller, Edward Falkingham, and replace him with his friend Charles Saunders. The changes reflected Anson's continuing concerns with the performance of Navy Board officials: both men had proved to be a barrier to progress and their removal would advance the cause of naval reform.

Anson wanted to appoint joint surveyors who would challenge the restrictions of conventional ship design embodied in the discredited 1745 establishment and he selected Thomas Slade, Master Shipwright at Deptford, and William Bately, Assistant Surveyor of the Navy, to replace Allin. They both proved to be sound choices and a period of unprecedented creativity in British ship design would follow. Anson had met Slade in 1747 when he was an assistant master shipwright at Woolwich, and his career had progressed rapidly as a result of the First Lord's patronage. Slade, who remained in post until he died in 1771, designed most of the navy's early 74-gun ships and frigates. He was also responsible for HMS *Victory* (100), which was ordered in 1758 and launched in 1765 but did not put to sea until 1778; it was to be rebuilt twice before serving as Nelson's flagship at the Battle of Trafalgar in 1805.

Ignoring the constraints of the 1745 Establishment, Slade produced designs for the first 74-gun ships of the *Dublin* class within three weeks of his appointment. Closely resembling the lines of the French warship *Invincible*, which had been captured in 1747, they were a new type of two-decker of 1,546 tons (an increase of more than 100 tons compared to previous 70-gun ships) and were the first to be designed around specific armament (in this case 14 pairs of 32-pounder guns). This revolutionary design 'stood for everything the old surveyors had been against: it was of foreign ancestry; it was a large two-decker, whereas they had put their faith in small three-deckers. [It meant] destroying the whole system by which ships had been designed for the last half-century'.[72] Anson had finally succeeded in overturning the 1745 Establishment and the rules which had previously determined British ship design. When he was forced to resign in 1756, the new Admiralty Board endorsed the new design and ordered two more 74-gun ships.

---

69   Wilkinson, *The British Navy*, p.94.
70   Lavery, *The Ship of the Line*, vol.I, p.97.
71   Quoted in Brian Lavery, 'Thomas Slade (1703/4–1771)', *Oxford Dictionary of National Biography*, <https://doi.org/10.1093/ref:odnb/64866>, accessed 21 September 2022.
72   Lavery, *The Ship of the Line*, vol.I, p.97.

On Anson's return to office in 1757, further orders were placed based on original British designs and, by 1759, fourteen 74-gun ships were in service (with a total of 28 being ordered before the end of the war). They were to play an important role in Hawke's decisive victory at Quiberon Bay in 1759 and following the battle three more 74-gun ships were ordered. The new ships were to influence the design of other warship classes, including the 64-gun ships, which were generally larger and more heavily armed than their predecessors; by 1762, these two new designs constituted nearly half of the 141 ships of the line then in service. They replaced the 70 and 60-gun third-rates in a revised rating system that Anson introduced towards the end of the Seven Years War, which was based on three main ship types – ships of the line, cruisers and frigates; light craft were unrated.[73] There is no doubt that the 74-gun ship 'was the great success of the 1750s, and it remained the most common type of ship of the line until well after 1815'.[74] When Anson died the period of innovation in ship design came to an abrupt end. This was confirmed early in 1763 when the Admiralty informed the Navy Board that it was of 'great importance to the King's service that every ship of the same class should be built so nearly to resemble each other that the masts, yards, furniture and stores provided for one may serve for every other of the like rank'.[75]

Anson also asked Slade to work on the design of the navy's smaller ships (fifth- and sixth-rates) and the 32-gun *Southampton* class frigates were among the first outputs. He drew on earlier French-derived designs, including the *Unicorn* and *Lyme* of 1748, which incorporated an unarmed lower deck 'so that the gunports could be raised some way above the waterline, allowing the ship to heel in a breeze and to fight in rough weather'.[76] Slade produced a new two-deck frigate that was more powerful and had improved sailing qualities compared to the smaller one-deck types it replaced. The *Southampton* class frigates carried 26 12-pounders on the upper deck and six 6-pounders on the quarterdeck. Slade designed further frigate classes during the Seven Years War, including the successful *Richmond* and *Niger* classes. The 32-gun frigates were another successful wartime design inspired by Anson and they continued in service until they were outclassed by larger French versions in the 1790s.

Anson's wartime strategy, which was heavily influenced by his experiences during the War of the Austrian Succession, was based on the deployment of the Western Squadron, which was re-established early in 1755. It had played a significant role in 1747–1748 when, according to Anson, 'all our great successes at sea arose entirely from it'. Its objectives in the Seven Years War were similar to those in the last war: to keep the French fleet at Brest and Rochefort; to prevent the dispatch of enemy reinforcements overseas; to intercept French merchant shipping; and to protect British trade. The squadron would maintain a distant blockade of Brest for much of the war with mixed results until a more effective close blockade of the port was established by Edward Hawke in 1759. He remained on station for months until bad weather forced him to abandon it, allowing the French to sail from Brest

---

73 P. W. Brock, 'Anson and His Importance as a Naval Reformer', *The Naval Review*, 17 (1929), pp.521–522, provides a summary of the revised rating system.
74 Brian Lavery, *The Arming and Fitting of English Ships of War 1660–1815* (London: Conway Maritime Press, 1998), p.121.
75 John B. Hattendorf et. al. (eds), *British Naval Documents 1204–1960* (London: Navy Records Society, 1993), p.493.
76 Lavery, *Anson's Navy*, p.35.

only to be defeated at Quiberon Bay. Anson justified the overriding priority he gave to the Western Squadron in the following terms:

> Our colonies are so numerous and so extensive that to keep a naval force at each equal to the united force of France would be impracticable with double our navy. The best defence therefore for our colonies as well as our coasts is to have such a squadron always to the westward as may in all probability either keep the French in port or give them battle with advantage if they come out. The large French ships of war which return home… must either go into Brest or the ports in the Bay [of Biscay], and an English squadron to the westward is the best, indeed the only, means to intercept them.[77]

The Western Squadron was to play a critical role in disrupting French trade and protecting British merchant shipping and, according to Anson:

> The whole trade of France to her colonies, whether going out or returning home, runs such risk of being intercepted by our western cruisers that the French insurance is from 25 to 30 per cent going out and from 40 to 45 per cent coming home, a burthen which no trade can bear, and which must destroy it. [Most British trade] comes in between Cape Clear [on the south-west coast of Ireland] and Ushant, a station where the French cruisers and privateers might do infinite mischief if they were suffered to go out or return in safety. During the last rebellion [i.e. the Jacobite rebellion, 1745], when the western cruisers were called in to defend our coasts, the number of captures and mischiefs done to our merchants were incredible. These are the benefits of which a Western Squadron is productive.

However, as Anson pointed out, these benefits were 'not cheaply gained. A fleet superior to what the enemy can send out must be always employed, otherwise the moment of weakness or absence may be seized; our ships must always be clean, otherwise the enemy coming fresh out of port may outsail us'. Adverse weather

> …wears out the ships, the masts and the rigging, and ruins the health and costs the lives of the seamen; it often disables a ship in a week which has been three months in preparing, and it demands a greater part of our naval force. Less than 30 ships of the line completed [and] manned will not keep 20 constantly at sea, even in the summer.[78]

Despite Anson's consistent focus on operations in home waters, in the initial stages of the conflict, the threat posed by the French in North America meant that priority was given to deploying the Royal Navy overseas. With Newcastle hoping to keep any conflict with

---

77 Herbert W. Richmond (ed.), *Papers Relating to the Loss of Minorca in 1756* (London: Navy Records Society, 1913), pp.94–95.
78 Richmond, *Papers Relating to the Loss of Minorca*, p.96. These notes form part of the defensive briefing prepared by Anson and Hardwicke for the Parliamentary enquiry into the loss of Minorca.

France confined to North America, the Government dismissed the possibility of deploying the Western Squadron aggressively in home waters because it would run the risk of starting a maritime war in Europe. On 24 March, as it was held in port, ministers confirmed plans to dispatch a naval force to North America to lie in wait for the French: 'a squadron not exceeding seven of the line should be sent as soon as ready to cruise off Louisbourg, with instructions to fall upon any French ships of war that shall be attempting to land troops in Nova Scotia or to go to Cape Breton or through the St Lawrence to Quebec'.[79] It was later increased to 11 ships of the line in response to the arrival of a French claim to the disputed territory in the Ohio Valley. With Hawke in command of the Western Squadron, Anson selected Edward Boscawen to command the ships destined for North America; he was the obvious choice as there 'was really no reputation of the last war which stood higher than his and was available for the post'.[80]

Boscawen departed on 26 April with orders to cruise off Louisbourg, where he was to do his best to capture any French warships or transports carrying troops or supplies he encountered. If they offered any resistance, 'you will employ the means at your disposal to capture and destroy them'.[81] Shortly afterwards, on 3 May, the French squadron carrying reinforcements for Canada, which had been preparing since January, departed from Brest. Commanded by Emmanuel-Auguste de Cahideuc, Comte Du Bois de la Motte, the squadron consisted of 19 ships of the line and six frigates. In response, Anson decided to reinforce Boscawen with six additional ships of the line and he was confident that the combined force would be strong enough to capture the whole French squadron. He selected Francis Holburne to command the second squadron and secured his promotion to rear admiral, although Boscawen was not particularly happy with the decision. He claimed that Holburne was not well thought of in the service and attributed his appointment to the fact that he had 'contrived to insinuate himself into the good graces of Lord Anson'.[82] The First Lord explained the urgency of Holburne's task: 'your getting to America, and joining Vice Admiral Boscawen before the French get to Louisbourg, is of such immense consequence to the Kingdom, that I must again intreat you to be very assiduous in making your passage in as little time as possible'.[83]

Although Holburne left England without delay, he did not reach Boscawen in time. Boscawen had arrived off Newfoundland on 3 June, with the French following three days later. In foggy conditions, the French squadron scattered and, two days later, Boscawen was only able to engage a small number of enemy ships. The *Alcide* (64) and *Lys* (64) were captured, while the *Dauphin Royal*, the third member of the group, escaped, with the rest of the French fleet, which had separated in the fog, avoiding an engagement. By the time Holburne arrived on 21 June, the opportunity to fight a decisive engagement had passed. The French fleet had reached its destination and reinforcements were landed at Louisbourg

---

79 Corbett, *England in the Seven Years War*, vol.I, p.43.
80 Corbett, *England in the Seven Years War*, vol.I, p.44.
81 Corbett, *England in the Seven Years War*, vol.I, p.45.
82 Edward Boscawen to Fanny Boscawen, 26 June 1755, in Peter Kemp (ed.), 'Boscawen's Letters to His Wife', *The Naval Miscellany*, vol.IV (London: Navy Records Society, 1952), p.194.
83 George Anson to Francis Holburne, 8 May 1755, in Montagu Burrows, *The Life of Edward Lord Hawke* (London: W. H. Allen, 1883), pp.230–231.

and Quebec, providing them with the means to continue the fight on land. Soon afterwards Britain learnt that Braddock had been mortally wounded as the British were defeated at the disastrous Battle of the Monongahela on 9 July. Despite this setback, the British now looked beyond the Ohio Valley to a more ambitious objective of taking the whole of Canada south of Quebec and Montreal, although little progress towards it would be made in 1755.

8

The Minorca Crisis, 1756–1757

Boscawen's limited engagement off Newfoundland in June 1755 had done nothing to weaken French naval power but it would have significant political consequences: diplomatic relations with Britain were severed and conflict between the two countries would no longer be confined to America. The operation had failed partly because Boscawen had not been provided with sufficient ships to intercept the French as they arrived off Newfoundland or to maintain a blockade of North America to prevent them from leaving. Anson had also not taken account of adverse local weather conditions, where visibility was often limited, making it difficult to intercept an entire enemy squadron. He should have taken advice from the 'captains in London who knew what the weather was like in those waters from their experience when guarding the Newfoundland fishery'.[1]

Anson may also be criticised for how Boscawen's orders were drafted – if he had borne in mind 'the formula that blows before war must be "all or not at all", it is scarcely possible [that they] would have been drafted so carelessly as to permit of his making the mistake he did'.[2] Boscawen and Holburne left for England in October, having maintained an ineffective blockade of the St Lawrence during the intervening period. Despite these initial setbacks, Horace Walpole was impressed with the progress that the Admiralty had made in the conflict so far and, in June, he made a rare positive reference to Anson: 'the spirit and expedition with which we have equipped so magnificent a navy has surprised [the French], and does exceeding honour to my Lord Anson, who had breathed new life into our affairs'.[3]

With priority being given to the dispatch of naval forces to North America in April and May, Anson delayed preparations for the departure of the Western Squadron, which was due to patrol off Brest. Edward Hawke faced problems with manning and victualling, but he was held in port because of a reluctance among some ministers to engage the French navy in home waters in the absence of a formal declaration of war. However, others argued that there were strong arguments in favour of using the squadron aggressively to disrupt French trade, with the aim of damaging its finances, reducing its uncertain supply of good seamen and

---

1   Daniel A. Baugh, *The Global Seven Years War 1754–1763: Britain and France in a Great Power Contest* (second edition, London: Routledge, 2021), p.100.
2   Corbett, *England in the Seven Years War*, vol.I, p.59.
3   Horace Walpole to Horace Mann, 15 June 1755, in Lewis (ed.), *The Yale Edition of the Correspondence of Horace Walpole*, vol.20, p.485.

making 'the whole Kingdom of France cry out against war'.[4] Newcastle asked Hardwicke to consult Anson, who thought that 'a cruise would be good for both fleet and crews' and suggested that Hawke should be authorised to attack any French squadron he encountered, but not single ships.[5] No immediate decision was taken and the squadron remained in port as Cabinet discussions intensified early in June following news of the departure of a French squadron, commanded by Hilarion Josselin, Comte Du Guay, from Brest, with orders to protect merchant ships heading for France. The expected return of Comte Du Bois de la Motte from North America in the autumn would provide another possible target.

On 14 July, while discussions on the Western Squadron's role continued, Anson sent a copy of Boscawen's letter of 21 June about his engagement with the French to Lord Hardwicke.[6] He was alarmed by what he read and wrote to Newcastle: 'We have done too much or too little. The disappointment this news causes troubles me greatly'. He replied to Anson: 'It gives me much concern that so little has been done, since anything has been done at all. Voilà the war has begun!'.[7] Anson agreed with Hardwicke's assessment and expected France to declare war imminently, but his prediction was not shared by other members of the inner committee and proved to be wide of the mark. Newcastle's position remained unchanged: he wished to avoid any aggressive action that might compel France to declare war at a time when arrangements for the defence of Hanover were being made, but other ministers favoured more aggressive action to avoid missing opportunities to disrupt French trade.

In George II's absence in Hanover, the Regency Council (which included Anson as one of the Lords Justices) discussed the role of the Western Squadron on 21 July and a compromise was agreed. As reported by George Bubb Dodington, the Treasurer of the Navy, ministers decided that Hawke should sail with 16 ships of the line to Torbay and wait there for further instructions, which were to be prepared by Lord Anson and Thomas Robinson. Hawke's primary responsibility would be the protection of British trade and he was authorised to intercept any French squadron he encountered and 'endeavour to seize and take by every means their ships and vessels'. But, drawing on Boscawen's recent experience, he was ordered not to attack individual French warships or merchantmen. Anson was persuaded to adopt the same position even though he believed that more aggressive action was necessary. It was reported that 'Lord Anson, as usual said little, but as an admiral, & First Lord of the Admiralty, thought it became him to seem rather inclined to the spirited side of the question'.[8] Anson's view, as he expressed it to Henry Fox, was there 'were a hundred objections to this course, but that, as France was certain to proclaim war in a few days, there was no harm in gratifying those at the upper end of the table by signing the document without protest'.[9]

When the formal declaration of war that Anson had expected failed to appear, Fox and other ministers wanted the instructions to be strengthened as relations with France

---

4　Quoted in Martin Robson, *A History of the Royal Navy. The Seven Years War* (London: I.B. Tauris, 2016), p.18.
5　Corbett, *England in the Seven Years War*, vol.I, p.52.
6　Edward Boscawen to George Anson, 21 June 1755; a draft is included in Kemp (ed.), 'Boscawen's Letters to His Wife', pp.192–193.
7　Quoted in Corbett, *England in the Seven Years War*, vol.I, p.58.
8　Clark (ed.), *The Memoirs*, p.169.
9　Giles Fox-Strangways, Earl of Ilchester, *Henry Fox, Lord Holland, His Family and Relations* (London: John Murray, 1920), vol.I, pp.263–264.

deteriorated. As a result of these representations, Newcastle called a meeting at which Anson was present and it was decided that Hawke should be authorised 'to seize and take, by every means in [his] power, all French ships and vessels, as well men of war and privateers as merchantmen', and revised orders were sent to him on 6 August.[10] Following Du Guay's seizure of the *Blandford* (20) on 13 August, these orders were extended to all other British warships at sea. The Western Squadron finally left Spithead on 28 July but because of bad weather did not arrive off Cape Finisterre until 23 August. With only a single frigate at his disposal, Hawke's search for Du Guay was unlikely to succeed and, shortly afterwards, he was forced to return to England as sickness and bad provisions took their toll. Anson planned to send out replacement ships, but he left it too late and De la Motte was able to return to France without being intercepted.

On 14 October, the Western Squadron returned to sea and, in Hawke's absence on leave, Admiral John Byng was appointed to the command. During a highly successful cruise, more than 300 French merchant ships and 6,000 seamen were seized, providing a welcome contrast to the failure to intercept French naval forces earlier in the year. Joseph Yorke later pointed to the longer-term deterrent effect of the Western Squadron's cruises, commenting that the 'much condemned & exploded measure of Lord Anson's, for taking the French ships before the open declaration of the last war has contributed (from the apprehension of a repetition) more than anything to repress the D[uke] of Choiseul's vivacity; of this I had some strong proofs & it gave me much pleasure'.[11]

Byng's experience in command – he had to return to port after only a month because of leaky ships and sickness – pointed to the significant costs of maintaining a constant presence off the French coast. Despite these problems, Anson was able to send the squadron, now under the command of Vice Admiral Henry Osborn (described by Augustus Hervey as a 'worthy good man'), back to sea again in January 1756, as fears of a French invasion grew.[12] It was to cruise off Brest for much of the year, with Anson selecting Hawke, Boscawen and then Knowles in succession to Osborn. Despite the difficulties of keeping the Western Squadron at sea for extended periods, its presence had paid dividends, as Anson reported later in the year: 'the French fleet is kept in; our coast and colonies are unmolested; the French trade and succours intended for America have been in part intercepted; and our trade in the midst of war has hitherto enjoyed the security of peace'.[13]

The French chose not to respond to Byng's mass seizures of her merchant ships and for the moment did not declare war, but, towards the end of 1755, they delivered an ultimatum, which included a demand for the restitution of their shipping. The Government rejected their demands, accelerating the drift towards a formal declaration of war. At this point, Anson received details of the French war plan, which gave priority to the war at sea and assumed that they would soon have 50 ships of the line and as many frigates in service. It

---

10 Ruddock F. Mackay, *Admiral Hawke* (Oxford: Clarendon Press, 1965), p.128.
11 Joseph Yorke to Edward Weston, 19 December 1764, in HMC, *Reports on the Manuscripts of... C. F. Weston Underwood* (London: H. M. Stationery Office, 1885), p.378. Choiseul was French First Minister of State, 1758–1770.
12 Erskine (ed.), *Augustus Hervey's Journal*, p.243.
13 Quoted in Richard Middleton, 'British Naval Strategy, 1755–1762: The Western Squadron', *The Mariner's Mirror*, 75 (1989), p.354.

suggested that their ships would be deployed in a defensive formation to match the distribution of the Royal Navy. Hardwicke consulted Anson about the plan and his view was that 'it was a weak one, and such as England may be well able to deal with'. Its main weakness was 'the great subdivision of their force, which aims at guarding as many points as we have to guard'. He also believed that it would take longer for the French to commission their new ships than they expected. The plan focused on the destruction of British trade and there was no reference to any proposal to invade England, which Hardwicke found surprising as he 'considered that an invasion undertaken in a formidable manner would hamper us by destroying our credit more than any war on our commerce'.[14]

The plan was also contrary to the intelligence that had been received in London since August 1755 about the build-up of 70,000 French troops in the Channel ports. The Government was also aware that a squadron of 12 ships of the line was fitting out at Toulon, which would be ready in the spring of 1756. Although it was not clear whether the Toulon fleet would be used to attack Gibraltar or Minorca, sail into the English Channel or head for Canada, by December 1755, Anson seems to have made his mind up. He wrote to Hardwicke: 'I think it would be a dangerous measure to part with your naval strength from this country, which cannot be recalled if wanted, when I am strongly of opinion that whenever the French intend anything in earnest, their attack will be against this country'.[15] However, he did not hold a consistent view on the issue as only a few months earlier he had expressed a different opinion in a letter to Lord Holderness when he said that fears of an invasion are not very strong and he thought 'the French too wise to attempt it'.[16]

Firmer information about French war aims was not received until February 1756 when the Government first became aware that they had prepared a fully developed plan for the invasion of England and were fitting out ships at Brest and Rochefort. However, it later became clear that these plans were intended to deceive the British and that the French were in fact preparing to launch an attack on Minorca, which would be mounted from Toulon, some 180 miles away. The island, which had been in British hands since 1708, was used as a base by the Royal Navy for operations against the French fleet in Toulon and elsewhere in the Mediterranean. Although the British were aware of the preparations at Toulon, there was continuing uncertainty about France's real intentions, with Anson and others believing that it was more likely that their ships were destined for Canada rather than Minorca.

Despite this uncertainty, it would have been prudent for Britain to have strengthened Minorca's defences and kept watch on Toulon, particularly as Anson had the naval forces available to meet this threat. At the end of 1755, the navy had 83 ships in service: there were 14 cruising in the Channel, 52 were fitting out in England, 11 were in the Caribbean, four were in the East Indies, and three were in the Mediterranean. Although he could have redeployed his forces, Anson's top priority remained the defence of home waters – and convoy duty – and he underestimated the threat to Minorca, with the result that no action was taken to reinforce the small British naval presence in the Mediterranean. Additional ships could have prevented the departure of the French from Toulon but the failure to act meant that by 8 April 1756 their expeditionary force was ready to leave for Minorca unhindered by a British presence.

---

14   Corbett, *England in the Seven Years War*, vol.I, p.86.
15   BL: Hardwicke Papers, Add. MS. 35,359, f.383, George Anson to the Earl of Hardwicke, 6 December 1755.
16   BL: Egerton MS. 2,444, f.42, George Anson to Lord Holderness, 9 May 1755.

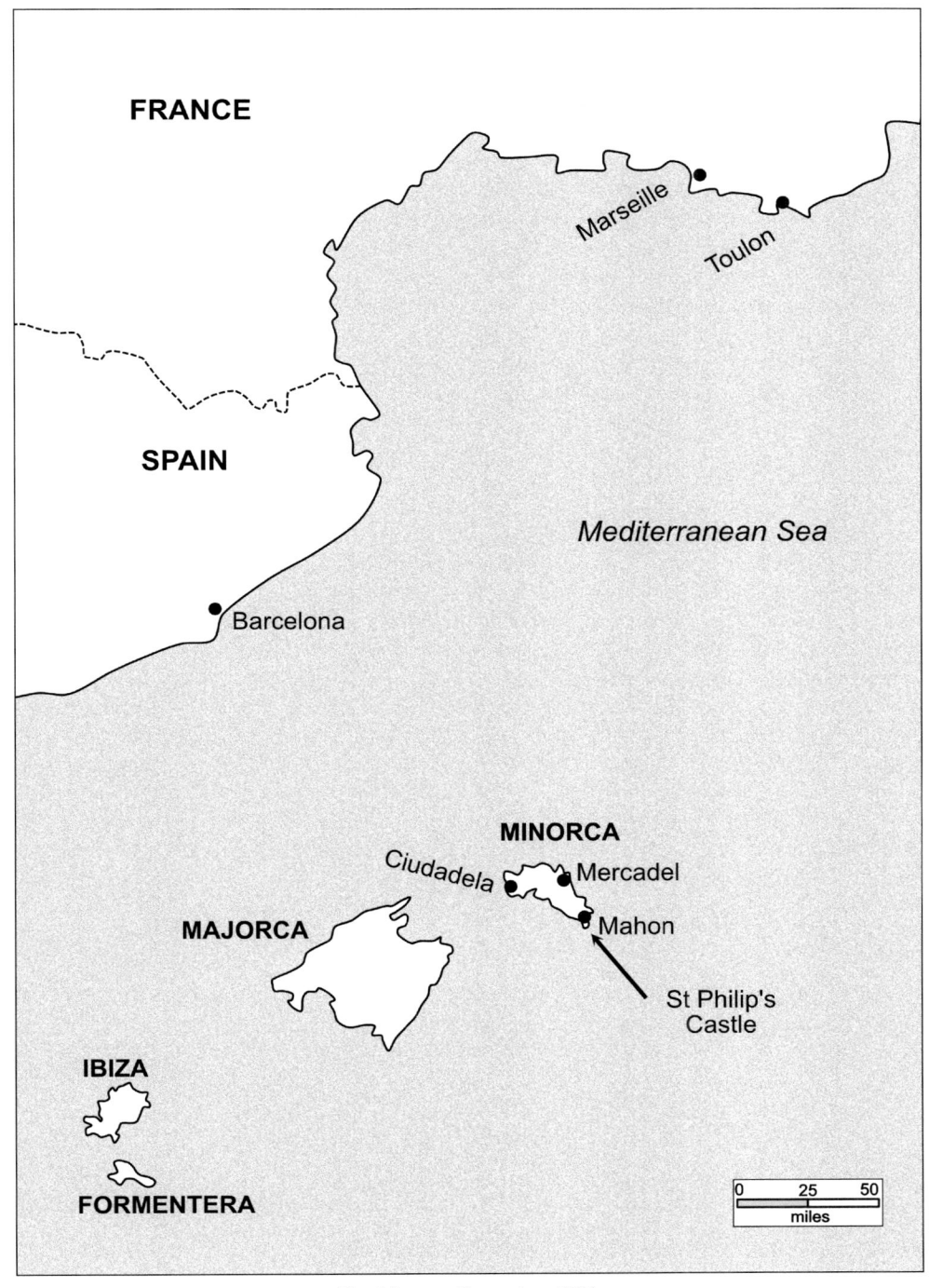

The Minorca Campaign, 1756.

In response to continuing fears of an invasion, on 27 February Anson ordered Hawke to blockade the Channel ports, but the arrival of new intelligence of a possible French attack on Minorca led to an urgent reassessment of the navy's priorities. In advance of an inner Cabinet meeting on 9 March, Newcastle asked Anson to prepare a squadron for service in the Mediterranean. The meeting considered the various intelligence reports and concluded that 'as strong a squadron as can be spared from hence be got ready to send into the Mediterranean'. Anson decided to allocate 10 ships of the line together with two ships from Commodore George Edgcumbe's Mediterranean squadron but with the French having 12 heavily armed ships available for the Minorca operation, Anson was providing 'neither superiority nor a margin for mishaps, whether caused by storms or combat'.[17]

Anson selected Admiral Byng to command the new squadron and a few days later he was promoted to admiral of the red. He was ninth on the list of flag officers and next in seniority to Anson himself. Rear Admiral Temple West was appointed as his second-in-command. Byng's appointment was a fateful decision that was to lead to the only major crisis in Anson's political career. Byng had joined the navy in 1718 and, like Anson, had served at the Battle of Cape Passaro, where his father had defeated the Spanish. Promoted to captain in 1727, he would spend a significant portion of his career in the Mediterranean, including service as the senior officer at Port Mahon. In 1747, he was appointed second in command to Vice Admiral Henry Medley in the Mediterranean and on Medley's death replaced him as commander in chief, a post he held until the end of the war. As mentioned above, he had a successful cruise in 1755 and, in selecting Byng, Anson, who 'was always mindful of the Western Squadron, must have taken favourable notice of his performance'.[18]

The second Earl of Hardwicke later defended his brother-in-law's choice, saying that 'he was fortunate in his choice of commanders except in that of Admiral Byng, and in him was only mistaken with the rest of his profession, for nobody ever suspected the capacity or courage of that unfortunate officer till the action off Mahon'.[19] However, Byng's earlier service under Medley had suggested that there were weaknesses in his character that Anson may have overlooked or been unaware of. In 1747, Byng had done nothing to prevent the French from taking the Austrian-held Lérins Islands off the south of France and his correspondence with Medley on the subject showed 'the same despondency, the same iteration of inability, the same assumption that the French had taken such measures as must prove fatal to the English cause, which pervaded his letters in 1756'.[20]

Despite the arrival of further intelligence confirming the scale of the French invasion fleet, Anson continued to give priority to the Western Squadron and did not increase the size of Byng's force. On 11 March, Anson issued Byng with orders to go to Portsmouth and take the squadron of 10 ships under his command and he arrived there nine days later. According to Augustus Hervey, Byng found that he was missing a frigate and that Anson had 'only sent the worst of the fleet while he kept the rest cruising at home, no hospital ship,

---

17 Baugh, *The Global Seven Years War*, p.159.
18 Daniel A. Baugh, 'John Byng (*bap.* 1704, *d.* 1757)', *Oxford Dictionary of National Biography*, <https://doi.org/10.1093/ref:odnb/4263 >, accessed 31 October 2022.
19 BL: Hardwicke Papers, Add. MS. 35,428, f.5, 'Memorial of Family Occurrences from 1760 to 1770 inclusive'.
20 HMC, *Report on the Manuscripts of Lady Du Cane*, p.xix.

no fireship, no store-ship, nor any tender'.[21] He later complained that his ships were 'the worst conditioned and mostly of the worst manned of any perhaps in his Majesty's service' and that his squadron was not powerful enough for the task in hand.[22] The last ship to join his squadron at Spithead, the *Intrepid* (64), the former French warship *Sérieux* captured in 1747, 'was not fit for a foreign voyage, and had neither water, provisions nor stores for that purpose'.[23]

Byng also discovered that he was short of 722 men, including 222 vacancies on his flagship *Ramillies* (90), but the Admiralty ordered him not to take men from six named ships at Portsmouth that were required for 'the most pressing service'.[24] Press gangs raised additional manpower but the squadron was still short of 336 men on its departure. On 24 March, the Admiralty informed him that five ships at Portsmouth under the command of Augustus Keppel were to join six other ships that were already at sea searching for the French, prompting Byng to comment that 'Lord Anson sent all the best ships cruising with his favourites'.[25] It is difficult to understand why Anson deployed as many as 11 fully-manned warships to deal with an 'unimportant French convoy', while Byng's strategically important mission was given lower priority and delayed as a result. It is clear that 'Byng could have sailed earlier – and with more ships – without the slightest risk to the safety of the British Isles'.[26]

Byng did not receive his instructions, which had been prepared by Anson, until 1 April. Issued on 30 March 1756, nine days later than expected, they informed him that it 'may be of the utmost consequences to the welfare of this nation that the squadron under your command should immediately put to sea'.[27] He should leave for Gibraltar with as many of his 10 ships as were ready, with the rest following as soon as possible and, on his arrival, he was to take Commodore Edgcumbe's Mediterranean squadron under his command. He was to carry 900 members of Lord Bertie's Regiment of Fusiliers, the 7th Foot, replacing the marines in his squadron who were being sent to other ships. The War Office ordered the Fusiliers to land at Gibraltar, where they would be replaced by a battalion taken from the Gibraltar garrison. Anson objected to this odd arrangement, pointing out that it was necessary for the Fusiliers to remain on board as they formed an essential part of each ship's crew following the departure of the marines. It was then decided that the Fusiliers should remain with the squadron and that Gibraltar should only provide an additional battalion from its garrison if Minorca was likely to be attacked. However, the circumstances in which Lieutenant General Thomas Fowke, the Governor of Gibraltar, was to send his troops to Minorca were not clearly defined.

On his arrival at Gibraltar, Byng was to establish whether a French squadron had passed through the Straits (with a likely destination of North America) and if that was the case, he was to detach sufficient ships to sail for Louisbourg. He was then to sail with his remaining

---

21   Erskine (ed.), *Augustus Hervey's Journal*, p.203.
22   Quoted in Richmond, *Papers Relating to the Loss of Minorca*, p.xix.
23   Dudley Pope, *At Twelve Mr Byng was Shot* (London: Secker & Warburg, 1987), p.89.
24   Quoted in Brian Tunstall, *Admiral Byng and the Loss of Minorca* (London: P. Allan, 1928), p.51.
25   Erskine (ed.), *Augustus Hervey's Journal*, p.204.
26   Pope, *At Twelve Mr Byng was Shot*, p.83.
27   Byng's instructions are printed in Pope, *At Twelve Mr Byng was Shot*, pp.344–346.

ships to Minorca. If the French had not passed through the straits, the entire squadron was ordered to proceed to Minorca 'without a moment's loss of time'.[28] If he found that the island had been attacked by the French, he was to use all possible means in his power for its relief. If no such attack had been made, he was to go to Toulon and prevent any French ships from leaving the port or intercept those that might escape. It is surprising that Anson gave so much more emphasis to America than the Mediterranean in his instructions and did not provide any guidance for the much more likely situation – the one that Byng actually faced – with Minorca occupied and the French navy stationed off the island.

Byng's acknowledgement of Anson's instructions was less than enthusiastic. While he intended to do all he could to frustrate the French plans, he was not optimistic, commenting that he would 'think myself the most fortunate if I am so happy to succeed in this undertaking'.[29] As a result of his manpower shortages, Byng did not leave Spithead until 6 April, which was far too late to intercept the French who would leave Toulon on 10 April. The squadron consisted of 12 ships of the line under Roland-Michel Barin, Marquis de la Galissonnière, carrying 15,000 troops commanded by Armand Jean du Plessis, Duc de Richelieu. After two days' delay because of bad weather, they arrived off Minorca on 17 April, untroubled by the British. As French troops landed and advanced towards Mahon, Edgcumbe's squadron abandoned the harbour and made for Gibraltar.

Anson was to be strongly criticised after the fall of Minorca for not sending Byng earlier with a stronger force and for failing to address his manning problems. It seemed strange that 'after more than a year of semi-war no reinforcement should have been sent to the Mediterranean and that no steps should have been taken to collect more seamen early in the year, when it was known that many ships would have to be manned in the summer'.[30] However, as George Lyttelton, first Lord Lyttelton, Chancellor of the Exchequer, reported, 'Lord Anson thought he had no more to spare, and it was hoped [Byng] would arrive at Minorca before the French could get thither, and being joined by Commodore Edgcumbe… would be more than a match for the Toulon expedition, but this hope has failed by a few days'.[31] With Anson still convinced that an attack on Minorca was probably no more than a diversion, he believed that Byng's squadron was powerful enough. His priorities remained the defence of England and the need to avoid the Western Squadron being exposed to a stronger French fleet in the Channel.

The first news of the French landing on Minorca was provided by the Spanish ambassador in London at the beginning of May and, according to Bubb Dodington, Newcastle received it 'with much warmth and anxiety'. Dodington reported that the Prime Minister held the navy responsible for the delays in Byng's departure: 'he laid a vast deal of blame, there [i.e., the Admiralty] – and without naming Lord Anson show'd himself extremely dissatisfy'd with him'.[32] A letter from the diplomat Joseph Yorke confirmed the news of the French

---

28 Pope, *At Twelve Mr Byng was Shot*, p.345.
29 Pope, *At Twelve Mr Byng was Shot*, p.111.
30 Tunstall, *Admiral Byng*, pp.56–57.
31 Maud Wyndham, *Chronicles of the Eighteenth Century. Founded on the Correspondence of Sir Thomas Lyttelton and his Family* (Boston: Houghton Mifflin Company, 1924), vol.II, p.211.
32 John Carswell and Lewis A. Dralle (eds.), *The Political Journal of George Bubb Dodington* (Oxford: Clarendon Press, 1965), p.340.

landing and was also extremely critical: 'I am afraid the Admiralty has been deceived in its intelligence about the Toulon squadron, and yet I don't know how that can be possible'. He continued:

> What have our fleets been lying in harbour for so long? Not for fear of the invasion, for that has never yet been probable and I have always asserted it, because I did not care sixpence for 100,000 men upon the coast opposite to you, when I did not see 10 ships to convey them. I am afraid the Administration will have brought a storm upon itself which will not easily be laid.[33]

On 7 May, during a period when he was organising the opposition in the Commons, William Pitt launched an attack on Newcastle, blaming him rather than Anson for the probable loss of Minorca, including the failure to mobilise the navy at an earlier date. According to Newcastle, Pitt had 'laid everything that was blamed upon me... He made great compliment to my Lord Anson, all at my expense'.[34] However, as the Minorca crisis developed, Pitt was to turn his attention to Anson's alleged shortcomings, saying that 'he was not fit to command a cock-boat upon the River Thames'.[35] Fox, who was now Secretary of State for the Southern Department, shared some of Pitt's concerns, pointing out to Budd Dodington that he would have dispatched a stronger squadron a month earlier, but his views did not prevail. He said that Lord Anson had assured him that Byng's squadron would 'beat anything the French had or could have in the Mediterranean'.[36]

Newcastle sought to reassure Fox by explaining Anson's view that Byng's squadron 'was undoubtedly strong enough, and that in all probability the French would not stay to meet him'. He also endorsed Anson's view that priority should be given to home defence. If Britain was defeated by a superior French fleet in the Channel, it 'would have been a more fatal thing than in the Mediterranean, and that the Ministers would have been represented as fools or knaves, that did not see that the preparations in Toulon were only a feint'. The real difficulty was 'that we are not equal to the work we have undertaken. We are not singly a match for France. We cannot provide for all services and all places where they may attack us'.[37]

On 18 May, Britain declared war on France, recognising that a general European war was inevitable. It also belatedly decided to send further reinforcements to the Mediterranean and five ships of the line under the command of Rear Admiral Thomas Broderick were dispatched, but they would not reach Gibraltar until 15 June, nearly a month after Byng's abortive engagement with the French off Minorca. When Byng arrived at Gibraltar on 2 May he learnt that the French had invaded and captured the whole island apart from St Philip's Castle, which was under siege. Byng had orders to carry troops from Gibraltar if Minorca were threatened, but the army council of war decided against sending them because it would weaken their defences while landing reinforcements would be difficult

---

33 BL: Hardwicke Papers, Add. MS. 35,364, f.91, Joseph Yorke to Lord Royston, 7 May 1756.
34 BL: Newcastle Papers, Add. MS. 32,864, f.486, Duke of Newcastle to the Earl of Hardwicke, 8 May 1756.
35 John Almon, *Anecdotes of the Life of the Right Honourable William Pitt, Earl of Chatham, and of the Principal Events of His Time* (London: L. B. Seeley, 1797), vol.I, pp.249–250.
36 Carswell and Dralle (eds.), *The Political Journal of George Bubb Dodington*, p.340.
37 Duke of Newcastle to Henry Fox, 8 May 1756, in Fox-Strangways (ed.), *Letters to Henry Fox*, pp.78–79.

now that the French were in occupation. Despite the council's formal decision, Lieutenant General Fowke offered to send reinforcements but Byng declined them as he saw no prospect of successfully intervening on the island.

Byng left Gibraltar on 8 May and, as he passed Palma, Majorca, he spotted a French frigate which left to warn La Galissonnière. At this point, he was joined by his old friend Augustus Hervey, captain of the *Phoenix*, who had called into Palma. His first impressions of the squadron, which he recorded in his *Journal*, were far from favourable: 'twas worse than I saw, for his ships being almost all the worst of the fleet, that even they were not manned, that the troops of Lord Bertie's Regiment, which were to be landed at Mahon, made up the compliment [sic] now of the fleet'.[38] When Byng arrived off Minorca on 19 May he dispatched three frigates with orders to make for Port Mahon to deliver a letter to Lieutenant General William Blakeney, the acting governor, but ordered their withdrawal when the French squadron came into sight.

Byng planned to attack the French without delay, but light winds meant that the two squadrons were unable to come near each other until the following day (20 May). Byng had 13 ships under his command compared to 12 in the French line, with neither side having a significant advantage. At 10:00 a.m. Byng turned towards the French who were to the southwest and soon afterwards formed a line of battle. He ordered his captains to clear their ships for action. With the British on the starboard tack and the French on the larboard, the two squadrons were 'steering converging courses, as if travelling down each arm of an invisible V inscribed on the surface of the sea'.[39] Byng and La Galissonnière struggled to gain the weather gauge, with the French losing the race as the wind changed direction.

In the early afternoon, Byng hoisted the signal to approach the enemy at an angle; when he was in the right position in relation to the French line, he would order each of his captains to tack and open fire on his respective opponent. The plan faltered because his captains had not been fully briefed on the plans and the available signals could not communicate them effectively. The *Defiance*, which was at the head of the British line, did not steer directly for the leading French ship, *Orphee*, but came round to larboard on a course parallel with the French but more than a mile distant from them. It was only when Byng issued the signal to engage the enemy that his ships turned towards their opposite number in the enemy line. The *Defiance* and other ships in the van division were much closer to the French than those in the rear, and they engaged the French at close quarters. However, the rear, under Byng, never came within effective gunshot. A disabled English ship in the van division caused chaos, with the ships next in line backing their sails (to cause them to move astern) rather than going around her. Byng did not issue signals to direct them to avoid the obstruction and only one ship in the rear division engaged the enemy.

With the British van unsupported, the French moved forward to attack and caused heavy damage, but when Byng's rear division got underway again, they abandoned their plan to cut his squadron in half because of the risks. The French then retreated but Byng decided not to pursue them, bringing the battle to an end. Explaining his decision, he said: 'after the enemy bore away and made sail as they so much out-sailed us, and a considerable part

---

38 Erskine (ed.), *Augustus Hervey's Journal*, p.203.
39 Pope, *At Twelve Mr Byng was Shot*, p.139.

of the fleet was unable to pursue, I judged it improper to pursue with part of the fleet an enemy superior at first, and still all of them fit for action, according to all appearances'.[40] In the days that followed the engagement, he did not attempt to engage the French again, communicate with St Philip's Castle, or land his soldiers. A council of war concluded that there was nothing the squadron could do, and agreed to return to Gibraltar in case the French decided to attack.

On 31 May, Lord Anson received Byng's dispatch of 4 May (together with a letter from Lieutenant General Fowke), which he had sent before leaving Gibraltar for Minorca. He believed that if he had arrived before the French, he could have prevented them from occupying the island, but because they had landed in strength he did not have enough troops to lift the siege of the castle. In his view 'the throwing of men into the castle will only enable it to hold out a little longer time and add to the number that must fall into the enemy's hands'. He would sail to Minorca 'where I shall be a better judge of the situation of affairs there' but offered no hope that he would be able to relieve Mahon. Anson was concerned by what he read, telling Newcastle that he would not 'be much pleased with [Byng's] letters, and less with the Governor of Gibraltar's, who has sent no troops for the relief of Port Mahon, and for the very extraordinary reason, *viz.* because he would then have had fewer for Gibraltar'.[41] Anson's view was shared by other members of the Cabinet who agreed that Fowke should be recalled in disgrace.

On 2 June, Henry Fox received an extract of La Galissonnière's dispatch on the battle from the Spanish ambassador, which was written in 'such general terms that no one reading it could have a very exact idea of what had happened', except for the fact that Byng had clearly not been victorious.[42] A meeting of the inner committee, attended by Anson, which took place the next day, relied on this evidence – and Byng's letter of 4 May – to conclude that Byng and West should be replaced and ordered home. It was also agreed that Hawke should succeed Byng and assume command in the Mediterranean with orders to do everything in his power to relieve St Philip's Castle if it could hold out until he arrived.[43] Charles Saunders was appointed as his second in command, a promotion which has been described as 'a stroke of real genius, and worthy of Anson's unerring eye for talent'.[44]

Anson was depressed by what he read in Byng's letter and by concerns expressed by Admiral Boscawen, now in command of the Western Squadron, about the strength of the French fleet. As he commented to Newcastle that 'I don't know how it comes to pass, that unless our commanders in chief have a very great superiority of the enemy they never think themselves safe; I wish it was possible to have it in all parts of the world, but that cannot be unless we know what was the destination of the French fleet'.[45] Soon afterwards, Anson decided that the captain of Byng's flagship *Ramillies* and her six lieutenants should also return home.[46] Although the reason for this decision was not recorded, it must have occurred

---

40 Pope, *At Twelve Mr Byng was Shot*, p.157.
41 BL: Newcastle Papers, Add. MS. 32,865, f.159, George Anson to the Duke of Newcastle, 31 May 1756.
42 Pope, *At Twelve Mr Byng was Shot*, p.169.
43 BL: Newcastle Papers, BL Add. MS. 32,865, ff. 211–212, Duke of Newcastle to George Anson, 5 June 1756.
44 Tunstall, *Admiral Byng*, p.157.
45 BL: Newcastle Papers, Add. MS. 32,865, ff.221–222, George Anson to the Duke of Newcastle, 6 June 1756.
46 TNA: ADM 3/64.

to Anson that Byng might be accused of cowardice and that the evidence of his own officers would be needed at a court-martial. Anson's fellow commissioner Boscawen thought that others should share the blame along with Byng. He wrote to his wife Fanny that:

> Mr Byng stayed at Gibraltar 10 days, for what I cannot divine. He also loitered five days at Spithead, upon frivolous pretences, but after all, why was he not ordered sooner? Everybody knew the French were arming against that place long before he was ordered, so that if he is to blame, he is not the only person to be blamed.[47]

Byng returned to Gibraltar on 20 June, four days after Rear Admiral Broderick's arrival, and they made plans for the combined squadron to sail to Minorca, but they had not left by the time Hawke arrived on 3 July. By this point the opportunity to relieve the garrison – or to disrupt the French supply route from Toulon to Minorca – had been missed as the whole island was now in French hands. Hawke delivered a letter to Byng from John Clevland, which said that 'His Majesty is so much dissatisfied with your conduct, that he has ordered their Lordships to recall yourself and Mr West'.[48] Augustus Hervey reported that he had seen Edward Hawke, who condemned the 'unprecedented infamous reports Lord Holland [Henry Fox], Lord Anson and the Duke of Newcastle encouraged everywhere against Mr Byng's character in order to raise the mob against him and turn all the resentment and just indignation of the people from themselves to Admiral Byng'.[49] Public disquiet grew during June with criticism focused on the Government despite the removal of Byng from his command. With leading ministers, including Anson, determined to evade responsibility, further action would be needed to redirect the blame onto Byng.

When Byng's formal dispatch, dated 25 May, finally arrived in London on 23 June, it was accompanied by a letter to Anson, which provided further evidence of his defeatist attitudes: 'when I sailed from Gibraltar I found it was the general opinion not to leave this place when there was so little, if any hopes of relieving Minorca, and [? not] much more hoping for the success we have had against a fleet superior to ours'.[50] On 25 June, after ministers had read the letters, they concluded that Byng was guilty of dereliction of duty and should be tried by court-martial under paragraph 12 of the Articles of War. They also decided that Byng's dispatch could not be published without significant cuts with the aim of ensuring, according to an historian of the Minorca crisis, that 'the public might receive as much information as possible, the French as little information as possible, and Byng as much blame as possible'.[51]

To accompany publication in *The London Gazette*, several national newspapers were briefed on Byng's shortcomings:

---

47 Edward Boscawen to Fanny Boscawen, 3 June 1756, in Kemp (ed.), 'Boscawen's Letters to His Wife', p.218.
48 Tunstall, *Admiral Byng*, p.169.
49 Erskine (ed.), *Augustus Hervey's Journal*, p.217.
50 John Byng to George Anson, 25 May 1756, in Yorke (ed.) *The Life and Correspondence*, vol.II, p. 293.
51 Tunstall, *Admiral Byng*, p.162; see Pope, *At Twelve Mr Byng was Shot*, pp.181–182, for details of the cuts to the text.

Though he [Byng] solicited the command, he *deferred* sailing from England till very pressing letters were sent him from authority; many *strange* delays happened in the course of the voyage; he *lost* seven days at Gibraltar, when the utmost expedition was necessary for the public service... the bad condition of the enemy's fleet occasioned their only maintaining a running fight; night and the cautiousness of our Admiral put an entire end to the skirmish...[52]

On 29 June, Fox instructed Anson to issue orders for Byng's arrest on his arrival in England and to make arrangements for his court-martial. He was also to ask Hawke to investigate Byng's role in the battle and his action 'subsequent thereto; and particularly as to his leaving the island of Minorca exposed to the French Fleet'.[53] Government briefings fuelled public anger against Byng and, by July, the campaign against him was 'in full swing: hired hacks prepared pamphlets, suborned journalists wrote malicious articles and lampoons'.[54] Effigies of Byng were burnt across the country and Wrotham Park, his estate in Hertfordshire, was attacked and narrowly escaped destruction. News of the surrender of St Philip's Castle on 29 June arrived in mid-July and the 'wrath of the ministry and the fury of the populace were excessive'.[55]

Despite the continuing popular anger directed at Byng, Ministers still feared that they would be held primarily responsible for the loss of Minorca. On 19 July, Newcastle wrote to Hardwicke expressing concern that the opposition would endeavour to place the blame '*singly* upon me, or if that can't be done, to make me answerable for other people's neglects or weaknesses'. Anson should prepare for the 'immediate trial and condemnation of Admiral Byng, if, as I think there can be no doubt, he deserves it'. The 'sea officers should be learnt to talk in this manner, and not to think to fling blame upon civil ministers. Your Lordship knows the little share *we* have in military operations, or in the choice of military men, either at sea or on land'.[56] At a Cabinet meeting the following day it was agreed that Anson should produce a defence of the Government's conduct. The Admiralty was to prove that no ships could have been sent to the Mediterranean before Byng's squadron was dispatched, that his ships were sufficient in number and had been made ready in time. The briefing was to show that Minorca could have been saved if Byng had done his duty.

Byng reached England on 26 July and, in response to a request for an explanation for his arrest, the Admiralty simply said that 'the directions for confining him were in pursuance of the King's pleasure, in order to his being brought to trial for his conduct and behaviour in the Mediterranean'.[57] He was initially confined on board the *Antelope* while the Government decided where to hold him as he awaited trial. Fox wrote to Anson on 30 July asking him 'to consider well what hands you trust him to' in order to avoid any possibility of

---

52   Quoted in Pope, *At Twelve Mr Byng was Shot*, p.183.
53   Pope, *At Twelve Mr Byng was Shot*, p.183.
54   Pope, *At Twelve Mr Byng was Shot*, p.187.
55   J. K. Laughton, 'John Byng (1704–1757', *The Dictionary of National Biography* (1886), <https://doi.org/10.1093/odnb/9780192683120.013.4263, accessed 31 October 2022.
56   BL: Newcastle Papers, Add. MS. 32,866, f.210, Duke of Newcastle to the Earl of Hardwicke, 19 July 1757.
57   Pope, *At Twelve Mr Byng was Shot*, p.196.

an escape, before expressing his view that he should be confined in the Tower of London.[58] In his reply to Fox, Anson agreed, explaining that 'I do think (from his former situation in the Fleet), he might have a chance to escape if he has any such intention. A letter is wrote to the Secretary of War for a strong guard to bring him to town from Portsmouth'.[59] The Government later changed its mind and on 9 August, Byng was taken to the Royal Hospital, Greenwich, where he was held until his court-martial began.

On 1 August, Anson chaired a meeting of the Admiralty Board to determine the charges that Byng should face. It decided that he should be charged with acting contrary to his instructions under the Twelfth Article of War: that on 20 May 'he did withdraw or keep back, and did not do his utmost to take, seize, and destroy the ships of the French king… [and] did not do his utmost to relieve St Philip's Castle… but acted contrary to and in breach of his instructions'.[60] Anson later addressed the question of whom Byng could call in his defence and, early in August, he agreed to his request for 37 witnesses but rejected a demand for 31 more. In his reply, Anson said the Board 'was desirous to give you the earliest opportunity of acquitting yourself, if possible, from so heavy a charge', but considered his request for additional witnesses 'merely as a scheme suggested to you to delay your being brought to trial. By the same means you may put off your trial forever'. Anson pointed out that as many as 20 officers who had served with him were available to give evidence and suggested that several of them 'must be presumed under a particular bias (as far as truth will permit) in your favour'.[61] His letter has been described by an historian of the Minorca crisis as 'monstrous and venomous', while Byng's reply was measured and included an explanation of why he needed additional witnesses.[62] Anson had no further role in organising Byng's trial as members of the court-martial were selected after he left office, and the appeal to save Byng's life was held when Lord Winchilsea was First Lord.

As Newcastle had predicted, the Government's neglect of Minorca increasingly became the focus of public attention and, by August, demands for a public enquiry were being made by local representatives across the country. The most important intervention came from the City of London, which criticised the failure 'to prevent or defeat an attack, after such early notice of the enemy's intentions' and called for 'the authors of our late losses and disappointment, to be enquired into and punished'.[63] It was accompanied by a threat to withdraw its financial support unless action was taken. Several leading newspapers published articles criticising the Government's failure to act in good time or reinforce the Minorca garrison. *The Evening Post* argued that the loss of Minorca 'cannot surely be looked upon by any person as an uncertain event of war, but as a certain event of the treachery, negligence, or incapacity of those who were entrusted with power, more than sufficient to preserve it'.[64]

Anson was among the senior ministers who were the subject of intense criticism in the press and other publications. It was widely believed that Byng was being prosecuted to protect Anson,

---

58   Henry Fox to George Anson, 30 July 1756, quoted in Pope, *At Twelve Mr Byng was Shot*, p.196.
59   BL: Anson Papers, Add. MS. 15,995, f.13, George Anson to Henry Fox, [1756].
60   Quoted in Pope, *At Twelve Mr Byng was Shot*, p.244.
61   Tunstall, *Admiral Byng*, pp.198–200.
62   Pope, *At Twelve Mr Byng was Shot*, p.218.
63   Pope, *At Twelve Mr Byng was Shot*, p.206.
64   Pope, *At Twelve Mr Byng was Shot*, p.210.

whose alleged failings as a strategist – including his obsession with an illusionary French invasion – had led to the loss of Minorca. It was claimed that he owed his appointment to his father-in-law, Hardwicke, that he lacked the energy needed to run the wartime navy, and that his promotions were based on favouritism rather than merit. He was mocked by the nickname 'Mute', reflecting the widely held view that he 'was a man of legendary taciturnity, which was interpreted as a sign of dull torpor'.[65] Anson felt compelled to ask the Solicitor-General for advice on whether one particularly damaging article in *The Gazetteer and London Daily Advertiser* was libellous. He decided to let the matter rest when he was advised against taking any action on the grounds that 'when so many more virulent papers against [the] Government have been published without any animadversion, it would be very injudicious to start with this'.[66]

It has been estimated that Anson appeared in some 33 hostile engravings and several pamphlets published in 1756–1757. Many prints drew on Anson's reputation as a gambler, implying that his 'intelligence assessments, planning and deployment of the fleet were so erratic that he was guilty of reckless gambling, not only with Britain's maritime and colonial fortunes but also with national survival itself'.[67] He was also subject to scurrilous gossip about his marriage based on the assertion that it was invalid because he was unable to consummate it. According to Walpole, Anson's 'incapacity grew the general topic of ridicule; and he was joined in all the satiric prints with his father-in-law, Newcastle, and Fox'.[68]

The first of several pamphlets attacking the Government published during the summer argued that Byng was 'a victim to state policy', which was necessary to 'divert the populace from diving too deep into political mysteries,[69] while a second pamphlet, which analysed the text deleted from Byng's dispatch, clearly held Anson responsible for the loss of Minorca although he was not mentioned by name. The second pamphleteer pointed to

> The insufficiency of the *English* fleet, the long delay in sending it, the want of stores and artificers at Gibraltar, the ordering the marines out of Mr Byng's squadron at Portsmouth, sending no troops to Mahon, no hospital-ships, fire-ships, or tenders, the sending him with foul and crazy ships, ill manned and old, the concealment of his vindication, and adding to his destruction by ten thousand calumniating inventions.[70]

The appearance of these critical pamphlets led Earl Waldegrave to comment that Anson was no more deserving of the 'violent clamour' raised against him than of the high reputation which proceeded it. He was:

---

65 John M. Cardwell, *Arts and Arms: Literature, Politics and Patriotism During the Seven Years War* (Manchester: Manchester University Press, 2004), p.89.
66 Quoted in Pope, *At 12 Mr Byng was Shot*, p.223.
67 Cardwell, *Arts and Arms*, pp.90–91.
68 Walpole, *Memoirs of the Reign of King George II*, vol.II, p.228.
69 *A Modest Apology for the Conduct of a Certain Admiral in the Mediterranean* (London: M. Cooper, 1756), p.v.
70 *An Appeal to the People: Containing, the Genuine and Entire Letter of Admiral Byng to the Secr. of the Ad---y* (London: J. Morgan, 1756), pp.74-75. See also [Paul Whitehead], *A Letter to a Member of Parliament in the Country, from His Friend in London, Relative to the Case of Admiral Byng* (London: J. Cooke, 1756) for similar criticisms.

In reality a good sea officer and had gain'd a considerable victory over the French in the last war, but nature has not endow'd him with those extraordinary abilities, which had been so liberally granted him by the whole nation… [Now] on the contrary, he is to be allow'd no merit whatsoever; the loss of Minorca is to be inputed to his misconduct, though many were equally, some infinitely more blameable; his slowness in business, is to be call'd negligence, and his silence and reserve, which formerly pass'd for wisdom, takes the name of dullness, and of want of capacity'.[71]

Newcastle decided to respond to these public attacks on the administration by initiating a contest which became 'three-cornered, the Ministers attacking Byng, Byng attacking the Ministers and the opposition attacking both'.[72] Critical articles inspired by the Government appeared in the press and an anti-Byng pamphlet, commissioned by Lord Hardwicke, was published. Produced by the Scottish poet and dramatist David Mallett, it explained why it had not been possible to supply Byng with a more powerful fleet or send it out at an earlier date. Anson supplied Mallett with Admiralty documents with Clevland's help and commented on the first draft. Hardwicke, who was 'not much enamoured with it', approved a final version and it was published anonymously as *The Conduct of the Ministry Impartially Examined*.[73] In November, Mallett was paid a fee of £300 for his labours from the Duke of Newcastle's secret service fund.[74]

As early as August, Newcastle had seen 'dangers on all sides, and no means of getting out of them' and considered the possibility of resigning even though responsibility for what had happened was not his alone. As he explained to Hardwicke: 'Though there is nothing I would not yield to, for the sake of the King and the public, the Army is absolutely under other direction [the Duke of Cumberland's] and the sea [Anson] does not love to be controlled, or even advised, yet I am to answer for any miscarriage in either'.[75] As public pressure intensified later in the year, ministerial changes came under discussion and Fox, as the responsible Secretary of State, considered his position.

Fox was a 'marked man' but did not hold himself responsible for what had happened and was unwilling to defend ministerial colleagues who had rejected his pleas to reinforce the Minorca squadron. As Bubb Dodington recorded in his diary: 'Lord Anson assur'd him, and took it upon himself, that Byng's squadron would beat any thing the French had, or could have, in the Mediterranean'.[76] Even Lord Hardwicke recognised that it might be necessary to sacrifice his son-in-law at a time when the survival of the administration was at stake, commenting to Newcastle on the absence of any 'proposal for bringing an efficient Parliamentary man into the Admiralty. This is indeed very necessary, for not only

---

71 Clark (ed.), *Memoirs*, p.186.
72 Tunstall *Admiral Byng*, p.190. A more balanced contemporary assessment may be found in *Impartial Reflections on the Case of Mr. Byng, As Stated in an Appeal to the people, &c. and a Letter to a Member of Parliament, &c* (London: S. Hooper, 1756).
73 [David Mallett], *The Conduct of the Ministry Impartially Examined. In a Letter to the Merchants of London* (London: S. Bladon, 1756).
74 BL: Anson Papers, Add. MS. 15,956, f.25, Earl of Hardwicke to George Anson, 10 October 1756.
75 Duke of Newcastle to the Earl of Hardwicke, 28 August 1756, in Yorke (ed.), *The Life and Correspondence*, vol.II, p.310.
76 Carswell and Dralle (eds.), *The Political Journal of George Bubb Dodington*, p.340.

the sake of the Board of Admiralty but of the whole administration, for on those affairs the chief stress will lie'.[77] Attempts to save the administration came to nothing when, on 14 October, Fox carried out his threat to resign and the plan to replace him with Pitt to ensure Newcastle's political survival failed. Pitt refused to join an administration with Newcastle at its head and, on 11 November, Newcastle, Hardwicke and Anson were forced to resign.

A new administration headed by William Cavendish, fourth Duke of Devonshire, was formed with Pitt as Secretary of State for the Southern Department, where he assumed responsibility for war policy. Anson would have no place in an administration dominated by Pitt, who 'strongly arraigns the conduct of the Admiralty and the management of our fleets and squadrons', and he was succeeded as First Lord by Richard Grenville-Temple, Earl Temple, Pitt's brother-in-law and close political ally.[78] The entire Anson Board, whose reputation had been irretrievably damaged by the loss of Minorca, was replaced except for Anson's ally Edward Boscawen, a leading naval critic of Byng, who now became the dominant member. He provided the only continuity with the previous administration and 'had every reason to justify the policy of his patron Anson'.[79] Pitt selected the other members of the new Board, which only remained in office until he was dismissed in April 1757. He reappointed them when he returned as Secretary of State in June and Anson was forced to accept them on his return to the Admiralty. The civilian members of Temple's Board were Gilbert Elliot, George Hay and Thomas Hunter, all of whom were Pitt's Parliamentary allies but had no relevant experience of naval issues. Apart from Boscawen, the naval members were Vice Admiral Temple West and Vice Admiral John Forbes. West, who received no blame for the Minorca debacle, was Lord Temple's cousin and a supporter of William Pitt. Forbes' appointment, on the other hand, was made on professional rather than political grounds.

The short-lived Board headed by Lord Temple was not associated with any innovations in policy and Lord Barrington, Secretary at War, pointed to the continuity of policy with its predecessor. It had maintained 'every effort in America, consistent with our safety at home, every effort at sea, and whatever this country can do besides, given to the support of our allies on the continent. I am told the Admiralty change nothing in what they find to have been Lord Anson's plan'.[80] As Walpole pointed out, Anson remained influential: 'Lord Hardwicke and Lord Anson were out of place, but were they out of power? Without hinting how soon they remounted to formal power, let it be remembered that at that moment, they commanded the House of Lords, and had a vast majority in the House of Commons'.[81] During the period he was out of office, Anson remained physically close to the centre of power, moving only a short distance from his former quarters at the Admiralty to Downing Street, and maintained his close connection with John Clevland.

Despite evidence of continuity in policy between the two boards, the new First Lord was quick to distance himself from his predecessor's approach to the Minorca problem, with Augustus Hervey reporting Lord Temple's view that the previous Board's behaviour

---

77 Quoted in Pope, *At 12 Mr Byng was Shot*, p.225.
78 Earl of Hardwicke to Joseph Yorke, 31 October 1756, in Yorke (ed.), *The Life and Correspondence*, vol. II, p.333.
79 Tunstall, *Admiral Byng*, p.205.
80 Yorke (ed.), *The Life and Correspondence*, vol II, p.362.
81 Walpole, *Memoirs of the Reign of King George II*, vol.II, pp.356–357.

towards Byng was 'quite shameful'. Anson's former colleague Henry Fox was also critical. Hervey said that Fox had 'insinuated to me that he had nothing to do with the proceedings against Mr Byng and disapproved Lord Anson's conduct on the whole'.[82] Walpole summed up the new Government's different attitude: it shows 'great tenderness to Byng, who had certainly been most inhumanly and spitefully treated by Anson'.[83] However, it soon became apparent that the change in approach was more apparent than real.

Shortly before Anson's departure from office, Lord Hardwicke feared that Anson would be targeted in the wide-ranging Parliamentary enquiry into the failures in America and Minorca that Pitt was demanding and those fears were soon to be realised. He wrote to his son Joseph: 'The affairs of the Admiralty consist of so many branches, and admit of such variety of opinions, that nobody knows how far enquiries may be carried. Ill success will be worked up into mistakes, mistakes into neglects, and neglects into crimes'.[84] It soon became clear that Anson also faced the risk of being impeached over his role in the loss of Minorca and other alleged failures. Pitt employed a leading lawyer to draw up articles of impeachment against Anson, focusing on the charge that he had failed to provide Byng with an adequate fleet. Although Pitt abandoned his plans for impeachment action, the Parliamentary enquiry, which he hoped would expose the failings of his predecessors, would soon begin.

As the new Board progressed arrangements for Byng's trial, it soon became clear that it was not necessarily any more sympathetic to him than its predecessors. The Devonshire administration's grip on power was uncertain and the influence of Newcastle and Fox (and their allies Hardwicke and Anson) was still felt. As Walpole commented, 'the chief friends of each remain in power',[85] increasing the prospect of securing Byng's conviction while defending their part – and that of Lord Anson – in the Minorca debacle. Newcastle was reassured when he was briefed on information provided by Lieutenant General Blakeney, which suggested that Byng could have communicated with St Philip's Castle and landed reinforcements, with the result that 'Marshal Richelieu and his army must have capitulated'. When Hardwicke received this intelligence, he informed Newcastle that 'the information is very material' and had 'communicated it to my Lord Anson, who will make the best use of it he can in his present private situation'.[86]

Byng's court-martial was convened on the *St George* at Portsmouth on 28 December. Vice Admiral Thomas Smith, a relation of Lord Temple, was appointed as president, but the other three admirals selected as members of the court were allies of Lord Anson. Francis Holburne, the most senior, had been sent to reinforce Boscawen off Louisburg early in 1755 but Anson later thought him 'subversive, an opinion that probably drew something from Holburne's

---

82 Erskine (ed.), *Augustus Hervey's Journal*, p.231.
83 Horace Walpole to Horace Mann, 29 November 1756, in Lewis (ed.), *The Yale Edition of the Correspondence of Horace Walpole*, vol.21, p.23.
84 Earl of Hardwicke to Joseph Yorke, 31 October 1756, in Yorke (ed.), *The Life and Correspondence*, vol.II, p.334.
85 Horace Walpole to Thomas Mann, 13 November 1756, in Lewis (ed.), *The Yale Edition of the Correspondence of Horace Walpole*, vol.21, p.17.
86 Earl of Hardwicke to the Duke of Newcastle, 6 December 1756, in Yorke (ed.), *The Life and Correspondence*, vol.II, p.355.

Scottish origins and his failure to adopt English "manners" as befitted a naval officer'.[87] The other two rear admirals – Harry Norris and Thomas Broderick – 'owed everything' to the former First Lord according to an historian of the Minorca crisis.[88] Nine captains were selected to sit on the court-martial, including Peter Denis and Augustus Keppel, both of whom had close connections with Anson. When the selection process was completed, Boscawen, who was consistently critical of Byng's conduct, was confident that 'we shall have a majority, and he will be condemned'.[89]

Although the witnesses examined during his trial focused on Byng's conduct at sea, some evidence about the Admiralty's role was also heard. Augustus Hervey, who appeared for the defence, later claimed that his evidence was intended to prove that 'the failure of that day's success should have ALL laid at the door of those infamous ministers who sent such a weak squadron out, after all the repeated intelligences they had had'.[90] Under cross-examination, Byng's former deputy, Vice Admiral Temple West, now a member of the Admiralty Board, acknowledged that some of Byng's ships were in poor condition and that several were undermanned. However, according to the Duke of Newcastle, the combined evidence provided by West and Blakeney 'seemed almost of themselves sufficient to condemn Mr Byng. If it should come out that the fleet was strong enough and sent in time enough to relieve the place, and that the loss was simply owing to the cowardice or fault of the Admiral, how are the Ministers to blame?'.[91]

On the day the trial ended – 19 January 1757 – a letter from the famous French writer Voltaire arrived in London, enclosing a letter from the Duc de Richelieu, who had returned to Paris after taking Minorca. Richelieu strongly defended Byng's record, saying that 'his reputation ought not to be attacked for being worsted, after having done everything that could be expected... All the measures taken by Admiral Byng were admirable'.[92] The letters were intercepted by the Post Office in London and passed to Lord Holderness, who sent copies to Anson. His reaction to this unwelcome intervention was to 'sink them' as they 'would do harm at the court-martial'.[93] The Government decided not to suppress the letters, but Anson's fears were not realised as Byng could not have received them in Portsmouth until several days after the end of the trial.

While the court's verdict was awaited, Anson was actively involved in preparing the previous administration's defence of its role as the House of Commons launched its enquiry. Hardwicke selected Philip Webb MP, a solicitor who had expert knowledge of constitutional law, to prepare a paper justifying the administration's response. He was provided with documents produced by John Clevland and Philip Stephens and Hardwicke asked him to use them to prove that 'consistently with the *probable safety of this country* a squadron could not have been sent *sooner* to the Mediterranean' nor could it 'have been made *stronger* when

---

87 J. K. Laughton and Ruddock F. Mackay, 'Francis Holburne (1704–1771)', *Oxford Dictionary of National Biography*, <https://doi.org/10.1093/ref:odnb/13483>, accessed 2 January 2023.
88 Pope, *At 12 Mr Byng was Shot*, p.241.
89 Walpole, *Memoirs of the Reign of King George II*, vol.II, p.287.
90 Erskine (ed.), *Augustus Hervey's Journal*, p.234.
91 Quoted in Tunstall, *Admiral Byng*, pp.238–239.
92 Quoted in Pope, *At Twelve Mr Byng was Shot*, p.277.
93 Quoted in Pope, *At Twelve Mr Byng was Shot*, p.278.

it was sent'. He was also asked to show that Byng's squadron was 'rather superior to Monr de la Galissonnière's or any other French squadron with which he was likely to meet'.[94]

By 26 January, Webb had completed a draft of the defence, with Hardwicke concluding (in a letter to Anson) that the papers were 'extremely well done… They appear to me to make a complete justification'.[95] However, Hardwicke wanted Anson's help in describing the Admiralty's role in more detail and in addressing the question of the practicability of sending part of the Western Squadron to the Mediterranean. As the document was being finalised Hardwicke suggested to Anson that he should 'not be sparing in laying any commands upon me, for this is a common cause, tho' it would be sufficient for me, if it were only yours'.[96] His reply has not survived, but Hardwicke reported that neither he nor Anson feared an investigation into their past decisions.[97]

The court found Byng guilty on 27 January and sentenced him to death. It was accompanied by a plea for mercy, a move supported by William Pitt, who used the verdict as a weapon to criticise the previous administration. The sentence produced a flurry of new attacks on Anson and other former ministers in the press and satirical prints. With doubts about the legality of the sentence being raised in the House of Commons and elsewhere, Lord Temple secured the King's agreement to seek legal advice and a panel of 12 judges unanimously agreed that it was a legal sentence. Following an intervention by Augustus Keppel, who wished to be absolved from his oath of secrecy as a member of the court-martial so that he could speak out, the Cabinet agreed to delay the execution. The Commons passed a Bill to enable this by a large majority, but when it was debated in the Lords, Lord Mansfield, who was president of the committee of judges, suggested that the members of the court-martial could be examined at the Bar of the House without the need for legislation. They would be questioned individually by Lord Hardwicke, and, on 2 March, they all defended their sentence while confirming that their application for mercy was unanimous.

According to Walpole, Hardwicke and Anson had taken the opportunity of a short delay to remind members of the court that 'their promotion depended on the Admiralty, and that Pitt and Temple could not protect them from Hardwicke, Newcastle and Anson, who might return to power at any moment'.[98] Hardwicke's critics claimed he was principally motivated by a 'desire to stem the public clamour and save his son-in-law', and his interrogation had the desired result, bringing the debate on Byng's fate to an end, with even Lord Temple declaring that all his doubts had been removed.[99] According to Byng's friend Augustus Hervey, Temple's unequivocal statement led 'most people imagine there was some compromise between the late and present administration to screen those most infamous delinquents, Lord Anson, Mr Fox, and the Duke of Newcastle'.[100]

---

94 Earl of Hardwicke to Philip Webb, 2 January 1757, in Yorke (ed.), *The Life and Correspondence*, vol.II, pp.356–357.
95 BL: Anson Papers, Add. MS. 15,956, f.27, Earl of Hardwicke to George Anson, 26 January 1757.
96 BL: Anson Papers, Add. MS. 15,956, f.29, Earl of Hardwicke to George Anson, 29 January 1757.
97 Earl of Hardwicke to George Anson, 6 December 1756, in Yorke (ed.), *The Life and Correspondence*, vol.II, p.376.
98 Tunstall, *Admiral Byng*, pp.267–268.
99 Quoted in Yorke (ed.), *The Life and Correspondence*, vol.II, p.345.
100 Erskine (ed.), *Augustus Hervey's Journal*, p.241.

Philip Yorke, First Earl of Hardwicke, mezzotint by J. McArdell. (Rijksmuseum)

George II rejected last-minute pleas for clemency from Lord Temple and others as he remained convinced that Byng was guilty of cowardice, a decision that also reflected the continuing influence of former ministers, including Anson. According to Walpole, Anson had been eager for Byng's execution, but as the date approached, he had some last-minute regrets:

> ...in midnight fits of weakness and wine, [Anson] held forth at Arthur's [a leading London club] on his anxiety to have Mr Byng spared; and even went so far as to break forth abruptly to Lord Halifax, the Admiral's relative by marriage, "Good God! My Lord, what shall we do to save poor Mr Byng?" The Earl replied, "My Lord, if you really mean it, no man can do so much towards it as yourself".[101]

Despite Anson's apparent reservations, it would not have been in his political interests to intercede on Byng's behalf and there is no evidence that he did so. The Duchess of Newcastle confirmed the widely held view that unless Byng 'was put to death, Lord Anson could not be at the head of the Admiralty'.[102] On 14 March, Byng was executed by firing squad on the quarterdeck of the *Monarch* (74).

The Commons enquiry into the Minorca expedition, which concluded on 3 May, focused on the conduct of Anson and his colleagues rather than on Byng's actions at sea. The inquiry report's resolutions exonerating former ministers were endorsed in a series of votes, except for the final resolution, which rejected one of the main criticisms levelled at Anson. Asserting that 'no greater number of ships of war could be sent into the Mediterranean than were sent on 6 April 1756', it briefly ran into difficulties when the opposition produced an amendment which stated the opposite. The amendment was defeated by a majority of 80, but as many as 115 members who voted for the amendment believed that Anson was at fault. It was a view shared by Walpole who summed up a widely held view when he pointed the finger of blame at former ministers rather than Byng. Minorca, he said, 'had been sacrificed by the negligence of Lord Anson and by the Duke of Newcastle's panic of an invasion'.[103]

---

101 Walpole, *Memoirs of the Reign of King George II*, vol.II, p.317. Walpole's verse on the subject: 'Proud Anson, do you feel no conscience sting, / While yours the errors, but the victim Byng? / In you 'tis most unjust to hasten fate / First multiply, e're you depopulate', is in Lewis (ed.), *The Yale Edition of the Correspondence of Horace Walpole*, vol.21, p.66.
102 Walpole, *Memoirs of the Reign of King George II*, vol.II, p.371.
103 Horace Walpole, *Memoirs of the Reign of King George III* (London: Bentley, 1845), vol.IV, p.142.

9

Wartime Cruise, 1757–1758

Early in April 1757, George II dismissed Pitt's first administration – and his Admiralty Board – and replaced it with a caretaker government under the Duke of Devonshire. Lord Winchilsea was appointed First Lord of the Admiralty – his second term of office – but he only remained in office for three months. With the conclusion of the Minorca enquiry in May, Newcastle was able to open negotiations with Pitt about forming a coalition to replace the Devonshire administration. Their differences were resolved in protracted negotiations, which led to the formation of the Pitt-Newcastle coalition and Anson's return as First Lord early in July, following a period when he had been ill with gout. Based on Newcastle's influence in the House of Commons, the coalition would have the Parliamentary support it needed to win the war. Pitt returned as Secretary of State for the Southern Department – a post he held until his resignation in 1761 – and Newcastle was appointed First Lord of the Treasury.

In Pitt's negotiations with Newcastle and Hardwicke, he had demanded the 'full restoration of his friends' and opposed Anson's return to the Admiralty as he continued to blame him for the loss of Minorca.[1] He did not, however, insist on Lord Temple's reappointment and Temple, who returned as Lord Keeper of the Privy Seal, was relieved at not being restored to office as he had 'found it the most uneasy situation that a man could possibly be in; for he was obliged to be continually turning, first to one admiral and then to another, to get explanations of the common terms and forms'.[2] Pitt turned instead to Henry Legge, a former Treasurer of the Navy and Chancellor of the Exchequer, as his preferred candidate. Lord Hardwicke thought it was 'a great instance of weakness that our friend, Mr Legge, should have such a hankering for the Admiralty'. However, Legge was soon to acknowledge that Anson 'was the most proper person' for the Admiralty if only he 'could get the better of some little inadvertences and mistakes in manner'. These included his reserved nature, a dislike of correspondence and a reluctance to consider unsolicited applications for appointments and promotions. Hardwicke was well aware of Anson's apparent shortcomings and,

---

1   Horace Walpole to Horace Mann, 1 June 1757, in Lewis (ed.), *The Yale Edition of the Correspondence of Horace Walpole*, vol.21, p.92.
2   Earl of Hardwicke to the Duke of Newcastle, 22 July 1757, in Yorke (ed.), *The Life and Correspondence*, vol.III, p.160.

as he explained to Newcastle, had 'taken a great deal of care to get them rectified and think I have succeeded'.³

In a series of meetings with George II about the formation of the coalition, Hardwicke made it clear that he could not join it unless Anson was found a place. He had been pressing for his return since the beginning of March even though it would not have been a popular move. Pitt said: 'Lord Anson being totally drop't, a hardship; and a point of honour to Ld. Hardwicke to mention him to the King'.⁴ As Hardwicke later reported to Anson, when the King objected to Pitt's proposal to make Legge First Lord, he then 'threw your Lordship in his way, but that I was far from knowing what the other person would say to it. His Majesty answered quick, "I shall like it extremely"'. On 15 June, Newcastle and Hardwicke met Pitt and the royal favourite and future prime minister John Stuart, third Earl of Bute, with the intention of persuading them to accept Anson's return. According to Hardwicke, it was Bute who first 'broke the ice, declared his particular respect for your Lordship, and did great justice to your character and merit in your profession, and declared that he knew these to be the sentiments of the place to which he belonged'.⁵

With Pitt's preferred candidate for First Lord (Henry Legge) now being appointed as Chancellor of the Exchequer, Pitt was content to support Anson's return to office, but his later claim that he was responsible for reinstating him was quite unjustified. In a speech to the House of Lords in 1770 as the Earl of Chatham, he said that:

> The state of facts laid before Parliament in… 1756, so entirely convinced me of the injustice done to his character that, in spite of the popular clamours raised against him, in direct opposition to the complaints of the merchants, and of the whole city… I replaced him at the head of the Admiralty and I thank God that I had resolution enough to do so.⁶

However, as we have seen, the credit for returning him to office must go to the King and Hardwicke rather than to Pitt, who had been one of his strongest critics since the fall of Minorca.⁷ But Pitt, who was again in charge of military strategy, appreciated that Anson's long experience would make him a valuable chief naval adviser as he pursued the war against France more aggressively. For Anson, working with a more proactive and demanding minister like Pitt was likely to reduce his influence in the short term, particularly as his reputation has been damaged by the Minorca debacle, but he gradually recovered his previous standing.

According to Hardwicke, Anson had been restored 'by the united voice of all parties and the concurrence of Savile House',⁸ and Lord Lyttelton reflected the majority view in

---

3   Earl of Hardwicke to the Duke of Newcastle, 22 July 1757, in Yorke (ed.), *The Life and Correspondence*, vol.III, pp.159–160.
4   William Pitt to Lord Bute, 15 June 1757, in Romney Sedgwick, 'Letters from William Pitt to Lord Bute, 1755–1758', in Richard Pares and A.J.P. Taylor (eds.), *Essays Presented to Sir Lewis Namier* (London: Macmillan, 1956), p.123.
5   BL: Anson Papers, Add. MS. 15,956, f.36, Earl of Hardwicke to George Anson, 18 June 1757.
6   *The Parliamentary History of England to the Year 1803*, vol.XVI, p.1100.
7   SRO: Anson Family Papers, D615/P(S)/1, Elizabeth Anson to George Anson, [25 June 1757].
8   Yorke (ed.), *The Life and Correspondence*, vol.II, p.404.

Parliament when he said that he took 'particular satisfaction in his being so honourably restored to an office which no other man in the kingdom is capable of filling with equal ability, and from which he had been removed by the clamour of faction and madness of the times'.[9] However, there were dissenting views among members of both political parties and popular opinion was against the appointment. Earl Waldegrave commented: 'the most surprising phenomenon was Lord Anson, returning to his old employment, in spite of his unpopularity, and of all the abuse which had been raised against him by the very men who were now to be his associates either at the Cabinet Council, or at the Board of Admiralty'.[10] The Duke of Devonshire, the former prime minister, commented that 'Lord Anson is said to be the most unpopular point of the whole system and has ruined the popularity of Mr Pitt and his party'.[11] According to Walpole, who gave Anson the nickname 'Admiral Almanzor', the City of London was 'indignant' at his reinstatement but, as he pointed out, 'when the chiefs are accorded, the mob of a faction are little regarded'.[12] His old adversary, Augustus Hervey, was also dismayed by the news 'for my own sake as he has ever been very adverse to me, for my country's sake as a most ignorant man, and for the sake of the service as a prejudiced weak head that was only led by three or four interested people nearly as ignorant as himself'.[13]

Pitt's agreement to Anson's return to office was subject to at least one major condition as he was unwilling to give him any say in the membership of the new Admiralty Board. He intended to restore the civilian members whom he had previously selected to serve under Lord Temple and who had served until their dismissal in April. Anson failed in his attempt to place Edward Hawke on the Board, with Vice Admiral Temple West being appointed to the vacancy for the third naval member, although this appointment was made for political rather than professional reasons. Despite this setback, Anson would have welcomed the continuation of two other experienced naval commissioners: Edward Boscawen, the sole survivor of Anson's previous Board, and Vice Admiral John Forbes, a former commander of the Mediterranean Squadron and member of Byng's court-martial. Despite Anson's lack of influence on the membership of the Board, Pitt offered him assurances that his dominant position would be respected and that the junior members would conform to his wishes. Board decisions were never taken by majority vote and the requirement that his written instructions should be signed by two other members of the Board did not represent an effective check on his power as his colleagues rarely if ever refused to sign.

Although Anson may have been reassured by Pitt's promises, Lord Winchilsea had his doubts and thought he was now in a 'much worse situation than when he was left in the island of Tinian; and that had it been his [Winchilsea's] case to have been left on that island, even there he would not have kept such company as his Lordship was now going into'.[14] He

---

9   Lord Lyttelton to the Earl of Hardwicke, 7 July 1757, in Harris, *The Life of Lord Chancellor Hardwicke*, vol.III, p. 147.
10   Clark (ed.), *The Memoirs*, p.208.
11   Quoted in Clark, *Dynamics of Change*, p.444.
12   Walpole, *Memoirs of the Reign of King George II*, vol.II, p.34. The nickname Almanzor is derived from John Dryden, *Almanzor and Almahide: or, the conquest of Granada by the Spaniards* (1672).
13   Erskine (ed.), *Augustus Hervey's Journal*, p.253.
14   Richard Rigby to the Duke of Bedford, 29 June 1757, in Russell, *Correspondence of John, Fourth Duke of Bedford*, vol.II, p.258.

offered 'to protect him whenever he should find it necessary against his own Board'. In view of the difficult negotiations that had led to the formation of the new coalition, Hardwicke advised Anson to accept the appointment on the terms offered and make 'no difficulty or hesitation' about Board membership as there was no prospect of making changes in the short term.[15] Although Pitt had not been receptive to his demands, Anson would also soon run into difficulties with Newcastle about Board membership when he selected Hawke to fill the vacancy created by the sudden death of Temple West in August 1757.

It was suggested at the time that Pitt was also able to impose a second condition on Anson's return to ensure that he had full control of a Board that was no longer in the hands of a political ally. Improbably, it was claimed that George II had restricted Anson's access to the Secretary of State's communications by agreeing that

> ...the correspondence with the naval officers, usually in the Admiralty, should be given to Mr. Pitt... the rule or custom being, the Secretary of State sends all the orders respecting the navy... to the Admiralty, while the secretary to that Board writes those orders out again in the form of instructions to the admiral or captain of the fleet... for whom they are designed.[16]

However, according to this account, 'during Mr. Pitt's administration, he wrote the instructions himself, and sent them to their Lordships to be signed, always ordering his secretary to put a sheet of white paper over the writing. Thus they were kept in perfect ignorance of what they signed'. There is, however, no evidence to suggest that such a bizarre arrangement was ever actually imposed or that Pitt used other means to interfere in the operation of the Board.[17]

With Anson reinstalled at the Admiralty, he focused almost exclusively on wartime priorities and – with one or two notable exceptions – thoughts of further reform were put to one side. He focused initially on restoring the Board's professional reputation which had declined under his two predecessors. As one of the junior Lords informed Newcastle: 'Affairs not only go on well... but infinitely better than in my Lord Temple's time'. Now they knew 'what they did, which was not the case formerly'.[18] He also resumed effective working relations with Lord Ligonier in the months following his appointment as commander in chief, replacing the Duke of Cumberland who resigned in September 1757. Serving as Pitt's principal wartime advisers, Anson and Ligonier provided 'an unprecedented example of cooperation between army and navy [and implemented] the strategic system by which Pitt proposed to win the greatest victory in English history'.[19]

The Board benefitted from the fact that Anson, as a leading member of the new administration, participated in meetings of the Cabinet and of the smaller inner committee or 'conciliabulum'. Apart from Anson, its members were Newcastle, Granville (the Lord

---

15   BL: Anson Papers, Add. MS. 15,956, f.36, Earl of Hardwicke to George Anson, 18 June 1757.
16   Almon, *Anecdotes*, vol.I, p.269.
17   Richard Middleton, 'Pitt, Anson and the Admiralty, 1756–1761', *History*, 55 (1970), p.189.
18   BL: Newcastle Papers, Add MS. 32,872, f. 285–288, Duke of Newcastle to the Earl of Hardwicke, 21 July 1757.
19   Fred Anderson, *Crucible of War: The Seven Years War and the Fate of the Empire in British North America 1754–1766* (London: Faber and Faber, 2000), p.215.

President), Hardwicke, Mansfield, the two Secretaries of State (Holderness and Pitt) and Ligonier. According to Lord Barrington, 'they meet continually, and their opinion is the advice given to the King. They always mean to agree and if they differ, they differ amicably. I am convinced at present there is not a man among them who wishes ill to the others'.[20] Anson became an influential voice in these informal meetings with Pitt increasingly valuing his advice as he sought to improve British military fortunes.

Pitt's main priority was winning the war in North America, where events had not so far gone in Britain's favour, while adopting a defensive strategy in Europe. This consisted of sending subsidies to Frederick II of Prussia who was fighting the French in Europe while developing plans for diversionary operations against France and her possessions. He made no change to the strategy which Anson had adopted at the beginning of the war of deploying the Western Squadron to maintain a blockade of the enemy coast with the aim of ensuring that the French fleet was confined to port and unable to reinforce her colonies. The economic impact of the blockade was enhanced by the presence of a large number of privateers, authorised by the Government, which disrupted French trade.

At the time Anson returned to office, the Royal Navy had 76 ships of the line and 20 50-gun ships in service compared to the French navy's 38 ships of the line and three 50-gun ships. There were nearly 63,000 men in British naval service although more were needed and by the end of the war, the fleet had increased to 300 ships, which were manned by some 82,000 mariners. But in mid-1757, British superiority over the French 'was not great enough because to accomplish its tasks the Royal Navy required a fleet two and a half to three times larger'.[21] By the spring of 1758, the navy equalled its maximum strength in the previous war and had achieved the required preponderance over the French: at this point the Royal Navy had 82 ships of the line, twenty-four 50-gun ships and 120 frigates and 70,000 seamen in service. As fleet numbers rose additional men were secured with difficulty and even during critical periods it was often necessary to lay up ships because of manpower shortages. There were also problems retaining recruits, with high levels of desertion and poaching by merchant ships and privateers being the main concerns. As we have seen, Anson is not associated with any significant changes to the recruitment process although he sought to improve the operation of press gangs and enhance recruitment incentives.

At first, the new administration made no significant changes to the navy's deployment, with two-thirds of the fleet being employed in the Channel, the Western Approaches, and the Mediterranean, with much of the remainder stationed in North America, and the East and West Indies. When Anson returned to office, the first attempt to capture Louisbourg was well underway, with Vice Admiral Francis Holburne commanding the naval squadron of 14 ships of the line and transports carrying 6,000 troops. Preparations had begun in January 1757, with John Campbell, fourth Earl of Loudoun, commander in chief in North America, assembling transports in New York to convey his troops to Halifax. In England, the squadron commanded by Holburne had been long delayed by bad weather and did not reach Halifax until 9 July. One of Anson's first acts was to provide Holburne with five more ships of the line, but they would not be sufficient to overcome the strong French naval

---
20　Quoted in Yorke (ed.), *The Life and Correspondence*, vol.III, pp.125–126.
21　Baugh, *The Global Seven Years War*, p.264.

presence at Louisbourg. Three French squadrons, including the main Brest squadron under the command of the Comte de la Motte, had managed to evade the Western Squadron when it was blown off station in a gale, arriving at Louisbourg on 20 June. When news of the strong French presence reached Halifax, the operation was abandoned and Holburne instituted a short-lived blockade of Louisbourg in September before bad weather forced him to call it off.

Shortly before the new ministry started work, the French began an advance on Hanover, forcing the Duke of Cumberland and the Army of Observation to retreat. Frederick II was compelled to withdraw from Bohemia and the Russians were planning to enter the fight. Pitt ruled out providing direct military assistance to Germany and was unwilling to accede to Frederick's request for the navy to be sent to protect Prussia's Baltic coast, a decision that Anson, who was facing manpower shortages, readily supported. He was more receptive to Frederick's suggestion of a diversionary expedition to the coast of France, which he hoped might persuade the French to withdraw most of their troops from Germany to strengthen their home defences. Action against France would also avoid the need to send British forces to Hanover. Ministers, including Anson, supported the idea because it represented 'a suitable compromise between those who said that the nation would be undone unless the French were stopped in Germany, and those who asserted that the nation would be equally ruined if British troops were the means of doing it'.[22]

The naval base of Rochefort was quickly selected as the proposed target, which remained a closely guarded secret, with Ligonier instructed to prepare a plan and Lieutenant General Sir John Mordaunt selected to command the combined expedition. Anson attended a ministerial meeting on 14 July, which confirmed the target and authorised naval and military preparations to continue as rapidly as possible. Anson selected Edward Hawke to command the squadron and appointed Vice Admiral Sir Charles Knowles as his second in command, neither of whom was enthusiastic about the project. Knowles had been appointed despite Anson's reservations, which he expressed to Hawke: 'Knowles' imprudence always hurts him, and he has enemies enough to seize every occasion that offers. I have always wished him well with all his indiscretion. His busy spirit constantly draws him into difficulties'.[23] Hawke's captains included Keppel, Howe, Denis and Byron, who had served with Anson on his voyage around the world. The squadron, which consisted of 16 ships of the line and 12 frigates, would escort 65 transports carrying more than 8,000 troops. Hawke's orders were to 'burn and destroy, to the utmost of your power, all docks, magazines, arsenals and shipping that shall be found [at Rochefort]'.

On 2 August, Anson attended a meeting to discuss the approaches to Rochefort, with Pitt, Ligonier, Mordaunt, Hawke, and Knowles among those present. Pitt had instigated the meeting to reassure Anson and the two commanders about the feasibility of the operation. They received a briefing from a French pilot, who advised them that a direct naval attack on Rochefort could be ruled out because of the difficulty of negotiating the River Charente, but a landing could be made at either Fouras or Châtelaillon, both of which were several miles from the target. Anson was present at a further ministerial meeting on 4 August, which

---

22 Middleton, *The Bells of Victory*, p.26.
23 George Anson to Edward Hawke, 19 October 1757, in Burrows, *The Life of Edward Lord Hawke*, p.339.

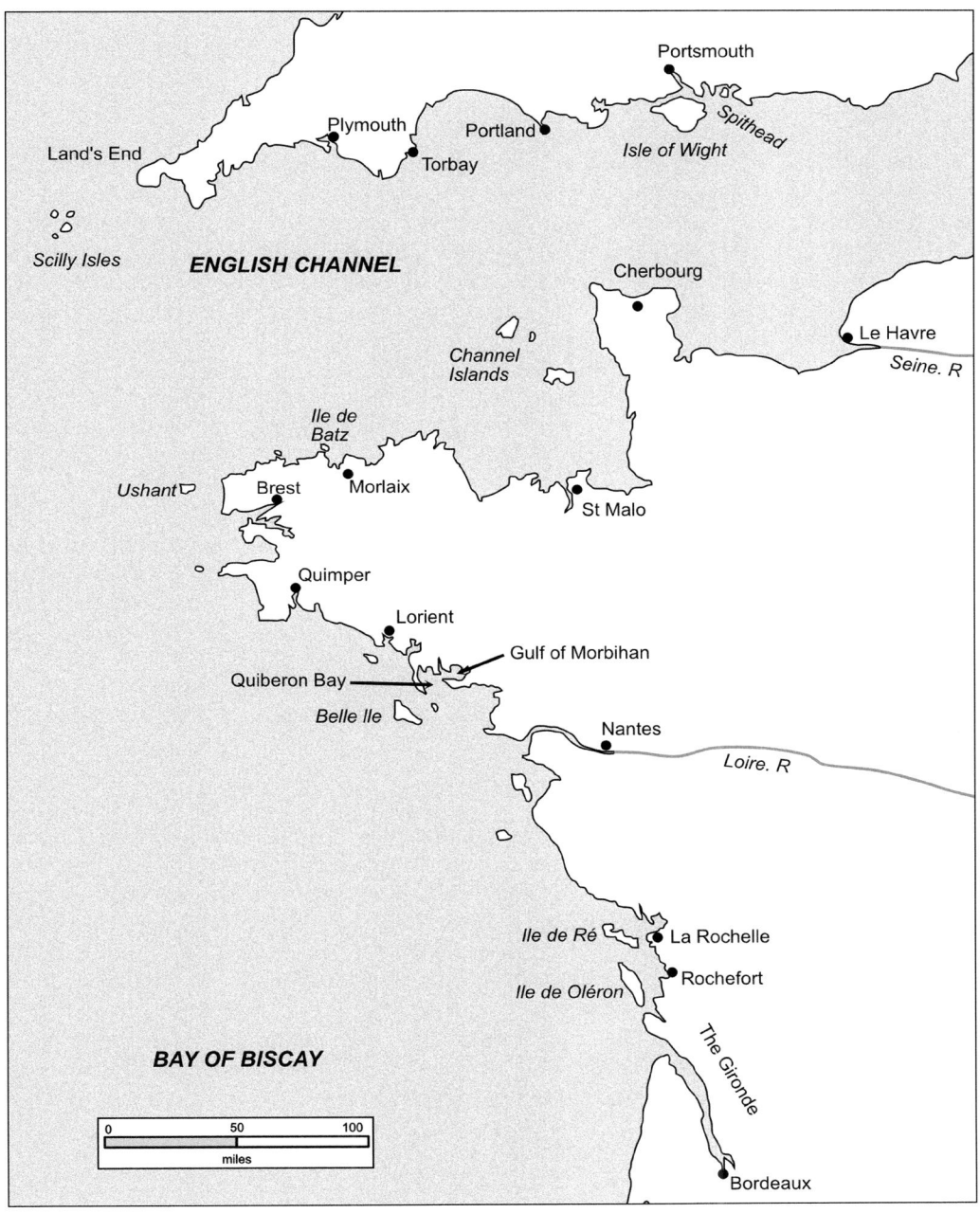

French Atlantic Coast.

confirmed that the expedition should still go ahead as a diversionary attack despite the arrival of news of Cumberland's defeat at the battle of Hastenback on 26 July. Cumberland was forced to retreat and agree to unfavourable terms at the Convention of Klosterzeven as the French took possession of Hanover. Under the instructions approved at the meeting, Mordaunt was only to land if it was safe to do so and he was to storm Rochefort rather than undertake a siege.

Preparations for the expedition were interrupted by a disagreement between Anson and Newcastle over the filling of a vacancy on the Admiralty Board, occasioned by the sudden death of Temple West on 9 August. Anson, who, as we have seen, headed a Board filled with Pitt's allies, wanted to strengthen his position by appointing Hawke to the vacancy. Pitt acknowledged that as Anson had not chosen any members of his Board, it was 'very proper he should recommend one now', but Newcastle was determined to select a successor himself.[24] When Anson met Newcastle to discuss the vacancy, he expressed his 'strong desire' for Hawke, but the Duke was determined to appoint Hans Stanley, to whom he had previously promised a place on the Board after his failure to secure a position in the new coalition. Although Hardwicke thought Stanley might be a useful ally in the Commons, Anson believed he would 'in all probability be very troublesome, and very likely a spy for [Bubb] Dodington'.[25]

Although Anson 'begged him at least to defer filling it up a little… to try if he could not accommodate both', Newcastle would not agree and Hardwicke could not change his mind. George II also wanted Hawke to go on the Board but did not press the point in the face of Newcastle's determination to preserve the Treasury's traditional role in making these appointments. The King approved Stanley's appointment and Anson considered resigning:

> It is certain that the office [of Lord Admiral] is not very desirable at this time – nor would it be a bad or discreditable reason for quitting it, that he had not been able to obtain so reasonable a wish as desiring to have an officer of the character of Sir Edward Hawke at the Board, before Mr Stanley.[26]

However, in the end, he accepted the decision and did no more than complain that the Board was 'always filled up, by the Duke of Newcastle, with persons of no use there, and of no weight or abilities elsewhere'.[27] Anson also apparently threatened to resign when Newcastle put a proposal from a naval lord direct to the King without consulting him first. According to Lady Anson, Newcastle then submitted the unspecified (and undated) proposal to a Cabinet meeting 'without making the least mention of it to the person at the head of that Board'.[28]

Both services faced recruitment difficulties as preparations for the Rochefort expedition continued but Anson was able to raise the 3,500 men needed through a general press. There were also delays in assembling the transports and Anson informed Pitt that it would

---

24 BL: Hardwicke Papers, Add. MS. 35,359, f.399, Elizabeth Anson to the Earl of Hardwicke, 10 August 1757.
25 BL: Hardwicke Papers, Add. MS. 35,359, f.399, Elizabeth Anson to the Earl of Hardwicke, 10 August 1757.
26 BL: Hardwicke Papers, Add. MS. 35,359, f.399, Elizabeth Anson to the Earl of Hardwicke, 10 August 1757.
27 BL: Hardwicke Papers, Add. MS. 35,359, f.399, Elizabeth Anson to the Earl of Hardwicke, 10 August 1757.
28 BL: Hardwicke Papers, Add. MS. 35,376, ff.182–183, Elizabeth Anson to Lord Royston, n.d.

be impossible to get them ready by his deadline. Although the story that Pitt planned to impeach him in the House of Commons was almost certainly apocryphal, it is quite possible 'that Anson grumbled, and that Pitt reminded him that his return to office was not intended to put a sponge over the Minorca affair, but to give him a chance of retrieving his reputation'.[29] The expedition did not depart from Cowes until 8 September – a month later than planned – entering Basque Roads on the 22nd and occupying the fort on the Île d'Aix, which controlled the approaches to Rochefort.

The army quickly ruled out a direct assault on Rochefort even though it was weakly defended, a decision that was mistakenly endorsed by Hawke. Fouras was eventually selected as an alternative but when the landing there was abandoned because of unfavourable winds, Hawke announced, on 29 September, that 'should the general officers of the troops have no further military operations to propose, considerable enough to authorise my detaining the squadron under my command longer here' he intended to return to England'.[30] Soon afterwards Mordaunt decided to bring the failed expedition to an end. As Hawke arrived back at Spithead, Anson wrote to his father-in-law about the outcome: 'I wish I could send your Lordship any agreeable news, but there seems to be a fatality about everything we undertake and that nothing succeeds'.[31]

Despite these setbacks, Anson thought that the navy had 'done well and all in their power [which] gives me satisfaction', but expressed disappointment at Hawke's conduct. The fact that Hawke had 'put his name to any council of war, when I warned him so strongly against it, astonishes and hurts me'. After a series of setbacks, the failure to attack Rochefort did nothing to lessen Anson's despondent mood as he reflected 'that not one event from the beginning of the war has come before us, that has not been unfortunate'.[32] By this time ministers were faced with a deteriorating situation in Germany and the failure of the first attempt to capture Louisbourg, which, as we have seen, was protected by the main Brest fleet and two other French squadrons. All three squadrons managed to evade the Western Squadron when they sailed through the Western Approaches on their return home in October. Only the news of Robert Clive's victory over the Nawab of Bengal at the Battle of Plassey in June, which gave the British control of Bengal, had relieved the gloom in London. The East India Company's operations against the French in India depended on naval support provided by a squadron of six ships under the command of Vice Admiral Charles Watson, which Anson had dispatched in 1754.

Following Hawke's return from France early in October, Pitt proposed that he should be sent back to Rochefort with orders to seize the Ile de Ré, but Anson and other ministers opposed the move because the Western Squadron was needed to intercept enemy forces returning to France and it was dropped. Amid popular anger at the failed operation, Mordaunt sought an enquiry into the conduct of the army and navy officers. Anson opposed the suggestion because army officers would be judging their naval counterparts, but a board of general officers was convened to look into the causes of the expedition's failure. It concluded that a landing and an attack could have been attempted, echoing Pitt's view that

---

29   Corbett, *England in the Seven Years War*, vol.I, p.191.
30   Mackay, *Admiral Hawke*, p.176.
31   BL: Hardwicke Papers, Add. MS. 35359, f.401, George Anson to the Earl of Hardwicke, 6 October 1757.
32   BL: Hardwicke Papers, Add. MS. 35359, f.401, George Anson to the Earl of Hardwicke, 6 October 1757.

there was a 'determined resolution, both in the naval and military commanders, against any vigorous exertion of the national power'.[33] Elizabeth Waldegrave reported that 'Lord Anson is very angry the court of inquiry has been so severe upon the sea, and says Sir E[dward] H[awke] will defend himself in Parliament'.[34] Mordaunt was subsequently court-martialled for disobeying orders and although he was acquitted, his reputation was damaged beyond repair.

When Parliament met at the end of 1757, the King's Speech included a commitment to prosecute the war vigorously, with George II promising 'to apply my utmost efforts for the security of my Kingdom, and for the recovery and protection of the possessions and rights of my Crown and subjects in America and elsewhere'. This would be achieved by the 'strongest exertion of his Majesty's naval force, as by all other adequate methods'.[35] When the inner committee had first discussed military priorities for 1758 at a meeting the previous August, Pitt expressed his determination to continue efforts to conquer Canada and, when news of the failure of the first Louisbourg expedition reached London in September, he decided to make a second attempt next year. Until the fortress was taken, it would be impossible to attack Quebec, which was 620 miles away up the St Lawrence. An assault on Quebec would follow the capture of Louisbourg and would be combined with two land operations – to recover the lakes of St George and Champlain and then advance towards Montreal, and attack Fort Duquesne with the aim of recovering the valley of the Ohio.

The prospects of success for a second Louisbourg expedition were now greater because of the reduced strength of the French navy, which would have no more than 25 ships of the line in service by mid-1758. However, France would give the highest priority to saving Louisbourg and Anson worked on plans to prevent her from sending reinforcements to North America so that the Royal Navy would maintain local superiority. This involved coordinating the actions of the three squadrons operating in the Western Approaches, the western Mediterranean, and off Nova Scotia. The Halifax squadron would be responsible for intercepting the French warships based at Louisbourg that were active in the area. With the opposing naval forces concentrated at these points, Anson assumed 'that the Atlantic Ocean was relatively secure… [and] troop transports and merchantmen could reasonably cross the Atlantic escorted by only a few warships'.[36] Without the need to provide a strong escort, British naval forces could cross the ocean more quickly or be diverted to other purposes.

Planning for the new expedition began at an inner committee meeting in September 1757 and continued for the next two months, with Pitt taking the leading role and Anson and Ligonier providing advice and undertaking more detailed preparations. An early decision was taken to keep eight ships of the line under Holburne's command in Halifax during the winter in readiness for next year's campaign, returning only his most badly damaged ships to England, and Anson issued orders to this effect on 21 September. He ordered naval stores

---

33 Quoted in Yorke (ed.), *The Life and Correspondence*, vol.III, p.117.
34 Lady Elizabeth Waldegrave to the Duke of Bedford, 26 November 1757, in Russell, *Correspondence of John, Fourth Duke of Bedford*, vol.II, p.306.
35 *The Journals of the House of Commons* (Reprinted 1803), vol.28, p.3.
36 Hugh Boscawen, *The Capture of Louisbourg, 1758* (Norman: University of Oklahoma Press, 2011), pp.50–51.

to be dispatched and arranged for the limited facilities at Halifax to be expanded. Anson recommended Boscawen to command the Louisbourg squadron after ruling out several more senior officers, including Holburne, following the failure of the first expedition. It proved to be a sound choice, with Boscawen, who had previous experience of amphibious operations, demonstrating 'fine leadership and command ability at the senior level, both afloat and onshore' during the operation.[37] Anson's choice for the second in command – Rear Admiral Sir Charles Hardy, Governor of New York, 1755–1757 – was also a success as his contributions 'to preparations for the expedition, the close watch, and the siege were significant'.[38] Major General Jeffrey Amherst was appointed to the overall command of the land forces.

On 19 December, Anson instructed the Navy Board to prepare Boscawen's warships and transports and give the work its highest priority. He attended a meeting of the inner committee on 27 December, which approved Boscawen's and Hardy's appointments and agreed that 65 transports should be hired. They would be needed to move most of the 14,000 troops required for the operation from New York to Halifax although another 2,000 men would need to be sent from England. They would be escorted by a squadron of 16 ships of the line, with several frigates and bomb vessels, which would be reinforced by the eight warships that had remained at Halifax during the winter. As result, Anson calculated that Boscawen would enjoy local naval superiority unless the French were able to send further reinforcements across the Atlantic. Early in 1758, Pitt expressed concern that the preparations were not proceeding quickly enough, and it was later claimed that he once more threatened Anson with impeachment unless the fleet was ready on time.[39]

Pressure from Pitt had its effect because there were no further delays, with Hardy leaving first on 21 January to implement an early blockade of Louisbourg. Boscawen, who received his final instructions on 27 January, left a month later but bad weather meant that it took him 11 weeks to cross the Atlantic and he did not enter Halifax until 9 May. Soon after Boscawen's departure, Anson's plan to prevent the French from sending reinforcements to Canada, using squadrons operating in Northern America, the Western Approaches and the Mediterranean, took effect. In March, the Western Squadron, which was under Hawke's command, was ordered to protect British trade and destroy any French ships he encountered. On 5 April, he launched a raid on a large French convoy bound for Louisbourg that was loading in Basque Roads and supplies to North America were severely disrupted as a result. It was the Western Squadron's first successful action since the beginning of the war three years earlier.

On 28 February, Admiral Henry Osborn, who was tasked with watching the exit from the Mediterranean, defeated three French ships of the line at Cartagena and subsequently blockaded the port. This did not prevent Augustus Hervey, who served as Osborne's staff officer, from criticising Anson for failing to provide sufficient ships to cover Cartagena and Toulon as well as the Straits of Gibraltar. He complained that:

---

37 Boscawen, *The Capture of Louisbourg*, p.320.
38 Boscawen, *The Capture of Louisbourg*, p.321.
39 Almon, *Anecdotes*, vol.I, pp.271–272.

> The same fatality attended the navy of England at this immediate era as it did at the taking of Minorca. I mean the same ignorant and obstinate First Lord of the Admiralty, Lord Anson, who only considered a few interested people that had sailed with him in his South-Sea voyage and were incapable of giving him better advice.[40]

These politically motivated criticisms seem wide of the mark as only five French convoys were able to evade the Royal Navy's blockade and none was able to reach Louisbourg, where only a small enemy naval force was present.

With preparations for the Louisbourg expedition completed, ministers turned their attention to operations in Europe and to negotiations with Frederick II who sought more naval and military assistance as he fought the French, Russians, and Austrians. Like other ministers, Anson continued to resist Frederick's demands for a fleet to be sent to the Baltic because even as the navy continued to expand, he did not have the ships available for such an operation. However, in September 1757 he had sent a small squadron to the Baltic, under the command of Commodore Charles Holmes, with instructions to patrol the River Ems. It protected Frederick's flank and supported his operation to capture Emden. Pitt was much more receptive to the Prussian demand that coastal operations against France should be restarted and planning for a new expedition soon began in London.

Early in April 1758, Pitt instructed Anson to assemble as many ships as possible for a new amphibious operation against France. Although the objective had not yet been defined, it was agreed that it should be confined to the English Channel so that the Western Squadron's primary role in home defence would not be compromised. A plan prepared by Ligonier, Lieutenant General Charles Spencer, third Duke of Marlborough, and Lord George Sackville, dated 11 May, recommended that the port of St Malo should be attacked, and it was approved at a meeting of ministers shortly afterwards. Anson gave his assent but his attitude to Pitt's coastal operations was increasingly ambivalent. He thought their only real benefit was in forcing the French to leave port by placing them 'under difficulties they cannot be relieved from but by risking their fleet'.[41]

Anson suggested that two squadrons should be organised in support of the expedition, which was to be led by the Duke of Marlborough, and they should operate separately: one would cover the landing, while the main force, under the command of Edward Hawke, would watch the enemy at Brest. He recommended that Captain Richard Howe, who had distinguished himself during the raid on Rochefort, should command the covering force. Anson's decision to divide the command reflected the navy's experience at Rochefort and his view that Howe would cooperate more effectively with the army than Hawke. At the beginning of May, with the troops assembling and the transports ready for service, Anson ordered Howe to Portsmouth to assume command.

The transports carried a newly designed landing craft which replaced the inadequate equipment used at Rochefort. Anson took the lead in overseeing the production of a new flat-bottomed boat and a successful design emerged. On 28 April, following an inspection of the first launch, the Admiralty directed the Navy Board to build 'with the utmost expedition

---

40 Erskine (ed.), *Augustus Hervey's Journal*, pp.269–270.
41 Elizabeth Anson to Lord Royston, 25 May 1758, in Corbett, *England in the Seven Years War*, vol.I, p.265.

Edward, Lord Hawke, mezzotint by J. McArdell. (Yale Centre for British Art)

as many launches of the same nature… as can be got completed and ready at Portsmouth by the 17th of next month'.[42] Two different sizes were produced but both designs were similar: they were flat-bottomed and clinker-built, with oars, sails and a detachable rudder. The larger type was 36 feet long, 10 feet 2 inches in breadth, carried 70 soldiers and could accommodate 20 oarsmen; the smaller version was 30 feet long, 9 feet 9 inches wide and equipped for 16 oarsmen.[43]

While preparations proceeded according to Pitt's timetable, they were overshadowed by Hawke's intemperate reaction to the news that an expedition was leaving for France, which he learnt on his return from a successful cruise with the Western Squadron. On 10 May,

---

42　Hugh Boscawen, 'The Origin of the Flat-Bottomed Landing Craft 1757–58', *National Army Museum Report* (1984), p.25.
43　David Syrett, 'The Methodology of British Amphibious Operations during the Seven Years and American Wars', *The Mariner's Mirror*, 58 (1972), p.273.

without any prior warning from Anson, Hawke discovered that he was to command the covering force, while Richard Howe, an officer 12 years his junior, was to lead the naval side of the landing. Hawke mistakenly believed that another attack on Rochefort was planned, suggesting that Anson had a lack of confidence in him after the failure of the previous year's expedition. Within hours he had written to the Admiralty complaining that a more junior officer would reap all the credit 'while it is probable I, with the capital ships, might be ordered to cruise in such a manner as to prevent his failing in this attempt'. Under the circumstances, he had no choice but to lower his flag, explaining that 'no consequence that can attend my striking it without orders shall ever outbalance with me the wearing it one moment with discredit'.[44]

Soon after he sent the ill-judged resignation letter, Hawke discovered that he was mistaken in his belief that the expedition was going back to Rochefort. On 12 May, he was summoned to a meeting of the Admiralty Board to explain his impetuous conduct. He acknowledged that he had acted 'hastily' and apologised, but his attempt to justify his conduct was feeble:

> He did not do it with any view of disregard or disrespect to the Board, but merely from thinking it would appear a slur upon him to the world and that they would say that he... was not thought fit... to carry on a service of consequence, and he thought he had better not serve at all, if he could not serve with honour.[45]

The Board concluded that Hawke was guilty of 'a high breach of discipline' in striking his flag without an order to do so.[46] Although Anson could not allow him to go unpunished – he was relieved of his command of the Western Squadron – no further action was taken. To fill the vacancy Hawke had created, Anson felt compelled to assume command of the squadron himself. As he explained to Lord Hardwicke, 'this step of Sir Edward Hawke has spread a very improper spirit of discontent in the fleet at Spithead [and] I could not avoid offering my service, which the King has accepted, though not very willingly agreeing to the necessity of it'.[47] Once he had decided to take command, he was keen to retain Hawke's services on the cruise and appointed him as his deputy.

Anson may well have had mixed feelings about leaving London at the height of the war and as he was on the point of departing, his brother-in-law Lord Royston reported to Lord Hardwicke that he 'did not appear to me so well as I could wish him, and his spirits in a flutter, but I hope this will go off when he gets down to Portsmouth'.[48] Elizabeth was also unhappy about his departure: 'I must wish it had not been necessary, since, besides other circumstances, the hurry and confusion of a departure so sudden and unexpected is in all respects thoroughly disagreeable'.[49] In a letter to his daughter, Lord Hardwicke, who approved of Anson's decision to offer his services, acknowledged her 'great anxiety' about his departure, while pointing out 'he has hitherto been protected & blessed with great

---

44   Edward Hawke to the Admiralty, 10 May 1758, in Mackay, *Admiral Hawke*, p.195.
45   Admiralty minute, quoted in Mackay, *Admiral Hawke*, p.197.
46   Quoted in Mackay, *Admiral Hawke*, p.197.
47   BL: Hardwicke Papers, Add. MS. 35,359, ff.393–394, George Anson to the Earl of Hardwicke, 13 May 1758.
48   Quoted in Mackay, *Admiral Hawke*, p.198.
49   BL: Hardwicke Papers, Add. MS. 35,359, f.403, Elizabeth Anson to the Earl of Hardwicke, 15 May 1758.

success' and suggesting she should 'rely upon the same good Providence for the future'. Hardwicke was more concerned about 'the danger of the public losing the benefit of his service, at least for some time [and] from the consequential trouble this event is likely to bring upon Lord Anson'.[50]

Despite giving Anson a welcome break from political debate and the burdens of routine administration, Hardwicke was worried about how the Admiralty Board would manage its business, expressing the hope that 'they will not take much upon them in his absence'.[51] It was a concern shared by Anson himself, particularly as his fellow Board member Edward Boscawen was also away. After a few weeks at sea, Anson was not reassured by the reports he received from London: 'Though I don't think the affairs of the Admiralty go on the better for my absence, I had not the least thoughts of leaving the chief command of the fleet, while any operations are carrying on against the enemy, which appear so material to the King's service'. He also had strong personal and professional motives for remaining at sea for as long as possible:

> The command of a squadron at sea has always been my principal object and passion, and tho' possibly nothing extraordinary in a military service may come in the way of this fleet, I have the satisfaction myself to know that I am rendering a very material service both to the King and publick in putting this squadron into a different state of discipline to whatever it has been in yet.[52]

As head of the Western Squadron, Anson was ordered 'to prevent any ships of the enemy, from Brest or elsewhere, from molesting the operations' of Howe's covering force, but his responsibilities extended well beyond protecting the expedition as he was asked to use every opportunity 'to annoy and distress the enemy, taking due care to protect the trade' and if the French fleet were to leave Brest he was to 'use the utmost endeavours to attack and destroy the same'.[53] He flew his flag in the first-rate *Royal George* (100) – the largest ship in the world at the time of her launch in 1756 – after transferring from the *Royal Sovereign* (100) following representations from the lower deck about her 'great age and weakness'.[54] The *Royal George* was to be Hawke's flagship at the Battle of Quiberon Bay the following year; in 1782, she sank as a result of an accident while anchored at Spithead with the loss of 800 lives.

Anson set sail from St Helens on 1 June after addressing the squadron's manpower shortages, which he resolved by stripping men from other ships. He departed with 21 ships of the line, while Howe's squadron consisted of one ship of the line, four 50-gun ships, and 10 frigates; he escorted 130 transports, which accommodated 14,000 troops in 16 battalions and nine troops of light horse. Anson accompanied Howe across the Channel in the direction of St Malo before sailing away to the west. He decided against a blockade of Brest because he hoped the French fleet would

---

50 Earl of Hardwicke to Elizabeth Anson, 16 May 1758, in Harris, *The Life of Lord Chancellor Hardwicke*, vol.III, p.168.
51 Earl of Hardwicke to Elizabeth Anson, 16 May 1758, in Harris, *The Life of Lord Chancellor Hardwicke*, vol.III, p.168.
52 BL: Hardwicke Papers, Add. MS. 35,359, f.413, George Anson to the Earl of Hardwicke, 22 July 1758.
53 George II to George Anson, 23 May 1758, quoted in Middleton, *The Bells of Victory*, p.70.
54 Rodger, *The Wooden World*, p.233.

leave the port to attack Howe's squadron, which would give him the opportunity to fight a decisive action at sea. He sent five ships to cruise off the north coast of Brittany, while the remainder of the fleet was stationed off the Île de Batz. From this position, he could send reinforcements towards Brest or provide support to Howe should he require it. Anson soon sent messages to the Admiralty complaining about his lack of frigates which made intelligence-gathering more difficult and suggested that no more than three months' provisions should be carried because his ships were cluttered with stores, which affected their ability to manoeuvre easily.[55]

Soon after their departure, Hawke was taken ill and Anson permitted him to return to Portsmouth. Anson thought his illness was explained by the 'uneasiness of his mind from his own late conduct, which with the assistance of [Rear Admiral Francis] Holburne, and a very bad man his secretary, had done much mischief in the Fleet'.[56] Now without a flag officer, Anson reorganised his fleet into three divisions and, with George II's approval, appointed two of his senior captains to command the rear and van with the temporary rank of commodore. When a replacement flag officer failed to arrive, Anson secured the promotion of three of the most senior captains to the rank of rear admiral – Philip Durell, Charles Holmes and Charles Steevens.

With no sign of the French navy venturing out to sea, Anson gave priority to the tactical training of the squadron to address the shortcomings he had discovered, developing a 'plan of discipline', which is in a 'great part new'. This initiative was necessary because he had never 'seen such an awkwardness in going thro' the common manoeuvres necessary to make an attack upon any enemy's fleet' and found that many captains 'had never seen a line of battle at all, and none of them more than once'. Anson did not seek to blame Hawke for these weaknesses, which would have been inappropriate because he was leading a much-enlarged fleet with many personnel changes. He claimed his new regime of frequent exercises soon brought benefits, with the result that 'what we now do in an hour, in the beginning took us eight, which convinces me that men never do anything well, that they are not accustomed to, and frequently practised in'.[57]

While he was at sea, Anson developed several new signals relating to the line of battle formation, which he circulated to his captains in a series of additional fighting instructions (as he had done in the last war). These included a direction, issued on 30 August, to take aggressive action when single enemy ships were forced out of their line while the main fleet remained in place. Anson said that when he lowered the signal for the line of battle

> ...every ship in the fleet is then to use his utmost endeavours, to take or destroy such ships of the enemy, as they may be opposed to, by engaging them as close as possible, and pursuing them if they are driven out of their line, without having any regard to the situation which was prescribed to themselves by the line of battle, before the signal was hauled down.[58]

---

55 Richard Middleton, 'British Naval Strategy', p.357.
56 BL: Hardwicke Papers, Add. MS. 35,359, f.410, George Anson to the Earl of Hardwicke, 5 July 1758.
57 Tunstall, *Naval Warfare in the Age of Sail*, p.106; BL: Hardwicke Papers, Add. MS. 35,359, ff.413–414, George Anson to the Earl of Hardwicke, 22 July 1758.
58 D. Bonner-Smith (ed.), *The Barrington Papers; Selected from the Letters and Papers of Admiral the Hon. Samuel Barrington* (London: Navy Records Society, 1937), vol.I. pp.232; John Creswell, *British*

He issued another signal which would direct ships to steer for their immediately opposite opponents 'notwithstanding I shall keep the signal for the line ahead flying'.[59] Despite these thorough preparations, Anson did not meet the enemy and or use the new signals in action.

Howe reached Cancale Bay, the landing point some nine miles east of St Malo, on 5 June and the troops were disembarked in the face of limited French opposition. They marched towards St Malo but were unable to enter the town because of its strong fortifications. After destroying 30 privateers and a larger number of merchantmen, they withdrew to the Bay and re-embarked. Possible raids on Granville, Cherbourg or Le Havre were then considered and dismissed, and the expedition returned to England on 1 July. Meanwhile, Anson, who was patrolling the coast from Brest to Rochefort, wrote to Elizabeth expressing 'his concern for the success of the enterprise, but hopes there is an end of it and all other such schemes together'.[60] Anson was highly critical of the army's performance, commenting in a letter to Lord Hardwicke that it 'does not make the figure it ought to do'. He had been surprised by the army's decision to re-embark so suddenly at Cancale Bay and its unwillingness to land at Granville. He also criticised the army's earlier performance in North America, and at Rochefort when 'your generals saw men upon the hills, and tho' they knew there were no regular troops in the country, they would not land'. He attributed these failings to the generals' 'feeling a want of experience in themselves, which makes them fearful of coming into action, or putting anything to the risk, which must be done in all operations of war, where success can never be certain'.[61]

Anson was aware that openly criticising the St Malo operation would 'hurt the King's affairs' and said to Lord Hardwicke that he would only express his real opinions to him. Despite his caution, Pitt became aware of Anson's apparent lack of enthusiasm for future coastal operations, as he indicated in a letter to Lord Bute:

> I am more than ever impatient to get it [the next expedition] away, finding by a letter from Lord Anson that his Lordship is laying in for a reason to come into port, before it is long. Whether this be all from his own movement, or by concert, to embarrass and render impractical farther operations on the coasts of France, I will not venture to decide. But it is too evident that difficulties and obstructions swarm upon me.[62]

Pitt was referring to Anson's letter of 5 July, which alerted him to the fact that he would not be able to remain on station much longer because of increasing sickness. Soon afterwards he informed the Admiralty that to tackle an outbreak of scurvy that was spreading among his crews, a period of shore leave and a diet of fresh vegetables were needed. He also expressed concern about the quality of the victuals on board, reporting to the Admiralty that the cheese was 'so bad, from its being ill made, and not sufficiently squeezed, that it [was] scarce

---

Admirals of the Eighteenth Century: Tactics in Battle (London: George Allen and Unwin, 1972), pp.105–107.
59   Quoted in Tunstall, *Naval Warfare in the Age of Sail*, p.106.
60   BL: Hardwicke Papers, Add. MS. 35,376, f.150, Elizabeth Anson to Lord Royston, 25 June 1758.
61   BL: Hardwicke Papers, Add. MS. 35,359, f.411, George Anson to the Earl of Hardwicke, [29 June 1758].
62   William Pitt to Lord Bute, 11 July 1758, in Sedgwick, 'Letters from William Pitt', p.157.

fit to eat'.[63] On 19 July, Anson returned to Plymouth for fresh supplies but, despite the uncertain health of the crew, he was determined to leave as soon as possible: 'nothing could be more disagreeable to a commanding officer, than being a few days in port, in a constant hurry to get the ships equipped and ready for the seas'.[64]

On 22 July, he left Plymouth for the Île de Batz with Charles Holmes, newly promoted to rear admiral, on board. With the prevailing winds driving him up the Channel, Anson soon moved from the Île de Batz to Ushant as the expeditionary force sailed from St Helens for a second time on 1 August. Now under the command of Lieutenant General William Bligh, it landed at Urville and marched on Cherbourg, which it captured in the second week of August. It was notable as the first successful landing in France since the Hundred Years War (1337–1453): during a short period of occupation, they seized 35 ships and 22 brass cannon and demolished parts of the harbour structure.

On 17 August, after a successful withdrawal, Howe's squadron sailed to Portland Roads for a refit. The captured weapons were sent to London, where Elizabeth Anson witnessed

> …the noble procession of nearly 300 dray-horses with the 20 Cherbourg canon, which all the Johns and Joans in town… are convinced must be the first brass ones that ever were seen in England. I have a great mind to have them sent to Woolwich, where there lies near 200, which my Lord took and never showed to anybody.[65]

Once the refit had been completed, Bligh and Howe decided to return to St Malo and landed at St Lunaire, about six miles away, on 4 September. Poor weather forced Howe to find an alternative anchorage at St Cast, which was some 20 miles to the west of St Malo. With the fleet now unable to support an attack on St Malo, Bligh was forced to abandon the operation and march his troops to St Cast. French troops appeared before the British rear-guard was evacuated from the beach and in the battle that followed 2,300 British troops were killed or wounded and some 800 taken prisoner while the French lost 300 men. While Anson was still at sea, the Government decided that there would be no more expeditions to the coast of France. St Cast was a costly failure and the expedition had resulted in very few troops being withdrawn from Germany, as the occupation of Hanover remained France's highest priority.[66]

Despite this setback, Pitt remained convinced of the diversionary value of coastal attacks and he would launch a successful operation against Belle Isle in 1762. For now, he prioritised offensive operations against other French possessions overseas, selecting the island of Gorée, which lay off the coast of West Africa, as a first target. Its capture, which required a small squadron and a battalion of troops, would consolidate British control of the slave trade. Augustus Keppel, who continued to benefit from Anson's patronage, was selected to command the squadron. It proved to be a sound choice because Keppel ensured that the combined operation was effectively coordinated and the island was captured on 29 December. Pitt also planned an expedition to the French Caribbean island of Martinique,

---

63 TNA: ADM 1/90, George Anson to the Admiralty, 20 June 1758.
64 BL: Hardwicke Papers, Add. MS. 35,359, f.414, George Anson to the Earl of Hardwicke, 22 July 1758.
65 Quoted in Barrow, *The Life of George Lord Anson*, p.314.
66 Middleton, *The Bells of Victory*, p.84.

which he saw as a 'set-off to Minorca', and early in September, he asked Anson to return home to help with the preparations.[67]

Anson remained on station until Howe had left the French coast, but he had already been forced to send home some 500 men who were ill from scurvy, reducing the size of his squadron by three ships. As he made his way to England, he ordered a division to remain on station to maintain the blockade of Brest and to try to intercept a French squadron returning from Quebec. Anson's friend Charles Saunders remained on station for another two months before returning to England. It was evident that Anson retained a high opinion of Saunders, 'in whom I could confide for keeping the fleet in such discipline, that I should have a pleasure in going on board it'.[68] However, Saunders had been unable to intercept the warships returning to Brest, underlining the need for Anson to consider a change of approach to the blockading of French ports although this took some time to be realised. During four years of war, the Western Squadron had failed to destroy the French fleet and it was evident that 'without a closer watch on Brest and the other ports, the chances of an interception were poor'.[69]

Anson's arrival in Portsmouth on 18 September marked the end of a largely uneventful cruise as his ships had only had the opportunity to fight two minor engagements with individual enemy frigates.[70] His powerful squadron had compelled the French fleet to remain in port denying him the opportunity to fight a decisive battle, but it allowed the landings to proceed without interruption. He was now needed back at the Admiralty as Pitt planned further naval operations across the globe, which fully occupied Anson until his death in 1762: he would only have one more opportunity to return to sea in command of a squadron when he escorted Queen Charlotte from Hanover in 1761.

By the time Anson returned home, news of the fall of Louisbourg had reached England. Hardy had established an effective blockade in April, and he was joined by Boscawen who arrived off Louisbourg early in June. A joint navy-army planning staff was established to ensure effective coordination between the two services and, on 8 June, troops were landed to the west of Louisbourg and when naval guns were in position onshore the siege began in earnest. On 21 July, Boscawen's guns destroyed three French ships of the line in Louisbourg harbour; the two remaining warships were stormed, with one being burnt and another captured, and three frigates were lost. The French, who had lost a significant proportion of their navy in the defence of Louisbourg, surrendered shortly afterwards. Boscawen decided it was too late in the year to proceed up the St Lawrence and the expedition against Quebec was postponed until 1759.

The taking of Louisbourg was Britain's first significant victory in the war and paved the way for the capture of Quebec and the destruction of French colonial power in North America in 1760. British losses were small compared to those of the French, but scurvy was prevalent among Boscawen's crews, as Anson was soon to discover. Elizabeth Anson reported that he had received a visit from 'Captain Rodney and two or three more captains

---

67 Williams, *The Life of William Pitt, Earl of Chatham*, vol.I, p.380.
68 George Anson to the Earl of Hardwicke, 29 June 1758, in Yorke (ed.), *The Life and Correspondence*, vol.III, p.215.
69 Middleton, 'British Naval Strategy', p.338.
70 Beatson, *Naval and Military Memoirs*, vol.II, pp.187–188.

returned from Louisbourg… whose company was so offensive from the state of their health, as to make it but just possible to bear the cabin with them, not even almost after they were gone'.[71] By 1758, the French gains made in the early stages of the war were a distant memory as the Royal Navy made considerable progress in destroying French overseas trade by capturing or sinking most of the French merchant fleet and intercepting neutral ships carrying French goods. These successes were attributable to Anson's Western Squadron, which protected British trade and allowed British cruisers to attack French merchantmen.

---

71 Quoted in Pack, *Admiral Lord Anson*, p.221.

10

Planning for Victory, 1758–1762

Now back at the Admiralty after his cruise with the Western Squadron, in the autumn of 1758 Anson worked on plans to capture the French-held island of Martinique, which had been initiated by Pitt with Clevland's support while he was away. Anson had no reservations about the feasibility of the project but was concerned that too many warships were leaving home waters at a time when the threat of a French invasion could reappear. However, he must have been reassured by the navy's recent successes and he supported the proposal in ministerial meetings. The expedition went ahead, leaving early in 1759, but the attempt to capture the island was abandoned following an ineffective naval bombardment of the main fortress; it was not to be taken until 1762. Commodore John Moore, who commanded the naval force, advised the army to make for Guadeloupe, where many French privateers were based, and the island was captured in May 1759.[1]

By the end of 1758, Anson's main priorities were organising the navy's contribution to the final conquest of Canada and defending Britain from a possible French invasion. The plan for Canada involved the army launching simultaneous attacks on several fronts, with Montreal (the French capital), Quebec, Fort Niagara and the southern frontier being the principal targets. An amphibious expedition starting from Louisbourg would proceed eastwards up the St Lawrence, with the aim of capturing Quebec. Pitt selected James Wolfe to command the expedition and urgent preparations began in the middle of December.

Wolfe worked on the plan of operations, including details of the naval force it would require and how it should be deployed, but Anson was responsible for preparing the fleet and selecting its commander. With Hawke ill and Boscawen in the Mediterranean, Augustus Hervey claimed that Anson first turned to Sir Charles Hardy as his first choice for the command. The former Governor of New York, who had served as Boscawen's second in command during the siege of Louisbourg, was 'well acquainted with all America [and] had shown Lord Anson several papers and charts'. However, according to Hervey, he was advised against appointing him, as there 'were those about Lord Anson who were jealous of Sir Charles's rank and getting too much credit by any command. This only confirmed me in my opinion of Lord Anson's principles and abilities being of the very lowest class'.[2]

---

1   Middleton, *The Bells of Victory*, p.87; Marshall T. Smelser, *The Campaign for the Sugar Islands: A Study of Amphibious Warfare* (Chapel Hill, North Carolina: University of North Carolina Press, 1955).
2   Erskine (ed.), *Augustus Hervey's Journal*, p.301.

With Hardy no longer in the running if Hervey's account is to be believed, Anson turned to Rear Admiral Charles Saunders, who had just returned from the Mediterranean, as a more obvious candidate. Anson's friend and protégé was, like his patron, a man of few words and, according to Walpole, 'he was a pattern of most steady bravery, united with the most unaffected modesty. No man said less, or deserved more' and it soon became clear that Anson had made an inspired appointment, which was approved by the King together with his promotion to vice admiral.[3] Saunders was to prove more than equal to the challenges of an 'operation beyond all experience', which involved carrying 'an expedition hundreds of miles up a distant river, through a hostile country, against a fortress capital defended by regular troops'.[4] Rear Admiral Philip Durell, who would spend the winter at Halifax, was appointed as his second in command. On 29 December, Anson ordered him to move up the St Lawrence to prevent French supplies from reaching Quebec. Anson selected Rear Admiral Charles Holmes, who had captured Emden early in 1758 and served under his command in the Western Squadron, as the third flag officer. Among his other appointments, Anson placed John Jervis, later Admiral of the Fleet Earl St Vincent, as commander of the *Scorpion* (14) under Saunders.

The squadron, which consisted of 14 ships of the line, six frigates, three bomb vessels and three fireships, was to accompany 20,000 tons of transports. There were delays in assembling the fleet, particularly the transports, and Anson had to ask the Navy Board 'to use the utmost dispatch' on more than one occasion.[5] There were two separate departures from Spithead. Rear Admiral Holmes, who had four ships of the line and five frigates under his command, departed on 14 February 1759. He escorted 66 empty transport ships across the Atlantic to New York, where they would embark 12,000 regular troops and head for Louisbourg, which was the assembly point. Saunders left England with the rest of the fleet a few days later; it consisted of 10 ships of the line and three bomb vessels, and a small number of transports carrying ordnance and supplies.

Following Saunders' departure, Anson turned his attention to the rumours of a French invasion of Britain, which were beginning to circulate in London in February. Developed by the Duc de Choiseul and Charles Fouquet, Duc de Belle-Isle, the plan involved capturing London and establishing a foothold in Scotland rather than attempting to occupy the whole country; it was intended to force Britain to the negotiating table. The two invasion flotillas would be protected by the French Atlantic and Mediterranean fleets, while a small diversionary force would be dispatched to Ireland. On 19 February, Anson hosted a meeting of the inner committee to discuss how to respond to the threat.[6] He was able to brief his colleagues on the strength of the fleet: there were 41 ships of the line at home (of which 21 were ready for service) and 59 overseas (in the Mediterranean, North America and the East and West Indies). The French had 43 ships of the line at home but, unlike the British figures, this total included their Mediterranean fleet.

As the French invasion plan involved joining their Mediterranean and Atlantic fleets, Anson suggested strengthening the British Mediterranean squadron. Six more ships

---

3   Walpole, *Memoirs of the Reign of King George II*, vol.III, pp.231.
4   Corbett, *England in the Seven Years War*, vol.I, p.400.
5   Middleton, *The Bells of Victory*, p.106.
6   Middleton, *The Bells of Victory*, pp.108–112.

were sent to the Mediterranean and, in March, Boscawen was appointed to command the squadron. He was ordered to prevent the French fleet from passing through the Straits of Gibraltar and to go in pursuit if he was unable to stop them. Anson had also received several reports about invasion preparations at Havre-de-Grâce (now Le Havre), where at least 150 flat-bottomed boats were being constructed. In consultation with Pitt, Anson planned a raid in which six bomb vessels and a covering force of 13 ships would destroy the landing craft. He selected George Rodney for the command, secured his promotion to rear admiral of the blue and issued orders for the raid. Anson's plan was successfully carried out on 3–5 July when 3,000 shells were fired at the port, causing major damage and disrupting the invasion preparations. A second bombardment followed and Rodney maintained a blockade of the port until early in 1761.

The February meeting also discussed the continuing manpower shortages in the navy, which had 71,000 men early in 1759 but more were needed at a time when the fleet was still expanding rapidly. Numbers had only increased slowly because of significant losses through desertion, scurvy and other illnesses. The 1758 Navy Act, which included provision for the more frequent payment of seamen's wages, had failed to produce a significant increase in recruits. Anson continued to rely on impressment, which was extended in scope, but the meeting also agreed to transfer some men from frigates as well as taking them from privateers and the merchant service.

On 8 May, amid continuing news of French invasion preparations, the inner committee agreed that the Western Squadron should sail from Spithead to Torbay and then make for the French coast. Anson had considered taking the command himself but, on 9 May, Hawke returned to the squadron. Anson's plans for the defence of Britain included creating 'a mighty chain of fleet and frigates along the coast', with Newcastle reporting that 'Lord Anson is taking all possible methods by fitting out small ships, and taking into pay privateers and colliers, and fitting up transports to be employed as frigates upon this occasion'.[7] Ministers were also concerned about Ireland's exposure to French attack and it is possibly this issue to which Walpole refers in a letter of 16 May: 'There has been a great quarrel between Mr Pitt and Lord Anson on the negligence of the latter – I suppose they will be reconciled by agreeing to hang some admiral, who will come too late to save Ireland, after it is impossible to save it'.[8]

In orders issued by Anson on 18 May, which were similar in most respects to those issued to the Western Squadron in previous years, Hawke was to protect British trade, monitor the French fleet at Brest and prevent an invasion. He was ordered to cruise off Ushant and Brest for 14 days before returning to Torbay unless the 'operations of the enemy... should make it necessary... to prolong your cruise or take any other station near the coast of Great Britain'. Hawke was additionally ordered to take steps to stop fresh supplies reaching Brest and dispatch 'such of the smaller ships of the line and frigates as you shall think sufficient to cruise on the most likely stations for intercepting the same'. When he returned to Torbay to

---

7   Horace Walpole to Horace Mann, 8 July 1759, in Lewis (ed.), *The Yale Edition of the Correspondence of Horace Walpole*, vol.21, p.306; BL: Hardwicke Papers, Add. MS. 32,892, f.256, Duke of Newcastle to the Earl of Hardwicke, 17 June 1759.
8   Horace Walpole to George Montagu, 16 May 1759, in Lewis (ed.), *The Yale Edition of the Correspondence of Horace Walpole*, vol.9, p.236.

revictual he was to ensure 'that none of the ships have ever less than two months' provisions on board'.[9] At this point, Anson envisaged that Hawke would make a series of short cruises as he wished to avoid the damage that might be caused if the fleet were to remain on station for an extended period. However, it soon became apparent to Hawke that longer cruises would be needed if he were to keep an effective watch on the French and – with reinforcements arriving and new victualling arrangements introduced – his close blockade of Brest would continue until November.

When he arrived off the French coast, Hawke formed a small inshore force, under the command of Augustus Hervey, which would patrol the principal coastal routes into Brest while the main force remained off Ushant. As a result, 'Brest was 'blocked up in the strictest sense, [which] was something never previously contemplated, let alone achieved, by the Royal Navy'.[10] Hervey's force was to benefit from Anson's decision later in the year to require every captain to chart the French coasts and undertake hydrographical surveys. In a period when captains produced their own charts, the Admiralty's knowledge of the French coast, including its ports and possible landing places, was patchy, but Anson's intervention helped to fill some of the gaps.

Keeping Hawke on station for an extended period would involve resupplying him at sea, which Anson had tried with good results during his cruise the previous year. The first supplies arrived on station early in July and were successfully unloaded but Hawke soon made complaints about the quality of the victuals being delivered as scurvy started to appear. Anson responded by sending Robert Pett, a victualling commissioner, to Plymouth to address the problem and supplies of fresh meat and vegetables were soon provided to returning ships. He arranged for four transports to be hired, enabling vegetables (which Anson thought were antiscorbutics), live cattle and beer to be dispatched regularly to the squadron at sea.

Although deliveries were disrupted in bad weather, the crews remained generally healthy, and the problem of scurvy was much reduced. Staying at sea for extended periods would also require reinforcements to be dispatched so that Hawke could send ships home to clean and refit. Anson had ships readily available, and they were dispatched without delay. A cleaning rota was agreed upon, with six ships of the line being sent home at a time. Although there were delays in turning ships around because of the poor facilities and inadequate staffing levels at Plymouth dockyard, Hawke now had 23 ships of the line under his command, which enabled him to maintain numerical superiority over the Brest fleet of 22 ships.

Despite an effective blockade of Brest, there was more than one false alarm in London that the threatened French invasion had begun. One such scare occurred on 1 August when reports of a threat to Scotland were discussed at Anson's house. Lord Hardwicke reported on Anson's measured response when Pitt and Ligonier arrived unexpectedly late in the evening:

> In not many minutes Lord Anson came home and then I was lugged into the consultation, which was entirely upon… intelligence from Scotland. Lord Ligonier's fears were for Fort George [Inverness] but my Lord Anson thinks from the course this

---

9 TNA: ADM 2/1331, *Instructions from the Lords of the Admiralty to Hawke,* 18 May 1759.
10 Middleton, 'British Naval Strategy', p.362.

fleet took, that was not their destination. My Lord Anson is also clear that they cannot be a French Fleet but is of opinion that they are Dutch merchant men going north about under the convoy of two men of war… It was thought proper not to do anything at present but strengthen the garrison at Fort George.[11]

A few days later intelligence about a possible raid on Dover was received, but soon afterwards, on 18–19 August, the first setback to the enemy's invasion plans came with Boscawen's victory at the Battle of Lagos Bay when he defeated the French Mediterranean Fleet under the Marquis de la Clue off the Portuguese coast. He destroyed two ships and captured three more, with eight taking refuge in Cadiz, where they were blockaded. Elsewhere invasion preparations were proceeding according to plan, with many transports being assembled in the Gulf of Morbihan in Brittany. Anson sent Hawke reinforcements (four frigates) and ordered him to give priority to destroying the transports as well as keeping watch on Brest.

Meanwhile, Anson received the first reports on the progress of the Quebec expedition, which was untroubled by the French navy because Hawke had blockaded Brest. Saunders had arrived off Louisbourg on 21 April but could not enter the harbour there because of pack ice. As a result, he could not proceed up the St Lawrence without delay as Anson had wanted and was forced to wait at Halifax until 13 May. He found Durell still at Halifax despite his instructions to move into the St Lawrence and, as a result, the French had managed to sail 16 transports into Quebec without being challenged. Saunders left Louisbourg on 1 June and successfully negotiated the hazards of the St Lawrence, which included crossing the Traverse, a difficult passage some 25 miles from Quebec. This 'mighty armada of 40 warships and 180 transport reached… Quebec without a single ship, not even a transport, being lost; among them were ships of the line much larger than any vessel that had ever been there before'.[12]

The French frigates based at Quebec escaped upriver as Saunders approached and he anchored in the south channel off the Île d'Orleans, an island some three miles east of Quebec. He arrived without opposition, but his position was exposed and he was soon attacked by French fireships. Louis Joseph de Montcalm, commander-in-chief of New France, responded to Wolfe's arrival by entrenching 12,000 troops in a defensive line extending from Quebec north-east to the village of Beauport and the Montmorency River. On 31 July, Wolfe landed troops on the French left flank on the eastern bank of the Montmorency River, but the attack was soon repelled.

In the meantime, Saunders established a gun battery on the shore opposite Quebec, which enabled him, on 18 July, to send some ships upstream beyond the city. This opened up the possibility of landing above Quebec and fighting the French in the open. The search for suitable landing sites continued for several weeks until Wolfe and Saunders decided on Anse au Foulon, a dangerous location, less than two miles from the city's western wall. It would mean scaling a steep cliff although there were only 100 French defenders based on the high ground above. During the early hours of 13 September, while Saunders launched a diversionary bombardment at Beauport, some 4,500 men climbed the cliff and reached

---

11 BL: Newcastle Papers, Add. MS. 32,893, f.413, Earl of Hardwicke to the Duke of Newcastle, 1 August 1759.
12 Baugh, *The Global Seven Years War*, p.353.

the Plains of Abraham. The French were taken by surprise and in the battle that followed they were decisively defeated. Both Montcalm and Wolfe were killed. Quebec surrendered soon afterwards, although the delay in taking the city – and Amherst's failure to reach the St Lawrence – meant that the British conquest of Canada would not be completed until Montreal surrendered in September 1760.[13]

In selecting Saunders for the Quebec command, Anson had helped to ensure that the expedition to Quebec was successful, with the navy making a major contribution to the outcome of the decisive battle. The historian Julian Corbett wrote that although 'he lacked the genius of Wolfe, his hand throughout was the surer of the two; and dazzling as was the final stroke by which Wolfe snatched victory from failure, the steadier flame of Saunders's exploit is worthy to burn beside it.'[14] Victory had depended on the effective coordination of the two services, with Saunders commenting that 'during this tedious campaign there had continued a perfect good understanding between the army and navy'.[15] It was an outcome that Saunders had worked hard to achieve, with George Townshend, who was Wolfe's successor, acknowledging 'how much we are indebted for our success to the constant assistance and support [of the navy], and the perfect harmony and correspondence which have prevailed throughout our operations'.[16]

News of the fall of Quebec, which reached London on 16 October, followed a series of British naval and military successes during the annus mirabilis or year of wonders, with Walpole writing that 'Our bells are worn threadbare with ringing for victories'.[17] However, the greatest success of the year – and one for which Anson had long prepared the ground – was yet to come as Hawke maintained his position at Brest and Robert Duff's squadron kept watch in Quiberon Bay, where the invasion fleet was assembling. As the close blockade continued, Anson's priorities remained unchanged: containing the French fleet at Brest and preventing the departure of the invasion force from Morbihan.

On 7 November, Hawke was forced off station by bad weather for the second time since June and a week later the French fleet of 18 ships of the line under the Comte de Conflans left Brest. The French invasion plan had been activated and Conflans was to go to Morbihan to pick up his transports and then head for Scotland. By the time news of the French escape reached Anson, who was confident that they would be intercepted and defeated, Hawke was heading towards the Gulf of Morbihan with 23 ships of the line under his command. On 20 November, the two fleets sighted each other west of Belle Isle when they were no more than 20 leagues apart. Conflans ordered his fleet to take refuge in the dangerous waters of Quiberon Bay, south of Morbihan, assuming that Hawke would not follow him because of the risks posed by rocks and reefs as nightfall approached. However, Hawke was undeterred and pursued him into the Bay, raising a signal for a general chase without forming a line. In

---

13 Charles P. Stacey, *Quebec, 1759: The Siege and the Battle* (Revised edition, Toronto: Robin Brass Studio, 2002); Arthur G. Doughty, *An Historical Journal of the Campaigns in North America for the Years 1757, 1758, 1759, and 1760 by Captain John Knox*. 3 vols. (Toronto: Champlain Society, 1914).
14 Corbett, *England in the Seven Years War*, vol.I, p.476.
15 Quoted in Robson, *A History of the Royal Navy*, p.125.
16 Edward Salmon, *Life of Admiral Sir Charles Saunders, KB* (London: Isaac Pitman, 1914), p.147.
17 Horace Walpole to George Montagu, 21 October 1759, in Lewis (ed.), *The Yale Edition of the Correspondence of Horace Walpole*, vol.9, p.251.

the confused fighting that followed, seven French warships were captured or sunk; six were driven into the River Vilaine and trapped there, and eight made for Rochefort. Two British ships of the line were lost due to grounding.[18]

The 'most decisive naval battle of the eighteenth century' marked the end of the enemy's invasion plans and, with the loss of its battle fleet, Britain now had control of the seas.[19] When Anson wrote to congratulate Hawke, he noted that many of his friends, including Keppel, Denis, Campbell and Howe, had distinguished themselves during the battle.[20] John Campbell, who was Hawke's flag captain at Quiberon Bay, returned to England with news of the great victory. As Anson took him to be presented at Court, he told Campbell that the King would knight him if he wished. 'Troth, my lord,' answered Campbell, 'I ken nae use that will be to me'. 'But,' said Anson, 'your lady may like it'. 'Aweel,' replied Campbell, 'his Majesty may knight her, if he pleases'. He was not in fact knighted but received 500 guineas from the King.[21]

There is no doubt that 'none of this would have been possible but for Anson's perseverance with the Western Squadron. The success at Quiberon was a vindication of his policy'.[22] As we have seen, Hawke was able, to maintain a blockade for months at a time as a result of radical changes in the victualling arrangements under Anson's control, which meant that, for the first time, fresh meat and vegetable were supplied regularly to the fleet at sea. The close blockade established by Hawke had been a pragmatic response to the circumstances he faced off Brest, but Anson may perhaps be criticised for not having developed the concept at a much earlier point in the war. Although there was no doubt about its value, logistical constraints and high costs pointed to the difficulties of regularly imposing a close blockade for extended periods.[23]

Despite Hawke's great victory, a watch on the enemy at Quiberon was still needed and, in December, Anson gained approval from ministers for a squadron under Boscawen to be dispatched to relieve Hawke and monitor the French ships at Morbihan and Rochefort. He soon received confirmation that the French still posed a potential threat at sea when six frigates under the command of the privateer captain François Thurot escaped from Dunkirk, which was still being blockaded. Thurot sailed around the coast of Scotland and put 600 men ashore at Carrickfergus in Ireland in February 1760 but was defeated off the Isle of Man a few days later. Anson also continued to maintain a strong presence in the Mediterranean to keep watch on French ships at Cadiz and Toulon, with Saunders taking command in May 1760.

Amid these successes, Anson suffered a devastating blow when Elizabeth died prematurely. Her health had always been delicate – she had been ill most recently in mid-1759 when a family party was cut short – but her sudden death at Moor Park on 1 June 1760 at the

---

18 Nicholas Tracy, *The Battle of Quiberon Bay. Hawke and the Defeat of the French Invasion* (Barnsley: Pen & Sword Maritime, 2010).
19 Robson, *A History of the Royal Navy*, p.141.
20 Rodger, *The Wooden World*, p.277.
21 Quoted in J.K. Laughton, 'John Campbell (1720?–1790)', *The Dictionary of National Biography* (1886), <https://doi.org/10.1093/odnb/9780192683120.013.4518>, accessed 21 September 2022.
22 Middleton, *The Bells of Victory*, p.145.
23 Erica M. Charters, *Disease, War, and the Imperial State: The Welfare of the British Armed Forces during the Seven Years' War* (Chicago: University of Chicago Press, 2014), p.330.

age of only 34 was quite unexpected. She had been ill for 10 days with 'an epidemic fever and sore throat', which her friend Catherine Talbot described as scarlet fever, but she appeared to be recovering.[24] Only a day earlier, Anson had informed Hardwicke that she was 'quite out of danger, and tho' her rash is not all out, she is easy and, to a degree, has recovered her sleep and spirits', but while writing to him her doctor had reported that her fever was increasing. Anson admitted that he did not 'understand their jargon and always feel when I have any of them in the house, as I always did in my ship when I had a pilot; being ignorant myself, I always doubted whether my pilot knew as much as he ought to do; but in both cases there is nothing else to trust to'.[25]

Jemima Yorke described Lord Anson as being in the 'highest distress' as a result of Elizabeth's untimely death. According to Lord Royston, he 'bore this loss with great philosophy, though he was deeply afflicted by it. His house never could forget the lively and cheerful sunshine... which she spread over it'. According to Lord Hardwicke, 'the storm and passion of his grief and the impression of his loss far exceeded what I could have imagined, especially from him, who has naturally a certain firmness and composure'. The Duke of Newcastle described Lady Anson as 'one of the best of women' while her father said 'she was the life and soul of our societies, was always desirous to please and capable of doing it'.[26] Jemima Yorke summed up the general reaction to her death:

> She was everything that was great and good and amiable. She fitted every station of life to perfection – daughter, wife, sister, friend; she was the joy and comfort of all; a busy active mind and excellent heart; she seemed designed by Providence as a common blessing to a large and united family, and a useful example to the world of uncommon talents.[27]

It was a blow from which Anson would never fully recover.

While the naval war had virtually ended, France redoubled her efforts in Germany and was significantly reinforcing her armies on the Rhine in 1760. Another diversionary attack on the French coast was needed to help Ferdinand and Pitt mentioned Boulogne or the Flanders coast as possibilities although he favoured the capture of Belle Isle, which could be used as a base for future naval operations against Brest and Rochefort. It could also be used as a bargaining counter in peace negotiations in order to obtain the return of Minorca and, at a ministerial meeting on 3 October, Pitt explained the advantages of his proposal. Anson said that the weather would be suitable for an attack until about mid-November, but he did not otherwise express a view. Newcastle, who referred to it as a 'hazardous, ridiculous measure,' was expecting 'to have been supported by my Admiral and General, but that was

---

24   Horace Walpole to Horace Mann, 20 June 1760, in Lewis (ed.), *The Yale Edition of the Correspondence of Horace Walpole*, vol.21, p.302; Catherine Talbot to Elizabeth Carter, 3 June 1760, in *A Series of Letters Between Mrs Elizabeth Carter and Miss Catherine Talbot, from the Year 1741 to 1770* (London: Rivington, 1809), vol.II, p.332.
25   George Anson to the Earl of Hardwicke, 31 May 1760, in Yorke (ed.), *The Life and Correspondence*, vol.II, pp.593–594.
26   Yorke (ed.), *The Life and Correspondence*, vol.II, p.580.
27   Quoted in Godber, *The Marchioness Grey*, pp.65–66.

not my good fortune', referring to Anson and Ligonier.[28] The majority agreed to continue preparations and Anson selected Augustus Keppel to command the naval squadron. Despite his silence, Anson was far from enthusiastic about the operation because of the time that the Western Squadron had already spent at sea in 1760 and because winter was fast approaching.

Keppel was present at a follow-up meeting on 8 October and expressed reservations about the plan because the water surrounding Belle Isle was too shallow and its defences had recently been strengthened. Pitt responded by suggesting that Hawke, who was still cruising in the area, should be asked to settle the question of the water's depth. Anson wrote to him on 9 October asking for a report on the issue and other matters raised at the meeting. In an accompanying note, Clevland said that Anson had asked for Hawke's 'private thoughts' on the plan to be sent to him separately. Unfortunately, Hawke did not follow Anson's instructions, instead sending a single letter, which confirmed Keppel's assessment, rejected the idea that it would be an effective diversion and expressed a preference for a landing on the mainland. When Anson received Hawke's letter of 17 October, he took it straight to the King and was able to convince him to oppose the scheme. Pitt was angry with Anson for not consulting him first but outraged by Hawke's response, in which he had clearly exceeded his remit. In one of his last decisions before his death, George II concluded that the Belle Isle plan was impractical and decided to cancel it while favouring an expedition to the mainland, as Hawke had proposed. However, Hawke's letter did not convince Pitt and he was determined to press ahead.[29]

Anson was among the first to learn of George II's death from a stroke on the morning of 25 October. As he reported to Lord Hardwicke, 'I had a note two hours ago with the melancholy account of the King's death, upon which I went immediately to Kensington'.[30] When George III was proclaimed King, he expressed a wish that all his ministers should continue to serve him and, like his colleagues, Anson confirmed that he had no plans to resign. The only change the new King made was the addition of Lord Bute to the Cabinet Council; as his principal adviser, he was to be present when further discussions on the Belle Isle expedition, which Pitt initiated, were held on 11 November. Although there was no longer a need for a diversion – the French offensive in the west had ended and Frederick II had advanced against the Russians and Austrians – Pitt believed that the possession of Belle Isle would still be useful as a bargaining counter at the peace negotiations. During the meeting, 'Pitt with great art endeavoured to draw Lord Anson and Lord Ligonier in to give their opinions for it, which they had not resolution not to give into'.[31] With no objections from the two service chiefs, the plan was approved and preparations for the last combined operation of the war in Europe began.

The expedition finally sailed on 29 March 1761 and the island was captured on 7 June. As Pitt intended, the occupation gave Britain additional diplomatic leverage and kept French

---

28   Quoted in Mackay, *Hawke*, p.268.
29   Middleton, *The Bells of Victory*, pp.166–169; Mackay, *Hawke*, pp.267–277.
30   George Anson to the Earl of Hardwicke, 25 October 1760, in Yorke (ed.), *The Life and Correspondence*, vol.III, p.253.
31   Peter D. Brown and Karl W. Schweitzer (eds.), *The Devonshire Diary: William Cavendish, Fourth Duke of Devonshire, Memoranda on State of Affairs 1759–1762*, Camden Society, Fourth Series, vol.XXVII (London: Royal Historical Society, 1982), p.58.

warships in port, but it had little impact on the course of the war in Germany, where France would capture Hesse by the end of the year although Hanover remained free. Pitt had also secured the agreement of ministers to two naval expeditions to the Caribbean – the occupation of Dominica and St Lucia and a second attempt to take Martinique – and an attack on the French naval base on Mauritius. Dominica and St Lucia were captured in 1761 and Martinique followed. Rodney, who was appointed as commander in chief of the Leeward Islands, was given responsibility for taking Martinique, with Anson selecting him over the heads of several more senior officers. Rodney soon justified his decision, displaying considerable tactical ability in the operation which led to the French surrendering the island in February 1762. The expedition to Mauritius, which Anson had also been working on, was abandoned because the military situation in India had improved.

Although Anson devoted most of his energies to wartime naval operations, he continued to maintain a close interest in scientific developments and supported two promising initiatives during his final months in office. In 1761, he was responsible for initiating an experimental programme to sheath ships with copper in response to a request from the Navy Board, which had reported that 'His Majesty's ships have lately returned from the West Indies, being remarkably eat by the worm, though they had been but a small time there'. The Board suggested that a frigate should be sheathed in copper which might prove as 'effectual as any other method we can at present think of'.[32] The Admiralty immediately ordered the hull of the frigate *Alarm* to be sheathed as an experiment to test whether it would reduce maintenance costs and improve performance. It was later repeated on a small number of other ships but had limited success because the copper sheathing reacted with the iron bolts of the hull, causing the latter to corrode rapidly. The problem was only solved when the Admiralty decided to replace the iron bolts with hardened copper hull bolts and by 1782 the whole fleet had been fitted with copper sheathing.

In 1762, Anson was also responsible for the decision to install lightning-conductors on British warships. The lightning rod had been invented 10 years earlier by Benjamin Franklin, later one of the Founding Fathers of the United States, and offered a means of preventing the damage that lightning could cause to wooden warships. However, the mechanism selected – a chain that was to be raised up the mast when a storm was expected – did not work well because lightning could strike without warning. There were also objections to the use of conductors on the spurious grounds that they would attract lightning to the ship. A successful replacement system was invented in 1820 but it was not adopted by the Royal Navy until 1841.

Early in August 1761, Anson briefly returned to the sea in command of a squadron of warships and yachts with orders to collect Princess Charlotte of Mecklenburgh-Strelitz from Germany. A few weeks before, on 8 July, George III had announced to the Privy Council his intention to marry the princess and he ordered Simon Harcourt, first Earl Harcourt, a diplomat, to lead a delegation to Hanover. A squadron would sail to Stade in Hanover and escort the princess to England; the King gave Anson 'a paper of instructions, a full sheet, all writ with his own Royal hand'.[33] This important new duty may have influenced the timing

---

32 Quoted in R. J. B. Knight, 'Early Attempts at Lead and Copper Sheathing', *The Mariner's Mirror*, 62 (1976), p. 293.
33 Harris, *The Life of Lord Chancellor Hardwicke*, vol.III, p.247.

Queen Charlotte's passage to England, painting by Richard Wright. (Royal Collection Trust)

of his promotion shortly afterwards, on 30 July, to Admiral of the Fleet, the highest rank in the Royal Navy and the equivalent of field marshal in the army. It was an unprecedented mark of royal favour because the rank should have passed, on the death of George Clinton, to Admiral Sir William Rowley, who was the senior admiral of the white. The rank would revert to Rowley when Anson died in 1762.

The new Queen would return to England in the principal royal yacht – the *Royal Caroline* (named after George II's wife) – which had been used to carry the King on his regular visits to the Continent since entering service in 1750. The King was normally escorted by Lord Anson as the highest-ranking Admiralty officer. On this occasion, the yacht was refitted and extravagantly redecorated before leaving for Stade: she was a 'wonderful boat, entirely gilt without, within all rich gilding, red damask, mahogany, and Turkey carpets'.[34] Horace Walpole was told 'the painting of the Charlotte yatch would certainly turn the Queen's stomach. I said, if her head is not turned, she may compound for anything else'.[35] The works cost £5,200, which was nearly half the amount (£12,390) spent on her original construction. On 25 July, Anson and other members of the Admiralty inspected the yacht and renamed

---

34 Alice D. Greenwood, *Lives of the Hanoverian Queens of England* (London: G. Bell and Sons, 1911), vol.II, p.13.
35 Horace Walpole to Horace Mann, 17 August 1761, in Lewis (ed.), *The Yale Edition of the Correspondence of Horace Walpole*, vol.21, p.525.

her the *Royal Charlotte*. Four other royal yachts, which carried members of the royal household, and an escort of four warships, two sloops and two cutters, assembled at Woolwich before sailing to Harwich on 3 August.[36]

At Harwich, Anson took command and flew his flag in the *Royal Charlotte*, with his old friend Peter Denis serving as captain. On 7 August, the squadron left for Cuxhaven, where the four largest warships anchored seven days later, and the smaller ships continued to the Elbe. Anson reached the port of Stade on 15 August and set out to meet the new Queen, who had been married by proxy at Strelitz. She left from Stade in 'the Admiralty barge, with the royal standard of England flying in the bow, preceded by Lord Anson's barge, with the union flag in her bow. The *Royal Charlotte* yacht was dressed up in all the different colours of all nations to receive her'.[37] Now flying his flag in the *Lynx* (14), Anson departed on 24 August and when he rejoined the warships anchored off Cuxhaven, he transferred his flag to the *Nottingham*.

The return journey across the North Sea was long and difficult, taking 10 days rather than the normal three after they departed from Cuxhaven. In stormy weather, they saw Flamborough Head before being driven back towards the Norwegian coast three times. Some of the ships were damaged but, according to Anson, 'the Princess bore remarkably well' and gave her 'the highest character for her affability, her vivacity and her understanding'.[38] Given the difficult conditions, Anson decided to land at Harwich, abandoning the original plan to disembark the Queen at Gravesend and then travel by small boat to Greenwich for a state welcome. Charlotte disembarked on 7 September and arrived in London on the following day, much later than expected. According to Lord Hardwicke, 'everybody at Court is in amazement how Lord Anson has made the passage, & suppose he has either sent to Lapland for a wind, or rowed her along'.[39]

The successful journey to Hanover was the last occasion on which Anson went to sea. With his health soon deteriorating, he spent the final few months of his life planning operations against Spain once war had been declared at the beginning of 1762. Britain's relations with Spain had deteriorated since Charles III's accession to the throne in August 1759: he was anti-British and favoured closer cooperation with France, signing the Family Compact in 1761. The agreement included secret clauses committing Spain to diplomatic and military support for France if a satisfactory peace settlement with Britain could not be concluded by May 1762.

Ministers met on 15 September to discuss how to respond to Spain's more aggressive foreign policy, with Pitt proposing a pre-emptive attack before Charles could come to the aid of the French. He argued that there was little doubt that Spain was preparing for war and it was in Britain's interest to strike first; her naval weakness meant that there was an opportunity to inflict a decisive defeat, but a majority led by Newcastle and Bute opposed the proposal. Anson, who remained loyal to Newcastle, presented a paper showing 'how the

---

36 *Nottingham* (60), *Winchester* (50), *Minerva* (32), *Tartar* (28) and the sloops *Hazard* (14) and *Lynx* (14).
37 John Lyon, 'A Journal of the Late Voyage to Stade, when the Rt. Hon. Lord Anson went for Her Majesty', *The British Magazine*, 2 (September 1761), p.481.
38 University of Nottingham: Newcastle Papers, C3878, eighth Earl of Kinnoull to the Earl of Lincoln (second Duke of Newcastle), 9 September 1761.
39 Lord Hardwicke to Lord Royston, [6 September 1761], in Harris, *The Life of Lord Chancellor Hardwicke*, vol.III, p.250.

fleet's 105 ships of the line and 82,000 men were fully employed. A war with Spain would mean an enormous expansion of responsibilities in the Mediterranean, the East and West Indies, as well as the area between Finisterre and Cape Verde'.[40] Although the Royal Navy was smaller than in 1760, it was still more than double the size of the Spanish navy and, with the French fleet largely demobilised, Anson, who was 'prone to alarmism', may be criticised for overreacting to the threat.[41]

The inner committee returned to the Spanish issue three days later when Pitt repeated his demand for an attack on Spain. But the majority were still not convinced that war was inevitable, and it was decided to seek assurances from Spain about her peaceful intentions while trying to keep her detached from France. Pitt submitted a minute to the King expressing his disagreement with the majority view and pressing for immediate action. Most ministers decided against sending their own notes to the King but agreed to present their views in person, which Anson and his colleagues did on 24 September. Lord Ligonier shared Anson's reservations, pointing to the strength of the Spanish army.

At a further ministerial discussion on 2 October, Pitt again pressed for action but the majority remained opposed. Anson pointed to a shortage of seamen and ships, with many being cleaned and repaired after their summer cruise off the coast of France. He reiterated his view that 'our ships were not in a condition to enter immediately into any material operation against Spain'.[42] Pitt thought this view was excessively cautious but it was one that George III was almost certain to accept as he had previously said that if Anson spoke out against action this would cut 'short at once any consideration of immediate operations'.[43] Subsequent events confirmed the accuracy of Pitt's judgement and suggested that Anson had allowed political loyalties to sway his judgement.

With ministers unwilling to support immediate action against Spain, Pitt resigned as Southern Secretary and was replaced by Lord Egremont. Ministers did, however, agree that Anson should inform the King that they believed significant reinforcements should be sent to the Mediterranean Fleet and that Admiral Saunders should be prepared for a Spanish attack. Shortly afterwards, Anson wrote in secret to Saunders asking him to explore the feasibility of attacking Cadiz, a possibility that had been suggested by Lord Howe. Despite this instruction, Anson explained why he did not believe that war was imminent:

> It is thought by some people here that Spain has an inclination to declare war against us, I own I am not of that opinion not seeing what advantage Spain can promise themselves from the measure, nor do I think their weight would be great though it was thrown into the scale of France in the present conjecture.[44]

Anson's judgement proved to be questionable as relations with Spain continued to deteriorate rapidly and Britain stepped up its naval preparations. She declared war against

---

40 Middleton, *The Bells of Victory*, p.193.
41 Jonathan R. Dull, *The French Navy and the Seven Years War* (Lincoln: University of Nebraska, 2005), p.207.
42 BL: Newcastle Papers, Add. MS. 32,929, f.18, *Minute*, 2 October 1761.
43 Middleton, *The Bells of Victory*, p.195.
44 SRO: D615/P(S)/1/10/34, George Anson to Charles Saunders, [October 1761].

Spain on 2 January 1762 and four days later ministers assembled to discuss proposals to attack Havana and Manila as 'the most effectual methods of distressing and attacking the Spaniards'.[45] Both proposals were unanimously agreed upon. The expeditions aimed to disrupt the main sources of Spanish trade rather than seize territory in the hope that they would persuade Spain to enter into peace negotiations. As the Duke of Newcastle reported, 'we began with my Lord Anson's project of attacking Havana, and, after hearing the facility with which his Lordship and Lord Ligonier apprehended there was in doing it, we all unanimously ordered the undertaking'.[46] Lord Egremont introduced the second proposal for an amphibious assault on Manila, which was at the centre of Spain's Pacific trading empire. Anson's support for the Manila proposal was crucial from the beginning: 'the expedition would not have been undertaken, had [he] not, in the strongest terms, recommended and pressed it upon Lord Egremont'.[47]

Early in 1762, there were 297 ships in service in the Royal Navy and Anson deployed the fleet in the Atlantic and Mediterranean to meet the combined Franco-Spanish threat. There were 18 ships of the line patrolling in the Mediterranean under Charles Saunders, whose aim was to prevent the French and Spanish fleets from joining together. He later detached ships in support of Portugal when the Spanish invaded that country. To guard against the danger that a combined Franco-Spanish naval force might evade the British fleet and sail into the Channel in support of a new invasion attempt, ministers agreed that the Western Squadron, under Hawke's command, should be redeployed to Plymouth from its current positions off the French coast. Naval resources would also be found for the Havana and Manila expeditions, undermining Anson's earlier argument about the difficulty of fighting France and Spain at the same time.

In the weeks leading up to the meeting on 6 January, Anson had been working on the proposal for a surprise attack on Manila. Pitt had considered the possibility of an operation against the Philippines before his resignation and consulted Anson 'on account of his knowledge of these seas'.[48] Their thinking was informed by a proposal originally made by Colonel (later Lieutenant General Sir) William Draper, who commanded the 79th Regiment in India, on his return to London on sick leave in the autumn of 1761. He spoke to Egremont and Anson about his ideas for an amphibious expedition against Manila and was asked to submit a written proposal. Anson agreed to support the idea in principle, and, at the end of December, he approached Thomas Rous, chairman of the East India Company, to ask whether the Company would participate in the operation. Shortly afterwards, the Board discussed the idea and agreed 'to give all possible assistance… towards the attempt intended against Manilha [sic]… consistently with the interests of the Company'.[49]

Following the meeting of the inner committee on 6 January, Anson met with East India Company officials on three occasions to discuss a draft plan for the operation. During these

---

45 Brown and Schweitzer (eds.), *The Devonshire Diary*, p.154.
46 Corbett, *England in the Seven Years War*, vol.II, p.247.
47 Almon, *Anecdotes*, vol.I, p.326.
48 Almon, *Anecdotes*, vol.I, p.325.
49 *Meeting of the Directors of the East India Company*, 30 December 1761, in Nicholas P. Cushner (ed.), *Documents Illustrating the British Conquest of Manila, 1762–1763*, Camden Society, Fourth Series, vol.8 (London: Royal Historical Society, 1971), p.11.

discussions, it was decided that the expedition should also conquer the Philippine island of Mindanao, where a permanent British base would be established, as it was recognised that Manila would eventually have to be returned to Spain. In echoes of the discussions leading up to his circumnavigation in 1740, Anson was briefed on the advantages that would follow if the expedition succeeded:

> All trade or intercourse betwixt the E. Indies and the Spanish American provinces in the South Seas will be effectually cut off during the war, at least... [and] from such proposed settlement the Spanish provinces in the South Seas, both of South and North America, may with great success be insulated and plundered on the part of Great Britain.[50]

On 19 January, following the discussions between Anson and Company officials, the Board gave conditional approval to its participation in the expedition, 'if it shall appear in India consistent with their interest and security'.[51]

Anson thought the expedition would require no more than five ships of the line, one or two frigates and two sloops. Except for the frigate *Argo* (28), these ships would be drawn from the East Asiatic squadron, which was based in Madras (Chennai) under the command of Vice Admiral Samuel Cornish, rather than from those operating in home waters. The naval force would be increased to eight ships of the line when Cornish was denied the use of large Indiamen as transports, which were needed to move 1,700 troops under Draper's command. The fact that the expedition did not involve the redeployment of naval forces from Europe to the Far East may have been one of the reasons that persuaded Anson to support it.

The plan has been described by an historian of the Manila expedition as 'very bold and not a little foolhardy' because it would rely on a small landing force and the condition of Cornish's ships was poor.[52] Cornish was also worried about the approaching monsoon season and the lack of hydrographic charts, but Anson had few concerns about the naval aspects of the expedition (and his judgement proved to be correct): 'as the voyage from the coast of Coromandel thither is chiefly thro' the Straits, no difficulty can occur with regard either to the victualling or transport of such a number of troops on board the squadron in a run of no more than six weeks'.[53] Anson's direct involvement in planning the expedition came to an end on 21 January when Draper, who was appointed to the rank of 'Brigadier General in the East Indies only', received George III's instructions and sailed for Madras to organise the forces under his command.[54]

Anson devoted much of his remaining time in office to planning the expedition to Cuba, which was a much larger venture than the operation against Manila. He accorded it a high

---

50   *Rough Sketch of an Expedition to M[anil]a, mentioned to Lord A[nson] on 8th, 11th, and 12th Inst. January 1762*, in Cushner (ed.), *Documents*, pp.12–15.
51   *Meeting of the Directors of the East India Company*, 19 January 1762, in Cushner (ed.), *Documents*, p.18.
52   Nicholas Tracy, 'The Capture of Manila 1762', *The Mariner's Mirror*, 55 (1969), p.313.
53   Nicholas Tracy, *Manila Ransomed: The British Assault on Manila in the Seven Years War* (Exeter: University of Exeter Press, 1995), p.25.
54   *Instructions of George III to William Draper, 21 January 1762*, in Cushner (ed.), *Documents*, pp.18–22.

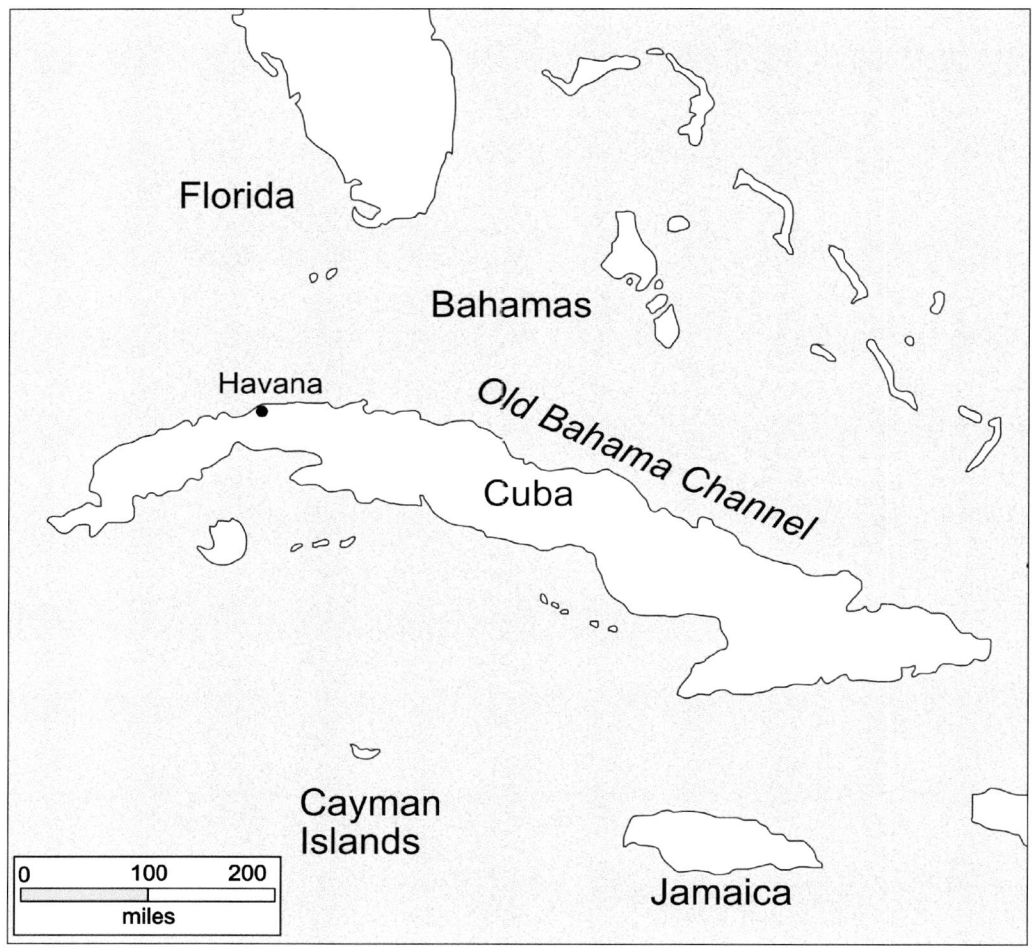

Cuba, 1762.

priority because Havana, a major centre of Spanish trade, was 'the site of the best naval base in the Caribbean, served as a rendezvous for homeward-bound *flotas*, commanded the communications between Spain and her American mainland colonies, and was reputedly rich in booty'.[55] The complex operation involved coordinating several naval and military units in widely dispersed locations, ensuring preparations were completed quickly and enabling the fleet to withdraw from Havana by the end of August when the hurricane season began.

Developed in conjunction with Ligonier, Anson's plan was based on information provided by Sir Charles Knowles, a former governor of Jamaica, who had conducted

---

55 David Syrett (ed.), *The Siege and Capture of Havana, 1762* (London: Navy Records Society, 1970), p.xiii.

operations against Cuba in the previous war against Spain and had visited Havana in 1756. The proposals, which demonstrated Anson's well developed planning skills, took account of seasonal weather and the need to confuse the enemy, thus ensuring the maximum surprise. Its success depended on the absence of a joint response by French and Spanish naval forces as the British approached the island. The most innovative aspect of Anson's plan was his decision to avoid using the normal (southerly) route to Cuba, which meant concentrating naval forces in Jamaica, then sailing west and arriving off the south coast of the island before proceeding to Havana on the north coast. Its main disadvantage was that the French and Spanish navies would have recognised a possible threat to Cuba if they had seen a concentration of British forces in Jamaica and would have responded.

To avoid this danger, Anson decided on an alternative route which meant approaching the island from the north through the Old Bahama Channel, a strait between Cuba and the Bahamas, basing it on an old Spanish chart in his possession. The channel, which was about 250 miles long, was a faster route because the fleet would benefit from the trade winds and have the advantage of surprise as it would remain undetected until it was in sight of the Cuban coast. This meant that the fleet would arrive off Havana before a rider on horseback could reach the capital to raise the alarm. But the plan was risky as the channel was narrow and dangerous – it was no more than 10 miles wide in places; the Spanish normally avoided using it and did not expect the British to do so. Sir Charles Knowles criticised this aspect of the plan, arguing that Anson was risking the whole fleet to save a week, but his fears proved to be unfounded. Newcastle, who had supported the venture in January, raised wider objections to the project in February that were equally misplaced, describing it as 'a most *expensive*, hazardous, uncertain expedition… to the Havana, when both ships and men are wanted elsewhere; a wild goose chase…'[56]

With Hawke and Saunders commanding in the Channel and Mediterranean respectively, Anson selected Vice Admiral Sir George Pocock to head the naval force. Pocock had wide experience in the East and West Indies and was well qualified for a role that required 'a man of the highest powers, not only as a fighting admiral, but as a navigator and seamen, and from both points of view no better choice could have been made'.[57] Anson's friend Augustus Keppel was appointed as second in command and nominated as Pocock's successor in the event of his death. On Lord Ligonier's recommendation, Keppel's brother George, third Earl of Albemarle, was appointed as head of the land forces even though he had no command experience. Anson's bold plan involved assembling troops based in several different locations on two continents and 'when we recollect how tiny were the administrative and operations staffs and how dire the effect of the weather upon sailing ships it was a remarkable example of the art of amphibious war.'[58]

Under Anson's plan, Pocock's squadron of seven ships of the line and one frigate was to escort transports carrying four infantry regiments and attached units of artillery and engineers. Apart from the 4,400 troops departing from England, additional men would

---

56 BL: Hardwicke Papers, Add. MS. 32,934, f.292, Duke of Newcastle to the Earl of Hardwicke, 12 February 1762.
57 Corbett, *England in the Seven Years War*, vol.II, p.248.
58 Rex Whitworth, *Field Marshal Lord Ligonier: A Story of the British Army, 1702–1770* (Oxford: Clarendon Press, 1958), p.366.

be assembled in North America and the West Indies. Pocock was to meet Major General Robert Monckton and Rear Admiral George Rodney, who were then commanding a force occupying Martinique, where they were to embark 8,000 troops, the largest contingent of the expeditionary force. The combined force of 15 ships and 13,000 men was then ordered to sail for Cape St Nicholas, the north-western point of Hispaniola, where they were to meet 4,000 troops arriving from New York.[59]

Anson acted swiftly to implement the agreed plan and the Admiralty issued orders to provide 10,000 tons of transport as early as 7 January. By 19 February, instructions were sent to Pocock as the troops, transports and supplies destined for Havana were being assembled at Spithead. On 25 February, Anson and two other Admiralty Lords, left for Portsmouth to see the embarkation of the troops and the accompanying fleet. They were accompanied by Queen Charlotte's brother, Prince Charles of Mecklenburg, and other Hanoverian visitors, including Count Frederick Kielmansegge. He described how 'the whole party went out [to the fleet] in several twelve-oared boats, in a kind of procession, to Spithead' and as it came on board Pocock's flagship, 'the Admiral saluted them with 21 guns [and] at the same moment all ships in the roads saluted, with as many guns, which was a splendid sight, as the ships were lying all around us, and gave us some idea of a naval action'.[60] Despite Anson's best efforts, a shortage of bedding – and bad weather – delayed Pocock's departure until 5 March. But the fact that he left for the Caribbean only two months after Ministers had agreed to the expedition was a measure of Anson's continuing effectiveness even as his health was beginning to fail. His organisation of the expedition 'indicated a degree of administrative skill and speed which was often lacking in preparations for other British military expeditions undertaken during the eighteenth century'.[61]

Anson left Portsmouth with a heavy cold and his health seems to have progressively deteriorated from this point. His past medical record was mixed: he had suffered from gout for many years and had experienced several bouts of illness since returning to England in 1744, often visiting Bath to immerse himself in the hot waters. Early in 1759, he was reported as being 'dangerously ill of a fever at his house at the Admiralty' but recovered rapidly.[62] However, on this occasion, now aged 65, he was not so fortunate: during March his illness progressed and it was feared that he might not recover. Anson's declining physical health may also have been affected by the continuing impact of Elizabeth's untimely death, which meant that since then he was likely to have been lonely with little purpose in life beyond his work. On 18 March, the Admiralty reported that he was 'somewhat better this evening, has had a little sleep, and his pains are easier, but his breathing is still much opprest [sic], upon the whole his Lordship appears better but is by no means yet to be thought out of danger'.[63]

---

59 Baugh, *The Global Seven Years War*, pp.518–527.
60 Frederick Kielmansegge, *Diary of a Journey to England in the Years 1761–1762* (London: Longmans & Co, 1902), p.260–262.
61 Syrett (ed.), *The Siege and Capture of Havana*, p.xv.
62 *The London Chronicle*, Vol 5, 6–8 February 1759, p.132.
63 Admiralty to the Duke of Newcastle, 18 March 1762 quoted in Pack, *Admiral Lord Anson*, p.251; see also John Clevland to Edward Weston, 19 March 1762, in HMC, *Reports on the Manuscripts of …C F Weston Underwood* (London: H. M. Stationery Office, 1885), p.328.

Although the immediate danger seemed to pass shortly afterwards – he was soon 'able to take an airing in his chariot' and returned to work before the end of March[64] – his health did not fully recover and he was advised to try the Bath waters under the supervision of his doctor William Oliver. While travelling to Bath, where he arrived on 15 April, Oliver reported that he was 'seized with a violent cough, attended with a constant and most copious discharge of a thin, frothy rheum'.[65] On this occasion, his stay in Bath did not produce any benefits and, on 26 April, Oliver thought he was 'much worse' while *The London Chronicle* noted 'Lord Anson was so bad, that there remained no hopes of his recovery'.[66] On 7 May, it was reported that Anson was on his way to London 'if he is ever able to reach it alive', while Walpole believed that he 'was in a very bad way'.[67] On 5 June, the day before his death, he left for Moor Park, but was taken ill early the following morning. He may have had a heart attack or stroke while walking 'a little in the gardens for the air. [He] came into the house, complained of being ill and laying down on his bed, expired without a groan' at about 9:00 a.m.[68]

On 21 June, Anson was interred in the family vault at Colwich alongside Elizabeth who had been buried there on 26 June 1760. He died before plans to create him Viscount Colchester, in recognition of his wartime services, could be finalised.[69] In the absence of a direct male heir, the patent was to have included a special remainder, which meant the viscountcy would have passed to George Adams, his sister Janette's son, on Anson's death. However, his existing peerage contained no such provision and the title became extinct with his passing. Under the terms of his will, which was proved on 16 June, he left the bulk of his estate to his brother Thomas, with Janette and George Adams receiving annuities of £300 a year each.[70] Thomas used his share of the inheritance further to enlarge the Shugborough estate and to rebuild George's townhouse in St James's Square. As we have seen, in a final tribute to his brother, Thomas commissioned a medal commemorating his victory at Cape Finisterre and his voyage around the world, which was circulated in 1769. When Thomas died in 1773, George Adams inherited Thomas's estate and took the name Anson.[71] His son Thomas (1767–1818) was created Viscount Anson of Shugborough and Orgreave in 1806.

Anson's passing was mourned by leading political figures and his family alike. No one was better placed to assess his contribution to public life than Lord Hardwicke, with whom he had been closely associated for the past 15 years. In a letter to the Duke of Newcastle, he said that:

---

64   *The London Chronicle*, vol.11, 6–8 April 1762, p.334.
65   BL: Newcastle Papers, Add. MS. 32,937, f.200, William Oliver to the Duke of Newcastle, 17 April 1762.
66   *The London Chronicle*, vol.11, 27–29 April 1762, p.408.
67   University of Nottingham: Newcastle Papers, C3381/1–2, H. Reade to the Earl of Lincoln (second Duke of Newcastle), 7 May 1762; Horace Walpole to George Montagu, 29 April 1762, in Lewis (ed.), *The Yale Edition of the Correspondence of Horace Walpole*, vol.10, p.27.
68   *The London Chronicle*, vol.11, 5–8 June 1762, p.538.
69   Keppel, *The Life of Augustus, Viscount Keppel*, vol.I, p.254.
70   TNA: PROB 11/876, Will of the Rt. Hon. George late Lord Anson Baron of Soberton, Co. Southampton.
71   Katherine Parker, 'Memorialising Anson, the Fighting Explorer: A Case Study in Eighteenth-Century Naval Commemoration and Material Culture', in Quintin Colville and James Davey (eds.), *A New Naval History* (Manchester: Manchester University Press, 2019), pp.133–150.

As I was intimately acquainted with his private, as well as his public virtues, nobody can be more sensible of the weight of this loss, both to his friends and to the nation. I could mention instances of his private generosity which few persons rise to... As he had the clearest military courage, I have sometimes wished that he had shewn a little more of the political kind; but that appearance was, in great measure, owing to a natural modesty and bashfulness, which he never got the better of.[72]

His brother-in-law Lord Royston (later second Earl of Hardwicke) said of him: 'This domestic connection was the greatest private happiness I have yet enjoyed. Too soon, alas, cut short; but such are earthly enjoyments!'[73] The Duke of Newcastle referred to the 'very great regard' that he had for Lord Anson and 'for the friendship with which he has honoured me for years', and said that 'there never was a more able, a more upright, or a more useful servant to his King and country, or a more sincere or valuable friend'.[74]

Anson did not live to see the successful outcome of the two operations against the Spanish empire that he had worked on during the last months of his life. Although Anson's Havana plan was briefly thrown off course by Rodney's decision to send most of his ships to Jamaica to meet a possible French and Spanish threat, corrective action was taken and Pocock arrived off Cuba on 6 June, the day on which Anson died, without interference from the enemy. He had successfully negotiated the Old Bahama Channel, which ranked 'as one of the riskiest feats of navigation of the age', and fully vindicated Anson's judgement.[75] Troops were landed some six miles to the east of Morro Castle, which dominated the entrance to Havana harbour, on the following day.

Operations proceeded slowly and the castle was only taken after a costly siege of 29 days, which led to the surrender of Havana on 12 August and brought the operation to a successful conclusion. Even though more than 5,000 British troops were killed or died of disease, the cost to Spain was far higher: apart from a loss of prestige, a third of her navy was trapped in Havana harbour, and over 100 brass guns and £750,000 in prize money (nearly £122 million in 2023 prices) were seized. The Keppel family were significant financial beneficiaries of the successful expedition, with Lord Anson having 'deliberately put them in a position where they might make a significant gain'. But he had also considered the question of leadership, which helped to ensure the success of the operation as earlier British operations in the Caribbean had failed because army and navy commanders 'wasted time arguing about strategy, and the delays allowed an onset of disease to bring failure. The Keppel brothers cooperated, and Pocock understood the situation'.[76]

The Havana campaign was a 'masterpiece of planning, of amphibious warfare, and of the exploitation of naval superiority', which provided a fitting conclusion to Anson's wartime service.[77] Lord Hardwicke later described it as an 'expedition of great consequence, extent and difficulty' that 'does the greatest honour to the memory of poor Lord Anson, who had

---

72   Quoted in Yorke (ed.), *The Life and Correspondence*, vol.II, p.157.
73   Harris, *The Life of Lord Chancellor Hardwicke*, vol.III, p.168.
74   Duke of Newcastle to Thomas Anson, 9 June 1762, in Anson, *The Life of Admiral Lord Anson*, p.181.
75   Rodger, *The Wooden World*, p.51.
76   Baugh, *The Global Seven Years War*, p.527.
77   Syrett (ed.), *The Siege and Capture of Havana*, p xxxiv.

so great a part in the formation and direction of it'. Although Pitt's allies were prepared to lay

> ...any ill success that might have attended it entirely as his [Anson's] door... the sea-officers agree that the lights which he gave them, and the charts which he furnished them with, did all prove right. Passing over some foibles (and no mortal man is without them) *take him for all in all* (as Shakespeare says), *I shall never see his like again* in that office.[78]

The second expeditionary force under Draper and Cornish did not arrive off Manila until 25 September after a six-week voyage from India. News of the outbreak of war with Britain had not reached the Philippines and, with the advantage of complete surprise and a poorly organized defence, the city fell on 6 October, with the result that 'the eastern fountain of Spanish wealth was as completely in our hands as the western'.[79] The British remained in occupation of Manila until April 1764 when it reverted to Spain. The Treaty of Paris, 1763, which ended the Seven Years War, did not refer to Manila because news of its capture did not reach Europe until more than two months after the treaty had been ratified and it was returned to Spain without any reciprocal British gain. Even if this last British conquest – Anson's final project – had served no strategic purpose, it provided another welcome example of British military success: 'the nation, already in full enjoyment of the sweets of peace, had still the satisfaction to receive from the remotest parts of the globe, the news of victories which augment her honour and her riches. There never had been a period more fortunate to Great Britain'.[80]

---

78 Earl of Hardwicke to the Duke of Newcastle, 2 October 1762, in Yorke (ed.), *The Life and Correspondence*, vol.III, p.418.
79 Corbett, *England in the Seven Years War*, vol.II, p.365.
80 *The Annual Register*, 1763, p.15.

Conclusion

When Anson rose from professional obscurity as the long-serving captain of a station ship in South Carolina to the command of a high-profile wartime expedition to Spanish South America he displayed many of the personal qualities that were to define him for the rest of his career. These included personal courage and single-mindedness in pursuit of a mission that he was determined to complete against the odds. His willingness to bear disproportionate losses in men and ships suggests that there was an element of ruthlessness in his character, which was also evident during the Minorca crisis. The official history of the expedition provides insights into his leadership style and gives examples of how he motivated his men. He was always on the alert for any signs of discontent among his crew and moved quickly to address them.

The example he provided while in command of the circumnavigation was to have a continuing impact on the development of the Royal Navy during the late eighteenth century: 'The stoicism and imperturbability shown by Anson under conditions of extreme stress were long remembered, and were soon incorporated into the evolving image of the British naval officer that was to reach iconic status in the age of Nelson'.[1] The voyage also provided the first evidence of Anson's well-developed ability to identify and promote his most able subordinates, giving them additional responsibility when the opportunity arose. They included Saunders, Saumarez, Brett, Denis and Keppel whose careers Anson continued to foster once he entered the Admiralty as he sought to give more weight to merit in a system that was largely based on seniority.[2] Anson's loyal colleagues were to disseminate his professional legacy, which included 'a tradition of devotion to duty, of aggressive attack and of taking his subordinates into his confidence… to future generations. Hawke learnt it from him, and the young Nelson learnt it from Hawke's follower, Captain William Locker'.[3]

Anson's good fortune as well as effective leadership played a part in the *Centurion*'s survival and luck was also evident in his interception of two elusive French convoys at the Battle of Cape Finisterre in 1747, leading to the Royal Navy's first decisive victory against France since the beginning of the war. As the first head of the newly-enlarged Western Squadron, he defined its role more clearly than any of his colleagues and prepared it thoroughly for combat. He raised professional standards to a new level by giving priority to

---

1   Williams, *The Prize of All the Oceans*, p.207.
2   Other officers serving on the circumnavigation who were to distinguish themselves during the Seven Years War included Hyde Parker, John Campbell, Lord Howe and John Byron.
3   N.A.M. Rodger, 'George, Lord Anson', in Peter Le Fevre and Richard Harding (eds.), *Precursors of Nelson: British Admirals of the Eighteenth Century* (London: Chatham Publishing, 2000), p.198.

training, adopting new tactical manoeuvres and actively managing his captains, encouraging them to pursue the enemy more aggressively than they had done in the past. The squadron's two decisive victories in 1747 convinced him that it should form the foundations of Britain's future naval strategy, a position he maintained throughout the Seven Years War. As Pitt later pointed out:

> While I had the honour of acting with Lord Anson, that able officer never ceased to inculcate upon the minds of his Majesty's servants the necessity of constantly maintaining a strong Western Squadron; and I must vouch for him, that while *he* was at the head of the marine it was never neglected.[4]

As mentioned above, Anson once said that he was 'no great politician', but he established himself quickly and effectively once he had decided on a political career.[5] Within months of returning home, he had found a parliamentary seat and forged an alliance with the Duke of Bedford, a leading member of the opposition, who would soon gain power. More important for his political career in the longer term were his developing links with leading members of the Whig establishment: his future father-in-law, Lord Hardwicke, Henry Pelham and the Duke of Newcastle. This close connection meant that he was the obvious candidate to succeed Lord Sandwich as First Lord of the Admiralty in 1751 and explains the considerable efforts that were made to secure his reappointment to the Admiralty in 1757 in the face of significant opposition as a result of the Minorca crisis. This strong political connection reinforced his position at the Admiralty where his high professional standing meant that he became the government's chief naval adviser almost from the beginning of his political career.

While it has been argued that 'no one else ever so successfully combined the roles of political and professional head of the navy', Anson's political career was not without its difficulties.[6] Although he remained loyal to the Whig establishment throughout his tenure as First Lord his relationship with Newcastle did not always run smoothly. Newcastle could not be sure that Anson would endorse his patronage recommendations and, in 1756, he expressed reservations about his advice during the Minorca crisis. He later insisted on maintaining Treasury control of appointments to the Admiralty Board against Anson's wishes. Despite these disagreements, their views on war policy were generally closely aligned even when there were strong arguments for a different course of action. One such example was their joint opposition to Pitt's sound proposals for a pre-emptive strike against Spain in 1761. This may be one of the examples that Hardwicke had in mind when he expressed his regret that Anson's political courage did not match his physical bravery. In explanation, he spoke of his 'natural modesty and bashfulness',[7] which meant that he never spoke in Parliament and was often silent in Cabinet meetings, but self-interest also shaped his political attitudes. For example, in 1751, as he was appointed as First Lord, he readily accepted Henry Pelham's retrenchment policies even though he believed that the post-war navy was underfunded.

---

4   *The Parliamentary History of England to the Year 1803*, vol.XVI, p.1100.
5   Woburn MSS: vol.XV, f.74, George Anson to the Duke of Bedford, 13 December 1746.
6   Rodger, 'George, Lord Anson', p.199.
7   Quoted in Yorke (ed.), *The Life and Correspondence*, vol.II, p.157.

Anson's record also raises some questions about his professional judgement, which include his incomplete instructions to Boscawen when he was sent to Canada in 1755 and his role as the Minorca crisis developed. In his fight for political survival in 1756–1757, Anson was determined to defend his own record and was unwilling to accept that the British presence in the Mediterranean should have been strengthened at a much earlier point. He also rejected the argument that Byng should have been provided with a more powerful squadron even though the Admiralty had readily available ships that could have been allocated to him. These decisions reflected Anson's preoccupation with the defence of home waters and his alarmism at the threat of a French invasion, real or imagined, which meant that the Mediterranean was accorded much less strategic priority than it really warranted. Contemporary observers were convinced that Anson could only survive if Byng took the whole blame for the debacle, and Anson's allies ensured that he paid the ultimate price. With his career in the balance, Anson did not attempt to intervene on his behalf as he faced execution even though he was perhaps in the best position to do so.

Despite these isolated lapses in judgement, Anson's professional reputation remains high and during his lifetime he was widely regarded as a man of integrity. He was the driving force behind several major reforms, mostly introduced in the 1740s, which laid the foundations of the more professional navy that was to fight three major wars against France by 1815. Measures to professionalise the officer corps were at the heart of these changes, including defining naval ranks, establishing an official uniform, and introducing a pension scheme to remove underperforming captains. He tackled the problem of naval discipline – a key priority for the Bedford group – by producing a new disciplinary code that would remain in force for more than a century. Establishing a Marine Corps to replace the previous regimental structure was another significant step in promoting good order on board ship as well as enhancing combat effectiveness.

Anson's patronage of Benjamin Robins' work on gunnery provides one example of his interest in advancing scientific knowledge in the interests of the navy. He was an active chair of the Board of Longitude, which successfully oversaw the development of a method for determining longitude at sea during his tenure, supported the need for the preparation of improved navigational charts, and encouraged medical research. He actively supported further exploration of the South Atlantic and Pacific in the interests of extending Britain's naval capabilities but, despite his best efforts, it did not prove possible to launch a new expedition until after his death.

Although Anson had an impressive record as a reformer, he did not introduce any significant changes to the management or resourcing of the Admiralty, the wider structure of naval administration or the operation of the royal dockyards. He ensured that these long-established administrative systems worked as efficiently as possible while using the private sector to increase shipbuilding capacity rather than depending solely on the royal yards.. Despite his efforts, these outdated structures often proved to be a significant barrier to progress. For example, the conservatism of the Navy Board delayed Anson's plans to develop new ship designs by more than a decade. Introduced during the Seven Years War, the new 74-gun ships and frigates that he had long wanted would stand the test of time and were still in service at the Battle of Trafalgar.

The benefits of Anson's long tenure at the Admiralty were realised during the Seven Years War when a more professional, better-disciplined navy took to the sea commanded by the able officers whose careers he had overseen over the past decade. Mobilisation proceeded largely according to plan and new ships gradually replaced the obsolete designs that he had long sought to jettison. The recruitment of seamen remained challenging and Anson relied on extending the scope of traditional methods rather than seeking more radical changes. Despite their limitations, the Admiralty recruited some 185,000 seamen and marines for service during the war, and found replacements for those killed in action or lost from desertion and disease, which 'required a conscious effort, ruthless determination and a very strong labour market'.[8] With one notable exception, his wartime appointments ensured that the best available flag officers, including Boscawen, Hawke, Pocock and Saunders, were appointed to head important expeditions. He selected Howe and Rodney for command over the heads of their more senior colleagues, while Adam Duncan, John Jervis and Samuel Hood, who were all to achieve great victories in the wars against France, 1793–1815, were first appointed as captains during his tenure at the Admiralty.

Although Anson's relationship with William Pitt did not always run smoothly, it produced positive results in the latter stages of the Seven Years War: 'Pitt's grip of major strategy and his broad view of the whole situation, backed by Anson's technical knowledge and spirit, formed a strong combination'.[9] Pitt later acknowledged the significant part that Anson had played in achieving victory against France and Spain and establishing Britain's new territorial empire. In 1770, as he commented in a debate in the House of Lords, 'to his wisdom, to his experience, and care (and I speak of it with pleasure) the nation owes the glorious naval successes of the last war'.[10] Although success in the early stages of the war eluded him, Anson continued to rely on the strategy of the Western Squadron, which eventually produced a decisive victory at the Battle of Quiberon Bay, under Hawke's leadership, in 1759. His victory had been made possible by the arrangements Anson made to resupply Hawke at sea while he was blockading Brest.

Under Anson's leadership, expeditionary forces were organised and supplied more efficiently and expeditiously than they had been in the past. Evidence of his well-developed planning skills is provided by his successful organisation of the Havana expedition in 1762, which was one of the most complex logistical exercises of the entire war. Completed in a short period with limited Admiralty support – at a time his health was rapidly failing – Anson's successful preparations explain why his high reputation as a naval administrator was fully justified.

Although Anson was not a traditional naval hero in the mould of a Nelson or Jervis, his tenure as First Lord had a lasting impact on the development of the navy and laid the foundations for its future success. His continuing influence was evident in the longevity of the new ship designs and weapons systems for which he was responsible, but his less tangible influence extended well beyond improvements in naval infrastructure and were even more important. Anson's role in developing and maintaining high professional standards, selecting the most able officers for high command, and recognising the important of scientific enquiry in the development of naval warfare, mark him out as one of Britain's most influential naval leaders.

---

8   Andrew Lambert, *War at Sea in the Age of Sail 1760–1850* (London: Cassell, 2000), p.123.
9   Brock, 'Anson and His Importance as a Naval Reformer', p.511.
10   *The Parliamentary History of England to the Year 1803*, vol.XVI, p.1100.

Bibliography

Manuscript Sources

Woburn Abbey, Bedford Estate Office
Papers of John Russell, fourth Duke of Bedford.

British Library
Papers of George, Lord Anson, Add. MS. 15,955-15,957.
Papers of John Perceval, second Lord Egmont, Add. MS. 47,001-47,015.
Papers of George Grenville, Add. MS. 42,083-42,088.
Papers of Philip Yorke, first Earl of Hardwicke, Add. MS. 35,349-36,278.
Papers of Thomas Pelham Holles, first Duke of Newcastle, Add. MS. 32,686–32,992; 33,046–33,048.
Papers of Sir John Norris, Add. MS. 28,134-28,137.

National Archives
Admiralty Board Correspondence, ADM 1; ADM 2.
Admiralty Board Minutes, ADM 3.
Secretaries of State Correspondence, SP 42.

National Maritime Museum
Papers of the Hartwell Family, HAR/4.
Papers of Edward, Lord Hawke, HWK/1-22.
Papers of John Montagu, first Earl of Sandwich, SAN/V/39; SAN/V/44; SAN/V/50.

Staffordshire Record Office
Anson Family Papers, D615/P(S).

Printed Primary Sources

Anon., *A Collection of Several Pamphlets, Very Little Known, Some Suppressed Letters, and Sundry Detached Pieces, Published in the Daily Papers Relative to the Case of Admiral Byng* (London: J. Lacy, 1756).

Anon., *An Appeal to the People: Containing, the Genuine and Entire Letter of Admiral Byng to the Secr. of the Ad---y* (London: J. Morgan, 1756).

Anon., *An Authentic Account of the Reduction of Louisbourg in June and July 1758* (London: W. Owen, 1758).
Anon., *Impartial Reflections on the Case of Mr. Byng, As Stated in an Appeal to the People, &c. and a Letter to a Member of Parliament, &c* (London: S. Hooper, 1756).
Anon., *A Letter to the Right Honourable Lord A---* (London: William Bizet, 1757).
Anon., *A Modest Apology for the Conduct of a Certain Admiral in the Mediterranean* (London: M. Cooper, 1756).
Anon., *The Naval Chronicle: Or, Voyages, Travels, Expeditions, Remarkable Exploits and Achievements, of the most Celebrated English Navigators, Travellers, and Sea-Commanders, From the Earliest Accounts to the End of the Year 1759*. 3 Vols. (London: J. Fuller, 1760).
Anon., *Remarks on a Pamphlet, Called, Considerations on the Bill for the Better Government of the Navy... by a Sea Officer* (London: 1749).
Anon., *The Report of the General Officers, Appointed by His Majesty's Warrant of the First of November 1757, to Enquire into the Causes of the Failure of the Late Expedition to the Coasts of France* (London: A Millar, 1758).
Anon., *The Trial of the Honourable Admiral John Byng, at a Court-Martial, as taken by Mr Charles Fearne, Judge-Advocate of his Majesty's Fleet* (Dublin: J. Hoey, 1757).
Astley, Thomas (ed.), *A New General Collection of Voyages and Travels*. 4 vols. (London: Thomas Astley, 1745–47).
Baugh, Daniel A. (ed.), *Naval Administration, 1715–1750* (London: Navy Records Society, 1977).
Bromley, John S. (ed.), *The Manning of the Royal Navy. Selected Public Pamphlets 1693–1873* (London: Navy Records Society, 1974).
Brown, Peter D. and Karl W. Schweizer (eds.), *The Devonshire Diary: William Cavendish, Fourth Duke of Devonshire, Memoranda on State of Affairs 1759–1762*, Camden Society, Fourth Series, vol. XXVII (London: Royal Historical Society, 1982).
Byron, John, *The Narrative of the Honourable John Byron (Commodore in a Late Expedition Round the World) Containing an Account of the Great Distresses Suffered by Himself and His Companions on the Coast of Patagonia from the Year 1740 till their Arrival in England, 1746* (London: S. Baker, G. Leigh & T. Davis, 1768).
Carswell, John and Lewis A. Dralle (eds.), *The Political Journal of George Bubb Dodington* (Oxford: Clarendon Press, 1965).
Chalmers, George, *An Estimate of the Comparative Strength of Britain, During the Present and Four Preceding Reigns; and of the Losses of her Trade from Every War since the Revolution* (London: John Stockdale, 1782).
Clark, J.C.D. (ed.), *The Memoirs & Speeches of James, 2nd Earl Waldegrave 1742–1763* (Cambridge: Cambridge University Press, 2002).
Climenson, Emily J. (ed.), *Elizabeth Montagu, the Queen of the Bluestockings, Her Correspondence from 1720 to 1761*. 2 vols. (London: John Murray, 1906).
Corbett, Julian S. (ed.), *Fighting Instructions, 1530–1816* (London: Navy Records Society, 1905).
[Corbett, Thomas], *An Account of the Expedition of the British Fleet to Sicily in the Years 1718, 1719 and 1720* (London: J. and R. Tonson, 1739).
Cushner, Nicholas P. (ed.), *Documents Illustrating the British Conquest of Manila, 1762–1763*, Camden Society, Fourth Series, vol.8 (London: Royal Historical Society, 1971).
Erskine, David (ed.), *Augustus Hervey's Journal. Being the Intimate Account of the Life of a Captain in the Royal Navy Ashore and Afloat, 1746–1759* (London: William Kimber, 1953).

Fox-Strangways, Giles, Earl of Ilchester (ed.), *Letters to Henry Fox, Lord Holland* (London: Roxburghe Club, 1915).

Gwyn, Julian (ed.), *The Royal Navy and North America: The Warren Papers 1736–1752* (London: Navy Records Society, 1973).

Hawke, Edward, *A Seaman's Remarks on the British Ships of the Line, From the 1st of January, 1756, to the 1st of January, 1782. With Some Occasional Observations on the Fleet of the House of Bourbon* (London: [1782]).

[Hervey, Augustus], *A Detection of the Considerations on the Navy Bill. By a Seaman* (London: W. Owen, 1749).

[Hervey, Augustus], *A Letter from a Friend in the Country to a Friend at Will's Coffee House; in Relation to Three Additional Articles of War* (London: J. Bromage, 1749).

Hattendorf, John B. et. al. (eds.), *British Naval Documents 1204–1960* (London: Navy Records Society, 1993).

Heaps, Leo, *Log of the Centurion. Based on the Original Papers of Captain Philip Saumarez on Board HMS Centurion, Lord Anson's Flagship during his Circumnavigation, 1740–44* (London: Hart-Davis, MacGibbon, 1973).

Historical Manuscripts Commission, *Report on the Correspondence and Papers of John Montagu, 4th Earl of Sandwich (1718–1792) in the Possession of Victor Montagu, Esq., of Mapperton, Beaminster, Dorset.* Compiled by Edward Warner (London: Royal Commission on Historical Manuscripts, 1976).

Historical Manuscripts Commission, *The Manuscripts of the Earl of Egmont* (London: H. M. Stationery Office, 1920–23).

Historical Manuscripts Commission, *Report on the Manuscripts of Lady Du Cane* (London: H. M. Stationery Office, 1905).

Historical Manuscripts Commission, *Reports on the Manuscripts of… C.F. Weston Underwood…* (London: Eyre & Spottiswoode, 1885).

[Hutchinson, J.], *The Private Character of Admiral Anson. By a Lady* (London: J. Oldcastle, [1747]).

Jucker, Ninetta S. (ed.), *The Jenkinson Papers, 1760–1766* (London: Macmillan, 1949).

Kemp, Peter (ed.), 'Boscawen's Letters to His Wife, 1755–1756, from the Falmouth Papers', *The Naval Miscellany*, vol. IV (London: Navy Records Society, 1952), pp.164–254.

Kielmansegge, Frederick, *Diary of a Journey to England in the Years 1761–1762* (London: Longmans & Co, 1902).

Lamb, Jonathan, Vanessa Smith and Thomas Nicholas (eds.), *Exploration and Exchange: A South Seas Anthology, 1680–1900* (Chicago: The University of Chicago Press, 2000).

Lavery, Brian (ed.), *Shipboard Life and Organisation 1731–1815*, Navy Records Society (Aldershot: Ashgate Publishing, 1998).

Lewis, Wilmarth S. (ed.), *The Yale Edition of Horace Walpole's Correspondence*. 48 vols. (New Haven: Yale University Press, 1937–1983).

Lind, James, *A Treatise of the Scurvy. In Three Parts. Containing an Inquiry into the Nature, Causes, and Cure, of that Disease. Together with a Critical and Chronological View of What has been Published on the Subject* (Edinburgh: A. Kincaid and A. Donaldson, 1753).

Lloyd, Christopher (ed.), *The Health of Seamen: Selections from the Works of Dr James Lind, Sir Gilbert Blane and Dr Thomas Trotter* (London: Navy Records Society, 1965).

Mackay, Ruddock F. (ed.), *The Hawke Papers: A Selection 1743–1771*, Navy Records Society (Aldershot: Scolar Press, 1990).

Matcham, Mary E. (ed.), *A Forgotten John Russell; Being Letters to a Man of Business 1724–1751* (London: Edward Arnold, 1905).
Osborn, Emily F.D. (ed.), *Political and Social Letters of a Lady of the Eighteenth Century 1721–1771* (London: Griffith Farran & Co, [1890]).
Philips, John, *An Authentic Journal of the Late Expedition under the Command of Commodore Anson* (London: J. Robinson, 1744).
Ranft, Brian McL. (ed.), *The Vernon Papers* (London: Navy Records Society, 1958).
Richmond, Herbert W. (ed.), *Papers Relating to the Loss of Minorca in 1756* (London: Navy Records Society, 1913).
Rodger, N.A.M., *Articles of War: The Statutes Which Governed Our Fighting Navies 1661, 1749 and 1866* (Havant: Kenneth Mason, 1982).
Rodger, N.A.M. (ed.), 'The Douglas Papers', *The Naval Miscellany*, vol. V, Navy Records Society (London: Allen and Unwin, 1984), pp.244–283.
Russell, John, *Correspondence of John, Fourth Duke of Bedford, Selected from the Originals at Woburn Abbey*. 3 vols. (London: Longman, Green, Brown and Longmans, 1842–46).
Sedgwick, Romney (ed.), *Letters from George III to Lord Bute, 1756–1766* (London: Macmillan, 1939).
Sedgwick, Romney, 'Letters from William Pitt to Lord Bute, 1755–1758', in Richard Pares and A.J.P. Taylor (eds.), *Essays Presented to Sir Lewis Namier* (London: Macmillan, 1956), pp.108–166.
Smith, D. Bonner (ed.), *The Barrington Papers; Selected from the Letters and Papers of Admiral the Hon. Samuel Barrington*. 2 vols. (London: Navy Records Society, 1937–1941).
Smith, W. J. (ed.), *The Grenville Papers: Being the Correspondence of Richard Grenville, Earl Temple, and the Right Hon. George Grenville, their Friends and Contemporaries*. 4 vols. (London: John Murray, 1852–1853).
Spavens, William, *The Narrative of William Spavens, Chatham Pensioner* (Louth: R. Sheardown, 1796).
Syrett, David (ed.), *The Rodney Papers: Selections from the Papers of Admiral Lord Rodney*. 2 vols, Navy Records Society (Aldershot: Ashgate, 2005–2007).
Syrett, David (ed.), *The Siege and Capture of Havana, 1762* (London: Navy Records Society, 1970).
Talbot, Catherine, *A Series of Letters Between Mrs Elizabeth Carter and Miss Catherine Talbot, from the Year 1741 to 1770*. 2 vols. (London: F. C. & J. Rivington, 1809).
Taylor, William S. and John H. Pringle (eds.), *The Correspondence of William Pitt, Earl of Chatham*. 4 vols. (London: John Murray, 1838–1840).
Thomas, Pascoe, *A True and Impartial Journal of a Voyage to the South-Seas, and Round the Globe, in His Majesty's ship the Centurion, Under the Command of Commodore George Anson* (London: S. Birt, 1745).
Walpole, Horace, *Memoirs of the Reign of King George II*. 3 vols. (London: H. Colburn, 1846).
Walpole, Horace, *Memoirs of the Reign of King George III*. 4 vols. (London: Bentley, 1845).
Walpole, Horace, *Reminiscences* (London: J. Sharpe, 1819).
Walter, Richard and Benjamin Robins *Anson's Voyage Around the World in the Years 1740–1744*. Glyndwr Williams (ed.) (Oxford: Oxford University Press, 1974).
[West, Temple], *An Examination and Refutation of a Late Pamphlet, Intitled, Considerations on the Navy Bill. By a Real Sea Officer* (London: S. Baker, 1749).

[Whitehead, Paul], *A Letter to a Member of Parliament in the Country, from His Friend in London, Relative to the Case of Admiral Byng* (London: J. Cooke, 1756).

[Wildman, William, Viscount Barrington], *Considerations on the Bill for the Better Government of the Navy*. By a Sea Officer (London: M. Cooper, 1749).

Williams, Glyndwr (ed.), *Documents Relating to Anson's Voyage Round the World 1740–1744* (London: Navy Records Society, 1967).

Wyndham, Maud M. (ed.), *Chronicles of the Eighteenth Century, Founded on the Correspondence of Sir Thomas Lyttelton and his Family*. 2 vols. (London: Hodder & Stoughton, 1924).

Yorke, Philip C. (ed.), *The Life and Correspondence of Philip Yorke, Earl of Hardwicke*. 3 vols. (Cambridge: Cambridge University Press, 1913).

[Young, John], *An Affecting Narrative of the Unfortunate Voyage and Catastrophe of His Majesty's Ship Wager, One of Commodore Anson's Squadron in the South Sea Expedition* (London: John Norwood, 1751).

Secondary Sources

Albion, Robert G., *Forests and Sea Power: The Timber Problem of the Royal Navy, 1652–1862* (Cambridge, Massachusetts: Harvard University Press, 1932).

Anderson, Fred, *Crucible of War: The Seven Years War and the Fate of the Empire in British North America 1754–1766* (London: Faber and Faber, 2000).

Anson, Walter V., *The Life of Admiral Lord Anson: Father of the British Navy, 1697–1762*. (London: John Murray, 1912).

Aspinall-Oglander, Cecil F., *Admiral's Wife: Being the Life and Letters of the Hon. Mrs. Edward Boscawen from 1719 to 1761* (London: Longmans & Co, 1940).

Barrow, John, *The Life of George Lord Anson: Admiral of the Fleet, Vice Admiral of Great Britain and First Lord Commissioner of the Admiralty* (London: John Murray, 1839).

Barrow, John, *The Life of Richard, Earl Howe, K.G., Admiral of the Fleet and General of Marines* (London: John Murray, 1838).

Baugh, Daniel A., *British Naval Administration in the Age of Walpole* (Princeton: Princeton University Press, 1965).

Baugh, Daniel A., *The Global Seven Years War 1754–1763: Britain and France in a Great Power Contest* (second edition, London: Routledge, 2021).

Baxter, Stephen B., *England's Rise to Greatness 1660–1763* (Berkeley: University of California Press, 1983).

Beatson, Robert. *Naval and Military Memoirs of Great Britain from 1727 to 1783*. 6 vols. (London: Longman, 1804).

Bellabarba, Sergio and Georgio Osculati, *The Royal Yacht Caroline, 1749* (London: Conway Maritime Press, 1986).

Black, Jeremy, *Pitt the Elder* (Cambridge: Cambridge University Press, 1992).

Boscawen, Hugh, *The Capture of Louisbourg, 1758* (Norman: University of Oklahoma Press, 2011).

Boudriot, Jean, *The Seventy-Four Gun Ship: A Practical Treatise on the Art of Naval Architecture*. 4 vols. (Rotherfield: Jean Boudriot Publications, 1986–1988).

Bradley, Peter T., *British Maritime Enterprise in the New World: From the Late Fifteenth to the Mid-Eighteenth Century* (Lewiston: Edwin Mellen Press, 1999).

Brewer, John, *The Sinews of Power: War, Money and the English State 1688–1783* (London: Unwin Hyman, 1989).
Brooks, Richard, *The Royal Marines: 1664 to the Present* (London: Constable, 2002).
Brown, Kevin, *Poxed and Scurvied. The Story of Sickness and Health at Sea* (Barnsley: Seaforth, 2011).
Browning, Reed, *The Duke of Newcastle* (New Haven: Yale University Press, 1975).
Browning, Reed, *The War of the Austrian Succession* (Stroud: Sutton, 1993).
Brunsman, Denver A., *The Evil Necessity: British Naval Impressment in the Eighteenth-Century Atlantic World* (Charlottesville: University of Virginia Press, 2013).
Buchet, Christian, *The British Navy, Economy and Society in the Seven Years War* (Woodbridge: The Boydell Press, 2013).
Burrows, Montagu, *The Life of Edward Lord Hawke* (London: W.H. Allen, 1883).
Callender, Geoffrey, *Sea Kings of Britain. Albemarle to Hawke (1660-1760)* (London: Longmans, Green & Co, 1909).
Campbell, John, *Naval History of Great Britain, Including the History and Lives of the British Admirals*. 8 vols. (London: John Stockdale, 1813).
Cardwell, John M., *Arts and Arms: Literature, Politics and Patriotism During the Seven Years War* (Manchester: Manchester University Press, 2004).
Chalus, Elaine, *Elite Women in English Political Life c.1754–1790* (Oxford: Clarendon Press, 2005).
Charnock, John, *Biographia Navalis; or, Impartial Memoirs of the Lives and Characters of Officers of the Navy of Great Britain from the Year 1660 to the Present Time*. 6 vols. (London: R. Faulder, 1794–1798).
Charteris, Evan, *William Augustus Duke of Cumberland and the Seven Years War* (London: Hutchinson, 1925).
Charters, Erica M., *Disease, War, and the Imperial State: The Welfare of the British Armed Forces during the Seven Years' War* (Chicago: University of Chicago Press, 2014).
Clark, J.C.D., *The Dynamics of Change. The Crisis of the 1750s and English Party Systems* (Cambridge: Cambridge University Press, 1982).
Clayton, Tim, *Tars: The Men Who Made Britain Rule the Waves* (London: Hodder & Stoughton, 2007).
Clowes, William L., *The Royal Navy: A History from the Earliest Times to the Present*. 7 vols. (London: Sampson Low, Marston and Company, 1897–1903).
Collinge, J.M., *Office-Holders in Modern Britain. Volume 7, Navy Board Officials 1660–1832* (London: Institute of Historical Research, 1978).
Conway, Stephen, *War, State and Society in Mid-Eighteenth Century Britain and Ireland* (Oxford: Oxford University Press, 2006).
Corbett, Julian S., *England in the Seven Years War. A Study in Combined Strategy*. 2 vols. (London: Longmans, Green & Co, 1907).
Corbett, Julian S., *Some Principles of Maritime Strategy* (London: Longmans, Green & Co, 1911).
Craik, Jennifer, *Uniforms Exposed: From Conformity to Transgression* (Oxford: Berg, 2005).
Creswell, John, *British Admirals of the Eighteenth Century: Tactics in Battle* (London: George Allen and Unwin, 1972).
Dickinson, Harry W., *Educating the Royal Navy: Eighteenth- and Nineteenth-Century Education for Officers* (London: Routledge, 2007).

Dull, Jonathan R., *The Age of the Ship of the Line: The British and French Navies, 1650–1815* (Lincoln: University of Nebraska, 2009).
Dull, Jonathan R., *The French Navy and the Seven Years War* (Lincoln: University of Nebraska, 2005).
Eder, Markus, *Crime and Punishment in the Royal Navy of the Seven Years War, 1755–1763* (Aldershot: Ashgate, 2004).
Fish, Shirley, *HMS Centurion, 1733–1769: An Historic Biographical-Travelogue of One of Britain's Most Famous Warships and the Capture of the Nuestra Senora de Covadonga Treasure Galleon* (Bloomington, Indiana: AuthorHouse, 2015).
Fish, Shirley, *The Manila-Acapulco Galleons: The Treasure Ships of the Pacific, with an Annotated List of the Transpacific Galleons 1565–1815* (Milton Keynes: AuthorHouse, 2011).
Fox-Strangways, Giles, Earl of Ilchester, *Henry Fox, first Lord Holland: His Family and Relations* (London: John Murray, 1920).
Gardiner, Robert, *The First Frigates. Nine-Pounder & Twelve-Pounder Frigates, 1748–1815* (London: Conway Maritime Press, 1992).
Gardiner, Robert, (ed.), *The Line of Battle: The Sailing Warship, 1650–1840* (London: Conway Maritime Press, 1992).
Glete, Jan, *Navies and Nations: Warships, Navies and State Building in Europe and America, 1500–1860*. 2 vols. (Stockholm: Almquist & Wiksell International, 1993).
Godber, Joyce, *The Marchioness Grey of Wrest Park*. Publications of the Bedfordshire Historical Record Society, vol. XLVII (Bedford: Bedfordshire Historical Record Society, 1968).
Goodwin, Peter G., *The Construction and Fitting of the Sailing Man of War, 1650–1850* (London: Conway Maritime Press, 1987).
Gradish, Stephen F., *The Manning of the British Navy During the Seven Years War* (London: Royal Historical Society, 1980).
Greenslade, M. W. (ed.), *A History of Staffordshire*. The Victoria History of the Counties of England, vol.17 (Oxford: Oxford University Press, 1976).
Gwyn, Julian, *An Admiral for America: Sir Peter Warren, Vice Admiral of the Red, 1703–1752* (Gainesville: University Press of Florida, 2004).
Gwyn, Julian, *The Enterprising Admiral: The Personal Fortune of Admiral Sir Peter Warren* (Montreal: McGill-Queen's University Press, 1974).
Haas, James M., *A Management Odyssey: The Royal Dockyards, 1714–1914* (Lanham: University Press of America, 1994).
Harding, Richard, *The Emergence of Britain's Global Naval Supremacy: The War of 1739–1748* (Woodbridge: The Boydell Press, 2010).
Harding, Richard, *The Evolution of the Sailing Navy, 1509–1815* (Basingstoke: St Martin's Press, 1995).
Harding, Richard, *Seapower and Naval Warfare 1650–1830* (London: Routledge, 2003).
Hartmann, Cyril H., *The Angry Admiral: The Later Career of Edward Vernon, Admiral of the White* (London: Heinemann, 1953).
Hood, Dorothy, *The Admirals Hood* (London: Hutchinson, 1942).
Intelligence Branch, Quartermaster-General's Department, *British Minor Expeditions 1746 to 1814* (London: Her Majesty's Stationery Office, 1884).
Kennedy, Paul M., *The Rise and Fall of English Naval Mastery* (London: Penguin Books, 2017).
Keppel, Thomas, *The Life of Augustus, Viscount Keppel*. 2 vols. (London: Henry Colburn, 1842).

Kinkel, Sarah, *Disciplining the Empire: Politics, Governance, and the Rise of the British Navy* (Cambridge: Harvard University Press, 2018).
Krulder, Joseph J., *The Execution of Admiral John Byng as a Microhistory of Eighteenth-Century Britain* (London: Routledge, 2021).
Lambert, Andrew, *Admirals: The Naval Commanders Who Made Britain Great* (London: Faber & Faber, 2008).
Lambert, Andrew, *Crusoe's Island: A Rich and Curious History of Pirates, Castaways and Madness* (London: Faber & Faber, 2016).
Lambert, Andrew, *War at Sea in the Age of Sail 1760–1850* (London: Cassell, 2000).
Langford, Paul, *A Polite and Commercial People: England 1727–1783* (Oxford: Oxford University Press, 1989).
Lavery, Brian, *Anson's Navy: Building a Fleet for Empire 1744–1763* (Barnsley: Seaforth, 2021).
Lavery, Brian, *The Arming and Fitting of English Ships of War 1660–1815* (London: Conway Maritime Press, 1998).
Lavery, Brian, *The Royal Navy's First Invincible 1744–1758* (Portsmouth: Invincible Conservations, 1988).
Lavery, Brian, *The Ship of the Line*. 2 vols. (London: Conway Maritime Press, 1983–1984).
Lawson, Philip, *George Grenville. A Political Life* (Oxford: Clarendon Press, 1984).
Layman, C.H., *The Wager Disaster: Mayhem, Mutiny and Murder in the South Seas* (London: Uniform Press, 2015).
Lees, James, *The Masting and Rigging of English Ships of War 1625–1860* (London: Conway Maritime Press, 1979).
Le Fevre, Peter and Richard Harding (eds.), *Precursors of Nelson: British Admirals of the Eighteenth Century* (London: Chatham Publishing, 2000).
Lewis, Michael, *England's Sea Officers: The Story of the Naval Profession* (London: George Allen & Unwin, 1939).
Lincoln, Margarette, *Representing the Royal Navy: British Sea Power, 1750–1815* (Aldershot: Ashgate Publishing, 2002).
Lloyd, Christopher, *The British Seaman 1200–1860: A Social Survey* (London: Collins, 1968).
Lloyd, Christopher, *The Nation and the Navy. A History of Naval life and Policy* (London: Cresset Press, 1954).
MacDougall, Philip, *London and the Georgian Navy* (Stroud: The History Press, 2013).
Macintyre, Donald, *Admiral Rodney* (London: P. Davies, 1962).
Mackay, Ruddock F., *Admiral Hawke* (Oxford: Clarendon Press, 1965).
Mackay, Ruddock F., and Michael Duffy, *Hawke, Nelson and British Naval Leadership 1747–1805* (Woodbridge: The Boydell Press, 2009).
McLeod, A.B., *British Naval Captains of the Seven Years War. The View from the Quarterdeck* (Woodbridge: The Boydell Press, 2012).
Marcus, Geoffrey, *Quiberon Bay: The Campaign in Home Waters, 1759* (London: Hollis & Carter, 1960).
Middleton, Richard, *The Bells of Victory: The Pitt-Newcastle Ministry and the Conduct of the Seven Years' War, 1757–1762* (Cambridge: Cambridge University Press, 1985).
Miller, Amy, *Dressed to Kill: British Naval Uniform, Masculinity and Contemporary Fashions, 1748–1857* (London: National Maritime Museum, 2007).

Morriss, Roger, *The Foundations of British Maritime Ascendancy: Resources, Logistics and the State, 1755–1815* (Cambridge: Cambridge University Press, 2010).

Morriss, Roger, *Naval Power and British Culture, 1760–1850: Public Trust and Government Ideology* (Aldershot: Ashgate Publishing, 2004).

Mundy, Godfrey B., *The Life and Correspondence of the Late Admiral Lord Rodney* (London: John Murray, 1830).

Murray, Arthur C., *An Episode in the Spanish War, 1739–1744: Admiral Lord Anson and Captain the Hon. George Murray, RN* (London: Seeley Service, 1952).

Murray, Arthur C., *The Five Sons of 'Bare Betty'* (London: John Murray, 1936).

Namier, Lewis B., *The Structure of Politics at the Accession of George III* (London: Macmillan, 1963).

Pack, Stanley W. C., *Admiral Lord Anson: The Story of Anson's Voyage and Naval Events of His Day* (London: Cassell, 1960).

Pack, Stanley W. C., *The Wager Mutiny* (London: Redman, 1964).

Padfield, Peter, *Guns at Sea* (New York: St Martin's Press, 1974).

Padfield, Peter, *Maritime Supremacy and the Opening of the Western Mind: Naval Campaigns that Shaped the Modern World* (London: John Murray, 1999).

Palmer, Michael A., *Command at Sea: Naval Command and Control Since the Sixteenth Century* (Cambridge, Massachusetts: Harvard University Press, 2005).

Peters, Marie, *The Elder Pitt* (London: Longman, 1998).

Peters, Marie, *Pitt and Popularity: The Patriot Minister and London Opinion during the Seven Years War* (Oxford: Clarendon Press, 1980).

Pocock, Tom, *Battle for Empire: The Very First World War 1756–63* (London: Caxton, 1998).

Pope, Dudley, *At 12 Mr Byng Was Shot* (London: Secker & Warburg, 1987).

Richmond, Herbert W., *The Navy in the War of 1739–48*. 3 vols. (Cambridge: Cambridge University Press, 1920).

Robinson, John M., *Shugborough* (London: The National Trust, 1989).

Robson, Martin, *A History of the Royal Navy. The Seven Years War* (London: I.B. Tauris, 2016).

Rodger, N.A.M., *The Admiralty* (Lavenham: Terence Dalton, 1979).

Rodger, N.A.M., *The Command of the Ocean: A Naval History of Britain, 1649–1815* (London: Allen Lane, 2004).

Rodger, N.A.M., *The Insatiable Earl: A Life of John Montagu, fourth Earl of Sandwich 1718–1792* (London: HarperCollins, 1993).

Rodger, N.A.M., *The Wooden World: An Anatomy of the Georgian Navy* (London: Collins, 1986).

Rodgers, Nicholas, *The Press Gang: Naval Impressment and its Opponents in Georgian Britain* (London: Continuum, 2007).

Ross, John, *Memoirs and Correspondence of Admiral Lord de Saumarez, from Original Papers*. 2 vols. (London: Richard Bentley, 1838).

Sainty, John C., *Office Holders in Modern Britain. Volume 4, Admiralty Officials, 1660–1870* (London: Athlone Press, 1975).

Salmon, Edward, *Life of Admiral Sir Charles Saunders, KB* (London: Isaac Pitman, 1914).

Sausmarez, Havilland de, *Captain Philip Saumarez, 1710–1747, and His Contemporaries. From Letters and Portraits at Sausmarez Manor, Guernsey. And an Account of the Origin of the Naval Uniform as Designed by Him* (Guernsey: Guernsey Press Company, 1936).

Simms, Brendan, *Three Victories and a Defeat: The Rise and Fall of the First British Empire, 1714–1783* (London: Allen Lane, 2007).
Smelser, Marshall, *The Campaign for the Sugar Islands 1759: A Study of Amphibious Warfare* (Chapel Hill: University of North Carolina, 1955).
Smith, Alan M., *Balchen's Victory. The Loss and Rediscovery of an Admiral and His Ship* (Barnsley: Seaforth, 2022).
Sobel, Dava, *Longitude: The True Story of a Lone Genius Who Solved the Greatest Scientific Problem of His Time* (New York: Walker, 1995).
Sobel, Dava, and William J.H. Andrewes, *The Illustrated Longitude* (London: Fourth Estate, 1998).
Somerville, Boyle, *Commodore Anson's Voyage into the South Seas and Around the World* (London: William Heineman, 1934).
Spinney, David, *Rodney* (London: George Allen and Unwin, 1969).
Starkey, David J., *British Privateering Enterprise in the Eighteenth Century* (Liverpool: Liverpool University Press, 2022).
Stroud, Dorothy, *Capability Brown* (Third edition, London: Faber and Faber, 1975).
Syrett, David, *Admiral Lord Howe. A Biography* (Staplehurt: Spellmount, 2006).
Syrett, David, *Shipping and Military Power in the Seven Years War: The Sails of Victory* (Exeter: University of Exeter Press, 2008).
Syrett, David, and R. L. DiNardo (eds.), *The Commissioned Sea Officers of the Royal Navy, 1660–1815* (London: Scolar Press for the Navy Records Society, 1994).
Taylor, Stephen, *Sons of the Waves: The Common Seaman in the Heroic Age of Sail* (New Haven: Yale University Press, 2020).
Thackeray, Francis, *A History of the Right Honourable William Pitt, Earl of Chatham* (London: C. and J. Rivington, 1827).
Tracy, Nicholas, *The Battle of Quiberon Bay, 1759: Admiral Hawke and the Defeat of the French Invasion* (Barnsley: Pen and Sword Maritime, 2010).
Tracy, Nicholas, *Manila Ransomed: The British Assault on Manila in the Seven Years War* (Exeter: University of Exeter Press, 1995).
Trew, Peter, *Rodney and the Breaking of the Line* (Barnsley: Pen and Sword Military, 2006).
Tunstall, Brian, *Admiral Byng and the Loss of Minorca* (London: P. Allan, 1928).
Tunstall, Brian, *Naval Warfare in the Age of Sail: The Evolution of Fighting Tactics 1650–1815*. Nicholas Tracy (ed.) (London: Conway Maritime Press, 1990).
Ware, Chris, *Admiral Byng: His Rise and Execution* (Barnsley: Pen and Sword Maritime, 2009).
Whitworth, Rex, *Field Marshal Lord Ligonier: A Story of the British Army, 1702–1770* (Oxford: Clarendon Press, 1958).
Wilkinson, Clive, *The British Navy and the State in the Eighteenth Century* (Woodbridge: The Boydell Press, 2004).
Williams, Basil, *The Life of William Pitt, Earl of Chatham*. 2 vols. (London: Longmans, Green & Co, 1915).
Williams, Glyndwr, *The Great South Sea: English Voyages and Encounters 1570–1750* (New Haven: Yale University Press, 1997).
Williams, Glyndwr, *The Prize of All the Oceans: The Triumph and Tragedy of Anson's Voyage Round the World* (London: HarperCollins, 1999).

Willis, Sam, *Fighting at Sea in the Eighteenth Century: The Art of Sailing Warfare* (Woodbridge: The Boydell Press, 2008).
Winfield, Rif, *British Warships in the Age of Sail 1714–1792: Design, Construction, Careers and Fates* (Barnsley: Seaforth, 2007).
Winfield, Rif, *The 50-Gun Ship* (London: Chatham Publishing, 1997).
Zerbe, Britt, *The Birth of the Royal Marines 1664–1802* (Woodbridge: The Boydell Press, 2013).

Articles and Chapters

Acland, Reginald, 'The Development of Naval Courts-Martial', *Journal of Comparative Legislation and International Law*, Third Series, 4 (1922), pp.35–59.
Acland, Reginald, 'The Naval Articles of War', *Journal of Comparative Legislation and International Law*, Third Series, 3 (1921), pp.190–201.
Aldridge, D. D., 'Admiral Sir John Norris, 1670 (or 1671)–1749: His Birth and Early Service, His Marriage and his Death', *The Mariner's Mirror*, 51 (1965), pp.173–183.
Barker, Derek, 'The Naval Uniform Dress of 1748', *The Mariner's Mirror*, 65 (1979), pp.243–253.
Baugh, Daniel A., 'George Anson (1697–1762)', in John B. Hattendorf (ed.), *The Oxford Encyclopedia of Maritime History* (Oxford: Oxford University Press, 2007), vol.I, pp.101–103.
Baugh, Daniel A., 'Great Britain's "Blue-Water" Policy, 1689–1815', *The International History Review*, 10 (1988), pp.33–58.
Baugh, Daniel A., 'Naval Power: What Gave the British Navy Superiority?', in Leandro Prados de la Escosura (ed.), *Exceptionalism and Industrialisation. Britain and its European Rivals, 1688–1815* (Cambridge: Cambridge University Press, 2004), pp.235–257.
Boscawen, Hugh, 'The Origin of the Flat-Bottomed Landing Craft 1757–58', *National Army Museum Report* (1984), pp.23–30.
Brock, Patrick W., 'Anson and His Importance as a Naval Reformer', *The Naval Review*, 17 (1929), pp.497–528.
Bruce, Anthony, 'Benjamin Robins and the Science of Naval Gunnery', *The Trafalgar Chronicle*, New Series 7 (2022), pp.37–47.
Bunn, James H., 'Commodore Anson's "Centurion" as Global Model of Self Repair', *Interdisciplinary Studies in Literature and Environment*, 14 (2007), pp.25–49.
Callender, Geoffrey, 'A New Portrait of Anson', *The Mariner's Mirror*, 6 (1920), pp.258–260.
Coats, Ann, 'Efficiency in Dockyard Administration 1660–1800: A Reassessment', in Nicholas Tracy (ed.), *The Age of Sail. The International Annual of the Historic Sailing Ship* (London: Conway Maritime Press, 2003), vol.I, pp.116–132.
Cock, Randolph, 'The Finest Invention in the World': The Royal Navy's Early Trials of Copper Sheathing, 1708–1770, *The Mariner's Mirror*, 87 (2001), pp. 446–459.
Conway, Stephen, Richard Harding and Helen J. Paul, 'Eighteenth-Century Britain: The Quintessential 'Contractor State?', *International Journal of Maritime History*, 25 (2013), pp.248–252.
Cowell, Peter, 'Admiral Byng: Justice Thwarted', *The Mariner's Mirror*, 106 (2020), pp.346–349.
Crimmin, Patricia K., 'Anson: Cape Finisterre, 1747', in Eric Grove (ed.), *Great Battles of the Royal Navy as Commemorated in the Gunroom, Britannia Royal Naval College, Dartmouth* (London: Arms and Armour, 1994), pp.71–78.

Crimmin, Patricia K., 'The Sick and Hurt Board and the Health of Seamen c.1700–1806', *Journal for Maritime Research*, 1 (1999), pp.48–65.
Cronin, James, 'An 'Island' of Cosmopolitan Culture: Anson's Voyage Round the World and the Library at Bowen's Court, Co. Cork', *History Ireland*, 19 (2011), pp.18–21.
Crowhurst, Patrick, 'The Admiralty and the Convoy System in the Seven Years War', *The Mariner's Mirror*, 57 (1971), pp.163–173.
Duffy, Michael, 'The Establishment of the Western Squadron as the Linchpin of British Naval Strategy', in M. Duffy (ed.), *Parameters of British Naval Power 1650–1850* (Exeter: University of Exeter Press, 1992), pp.60–81.
Frost, Alan and Glyndwr Williams, 'The Beginnings of Britain's Exploration of the Pacific Ocean in the Eighteenth Century', *The Mariner's Mirror*, 83 (1997), pp.410–418.
Gardiner, Robert, 'The First English Frigates', *The Mariner's Mirror*, 61 (1975), pp.163–172.
Gardiner, Robert, 'The Frigate Designs of 1755–57', *The Mariner's Mirror*, 63 (1977), pp.51–69.
Gordon, Eleanora A., 'Scurvy and Anson's Voyage Around the World 1740–1744. An Analysis of the Royal Navy's Worst Outbreak', *American Neptune*, 44 (1984), pp.155–166.
Gradish, Stephen F., 'Wages and Manning: The Navy Act of 1758', *The English Historical Review*, 93 (1978), pp.46–67.
Haas, James M., 'The Royal Dockyards: The Earliest Visitations and Reform, 1749–78', *Historical Journal*, 13 (1970), pp.191–215.
Haas, James M., 'Work and Authority in the Royal Dockyards from the Seventeenth Century to 1870', *Proceedings of the American Philosophical Society*, 124 (1980), pp.419–428.
Hackman, W. Kent, 'The British Raid on Rochefort 1757', *The Mariner's Mirror*, 64 (1978), pp.263–275.
Harding, Richard, 'America, the War of 1739–48 and the Development of British Global Power', *Journal of Maritime Research*, 6 (2004), pp.1–20.
Harding, Richard, 'The Expedition to Lorient, 1746', in Nicholas Tracy (ed.), *The Age of Sail. The International Annual of the Historic Sailing Ship* (London: Conway Maritime Press, 2003), vol. I, pp.34–54.
Harding, Richard, 'Leadership Networks and the Effectiveness of the British Royal Navy in the Mid-Eighteenth Century', in R. Harding and Agustín Guimerá (eds.), *Naval Leadership in the Atlantic World. The Age of Reform and Revolution, 1700–1850* (London: University of Westminster Press, 2017), pp.21–34.
Harding, Richard, '"Neglect or Treason": Leadership Failure in the Mid-Eighteenth Century Royal Navy', in Helen Doe and R. Harding (eds.), *Naval Leadership and Management, 1650–1950: Essays in Honour of Michael Duffy* (Woodbridge: The Boydell Press, 2012), pp.43–57.
Harris, J. R., 'Copper and Shipping in the Eighteenth Century', *Economic History Review*, 19 (1966), pp.550–568.
Hattendorf, John B., 'Byng: Cape Passaro, 1718', in Eric Grove (ed.), *Great Battles of the Royal Navy as Commemorated in the Gunroom, Britannia Royal Naval College, Dartmouth* (London: Arms and Armour, 1994), pp.64–70.
Hemingway, Peter, 'The Norris Committee: The 1745 Establishment of Dimensions and the Origins of the 74-Gun Ship', *The Mariner's Mirror*, 96 (2010), pp.75–80.
Hemingway, Peter, 'Sir Jacob Acworth and Experimental Ship Design during the Period of the Establishments', *The Mariner's Mirror*, 96 (2010), pp.149–160.

Houston, R.A., 'New Light on Anson's Voyage, 1740–4: A Mad Sailor on Land and Sea', *The Mariner's Mirror*, 88 (2002), pp.260–270.
James, Brian, 'The Battle that Gave Birth to an Empire', *History Today*, 59 (2009), pp.26–32.
James, G.F., 'The Admiralty Establishment 1759', *Bulletin of the Institute of Historical Research*, 16 (1938), pp.24–27.
Jones, James R., 'Limitations of British Sea Power in the French Wars 1689–1815', in Jeremy Black and Philip Woodfine (eds.), *The British Navy and the Use of Naval Power in the Eighteenth Century* (Leicester: Leicester University Press, 1988), pp.33–49.
Kinkel, Sarah, 'Disorder, Discipline, and Naval Reform in Mid-Eighteenth-Century Britain', *The English Historical Review*, 128 (2013), pp.1451–1482.
Kinkel, Sarah, 'The King's Pirates? Naval Enforcement of Imperial Authority, 1740–76', *The William and Mary Quarterly*, 71 (2014), pp.3–34.
Kinkel, Sarah, 'Saving Admiral Byng: Imperial Debates, Military Governance and Popular Politics at the Outbreak of the Seven Years' War', *Journal for Maritime Research*, 13 (2011), pp.3–19.
Landes, David S., 'Finding the Point at Sea', in William J. H. Andrewes (ed.), *The Quest for Longitude* (Cambridge, Massachusetts: Harvard University, 1996), pp.19–30.
Lavery, Brian, 'The Origins of the 74-Gun Ship', *The Mariner's Mirror*, 63 (1977), pp.335–350.
Luff, P. A., 'Mathews v. Lestock: Parliament, Politics and the Navy in Mid-Eighteenth-Century England', *Parliamentary History*, 10 (1991), pp.45–62.
Manwaring, G. E., 'The First Naval Uniform for Officers: The Story of the Blue and White Costume of 1748', *The Mariner's Mirror*, 6 (1920), pp.105–114.
Marcus, Geoffrey, 'Hawke's Blockade of Brest', *Journal of the Royal United Service Institution*, 104 (1959), pp.475–488.
Markham, Albert H., 'Lord Anson', in J. K. Laughton (ed.), *From Howard to Nelson: Twelve Sailors* (London: Lawrence and Bullen, 1899), pp.161–193.
Markley, Robert, 'Anson at Canton, 1743: Obligation, Exchange, and Ritual in Edward Page's "Secret History"', in Linda Zionkowski and Cynthia Klekar (eds.), *The Culture of the Gift in Eighteenth-Century England* (Basingstoke: Palgrave Macmillan, 2009), pp.215–234.
Middleton, Richard, 'British Coastal Expeditions to France, 1757–1758', *Journal of the Society for Army Historical Research*, 71 (1993), pp.74–92.
Middleton, Richard, 'British Naval Strategy, 1755–1762: The Western Squadron', *The Mariner's Mirror*, 75 (1989), pp.349–367.
Middleton, Richard, 'The Duke of Newcastle and the Conduct of Patronage during the Seven Years' War, 1757–1762', *British Journal for Eighteenth-Century Studies*, 12 (1989), pp.175–186.
Middleton, Richard, 'Naval Administration in the Age of Pitt and Anson, 1755–1763', in Jeremy Black and Philip Woodfine (eds.), *The British Navy and the Use of Naval Power in the Eighteenth Century* (Leicester: Leicester University Press, 1988), pp.109–128.
Middleton, Richard, 'Pitt, Anson and the Admiralty, 1756–1761', *History*, 55 (1970), pp.189–198.
Middleton, Richard, 'The Visitation of the Royal Dockyards, 1749', *The Mariner's Mirror*, 77 (1991), pp.21–30.
Moscoso, Sabrina G., 'George Anson's Voyage to the Pacific and the Defense at the Margins of the Empire', *Terræ Incognitæ*, 51 (2019), pp.219–234.
Murray, Oswyn A. R., 'The Admiralty', *The Mariner's Mirror*, 24 (1938), pp.204–225.

Parker, Katherine, 'Memorialising Anson, the Fighting Explorer: A Case Study in Eighteenth-Century Naval Commemoration and Material Culture', in Quintin Colville and James Davey (eds.), *A New Naval History* (Manchester: Manchester University Press, 2019), pp.133–150.

Parker, Katherine, 'Rewriting Admiral Anson as Naval Hero: Biographical Depictions of George Anson from the Eighteenth Century to the Mid-Twentieth Century', *The Trafalgar Chronicle*, 24 (2014), pp.81–94.

Parker, Katherine, 'The Savant and the Engineer: Exploration Personnel in the Narbrough and Anson Voyage Accounts', *Terræ Incognitæ*, 49 (2017), pp.6–20.

Pearsall, Alan W. H., 'Lord Anson: Sailor-Statesman or Not?', in Abigall T. Siddall (ed.), *Soldier-Statesmen of the Age of Enlightenment: Records of the 7th International Colloquy on Military History* (Manhattan, Kansas: Sunflower University Press, 1984), pp.270–279.

Pearsall, Alan W. H., 'Naval Aspects of the Landings on the French Coast, 1758', in N.A.M. Rodger (ed.), *Naval Miscellany*, vol. V, Navy Records Society (London: Allen and Unwin, 1984), pp.207–243.

Quirino, Carlos, 'Anson's Capture of the Manila Galleon', Philippine Historical Association, *Historical Bulletin*, 4 (1960), pp.39–51.

Rodger, N.A.M., 'Commissioned Officers Careers in the Royal Navy, 1690–1815', *Journal of Maritime Research*, 3 (2001), pp.85–129.

Rodger, N.A.M., 'George, Lord Anson', in Peter Le Fevre and Richard Harding (eds.), *Precursors of Nelson: British Admirals of the Eighteenth Century* (London: Chatham Publishing, 2000), pp.177–199.

Rodger, N.A.M., 'The Idea of Naval Strategy in Britain in the Eighteenth and Nineteenth Centuries', in Geoffrey Till (ed.), *The Development of British Naval Thinking: Essays in Memory of Bryan McLaren Ranft* (Abingdon: Routledge, 2006), pp.19–33.

Rodger, N.A.M., 'Image and Reality in Eighteenth Century Naval Tactics', *The Mariner's Mirror*, 89 (2003), pp.280–296.

Ryan, Hugh, 'George Anson's Voyage Round the World, by Richard Walter', *Proceedings of the Royal Institution of Great Britain*, 39 (1963), pp.529–534.

Stitt, F.B., 'Admiral Anson at the Admiralty, 1744–1762', *Staffordshire Studies*, 4 (1991–1992), pp.35–76.

Syrett, David, 'The British Landing at Havana: An Example of an Eighteenth-Century Combined Operation', *The Mariner's Mirror*, 55 (1969), pp.325–331.

Syrett, David, 'The Methodology of British Amphibious Operations during the Seven Years and American Wars', *The Mariner's Mirror*, 58 (1972), pp.269–280.

Thompson, Edgar K., 'George Anson in the Province of South Carolina', *The Mariner's Mirror*, 53 (1967), pp.279–280.

Toynbee, Paget, 'Horace Walpole's Journals of Visits to Country Seats', *The Volume of the Walpole Society*, 16 (1927–28), pp.9–80.

Tracy, Nicholas, 'The Capture of Manila 1762', *The Mariner's Mirror*, 55 (1969), pp.311–323.

Watt, James, 'Commodore Anson's Circumnavigation (1740–1744): The Bequests of Disaster at Sea', *Transactions & Studies of the College of Physicians of Philadelphia*, series 5, 7 (1985), pp.223–238.

Watt, James, 'Some Consequences of Nutritional Disorders in Eighteenth-Century British Circumnavigations', in J. Watt, E. J. Freeman and W. F. Bynum (eds.), *Starving Sailors. The*

Influence of Nutrition upon Naval and Maritime History ([London]: National Maritime Museum, 1981), pp.51–71.

Wickwire, Franklin B, 'Admiralty Secretaries and the British Civil Service', *Huntington Library Quarterly*, 28 (1965), pp.235–254.

Williams, Glyndwr, 'Anson at Canton, 1743: A Little Secret History', in Cecil H. Clough and P.E.H. Hair (eds.), *The European Outthrust and Encounter. The First Phase c.1400–c.1700: Essays in Tribute to David Beers Quinn on His 85th Birthday* (Liverpool: Liverpool University Press, 1994), pp. 271–290.

Williams, Glyndwr, 'Commodore Anson and the Acapulco Galleon', *History Today*, 17 (1967), pp.525–532.

Williams, Glyndwr, 'George Anson's Voyage Round the World: The Making of a Best-Seller', *Princeton University Library Chronicle*, 64 (2003), pp.289–312.

Williams, Glyndwr, '"To Make Discoveries of Countries Hitherto Unknown": The Admiralty and Pacific Exploration in the Eighteenth Century', *The Mariner's Mirror*, 82 (1996), pp.14–27.

Woodfine, Philip, 'Ideas of Naval Power and the Conflict with Spain, 1737–1742', in Jeremy Black and P. Woodfine (eds.), *The British Navy and the Use of Naval Power in the Eighteenth Century* (Leicester: Leicester University Press, 1988), pp.71–90.

Zirker, P. A., 'The Anson Squadron Narratives: A Modern View', *The Mariner's Mirror*, 51 (1965), pp.321–341.

Theses

Haas, James M., 'The Rise of the Bedfords, 1741–1757: A Study in the Politics of the Reign of George II', PhD thesis, University of Illinois, 1960.

Hemingway, Peter, 'The Work of the Surveyors of the Navy during the Period of the Establishments: A Comparative Study of Naval Architecture between 1672 and 1755', PhD thesis, University of Bristol, 2002.

Humphries, George P., 'Admiral George Anson's Administration of the British Admiralty, 1745–1762', Ph.D. thesis, Emory University, 1953.

McLean, Samuel A., 'The Westminster Model Navy: Defining the Royal Navy, 1660–1749, PhD thesis, King's College London, 2017.

Internet Sources

Baker, Andrew, *Thomas Anson of Shugborough and the Greek Revival* (2021), <https://moam.info/andrew-baker-thomas-anson-and-the-greek-revival_5a04b7491723dd1fb33b4212.html>, accessed 23 October 2022.

Baugh, Daniel A., 'John Byng (*bap.* 1704, *d.* 1757)' *Oxford Dictionary of National Biography*, <https://doi.org/10.1093/ref:odnb/4263>, accessed 31 October 2022.

Chalus, Elaine, 'Elizabeth Anson [née Yorke], Lady Anson (1725–1760)', *Oxford Dictionary of National Biography*, <https://doi.org/10.1093/ref:odnb/68350>, accessed 21 September 2022.

Coats, Ann V., 'John Clevland (1706–1763)', *Oxford Dictionary of National Biography*, <https://doi.org/10.1093/ref:odnb/64851>, accessed 21 September 2022.

Howse, Derek, 'John Campbell (*b. in or before* 1720, *d.* 1790)', *Oxford Dictionary of Biography*, <https://doi.org/10.1093/ref:odnb/4518>, accessed 21 September 2022.

Laughton, John Knox, 'George Anson, Lord Anson (1697–1762)', *The Dictionary of National Biography* (1885), <https://doi.org/10.1093/odnb/9780192683120.013.574>, accessed 14 September 2022.

Powell, Martyn J., 'John Russell, fourth Duke of Bedford (1710–1771)', *Oxford Dictionary of National Biography*, <https://doi.org/10.1093/ref:odnb/24320>, accessed 3 January 2023.

Rodger, N.A.M., 'George Anson, Baron Anson (1697–1762)', *Oxford Dictionary of National Biography*, < https://doi.org/10.1093/ref:odnb/574>, accessed 1 November 2022.

General Index

Acapulco 25, 27-28, 45-47, 55, 57, 72-74, 78
Acworth, Jacob 84, 86-88, 130, 135
Aix-la-Chapelle, Peace of 83, 102, 146
Allin, Joseph 23, 88, 152
Anson, Elizabeth, Lady, (née Yorke) 103-104, 109, 116-120, 125, 129, 132, 137, 140-144, 188, 192, 195-197, 205-206, 216-217
Anson, Thomas 11-12, 30, 71, 74, 77, 106, 108-109, 129, 143-144, 217
Antigua 134
Anville, Jean-Baptiste de La Rochefoucauld de Roye, Duc d' 90, 92, 94-95
Articles of War 43, 113, 126, 168

Bahamas 17-18, 215
Baltic 14-15, 184, 190
Barnett, Cdre Curtis 73, 81
Barrington, William Wildman, Viscount 98, 126, 133, 173, 183
Bately, William 152
Bath 216-217
Bath, William Pulteney, Earl of 78, 109, 121
Bedford, John Russell, Duke of 78-87, 89-90, 92-98, 103, 105, 110, 112-116, 124, 129, 133, 135, 221-222
Belle Isle 98-99, 196, 204, 206-207
Biscay, Bay of 31, 93, 99-100, 154
Blakeney, Lt Gen. William 166, 174-175
Bligh, Lt Gen. William 196
Bocca Tigris 63, 68
Boscawen, Adm. Hon Edward 93-94, 97, 99, 101, 105, 111, 115-116, 118, 135-136, 149, 155, 157-159, 167-168, 173-175, 181, 189, 193, 197, 199, 201, 203, 205, 222-223
Boscawen, Frances Evelyn 'Fanny' 97, 116, 118, 136, 168
Bowling Green 20-21

Brest 84, 89-92, 94-96, 98-99, 147, 153-155, 157-160, 184, 187, 190, 193-195, 197, 201-206, 223
Brett, Capt. Sir Peircy 34, 41, 43, 62, 65, 74, 81, 84, 92, 97, 106, 116, 121, 129, 137, 144, 220
Broderick, Rear Adm. Thomas 165, 168, 175
Bubb Dodington, George 158, 164-165, 172, 186
Buenos Aires 33, 38, 42
Bute, John Stuart, Earl of 180, 195, 207, 210
Byng, Adm. Sir George; see Torrington
Byng, Vice Adm John 15, 72, 127, 129, 148, 159, 162-176, 178, 181, 222
Byron, Cdre John 'Foul-Weather Jack' 123, 184

Cadiz 25, 93, 95, 203, 205, 211
Callao 27, 41-42, 47
Campbell, Capt. John 92, 106, 123, 140, 205
Canada 79, 85, 96-98, 100, 103, 147, 155-156, 160, 188-189, 199, 204, 222
Canton 41, 47, 51-52, 55, 61, 63-65, 68-69, 74-75, 112, 122, 144
Cape Breton 100, 146, 155
Cape Espiritu Santo 46, 54-57
Cape Finisterre 30, 93-95, 100, 159, 211: First Battle of 16, 19, 21, 23, 85, 88, 95, 98, 105-106, 135-136, 143, 217, 220; Second Battle of 29, 85, 107
Cape Horn 26-28, 31, 34-35, 38, 41-42, 47-48, 54, 122
Cape Passaro, Battle of 15-16, 162
Chamberlain, Capt. Peter 13-15
Charlotte, Queen 197, 209, 216
Carshalton 120
Charleston, South Carolina 17-23, 25
Chatham 13, 125, 150, 180
Cheap, Capt. David 29, 33-34, 41
Cherbourg 195-196

Chesterfield, Philip Stanhope, Earl of 114
Chile 26-28, 34, 38-39, 41
China 47, 50-53, 55, 62-69, 74, 77, 112, 122, 144
Choiseul, Étienne François, Duc de 159, 200
Clevland, John 82, 135-137, 168, 172-173, 175, 199, 207
Conflans, Hubert de Brienne, Comte de 94, 204
Corbett, Thomas 75, 82, 97, 135, 204
Cornish, Vice Adm. Samuel 213, 219
Cracherode, Lt Col Mordaunt 27
Cuba 15, 31, 213-215, 218
Cumberland, HRH Prince William Augustus, Duke of 127, 130, 147, 150, 172, 182, 184, 186

Denis, Capt. Peter 29, 43, 45, 59, 62, 64, 69, 71, 74, 97, 101, 103, 106, 109, 129, 175, 184, 205, 210, 220
Deptford 84, 87-88, 152
Devonshire, William Cavendish, Duke of 173-174, 179, 181
Dockyards 18, 50, 71, 77, 82, 86-88, 90, 93-94, 97, 126, 130-132, 134-135, 144-146, 150, 202, 222; see also Chatham, Deptford, Plymouth, Portsmouth, Woolwich
Draper, Brig. Gen. William 212-213, 219
Du Guay, Hilarion Josselin, Comte 158-159
Durell, Rear Adm. Philip 194, 200, 203

East India Company 26, 47, 51-52, 63-64, 67, 69, 122, 125, 187, 212
Edgcumbe, Cdre George 162-164
English Channel 69, 90-91, 160, 190

Falkingham, Edward 152
Falkland Islands 122-124
Fighting Instructions 16, 99, 101, 106-107, 126, 194
Florida 18
Forbes, Vice Adm. John 173, 181
Fowke, Lt Gen. Thomas 163, 166-167
Fox, Henry 147, 150, 158, 165, 167-174, 176

Gadsden, Thomas 21
Galissonnière, Roland-Michel Barin, Marquis de la 164, 166-167, 176
George I 12, 78
George II 27, 31, 53, 67, 72, 75, 79, 103-104, 111-112, 123, 129, 133-134, 138-139, 146-147, 153, 158, 169-170, 172, 176, 178-180, 182-183, 186, 188, 192-194, 200, 205, 207, 209

George III 207-209, 211, 213, 218
Gibraltar 30, 134, 160, 163-169, 171, 189, 201
Goodwin, John 86
Gorée 196
Gower, John Leveson-Gower, Earl 78, 109
Granville, John Carteret, Earl 78, 147, 182
Guadeloupe 199

Haddock, Capt. Richard 130
Half-pay 14-15, 21, 23, 25, 75, 81, 110, 113, 127-129, 135; see also 'Yellow Admirals'
Halifax, Nova Scotia 92, 134, 178, 183-184, 188-189, 200, 203
Hardwicke, Philip Yorke, Earl of 13, 70, 77-78, 80, 116-120, 132, 134-135, 137-138, 147, 158, 160, 162, 169, 171-177, 179-180, 182-183, 186, 192-193, 195, 202, 206-207, 210, 217-218, 221
Hardy, Rear Adm. Sir Charles 189, 197, 199-200
Harrison, John 24, 140
Havana 23, 212, 214-216, 218, 223
Hawke, Adm. Sir Edward 79, 85, 106-107, 115, 129, 137, 147, 153, 155, 157-159, 162, 167-169, 181-182, 184, 186-187, 189-194, 199, 201-205, 207, 212, 215, 220
Hedon 29, 78, 80, 109
Hervey, Capt. Augustus 104, 128-130, 159, 162, 166, 168, 173-176, 181, 189, 199-200, 202
Holburne, Rear Adm. Francis 155, 157, 174, 183-184, 188-189, 194
Holderness, Robert Darcy, Earl of 147-148, 160, 175, 183
Holmes, Rear Adm. Charles 190, 194, 196, 200
Holywell Farm 77
Howe, Capt. Richard, Viscount 184, 190, 192-197, 205, 211
Hutchinson, Mrs J. 19-20

Jacobites 84, 89, 91, 109, 154
Jamaica 14, 79, 134, 140, 214-215, 218
Johnson, Samuel 73, 142
Jonquière, Jacques-Pierre de Taffanel, Marquis de la 95, 99-103
Juan Fernandez Islands 34-35, 38-42, 69, 122-123

Keppel, Cdre Augustus 44, 62, 66-67, 72, 106, 110, 112, 129, 147, 163, 175-176, 184, 196, 205, 207, 215, 218, 220
Kidd, Capt. Dandy 27, 33-34

Lagos Bay, Battle of 203
Le Havre 195, 201
Legge, Capt Edward 27, 41
Legge, Henry 81, 83, 87-88, 179-180
Lestock, Adm. Richard 15, 79, 93, 95
Ligonier, Field Marshal Sir John 147, 182-184, 188, 190, 202, 207, 211-212, 214-215
Lorient 90, 93
Louisbourg 85, 90, 94-95, 146, 155, 163, 183-184, 187-190, 197-200, 203

Macao 40, 50-55, 63-65, 67-68, 71, 74, 112
Macclesfield, Thomas Parker, Earl of 13-14, 17, 78
Madeira 31-33
Madras 100, 213
Manila 25-26, 45-47, 52, 54-58, 64, 68-69, 73, 212-213, 219
Marines 30, 40, 52, 79, 83, 149-151, 163, 171, 223
Marlborough, Lt Gen. Charles Churchill, Duke of 190
Martin, Vice Adm. William 85, 90-93
Martinique 95, 196, 199, 208, 216
Mathews, Adm. Thomas 15, 79, 106
Mauritius 105, 208
Mexico 31, 45-49, 52, 54-55, 69, 121
Millechamp, Lawrence 38, 46, 49, 59, 68, 75
Minorca 72, 91, 127, 134, 136-137, 146, 148, 157, 160-175, 178-180, 187, 190, 197, 206, 220-222
Mitchell, Capt. Matthew 27, 33
Montagu, Capt. William 'Mad' 98, 102
Montero, Don Gerónimo 57-58, 60-62
Moor Park 120, 140-143, 205, 217
Moore, Cdre John 199
Morbihan, Gulf of 203-205
Mordaunt, Lt Gen. Sir John 184, 186-188
Motte, Emmanuel-Auguste de Cahideuc, Comte Du Bois de la 155, 158-159, 184
Murray, Capt. George 27, 33-34, 41

Navy Board 23, 28, 82, 86-89, 94, 97, 130-132, 135, 145-146, 152-153, 189-190, 200, 208, 222
Newcastle, Thomas Pelham-Holles, Duke of 13, 27, 30, 69-72, 74, 78, 80, 82, 84, 114-116, 118-119, 132-135, 138-139, 147, 154, 158-159, 162, 164-165, 167-176, 178-180, 182, 186, 201, 206, 210, 212, 215, 217-218, 221

Newfoundland 155, 157
Norris, Adm. of the Fleet Sir John 14, 23, 25-26, 87, 129, 132
Norris, Capt. Richard 27, 33,

Oakedge Hall 11-12
Officers, Royal Navy, careers of 15, 29, 41, 71, 74-76, 79, 83, 110-113, 116, 124, 126-130, 132, 135-137-138, 222-223; promotion 13-14, 82, 110-111, 132, 136, 138-139, 179, 220; ranks, 111-112, 116; retirement 110; see also Half-pay, 'Yellow Admirals'
Ogle, Adm. Sir Chaloner 79, 111, 129
Ordnance, Board of 82, 93, 126, 147, 200
Orford, Earl of: See Walpole, Robert
Osborn, Adm. Henry 72, 159, 189

Paita 42-46, 54, 71
Panama 25-28, 41-43, 45
Patronage 12-13, 23, 25, 70, 77, 80, 84, 125-126, 136-139, 152, 173, 196, 200, 221-222
Patterson, Lt Col James 150
Pearl River 53, 63
Pelham, Henry 72, 74, 78, 103, 133-134, 137, 144, 147, 150, 221
Peru 26-28, 31, 42-43, 45, 73, 121
Philippines 25, 45-47, 54-55, 64, 68, 212, 219
Pitt, William 78, 134, 141-142, 146-147, 149, 165, 173-174, 176, 179-184, 186-191, 195-197, 199, 201-202, 206-208, 210-212, 219, 221, 223
Pizarro, *Jefe de Escuadra* José Alfonso 31, 33-34, 38, 41-42, 73
Plymouth 31, 87-90, 93-95, 97-98, 150, 196, 202, 212
Pocock, Vice Adm. Sir George 137, 139, 215-216, 218
Pondicherry 105
Porto Bello 25, 79
Portsmouth 14, 23, 25-26, 30-31, 71-72, 77, 86, 92-93, 95, 97, 103-104, 121, 125, 150, 162-163, 170-171, 174-175, 190-192, 194, 197, 216
Press gangs 29, 148, 163, 183

Quebec 23, 85, 102-103, 146, 155-156, 188, 197, 199-200, 203-204
Quiberon Bay, Battle of 153-154, 193, 204-205

Recruitment 29, 54, 68-69, 71, 148-150, 183, 186, 201, 223; see also Press gangs

GENERAL INDEX

Richelieu, Armand Jean du Plessis, Duc de 164, 174-175
Robins, Benjamin 121, 125-126, 222
Rochefort 90, 92-93, 95, 98-99, 153, 160, 184, 186-187, 190, 192, 195, 205-206
Rodney, Rear Adm. George 47, 119, 130, 197, 201, 208, 216, 218, 223
Rowley, Adm. William 106, 135, 209

St Cast, Battle of 196
St Malo 88, 190, 193, 195-196
St Philip's Castle 165, 167, 169-170, 174
Sandwich, John Montagu, Earl of 78, 80-84, 86, 89-91, 98, 107, 113-116, 126, 129-130, 132-133, 135-136, 144, 146, 150, 221
Saumarez, Capt. Philip 29, 31, 35, 39-42, 47, 50, 58, 61-63, 66-67, 75-76, 84, 97, 106, 112, 220
Saunders, Vice Adm. Sir Charles 34, 40-41, 51, 74, 106, 109, 129, 152, 167, 197, 200, 203-205, 211-212, 215, 220, 223
Scurvy 28, 34-35, 38-40, 46, 48-49, 69, 71, 93, 95-96, 124-125, 195, 197, 201-202
Seven Years War 23, 81, 83, 88, 106, 110, 129, 133-134, 137-138, 144-146, 153, 219, 221-223
Shugborough Hall 11-12, 67, 77, 119, 143-144, 217
Sick and Hurt Board 82
Slade, Benjamin 24, 86, 89, 152-153
South Carolina 17-18, 20-23, 25, 220; see also Charleston
South Sea Company 21, 26
Spithead 14, 25, 30, 35, 41, 69, 93, 98, 147, 159, 163-164, 168, 187, 192-193, 200-201, 216

Temple, Richard Grenville-Temple, Earl 173-174, 176, 178-179, 181-182
Thomas, Pascoe 35, 40, 43, 47, 55, 60-61, 65
Tinian 49-51, 57, 69, 181
Torbay 158, 201
Torre, Gaspar de la 55

Torrington, Adm. George Byng, Viscount 15-17
Toulon 91, 160, 164-165, 168, 189, 205; Battle of 15, 79, 84, 135

Uniforms, naval 66, 112-113, 222
Ushant 94-95, 154, 196, 201-202

Valdivia 34-35, 38-39
Vere, Vere Beauclerck, Lord 80, 84, 115-116, 132
Vernon, Adm. Edward 25, 38, 41-42, 79, 84-86, 90-91, 97, 104, 106, 115
Victualling Board 82, 138, 202, 205

Wager, Adm. Sir Charles 25-27, 133
Wales, HRH Frederick, Prince of 104, 127, 129
Walpole, Horace 19, 73, 77, 97, 103-105, 109, 118-119, 121, 127, 129, 132, 142, 157, 171, 173-174, 176, 178, 181, 200-201, 204, 209, 217
Walpole, Robert (Earl of Orford) 25-28
Walter, Richard 51, 120-121
War of the Spanish Succession 13, 15
Warren, Vice Adm. Sir Peter 21, 23, 25, 85, 96-99, 101-104, 106, 111-112, 127-128, 130
Warship design, Anson's influence on 87-89, 152-153, 222; first frigates 89, 152-153; introduction of 74-gun ship 87-88, 94, 152-153
West, Vice Adm. Temple 162, 173, 175, 181-182, 186
Western Approaches 25, 90-91, 183, 187-189
Western Squadron 16, 83, 89-94, 96-98, 106, 109, 111, 136, 146, 148, 153-155, 157-159, 162, 164, 167, 176, 183-184, 187, 189-193, 197-201, 205, 207, 212, 220-221, 223
Winchilsea, Daniel Finch, Earl of 74-75, 80-81, 170, 179, 181
Wolfe, Maj. Gen. James 199, 203-204
Woolwich 84, 89, 131, 152, 196, 210
Wrest Park 118-119

'Yellow Admirals' 110

Index of Ships

Alarm (Br. 32) 208
Anna (Br. storeship) 11, 27, 35, 40, 42
Antelope (Br. 50) 169
Argo (Br. 28) 213
Asia (Sp. 64) 31, 42

Barfleur (Br. 90) 17
Blandford (Br. 20) 159
Bristol (Br. 50) 98, 102

Centurion (Br. 60, later re-rated 50) 23-25, 27, 29-31, 33-35, 38-66, 68-69, 71-77, 83-84, 87-89, 92, 97, 98n, 101, 103, 106, 121-123, 143-144, 147, 220
Centurion Prize (Br. galleon, ex-*Nuestra Señora de Covadonga*) 62-65, 68
Covadonga: see *Nuestra Señora de Covadonga*

Dartmouth (Fr. 18, ex-Br. Indiaman) 100n, 102
Dauphin Royal (Fr. 70) 155
Defiance (Br. 60) 98, 101-102, 166
Devonshire (Br. 66) 98, 101-102
Diamond (Br. 40) 23
Dublin (Br. 74) 152

Elizabeth (Fr. 64) 84, 143
Emeraude (Fr. 24) 100n, 102
Esperanza (Sp. 50) 31, 42
Essex (Br. 70) 140

Falcon (Br. 14) 99, 102
Falkland (Br. 50) 98

Garland (Br. 20) 18, 23
Gibraltar (Br. 20) 136
Gloire (Fr. 46) 100n, 102
Gloucester (Br. 50) 27, 33-35, 38, 40, 42, 45-49, 75-76

Guipuscoa (Sp. 66) 31

Hampshire (Br. 50) 14-15
Happy (Br. 10) 23
Harrington (Br. Indiaman) 64
Hermonia (Sp. 40) 31, 42

Industry (Br. storeship) 27, 33
Intrepid (Br. 64, ex-*Sérieux*) 163
Inverness (Br. 22) 99
Invincible (Fr. 74) 88, 100-102, 152

Jason (Fr. 52) 100

Kent (Br. 64) 98

Lion (Br. 58) 84, 143
Lyme (Br. 28) 89, 153
Lynx (Br. 14) 210

Mercure (Fr. hospital ship) 95
Modeste (Fr. 22) 100n, 102
Monarch (Br. 74) 178
Monmouth (Br. 66) 14
Monmouth (Br. 64) 98n, 102
Montagu (Br. 60) 15-16

Namur (Br. 74) 97-99, 101
Norwich (Br. 50) 147
Nottingham (Br. 60) 97-98, 102, 210
Nuestra Señora de Aranzazu (Sp. merchantman) 42; see also *Tryal Prize*
Nuestra Señora de Carmin (Sp. merchantman) 43
Nuestra Señora de Covadonga (Sp. galleon) 55, 57-63, 65, 68-69, 71, 75-77; see also *Centurion Prize*
Nuestra Señora del Monte Carmelo (Sp. merchantman) 42

INDEX OF SHIPS 245

Orphee (Fr. 64) 166

Pearl (Br 40) 27, 33-35, 40
Phoenix (Br. 20) 130, 166
Pilar (Sp. galleon) 46, 54-55, 58
Porcupine (Br. 16) 123
Prince George (Br. 90) 98, 101-102

Ramillies (Br. 90) 163, 167
Raven (Br. 10) 123
Rosario (Sp. galleon) 55
Royal Caroline (Br. yacht) 209; see also *Royal Charlotte*
Royal Charlotte (Br. yacht, ex-*Royal Caroline*) 210
Royal George (Br. 100) 193
Royal Sovereign (Br. 100) 193
Ruby (Br. 54) 13-14
Rupert (Br. 60) 16

St George (Br. 90) 174, 188
Salisbury (Br. 50) 124
San Esteban (Sp. 40) 31, 42
Santa Teresa de Jesus (Sp. merchantman) 43
Scarborough (Br. 20) 17-18
Scorpion (Br. 14) 200
Sérieux (Fr. 64) 100-102, 163; see also *Intrepid*

Severn (Br. 50) 27, 35, 40, 81
Shark (Br. 10) 17
Solebay (Br. 24) 21
Solidad (Sp. merchantman) 44
Southampton (Br. 32) 153
Squirrel (Br. 20) 18, 23

Tavistock (Br. 10) 98
Tryal (Br. 8) 27, 33-34, 38-40, 42-43
Tryal Prize (Br. 20, ex-*Nuestra Señora de Aranzazu*) 43, 47, 75-76
Tygre (Fr. privateer, 26) 88-89

Unicorn (Br. 28) 89, 153

Victory (Br. 100) 152
Vigilante (Fr. 22) 100n, 102
Viper (Br. 10) 99
Volante (Sp.44) 16

Wager (Br. 24) 27, 29, 33-34, 38, 40-41, 133, 123
Weazle (Br. 8) 17
Windsor (Br. 60) 98n, 101

Yarmouth (Br. 64) 92-93, 97-98, 102

From Reason to Revolution – Warfare 1721-1815

http://www.helion.co.uk/series/from-reason-to-revolution-1721-1815.php

The 'From Reason to Revolution' series covers the period of military history 1721–1815, an era in which fortress-based strategy and linear battles gave way to the nation-in-arms and the beginnings of total war.

This era saw the evolution and growth of light troops of all arms, and of increasingly flexible command systems to cope with the growing armies fielded by nations able to mobilise far greater proportions of their manpower than ever before. Many of these developments were fired by the great political upheavals of the era, with revolutions in America and France bringing about social change which in turn fed back into the military sphere as whole nations readied themselves for war. Only in the closing years of the period, as the reactionary powers began to regain the upper hand, did a military synthesis of the best of the old and the new become possible.

The series will examine the military and naval history of the period in a greater degree of detail than has hitherto been attempted, and has a very wide brief, with the intention of covering all aspects from the battles, campaigns, logistics, and tactics, to the personalities, armies, uniforms, and equipment.

Submissions

The publishers would be pleased to receive submissions for this series. Please contact series editor Andrew Bamford via email (andrewbamford@helion.co.uk), or in writing to Helion & Company Limited, Unit 8 Amherst Business Centre, Budbrooke Road, Warwick, CV34 5WE

Titles

No 1 *Lobositz to Leuthen: Horace St Paul and the Campaigns of the Austrian Army in the Seven Years War 1756-57* (Neil Cogswell)

No 2 *Glories to Useless Heroism: The Seven Years War in North America from the French journals of Comte Maurés de Malartic, 1755-1760* (William Raffle (ed.))

No 3 *Reminiscences 1808-1815 Under Wellington: The Peninsular and Waterloo Memoirs of William Hay* (Andrew Bamford (ed.))

No 4 *Far Distant Ships: The Royal Navy and the Blockade of Brest 1793-1815* (Quintin Barry)

No 5 *Godoy's Army: Spanish Regiments and Uniforms from the Estado Militar of 1800* (Charles Esdaile and Alan Perry)

No 6 *On Gladsmuir Shall the Battle Be! The Battle of Prestonpans 1745* (Arran Johnston)

No 7 *The French Army of the Orient 1798-1801: Napoleon's Beloved 'Egyptians'* (Yves Martin)

No 8 *The Autobiography, or Narrative of a Soldier: The Peninsular War Memoirs of William Brown of the 45th Foot* (Steve Brown (ed.))

No 9 *Recollections from the Ranks: Three Russian Soldiers' Autobiographies from the Napoleonic Wars* (Darrin Boland)

No 10 *By Fire and Bayonet: Grey's West Indies Campaign of 1794* (Steve Brown)

No 11 *Olmütz to Torgau: Horace St Paul and the Campaigns of the Austrian Army in the Seven Years War 1758-60* (Neil Cogswell)

No 12 *Murat's Army: The Army of the Kingdom of Naples 1806-1815* (Digby Smith)

No 13 *The Veteran or 40 Years' Service in the British Army: The Scurrilous Recollections of Paymaster John Harley 47th Foot – 1798-1838* (Gareth Glover (ed.))

No 14 *Narrative of the Eventful Life of Thomas Jackson: Militiaman and Coldstream Sergeant, 1803-15* (Eamonn O'Keeffe (ed.))

No.15 *For Orange and the States: The Army of the Dutch Republic 1713-1772 Part I: Infantry* (Marc Geerdinck-Schaftenaar)

No 16 *Men Who Are Determined to be Free: The American Assault on Stony Point, 15 July 1779* (David C. Bonk)

No 17 *Next to Wellington: General Sir George Murray: The Story of a Scottish Soldier and Statesman, Wellington's Quartermaster General* (John Harding-Edgar)

No 18 *Between Scylla and Charybdis: The Army of Elector Friedrich August of Saxony 1733-1763 Part I: Staff and Cavalry* (Marco Pagan)

No 19 *The Secret Expedition: The Anglo-Russian Invasion of Holland 1799* (Geert van Uythoven)

No 20 *'We Are Accustomed to do our Duty': German Auxiliaries with the British Army 1793-95* (Paul Demet)

No 21 *With the Guards in Flanders: The Diary of Captain Roger Morris 1793-95* (Peter Harington (ed.))

No 22 *The British Army in Egypt 1801: An Underrated Army Comes of Age* (Carole Divall)

No 23 *Better is the Proud Plaid: The Clothing, Weapons, and Accoutrements of the Jacobites in the '45* (Jenn Scott)

No 24 *The Lilies and the Thistle: French Troops in the Jacobite '45* (Andrew Bamford)

No 25 *A Light Infantryman With Wellington: The Letters of Captain George Ulrich Barlow 52nd and 69th Foot 1808-15* (Gareth Glover (ed.))

No 26 *Swiss Regiments in the Service of France 1798-1815: Uniforms, Organisation, Campaigns* (Stephen Ede-Borrett)

No 27 *For Orange and the States! The Army of the Dutch Republic 1713-1772: Part II: Cavalry and Specialist Troops* (Marc Geerdinck-Schaftenaar)

No 28 *Fashioning Regulation, Regulating Fashion: Uniforms and Dress of the British Army 1800-1815 Volume I* (Ben Townsend)

No 29 *Riflemen: The History of the 5th Battalion 60th (Royal American) Regiment, 1797-1818* (Robert Griffith)

No 30 *The Key to Lisbon: The Third French Invasion of Portugal, 1810-11* (Kenton White)

No 31 *Command and Leadership: Proceedings of the 2018 Helion & Company 'From Reason to Revolution' Conference* (Andrew Bamford (ed.))

No 32 *Waterloo After the Glory: Hospital Sketches and Reports on the Wounded After the Battle* (Michael Crumplin and Gareth Glover)

No 33 *Fluxes, Fevers, and Fighting Men: War and Disease in Ancien Regime Europe 1648-1789* (Pádraig Lenihan)

No 34 *'They Were Good Soldiers': African-Americans Serving in the Continental Army, 1775-1783* (John U. Rees)

No 35 *A Redcoat in America: The Diaries of Lieutenant William Bamford, 1757-1765 and 1776* (John B. Hattendorf (ed.))

No 36 *Between Scylla and Charybdis: The Army of Friedrich August II of Saxony, 1733-1763: Part II: Infantry and Artillery* (Marco Pagan)

No 37 *Québec Under Siege: French Eye-Witness Accounts from the Campaign of 1759* (Charles A. Mayhood (ed.))

No 38 *King George's Hangman: Henry Hawley and the Battle of Falkirk 1746* (Jonathan D. Oates)

No 39 *Zweybrücken in Command: The Reichsarmee in the Campaign of 1758* (Neil Cogswell)

No 40 *So Bloody a Day: The 16th Light Dragoons in the Waterloo Campaign* (David J. Blackmore)

No 41 *Northern Tars in Southern Waters: The Russian Fleet in the Mediterranean 1806-1810* (Vladimir Bogdanovich Bronevskiy / Darrin Boland)

No 42 *Royal Navy Officers of the Seven Years War: A Biographical Dictionary of Commissioned Officers 1748-1763* (Cy Harrison)

No 43 *All at Sea: Naval Support for the British Army During the American Revolutionary War* (John Dillon)

No 44 *Glory is Fleeting: New Scholarship on the Napoleonic Wars* (Andrew Bamford (ed.))

No 45 *Fashioning Regulation, Regulating Fashion: Uniforms and Dress of the British Army 1800-1815 Vol. II* (Ben Townsend)

No 46 *Revenge in the Name of Honour: The Royal Navy's Quest for Vengeance in the Single Ship Actions of the War of 1812* (Nicholas James Kaizer)

No 47 *They Fought With Extraordinary Bravery: The III German (Saxon) Army Corps in the Southern Netherlands 1814* (Geert van Uythoven)

No 48 *The Danish Army of the Napoleonic Wars 1801-1814, Organisation, Uniforms & Equipment: Volume 1: High Command, Line and Light Infantry* (David Wilson)

No 49 *Neither Up Nor Down: The British Army and the Flanders Campaign 1793-1895* (Phillip Ball)

No 50 *Guerra Fantástica: The Portuguese Army and the Seven Years War* (António Barrento)

No 51 *From Across the Sea: North Americans in Nelson's Navy* (Sean M. Heuvel and John A. Rodgaard)

No 52 *Rebellious Scots to Crush: The Military Response to the Jacobite '45* (Andrew Bamford (ed.))

No 53 *The Army of George II 1727-1760: The Soldiers who Forged an Empire* (Peter Brown)

No 54 *Wellington at Bay: The Battle of Villamuriel, 25 October 1812* (Garry David Wills)

No 55 *Life in the Red Coat: The British Soldier 1721-1815* (Andrew Bamford (ed.))

No 56 *Wellington's Favourite Engineer. John Burgoyne: Operations, Engineering, and the Making of a Field Marshal* (Mark S. Thompson)

No 57 *Scharnhorst: The Formative Years, 1755-1801* (Charles Edward White)

No 58 *At the Point of the Bayonet: The Peninsular War Battles of Arroyomolinos and Almaraz 1811-1812* (Robert Griffith)

No 59 *Sieges of the '45: Siege Warfare during the Jacobite Rebellion of 1745-1746* (Jonathan D. Oates)

No 60 *Austrian Cavalry of the Revolutionary and Napoleonic Wars, 1792–1815* (Enrico Acerbi, András K. Molnár)

No 61 *The Danish Army of the Napoleonic Wars 1801-1814, Organisation, Uniforms & Equipment: Volume 2: Cavalry and Artillery* (David Wilson)

No 62 *Napoleon's Stolen Army: How the Royal Navy Rescued a Spanish Army in the Baltic* (John Marsden)

No 63 *Crisis at the Chesapeake: The Royal Navy and the Struggle for America 1775-1783* (Quintin Barry)

No 64 *Bullocks, Grain, and Good Madeira: The Maratha and Jat Campaigns 1803-1806 and the emergence of the Indian Army* (Joshua Provan)

No 65 *Sir James McGrigor: The Adventurous Life of Wellington's Chief Medical Officer* (Tom Scotland)

No 66 *Fashioning Regulation, Regulating Fashion: Uniforms and Dress of the British Army 1800-1815 Volume I* (Ben Townsend) (paperback edition)

No 67 *Fashioning Regulation, Regulating Fashion: Uniforms and Dress of the British Army 1800-1815 Volume II* (Ben Townsend) (paperback edition)

No 68 *The Secret Expedition: The Anglo-Russian Invasion of Holland 1799* (Geert van Uythoven) (paperback edition)

No 69 *The Sea is My Element: The Eventful Life of Admiral Sir Pulteney Malcolm 1768-1838* (Paul Martinovich)

No 70 *The Sword and the Spirit: Proceedings of the first 'War & Peace in the Age of Napoleon' Conference* (Zack White (ed.))

No 71 *Lobositz to Leuthen: Horace St Paul and the Campaigns of the Austrian Army in the Seven Years War 1756-57* (Neil Cogswell) (paperback edition)

No 72 *For God and King. A History of the Damas Legion 1793-1798: A Case Study of the Military Emigration during the French Revolution* (Hughes de Bazouges and Alistair Nichols)

No 73 *'Their Infantry and Guns Will Astonish You': The Army of Hindustan and European Mercenaries in Maratha service 1780-1803* (Andy Copestake)

No 74 *Like A Brazen Wall: The Battle of Minden, 1759, and its Place in the Seven Years War* (Ewan Carmichael)

No 75 *Wellington and the Lines of Torres Vedras: The Defence of Lisbon during the Peninsular War* (Mark Thompson)

No 76 *French Light Infantry 1784-1815: From the Chasseurs of Louis XVI to Napoleon's Grande Armée* (Terry Crowdy)

No 77 *Riflemen: The History of the 5th Battalion 60th (Royal American) Regiment, 1797-1818* (Robert Griffith) (paperback edition)

No 78 *Hastenbeck 1757: The French Army and the Opening Campaign of the Seven Years War* (Olivier Lapray)

No 79 *Napoleonic French Military Uniforms: As Depicted by Horace and Carle Vernet and Eugène Lami* (Guy Dempsey (trans. and ed.))

No 80 *These Distinguished Corps: British Grenadier and Light Infantry Battalions in the American Revolution* (Don N. Hagist)

No 81 *Rebellion, Invasion, and Occupation: The British Army in Ireland, 1793 -1815* (Wayne Stack)

No 82 *You Have to Die in Piedmont! The Battle of Assietta, 19 July 1747. The War of the Austrian Succession in the Alps* (Giovanni Cerino Badone)

No 83 *A Very Fine Regiment: the 47th Foot in the American War of Independence, 1773–1783* (Paul Knight)

No 84 *By Fire and Bayonet: Grey's West Indies Campaign of 1794* (Steve Brown) (paperback edition)

No 85 *No Want of Courage: The British Army in Flanders, 1793-1795* (R.N.W. Thomas)

No 86 *Far Distant Ships: The Royal Navy and the Blockade of Brest 1793-1815* (Quintin Barry) (paperback edition)

No 87 *Armies and Enemies of Napoleon 1789-1815: Proceedings of the 2021 Helion and Company 'From Reason to Revolution' Conference* (Robert Griffith (ed.))

No 88 *The Battle of Rossbach 1757: New Perspectives on the Battle and Campaign* (Alexander Querengässer (ed.))

No 89 *Waterloo After the Glory: Hospital Sketches and Reports on the Wounded After the Battle* (Michael Crumplin and Gareth Glover) (paperback edition)

No 90 *From Ushant to Gibraltar: The Channel Fleet 1778-1783* (Quintin Barry)

No 91 *'The Soldiers are Dressed in Red': The Quiberon Expedition of 1795 and the Counter-Revolution in Brittany* (Alistair Nichols)

No 92 *The Army of the Kingdom of Italy 1805-1814: Uniforms, Organisation, Campaigns* (Stephen Ede-Borrett)

No 93 *The Ottoman Army of the Napoleonic Wars 1798-1815: A Struggle for Survival from Egypt to the Balkans* (Bruno Mugnai)

No 94 *The Changing Face of Old Regime Warfare: Essays in Honour of Christopher Duffy* (Alexander S. Burns (ed.))

No 94 *The Changing Face of Old Regime Warfare: Essays in Honour of Christopher Duffy* (Alexander S. Burns (ed.)

No 95 *The Danish Army of the Napoleonic Wars 1801-1814, Organisation, Uniforms & Equipment: Volume 3: Norwegian Troops and Militia* (David Wilson)

No 96 *1805 – Tsar Alexander's First War with Napoleon* (Alexander Ivanovich Mikhailovsky-Danilevsky, trans. Peter G.A. Phillips)

No 97 *'More Furies then Men': The Irish Brigade in the service of France 1690-1792* (Pierre-Louis Coudray)

No 98 *'We Are Accustomed to do our Duty': German Auxiliaries with the British Army 1793-95* (Paul Demet) (paperback edition)

No 99 *Ladies, Wives and Women: British Army Wives in the Revolutionary and Napoleonic Wars 1793-1815* (David Clammer)

No 100 *The Garde Nationale 1789-1815: France's Forgotten Armed Forces* (Pierre-Baptiste Guillemot)

No 101 *Confronting Napoleon: Levin von Bennigsen's Memoir of the Campaign in Poland, 1806-1807, Volume I Pultusk to Eylau* (Alexander Mikaberidze and Paul Strietelmeier (trans. and ed.))

No 102 *Olmütz to Torgau: Horace St Paul and the Campaigns of the Austrian Army in the Seven Years War 1758-60* (Neil Cogswell) (paperback edition)

No 103 *Fit to Command: British Regimental Leadership in the Revolutionary & Napoleonic Wars* (Steve Brown)

No 104 *Wellington's Unsung Heroes: The Fifth Division in the Peninsular War, 1810-1814* (Carole Divall)

No 105 *1806-1807 – Tsar Alexander's Second War with Napoleon* (Alexander Ivanovich Mikhailovsky-Danilevsky, trans. Peter G.A. Phillips)

No 106 *The Pattern: The 33rd Regiment in the American Revolution, 1770-1783* (Robbie MacNiven)

No 107 *To Conquer and to Keep: Suchet and the War for Eastern Spain, 1809-1814, Volume 1 1809-1811* (Yuhan Kim)

No 108 *To Conquer and to Keep: Suchet and the War for Eastern Spain, 1809-1814, Volume 2 1811-1814* (Yuhan Kim)

No 109 *The Tagus Campaign of 1809: An Alliance in Jeopardy* (John Marsden)

No 110 *The War of the Bavarian Succession, 1778-1779: Prussian Military Power in Decline?* (Alexander Querengässer)

No 111 *Anson: Naval Commander and Statesman* (Anthony Bruce)

No 112 *Atlas of the Battles and Campaigns of the American Revolution, 1775-1783* (David Bonk and George Anderson)

No 113 *A Fine Corps and will Serve Faithfully: The Swiss Regiment de Roll in the British Army 1794-1816* (Alistair Nichols)